DOS/VSE
Assembler
Language

DOS/VSE
Assembler
Language

A professional subset PLUS

Table handling ● Translation and bit manipulation ●
SAM ● ISAM ● DAM ● VSAM ●
Writing macro definitions ● Floating point arithmetic ●
Structured program development

Kevin McQuillen
Anne Prince

Mike Murach & Associates, Inc.

4697 West Jacquelyn Avenue
Fresno; California 93722
(209) 275-3335

Editorial team

Anne Prince
Mike Murach

Production team

Steve Ehlers
Lori Davis
Carl Kisling

Related products

Instructor's Guide for *DOS/VSE Assembler Language* by Anne Prince

DOS/VSE JCL by Steve Eckols
Instructor's Guide for *DOS/VSE JCL*

DOS/VSE ICCF by Steve Eckols

Library of Congress Catalog Card Number: 85-63465

ISBN: 0-911625-31-3

Contents

Preface

This book is a long overdue revision of the first book we ever published back in 1974: *System/360-370 Assembler Language (DOS)*. The first edition was used by more than 200 colleges and junior colleges for classroom instruction, and it was used in thousands of businesses for inhouse training. Nevertheless, we feel that this second edition is a major improvement over the first edition. It covers everything that the first edition did, but it does so in a more organized fashion. In addition, this book covers VSAM file handling and structured programming in assembler language, which the first edition didn't cover.

What this book does

When you develop a text for an assembler language course, one of the first jobs is deciding what the objectives of the course should be. Should you try to teach the student to write application programs in assembler language, to write special-purpose subprograms in assembler language, to do systems programming tasks in assembler language, or what? To complicate the problem, data processing is constantly changing so a reasonable objective of ten years ago isn't necessarily reasonable today. Furthermore, assembler language is far too extensive to cover completely in a single book, so you have to limit your objectives. As a result, we settled on three overall objectives for this book.

The first objective is to present an introduction to assembler language that will be useful to anyone who uses a DOS/VSE system, whether or not he or she ever writes programs in assembler language. If you've ever worked on an IBM mainframe, you know that all functions eventually get reduced to assembler language, so a knowledge of assembler language will help you use high-level languages and your VSE system more effectively. With this in mind, section 2 presents an introduction to assembler language that we feel is the least you should know about assembler language if you work on an IBM mainframe.

The second objective of this book is to teach you how to write special-purpose subprograms in assembler language that can be called by high-level languages like COBOL or PL/I. That's one reason why chapter 8 emphasizes subprogram linkage. Once you understand this linkage, you can write assembler language subprograms that do any of the functions presented in the other chapters of the book.

The third objective of this book is to prepare you to do systems programming tasks in assembler language: tasks like modifying a third-party application package, providing an exit routine for an operating system module, or writing an inhouse utility. Because this book doesn't begin to cover all of the capabilities of assembler language, I'm not saying that you'll be able to do all systems programming tasks once you complete it. But you should be able to do some systems programming tasks. More important, you should be able to research the related IBM manuals on your own so you'll be able to do whatever assembler language tasks you're assigned. To make this possible, section 4 shows you how to use the I/O macros for both the native access methods and for VSAM. This is a critical requirement that is missing in many competing texts.

Although it's not an objective, you should also be able to write application programs in assembler language when you complete this book. That was an objective for the first edition of this book, because in 1974 assembler language was second only to COBOL when it came to languages used for application programming. Today, however, few companies use assembler language for application programming. Although you may be asked to modify or rewrite an old application program, chances are slim that you'll be asked to write a new application program in assembler language.

Who this book is for

This book is for anyone who wants to learn assembler language as it is implemented on a DOS/VSE system. Since this book assumes that you have no data processing experience, the first three chapters present the hardware and software background you need for assembler language programming. As a result, if you've had experience with IBM mainframes, DOS/VSE, or programming, you may be able to skip some or all of these background chapters.

If you review the programming examples in this book, you'll see that most of them are simplifications of application programs. Remember, then, that their purpose is to illustrate the use of assembler language, not to teach application programming. We used application programs as examples because we felt they're easier to understand than systems programs. Once you learn assembler language by studying these examples, you can apply assembler language to whatever type of programmming problem you're assigned.

With that in mind, we feel that this book is suitable for independent study, an informal course, or a formal course in college or industry. It can be used in a data processing or a computer science curriculum. It can be used for a short course or a full-semester course. And, if it is supplemented by IBM manuals, it can be used as the basis for an in-depth, two-semester course.

Section	Chapters	Section title	Prerequisites	Design
1	1-3	Required background	None	Sequential
2	4-8	A professional subset of assembler language	Section 1	Sequential
3	9-12	Assembler language capabilities by function	Section 2	Random
4	13-16	Assembler language for DASD access methods	Section 2	Random after chapter 13
5	17-19	Program development techniques	Chapter 5 or Section 2	Sequential

Figure P-1   The basic organization of this book

How to use this book

If you're reading this book as part of a course, your instructor should guide you through it. On the other hand, if you're reading this book on your own, you should realize that the chapters don't have to be read in sequence. Instead, they are grouped into five sections as indicated by the table in figure P-1. As the table shows, you can continue with any of the other sections in this book after you complete the first two sections.

This type of organization, which we call *modular organization*, gives you a number of options as you use this book. If, for example, you want to learn how to use the DASD access methods after you complete section 2, you can go directly to section 4. Similarly, if you're ready to assemble and test your programs after you complete section 2, you can go directly to section 5. In fact, you can read chapters 17 and 18 any time after you complete chapter 5 in section 2. However, you must complete all of section 2 before you can read chapter 19.

Within each section, the chapters are designed in a sequential or random manner, as indicated by the table in figure P-1. If the chapters are sequential within a section, you have to read them in sequence. But if they are random, you can read them in whatever sequence you prefer and you can skip the chapters that don't pertain to your work. In section 3, for example, you may only be interested in chapter 11. If so, you can read it right after you complete section 2 and you can skip chapters 9, 10, and 12. If you check the design for section 4, you can see that it's random after you read chapter 13. This means that you can read chapters 14 through 16 in any order you prefer once you read chapter 13 in this section.

We used modular organization for this book for two reasons. First, it makes your learning more efficient because you learn a professional subset of assembler language in section 2. After that, you can easily add assembler language elements to this subset until you reach the level of expertise you desire. Second, the modular organization makes the book more useful to you as a reference after you've read the book for the first time because it groups the assembler language elements by function. Incidentally, modular organization is a unique feature of most of our books.

To help you learn from this book, each topic or chapter is followed by terminology lists and behavioral objectives. If you feel you understand the terms in each terminology list, it's a good indication that you've understood the content of the topic or chapter you've just read. In other words, we don't expect you to be able to define the terms in a list, but you should recognize and understand them. Similarly, if you feel that you can do what each objective requires, it's a good indication that you've learned what we wanted you to learn in each topic or chapter.

To give you a chance to apply your learning, appendix B presents a comprehensive case study. You can start working on this case study when you complete chapter 5. Then, as you complete each new chapter, the case study asks you to modify or enhance the basic program that you developed for chapter 5. Whether or not you have access to a DOS/VSE computer system so you can actually test your case study program, we recommend that you code the phases of the case study because that's a critical test of your learning progress. If you can code and test all phases of the case study so they work correctly, we feel that this book has accomplished its primary objectives.

Related products

Throughout this book, you'll learn the VSE JCL that you need for the assembler language functions that you'll be using. However, since this is an assembler language book, the JCL is presented at a low level. As a result, you may want to learn more about VSE JCL when you complete this book. If so, we recommend our book by Steve Eckols called *DOS/VSE JCL*. In addition to VSE JCL, it shows you how to use ICCF, POWER, some common utilities, and much more. If you use *DOS/VSE JCL* in conjunction with this book, you should end up knowing a great deal about your VSE system.

If you're an instructor in a school or a business, you will probably be interested in the *Instructor's Guide* that is available with this book. It presents complete solutions for the case study in appendix B. It gives you ideas and summary information for administering a course in DOS assembler language. And it gives you masters for most of the figures in the text so you can make overhead transparencies for them.

Related reference manuals

Although you shouldn't have much need for IBM manuals when you use this book, you may want to refer to them occasionally. As a result, I've listed the related reference manuals in figure P-2. As you can see, except for the Principles of Operation manual and Reference Card, the titles don't specify a particular system. That is because DOS/VSE is essentially the same no matter which processor it runs on. So, in general, you can use the

Order no.	Title
GA22-7000	System/370 Principles of Operation
GA22-7070	IBM 4300 Processors Principles of Operation
GC33-4010	OS/VS—DOS/VSE—VM/370 Assembler Language
GC33-4024	Guide to DOS/VSE Assembler
GX20-1850	System/370 Reference Card
SC24-5144	Using VSE/VSAM Commands and Macros
SC24-5146	VSE/VSAM Messages and Codes
SC24-5211	VSE/Advanced Functions Macro Reference
ST24-5210	VSE/Advanced Functions Macro User's Guide

Figure P-2   Related IBM reference manuals

same manuals whether you're using a System/370, 4300, or any other system that supports DOS/VSE.

As you work your way through this book, you may want to refer continually to two of the IBM manuals to see how they relate to the book. These manuals are *Principles of Operation* and *DOS/VSE Assembler Language*. In addition, you'll be referred to other manuals in various chapters of this book. If you want a quick reference for just the elements that are presented in this book, you can use the reference summary in appendix A.

Conclusion   Obviously, we believe that this book will help you learn DOS/VSE assembler language better than any competing product will. We're confident that this book will teach you a usable subset of assembler language and that it will let you learn as efficiently as possible.

If you have comments about this book, we welcome them. If you check the last few pages of this book, you'll find a postage-paid comment form. You'll also find a postage-paid order form in case you want to order any of our other products. We hope you find this book useful, and thanks for being our customer.

Mike Murach, Publisher
Fresno, California
December, 1985

Section 1

Required background

Before you can learn to develop programs in assembler language, you need some data processing background. The three chapters in this section present the minimum background that you need for this programming course. Chapter 1 introduces you to IBM mainframes because these are the machines that you use DOS/VSE assembler language on. Chapter 2 introduces you to the DOS/VSE operating system that you'll be using on an IBM mainframe. Chapter 3 presents a procedure for developing assembler language programs along with the job control language you'll need for translating and testing your programs.

Of course, if you already have programming experience or experience with a DOS/VSE system, you may already know much of the material in this section. If so, you can review the objectives and terminology lists at the end of each chapter or topic to see whether you need to study it.

Chapter 1

An introduction to IBM mainframes

This chapter introduces you to the hardware components of an IBM mainframe system. Since you probably have had some previous exposure to data processing and programming, this chapter only presents those introductory concepts that are necessary for assembler language programming. If you're already familiar with IBM hardware, much of the material in this chapter will be review for you. If so, you can review the terminology and objectives at the end of the chapter to determine whether or not you need to read it.

For mainframe systems, IBM manufactures dozens of hardware devices. Moreover, most are available in different models and with a variety of features. As a result, this chapter won't try to teach you about all the devices that can be part of an IBM mainframe system. Instead, it describes three general types of components.

The first type is processors, the central components in mainframe systems. The second type includes all the peripheral devices that are used to transmit data to and receive data from the processor. The third type consists of intermediate devices, called channels, that manage the data transfer between peripheral devices and the processor.

PROCESSORS

The center of an IBM mainframe system is the *processor*; all the other devices that make up the system configuration attach to it in some way. For the purposes of this book, you can think of the processor as consisting of two main parts: the central processing unit and main storage. The *central processing unit* (or *CPU*) is a collection of circuits that execute program instructions for calculation and data manipulation. *Main storage* (or *main memory*) is the high-speed, general-purpose, electronic storage that contains both the data the CPU operates upon and the program instructions it executes.

2

To refer to the amount of main storage a system provides, the symbol *K* has traditionally been used. Because the word *kilo* refers to 1000, one K refers to approximately 1,000 storage positions. Thus, "a 128K system" means a computer system with approximately 128,000 storage positions in its main storage. I say "approximately" because one K is actually 1,024 storage positions.

Today, however, mainframe computers are sold with much larger memories than can be expressed conveniently in Ks. For instance, a small IBM mainframe will have at least one megabyte of storage (expressed as 1*M*). The term *megabyte* refers to approximately 1,000,000 positions, or *bytes*, of storage. More precisely, a megabyte is 1,024K, or 1,024 times 1,024 bytes of storage. In chapter 4, you'll learn more precisely what a byte is.

Most IBM mainframes today run on processors that are members of the *System/360-370 family*. The System/360-370 family is a group of general-purpose processors that have developed over a 20-year span, beginning with the System/360 models of the mid-1960s and continuing with the System/370s and the 3030s of the 1970s. The 3080s and 4300s are current today.

Of course, as IBM has developed new System/360-370 processors, it has used contemporary technologies to create better, faster, and cheaper machines. As a result, although the IBM mainframe processors of today are direct descendants of the System/360s, those older machines are all but obsolete.

For the purposes of this book, we assume that you are *not* using a System/360 processor since only a few are still in use. In addition, we want you to know that any reference we make to a System/370 means a System/370 or any of its successors in the System/360-370 family of computers. As far as assembler language goes, it works the same way on a 370 as it does on any of the successors.

INPUT/OUTPUT EQUIPMENT

The second group of mainframe devices consists of the peripheral devices connected to the processor. Collectively, these devices are called *input/output devices*, or just *I/O devices*. Input devices send data to the processor, and output devices receive data from it. Some machines can perform both functions.

If you have any data processing experience at all, you are probably familiar with printers, terminal devices, direct access storage devices, and tape devices. These are the most commonly used I/O devices today. In addition, you may be familiar with card devices. Although card devices were used extensively in the past, they are practically obsolete today. In any event, because so many devices can be part of an IBM mainframe, I'm not going to try to cover them all. Instead, because this book emphasizes the programming for direct access storage devices, I'm going to focus on some details you need to know about them.

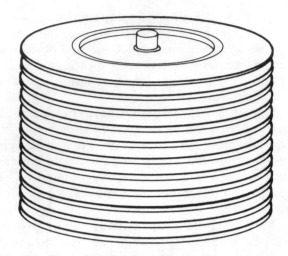

Figure 1-1   Conceptual illustration of a disk pack

Characteristics of direct access storage devices

A *direct access storage device* (*DASD*) makes it possible to access any record quickly. Because DASDs, regardless of their type, allow direct and rapid access to large quantities of data, they've become a key component of mainframe systems. They're used not only to store user programs and data, but also to store programs and data for operating system functions.

The most common type of DASD is the *disk drive*, a unit that reads and writes data on a *disk pack*. A disk pack, illustrated conceptually in figure 1-1, is a stack of metal platters that are coated with a metal oxide material. Data is recorded on both sides of the platters. A disk pack can be removable or it can be fixed in a permanent, sealed assembly inside the drive.

On each recording surface of a disk pack, data is stored in concentric circles called *tracks* as illustrated conceptually in figure 1-2. Although the number of tracks per recording surface varies by device type, the surface illustrated in figure 1-2 has 200 tracks, numbered from 000 to 199.

The data stored on a track is read by the DASD's *access mechanism*, which is an assembly that has one read/write head for each recording surface. This is illustrated conceptually in figure 1-3, which shows a side view of an access mechanism. As you can see, the access mechanism is positioned over the same track on all recording surfaces at the same time. As a result, all of these tracks can be operated upon, one after another, without the access mechanism having to move.

The tracks that can be accessed by a single positioning of the access mechanism make up a *cylinder*. As a result, there are as many cylinders on

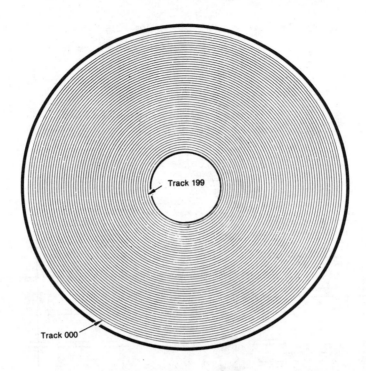

Figure 1-2   Conceptual illustration of the tracks on a disk surface

a disk pack as there are tracks on a single recording surface. So if there are 200 tracks on each recording surface of a disk pack, the entire pack contains 200 cylinders.

IBM mainframe DASD types

In concept, one DASD's operation is about the same as another's, but they vary in speed and capacity. Although you don't need to know the technical distinctions among all types of IBM DASDs, you do need to understand the two broad categories into which they're grouped: CKD and FBA.

Count-key-data (CKD) devices make up the first category and include devices that can be found on most IBM mainframe systems. The second category is *fixed-block architecture (FBA) devices*. At present, only two FBA units are available, and they run only under the DOS/VSE operating system and then only on 4300 processors.

CKD concepts   Figure 1-4 illustrates the CKD format. In this format, each record on a track is preceded by a *count area* and a *key area*. Since the illustration, which represents only one track, has four data areas, there are four count and four key areas on the track.

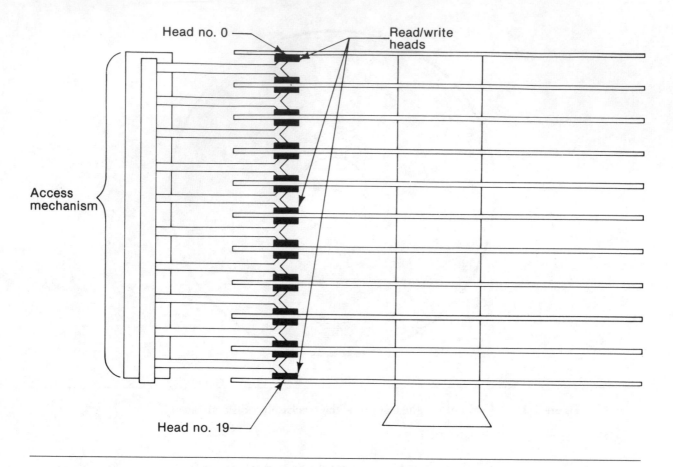

Figure 1-3   Conceptual illustration of a side view of an access mechanism

The count areas contain the disk addresses and lengths of the data areas following them. The key areas, which may be from 1 to 256 bytes in length, contain the control data that uniquely identifies the records in the file. For example, in a file of inventory master records, the part number would logically be recorded in the key area. In a file of payroll master records, the employee number would be recorded in the key area.

The difference between count and key, then, is that the count area contains a disk address that uniquely identifies a record location on the disk pack, and the key area contains a control field that uniquely identifies a record in a file. If the organization of a file doesn't require records with keys, the file can be defined without key areas, but all files require count areas. As you will see later, both count and key areas can be used to locate records that are being directly accessed.

In addition to count, key, and data areas, each track in the count-key-data format has a *home address*. The home address, which comes immediately before the first count area on a track, uniquely identifies each of the tracks on a disk pack. So, on a pack that contains 200 tracks and 20 recording surfaces, there are 4000 different home addresses.

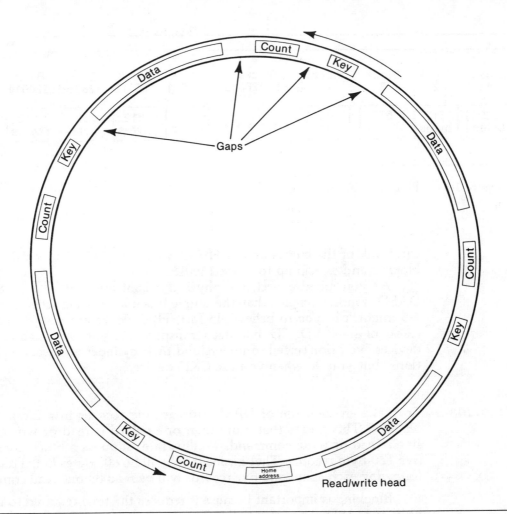

Figure 1-4   Count-key-data format on one track of a disk

Any programming references to data records on a CKD disk device are eventually reduced to cylinder number, head number, and either record number or key. The cylinders are numbered 0 through the number of tracks minus 1, the heads 0 through the number of recording surfaces minus 1, and record numbers start at 0 and go through the maximum number of records that can be stored on the track. Because record number 0 is used by the Disk Operating System, the first data record on a track is always record number 1. Thus, record number 1 on track 0 of cylinder 0 is actually the first data record on the first track of the first cylinder of a disk.

FBA concepts   On an FBA DASD, you can think of the entire disk area of a device as a string of blocks starting with block 0 and extending up to the capacity of the unit. Each block contains a fixed number of bytes that are available for user data: 512. To illustrate, figure 1-5 shows how you

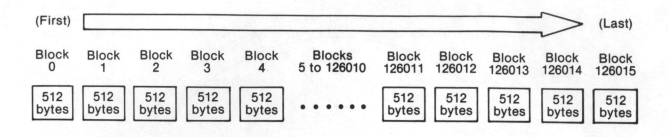

Figure 1-5   Blocks on an FBA DASD

can think of the blocks on one FBA device, the 3310; the records start at block 0 and extend up to block 126015.

As you might expect, the physical organization of data on an FBA DASD is more complex than the simple block addressing scheme in figure 1-5 might lead you to believe. In fact, FBA blocks are mapped onto the tracks of an FBA DASD, but that's transparent to you. When you use FBA devices, you don't need to understand their cylinder and track organizations, but you do when you use CKD devices.

Blocked records

To make efficient use of DASD storage, the records in a file are often *blocked*. This means that more than one record is read or written by a single read or write command. To illustrate, suppose a block consists of five 120-byte records. That means there will be 600 bytes in the data area following each count and five records will be read by one read command.

Blocking is important because it reduces the time required to read or write a DASD file sequentially. To read or write a record or block of records sequentially, a program must first search for the record or block on the selected track. To do this, the disk drive waits for the next record or block in sequence to rotate to the access mechanism so it can be read. This waiting period is called *rotational delay*, and on the average it takes one-half the time required for the disk to make one complete rotation. With unblocked records, one rotational delay is required for each record to be read or written. But if the records are blocked, only one rotational delay is required for each block. By eliminating rotational delay, blocking can significantly reduce the time required to read the records in a file sequentially.

Blocking can also affect the storage capacity of a disk pack. On a 3350 pack, for example, one track can hold 30 456-byte records when they're unblocked. That means that 10,000 456-byte records take over 333 tracks, or over 11 cylinders. But if the records are blocked with ten records to a block, four blocks can be recorded on each track, or a total of 40 records per track. Then, the entire file requires only 250 tracks, or eight and one-third cylinders.

CHANNELS

When I said before that a particular device can be attached to the processor, I simplified the relationship between the processor and the I/O devices. Although it may seem like a peripheral device is attached directly to the processor, it's actually attached to an intermediate device called a *channel*. A channel is a small computer that executes I/O instructions called *channel commands*.

A channel on an IBM mainframe may be one of three types: (1) a selector, (2) a byte multiplexer, or (3) a block multiplexer. A *selector channel* is designed to operate with only one device at a time, and transfers data byte by byte until a complete record has been transferred. In contrast, *multiplexer channels* operate with more than one I/O device at a time by interleaving data items. A *byte multiplexer* is usually used to attach several low-speed I/O devices like card devices and printers to the processor. It transfers data one byte at a time. A *block multiplexer* is used to attach higher-speed devices like tape units and DASDs and transfers data in blocks rather than bytes.

Because the channel performs the I/O operations, it frees the processor to execute other instructions. As a result, processing and I/O operations can be overlapped, and overall system performance is improved. In chapter 4, you will learn more about overlap.

SYSTEM CONFIGURATIONS

With such variety in IBM mainframe processors and input/output devices, the number of possible *system configurations* is practically limitless. As a result, one IBM mainframe configuration is likely to be different from another. At this time, then, I'll present only one configuration to help you understand the system you're going to use.

Figure 1-6 represents a small 4300 configuration. In fact, this is nearly the smallest system that can be configured under DOS/VSE. At the center of the system is a 4331 Model 1 with 1M of main memory. Attached to the processor is a collection of devices you might find on a small VSE system.

Although multiplexer channels are standard equipment on larger 4300s, they're optional on smaller 4300s. An alternative to using multiplexers on small systems is to install *I/O adapters*. I/O adapters are housed inside the processor cabinet and perform functions similar to multiplexers, but they're limited because only a few types of devices can be attached to them. The DASD adapter allows 3310, 3370, and 3340/3344 disk devices to be attached to the processor. The 8809 Magnetic Tape Adapter allows direct attachment of up to six 8809 magnetic tape drives. And the Display/Printer Adapter allows direct attachment of local terminals and printers. In the system in figure 1-6, five 3310 disk devices are attached to the DASD adapter; one 8809 tape drive is attached to the tape adapter; and one 3262 band printer, one 3278-2A system console, and four 3178 display stations are attached to the display/printer adapter.

Figure 1-6 also shows the *device addresses* of the system's hardware components. For instance, the device address of the first 3178 terminal is

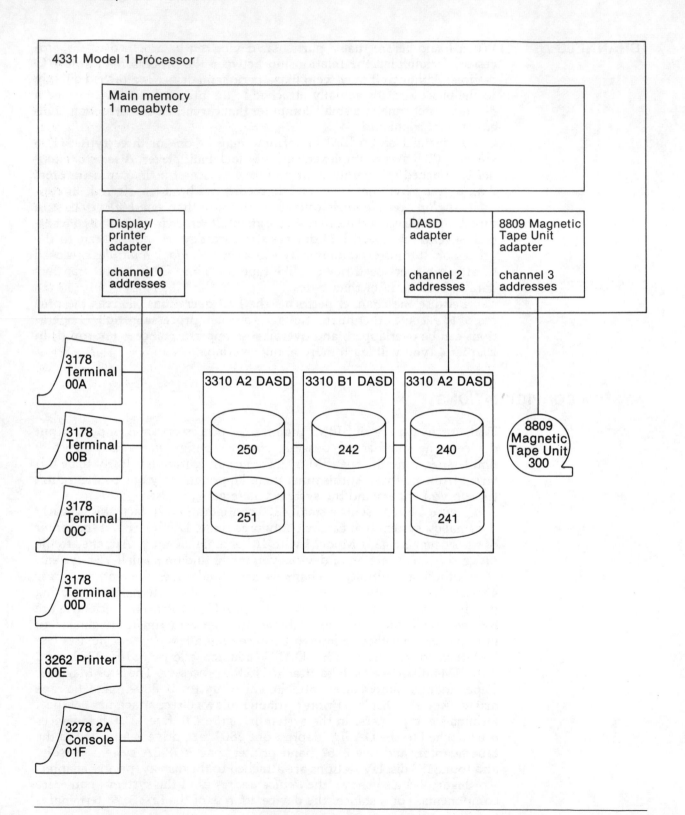

Figure 1-6   A small 4300 configuration

00A. Notice that all of the device addresses are three characters long. Actually, they are three digits long, but the digits are hexadecimal instead of decimal. As you will see in chapter 4, hex digits range from 0 to F, not from 0 to 9.

The first of the three digit positions in a device address represents the channel address of the device. On the smaller 4300s, channel 0 is the byte multiplexer channel. Since channel 0 is used to address devices attached to the display/printer adapter, the addresses of the terminals, system console, and printer in figure 1-6 all begin with a zero and they range from 00A to 01F. Similarly, the DASD adapter is on channel 2 and the tape adapter is on channel 3 in figure 1-6, so the addresses for the 3310s start with a 2 and range from 240 to 251 while the address for the 8809 tape unit is 300.

DISCUSSION

This chapter certainly isn't meant to be a comprehensive treatment of the hardware components that might be on your system. Before you can develop assembler language programs, though, you need to know something about your system configuration. In particular, you need to know what I/O devices you're going to be using. You also need to know the addresses of these devices. Later on in this book, you'll see how you use this hardware knowledge during the development of a program.

Terminology

processor	count area
central processing unit	key area
CPU	home address
main storage	blocked records
main memory	rotational delay
K	channel
kilo	channel command
M	selector channel
megabyte	multiplexer channel
byte	byte multiplexer
System/360-370 family	block multiplexer
input/output device	system configuration
I/O device	I/O adapter
direct access storage device	device address
DASD	
disk drive	
disk pack	
track	
access mechanism	
cylinder	
count-key-data device	
CKD device	
fixed-block architecture device	
FBA device	

Objectives

1. Find out the following about the I/O devices you will be using when you write assembler language programs:

   the model number and device address of the printer
   the model numbers, types, and device addresses of the DASD units

2. Describe the differences between count-key-data and fixed-block architecture DASDs.

3. Explain what blocked records are.

Chapter 2

An introduction to DOS/VSE

In order to write an assembler language program that will execute properly, you must know how to coordinate your program with your computer's
operating system. An operating system is a collection of programs designed to improve the efficiency of a computer system. Today, on the mainframes in the System/370 family, the two most popular operating systems
are called DOS/VSE and OS/MVS. This book teaches you how to
develop assembler language programs on an IBM mainframe that uses the
DOS/VSE operating system; another one of our books teaches you
assembler language for OS/MVS systems.

This chapter introduces you to DOS/VSE (or just VSE, as I'll call it
from now on) and to some of the other programs that make up a typical
VSE system. First, I'll describe how the system control programs manage
processor storage. Then, I'll present some details on how VSE manages the
user data it stores; this emphasizes DASD storage. Finally, I'll describe the
VSE library structure and introduce you to other components of a production system.

If you're already familiar with VSE, of course, this chapter will be
review for you. If it is, you can review the terminology and objectives at
the end of the chapter to decide whether or not you need to read it.

HOW VSE MANAGES PROCESSOR STORAGE

Although VSE performs a variety of functions, the most important one is
probably processor storage management. So, I will begin your introduction to VSE by describing how it manages processor storage. First, I will
describe multiprogramming; then, I will describe virtual storage.

Multiprogramming A common feature of mainframe computer systems is *multiprogramming*. When a system provides multiprogramming, it allows a single processor to execute more than one program at the same time. Actually, that's somewhat misleading, because only one program is executing at a given instant even though multiple programs are present in storage at the same time. Nevertheless, it looks like multiple programs are executing at one time.

Multiprogramming is important because it improves the overall productivity of a computing installation. Because internal processing speeds are far greater than input and output operation speeds and because most business applications do relatively little processing between I/O operations, a processor that executes only one program at a time is idle a large percentage of the time while the program waits for an I/O operation to finish. To make better use of this wasted time, multiprogramming allows additional programs to be in storage so their instructions can be executed while the first program waits for its I/O operation to be completed.

The central component of VSE, the *supervisor program*, or just *supervisor*, determines what program should be executing at any moment. A program that's executing is said to be in control of the system. When the program that's in control of the system must wait for an I/O operation to complete, it passes control back to the supervisor. The supervisor then passes control to another program.

The supervisor uses a scheme of priorities to determine what program should execute next. *Priority* is a "rank" that determines a program's eligibility for receiving system services. If several programs are waiting to resume execution, the supervisor passes control to the one with the highest priority. This process of passing control among programs of different priorities is called *task selection*.

The priority associated with a particular program is determined by the *partition* that it is executing in. On a VSE system, the available processor storage (that is, storage not required by the VSE system control programs) is divided into from two to 12 partitions. One partition is the *background partition*, which is for the lowest priority jobs. The remaining partitions are *foreground partitions*, which are for higher priority jobs. Although a system operator can change a partition's priority, generally Foreground-1 is for the highest priority jobs and Foreground-11 is for the lowest priority jobs. A user's program may run in any one of the available partitions.

All programs, including the supervisor, execute in the processor's *address space*. You can think of the address space as a string of bytes as long as the amount of storage on the system. For example, a 16 megabyte address space begins at byte 0 (numbering begins with 0, not 1) and extends to byte 16,777,215. Locations within the address space are identified by their displacement from its beginning.

Figure 2-1 illustrates the address space layout for a 16M four-partition VSE system. Here, the supervisor resides in the lowest portion of the address space. In other words, the supervisor area begins at 0K and extends upward. Since a typical supervisor requires 222K, its address range is 0K to 222K.

After the supervisor comes the storage available to the user pro-

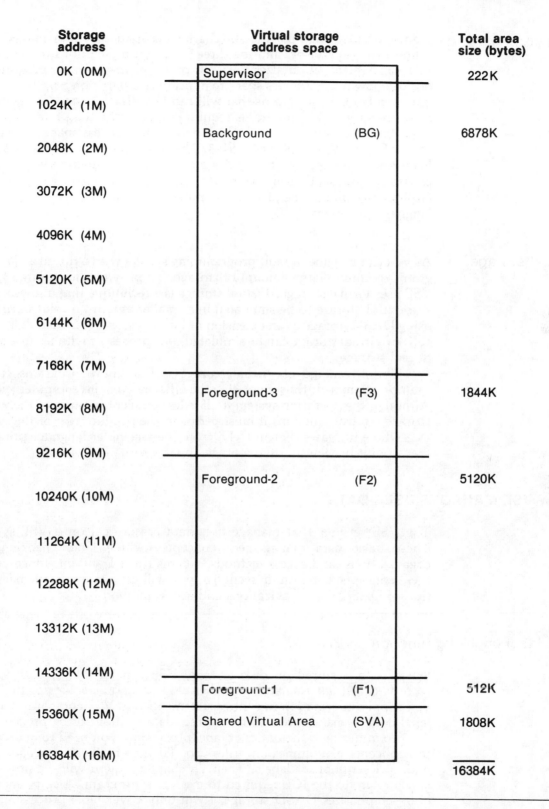

Storage address	Virtual storage address space		Total area size (bytes)
0K (0M)	Supervisor		222K
1024K (1M)			
	Background	(BG)	6878K
2048K (2M)			
3072K (3M)			
4096K (4M)			
5120K (5M)			
6144K (6M)			
7168K (7M)			
	Foreground-3	(F3)	1844K
8192K (8M)			
9216K (9M)			
	Foreground-2	(F2)	5120K
10240K (10M)			
11264K (11M)			
12288K (12M)			
13312K (13M)			
14336K (14M)			
	Foreground-1	(F1)	512K
15360K (15M)	Shared Virtual Area	(SVA)	1808K
16384K (16M)			16384K

Figure 2-1   VSE address space usage on a four-partition system

grams, divided into partitions. The background partition immediately follows the supervisor, and the three foreground partitions follow it. As you can see, partition sizes vary. In practice, the systems programmer decides how much address space to allocate to a partition based on the requirements of the programs that will run in it. In this case, for example, F2's (Foreground-2's) programs require more storage than F1's.

Note in figure 2-1 that the high end of the address space is occupied by the *Shared Virtual Area*, or *SVA*. The word *shared* in the name should help you remember that the SVA's most important function is to contain program modules that are shared throughout the system. Most of these are I/O modules, some of which are likely to be used by your assembler language programs.

Virtual storage

As you can imagine, a multiprogramming system with a dozen active programs requires a large amount of storage. To provide the required space, VSE uses virtual storage. *Virtual storage* is a technique that allows a large amount of storage to be simulated in a smaller amount of *real storage* by using DASD storage as an extension of internal storage. Under VSE, up to 16M of virtual storage can be simulated on a processor with as little as 1M of real storage.

The advantage of virtual storage is that more programs can be multiprogrammed, thus increasing the efficiency of the computer system. Although the operating system itself is less efficient because of the virtual storage control functions it must perform, the productivity of the system as a whole increases. Fortunately, from the assembler language programmer's point of view, virtual storage appears to be real storage.

HOW VSE MANAGES USER DATA

The VSE services that manage user data are critical on a VSE system. These basic data management concepts include label checking, file organizations, and access methods. At this time, I will introduce you to these concepts. Later on, in section 4, you will get a more detailed description of DASD file organizations and access methods.

VSE label checking function

When data is stored on disk or tape, VSE can identify it with special records called *labels*. Later on, when your program processes the data, you supply information in control statements that VSE compares with the label data to make sure that the correct data is about to be processed.

To understand the basics of label processing, you need to understand the concepts of volumes and files. So, I'll present these concepts along with a description of labels. Then, in chapter 3, you will see how these labels relate to the JCL required to execute a program. Again, since this book emphasizes DASD storage, I will only cover label processing as it applies to disk files.

Volumes   A *volume* is a storage unit that can be mounted on an input/output device. For disk devices, a volume is a disk pack. As you learned in chapter 1, disk packs can be either fixed or removable.

A typical VSE shop has many volumes. As a result, they need to be labelled to insure that operators use the correct volumes at the correct times. Removable disk packs should have *external labels* so system operators can select the proper volumes for particular applications. External labels are often handwritten and attached to the outside of the disk pack.

Just as important as external labels are the *internal labels* that VSE writes on disks. Internal labels are data stored on the disk, just like the records of a file. Then, when I/O operations are to be performed on the files of a particular volume, VSE can read the internal *volume label* to verify that the correct volume is mounted.

Each VSE disk pack *must* have a standard volume label. A *standard label* is one written in VSE format. A volume with standard labels has a *VOL1 label* that contains all the information VSE needs to perform its label checking functions. A disk volume may also have from one to seven supplementary volume labels called VOL2 through VOL8. However, these are strictly for information since VSE doesn't use them when it checks volume labels.

Probably the most important data in the VOL1 label is the *volume serial number*, or *volser*. The volser is a six-character name that uniquely identifies the volume. When a disk pack or DASD with a non-removable pack is initialized, it should be assigned a volser that's unique in your installation.

Files   The user data recorded on a volume is organized in one or more *files*. A file is a collection of related records that are treated as a unit. For instance, an employee file might contain one record for each of a firm's employees. Within a file, each record contains the same data elements as all the other records in the file.

The simplest case of a file-volume relationship is a single file on a single volume. Although it isn't common for a disk volume to contain only one file, it's not unheard of, particularly when a large file is stored on a DASD with removable packs. Logically, such a disk is called a *single-file volume*. It's much more likely, though, that a disk volume will hold several or many files. Then, it's called a *multi-file volume*.

Some files are too large to fit on a single volume. That doesn't mean that the file can't be stored, however, because it's possible for parts of a one file to be stored on different volumes in a *multi-volume file*. Large multi-volume files can reside on DASDs, but you're more likely to find them on tape because tape is an economical storage medium for large files.

All DASD files must have standard *file labels*. These labels are stored in a special area on the disk volume called the *VTOC*, or *volume table of contents*. The VTOC contains one or more entries for each file on the volume. The entries identify the files and specify their locations on the pack.

Figure 2-2 illustrates this concept for a DASD volume with six files. In this example, each file is contained in one contiguous area of storage, or *extent*, but that's not a requirement for DASD files. In addition, the volume contains three free extents. Notice that the file labels aren't adjacent to the files, but are stored together in the VTOC. Each file label contains the location information VSE uses to access the file. Notice, also, that the VTOC itself is a file; the records it contains are the labels for the other files on the volume.

As you'd expect, figure 2-2 simplifies the organization of data on a DASD. First, a typical DASD volume contains more than six files. Second, some files in a production environment may reside in more than just one extent. And third, although figure 2-2 suggests a sequential relationship between file positions on the volume and label entries in the VTOC, that's not necessarily the case.

File organizations

In addition to providing label checking functions to protect your installation's data, VSE also provides you with different ways to organize data on DASDs to meet different application requirements. *File organization* refers to the way an application views a file's structure. On a DASD, a file can have three organizations: (1) sequential organization, (2) indexed sequential organization, and (3) direct organization.

Sequential organization   In a file with *sequential organization*, records are stored one after another in consecutive order. Often, a data element within each record contains a key value that's used to sequence the records of the file in a particular order. To process the records in a sequential file, an application program normally reads or writes one record at a time in sequence. This is called *sequential processing*.

Indexed sequential organization   Using *indexed sequential organization*, it's possible to store records sequentially, but to access any one of them directly. To do this, an indexed sequential file contains two sections: a data section and an index section. Within the index section, each index entry contains a key field value and the location of the corresponding record within the data section of the file. Using this method of file organization, each key field must have a unique value. Then, if a record's key value is known, it's possible to access the record directly by retrieving its disk location from the index. On the other hand, it's possible to access the records sequentially without using the index because the records were stored sequentially on the DASD in the first place. When you process records on a direct, rather than a sequential, basis, it is often referred to as *random processing*.

Direct organization   Like a record in a file with indexed sequential organization, a record in a file with *direct organization* can be accessed directly (randomly). Unlike a file with indexed sequential organization, though, a file with direct organization doesn't have an index. Instead, direct organization depends on a direct relationship between data in each record and a DASD address. The address is usually calculated using a for-

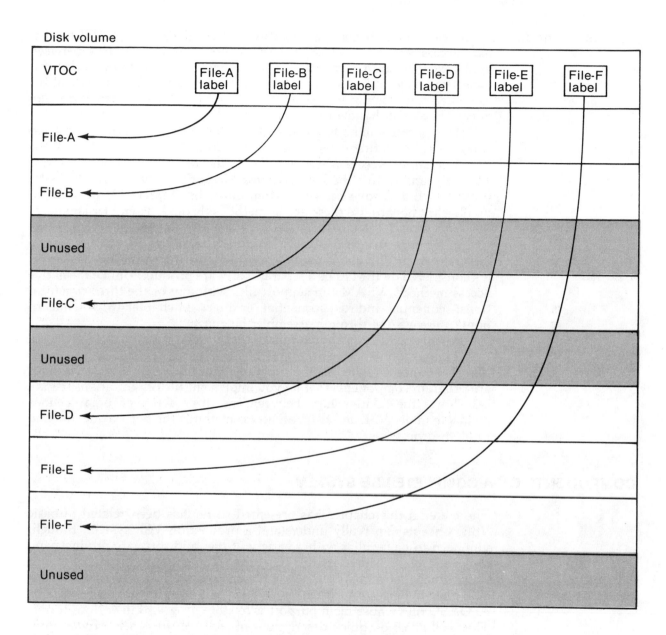

Figure 2-2   DASD labels and files on one disk volume

mula that derives it from data in the record. This is called a *transformation algorithm*. When direct organization is used, access to the records can be rapid, but in most cases the programming complexities involved don't warrant its use.

Access methods

To process files with these different types of organizations, a VSE system uses access methods. An *access method* serves as an interface between application programs and the physical operations of storage devices. When you code an I/O instruction in an assembler language program, for example, you actually invoke an access method. Access methods relieve you of having to handle the complex details of using I/O devices.

The access methods available to you under VSE fall into two categories. In the first category are the VSE *native access methods*: *SAM* (the *Sequential Access Method*), *ISAM* (the *Indexed Sequential Access Method*), and *DAM* (the *Direct Access Method*). They're a fundamental part of VSE and have been for a long time. In chapters 13, 14, and 15, you'll learn how to use these access methods through assembler language.

The second category includes only one access method: *VSAM* (the *Virtual Storage Access Method*). Practically speaking, VSAM is now an integral part of VSE and is used for most DASD file processing. However, it's considered by IBM to be a separate software product. Unlike the native access methods, VSAM can support files with any of the three organizations: sequential, indexed sequential, or direct. In chapter 16, you'll learn how to use VSAM through assembler language.

At this point, you should realize that there is a difference between a file's organization and the access method that processes it. Organization is a logical concept related to the programs that use a file. Access methods are program components that let you implement file organizations. Figure 2-3 shows the relationships between the three types of organizations available under VSE and the VSE access methods for both sequential and random processing.

COMPONENTS OF A COMPLETE VSE SYSTEM

The material this chapter has presented so far has been related to basic VSE concepts. To really understand a production VSE system, though, you need to be familiar with a variety of files and software products and their interrelationships. At this time, then, I'm going to introduce you to some other files and software components you're likely to find on your VSE system. First, you'll learn about VSE libraries. Those are the specialized DASD files whose main purpose is to store programs in various forms. Then, I'll give you quick descriptions of some of the other software products that supplement VSE on a typical production system.

VSE libraries

The software components that make up a complete VSE system number in the hundreds, and they're all stored on DASD. As you can imagine, managing all of them as separate DASD files would be inefficient and could easily get out of control. So to help systems personnel keep track of the components, VSE components are stored in special files called libraries. In addition, you can use libraries to store user-written programs.

A VSE *library* is a DASD file that contains a collection of related pro-

Sequential processing

Organization

	SAM	ISAM	DAM	VSAM
Sequential	Supported			Supported
Indexed sequential		Supported		Supported
Direct				Supported

Random processing

Organization

	SAM	ISAM	DAM	VSAM
Sequential				Supported
Indexed sequential		Supported		Supported
Direct			Supported	Supported

Figure 2-3   Access methods and file organizations for sequential and random processing

gram sub-files, or *members*. For example, one library may contain the source code for a group of programs. Then, the source code for any one program is a member of that library. All of a library's members are listed in the library's *directory*. So the system can directly access any member, the directory specifies each member's name, location, and size.

When you're developing a program on a VSE system, you go through a standard series of steps before you can execute it. First, you code the program. Second, you compile (or assemble) it. Third, you link edit the program. And fourth, you code the control statements to invoke it. (You'll learn more about these steps in the next chapter.) As figure 2-4 shows, the four types of VSE libraries correspond to the outputs of each of these four steps.

Source statement libraries   The output of the coding step is a source program in whatever language you use (such as COBOL, assembler, or PL/I). In a traditional DOS environment, the source program was keypunched into a deck of cards. Today, it is much more common for programs to be entered using some type of interactive program development system. In any case, when a program is complete, it is added as a member to a *source statement library*, or *SSL*. A member in an SSL is called a *book*.

Relocatable libraries The output of the compilation (or assembly) step is a relocatable module. A relocatable module is stored in a *relocatable library*, or *RL*, and is called an *object module*.

Core image libraries Before an object module can be executed, it has to be processed by the linkage editor program. The output of the linkage editor step is an executable module called a *phase*. Phases are stored as members in *core image libraries*, or *CILs*.

Procedure libraries When a program is complete, you use job control statements to execute it. Job control statements can be stored in a *procedure library*, or *PL*. A member in a PL is a *procedure*. Job control statements are also known as *job control language*, or *JCL*.

System libraries and private libraries When you read IBM VSE literature, you'll find references to "the" source statement library or "the" core image library. That's because early versions of DOS allowed only one of each type of library. Those were the *system libraries*.

Today, VSE still supports only one system library of each type, and they all reside in a special file called the *system residence file*, or just *SYSRES*. However, you can use an unlimited number of libraries located outside SYSRES; they're called *private libraries*. "Private" simply means that a library is outside the SYSRES file; it doesn't mean that access to a private library is restricted. When you develop programs for this course, your procedures, source books, object modules, and phases will most likely be stored in private libraries.

VSE software components

A production VSE system uses a variety of related software products. Some of these are components of the operating system itself; others are separately licensed products. However, the practical distinction between programs in the two groups isn't clear. A fully functioning VSE system must use some separately licensed products and may not use all of the facilities of the basic operating system. As a result, in addition to being familiar with the critical components of VSE itself, you also need to know about some of the other IBM software products that make up a complete system.

VSE/POWER *POWER* provides a function that helps a VSE system operate efficiently; it's called *spooling*. Spooling manages card devices and printers for application programs by intercepting program I/O requests for those devices and routing them to or from disk files instead. For example, if a processing program attempts to print a line on a printer, the line is spooled to a disk file. Because DASDs are faster than printers, spooling allows the processing program to resume execution more rapidly. Later, when the processing program has finished execution, the print lines temporarily stored on DASD are actually printed.

The benefits of spooling are twofold. First, programs can execute

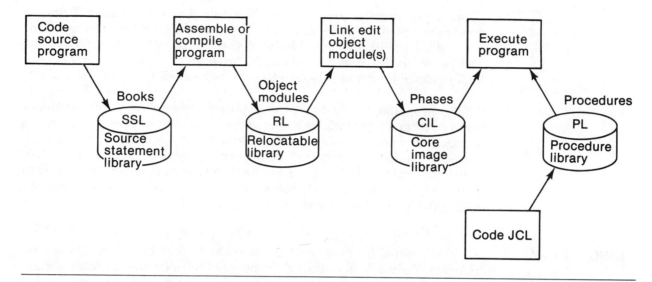

Figure 2-4   Program development and the VSE libraries

more rapidly because their I/O requests are satisfied at DASD rather than printer or card device speeds. Second, and probably more important, several programs that would otherwise require exclusive control of the same card devices and printers can execute at the same time. Without spooling, a program that writes to a printer has complete control of the device until it has finished executing, so other programs that need to do printer output have to wait.

Normally, POWER runs in a high priority partition and provides spooling services for all lower priority partitions. In addition, POWER serves as a job scheduler. To do this, it uses a scheme of classes and priorities to determine when and in what partition a program will execute. POWER also routes output to appropriate devices and is used to control those devices.

Language translators and the linkage editor   *Language translators* are the programs that convert source programs into object modules. One language translator, the *assembler*, is supplied as a part of VSE. Other language translators like the COBOL and FORTRAN IV compilers are separate products.

The *linkage editor* program, supplied as part of VSE, converts an object module into an executable phase and combines multiple object modules into a single phase. In chapter 3, you'll learn how to use both the assembler and the linkage editor.

Library maintenance programs   Not only does the linkage editor combine modules to create phases, but it's also used to add (or *catalog*) phases to core image libraries. In addition to the linkage editor, though, VSE includes several other specialized programs that perform library maintenance functions. Collectively, they're called the *VSE Librarian*.

Utility programs   Certain routine processing functions are common to most computer installations, such as copying files and sorting and merging records from one or more files. As a result, most shops use a set of general-purpose *utility programs* (or *utilities*) to perform these functions. With utility programs, specialized programs don't have to be created to perform common functions. Instead, you supply parameters to a general-purpose utility program to specify the exact processing it should do.

DISCUSSION   As you can tell by now, a VSE system is a complex collection of components. To use VSE effectively, you need to understand multiprogramming and virtual storage. You need to know how volumes, libraries, and files are organized. And, you need to know what capabilities your system software provides. But this chapter only presents the minimum you need to know to get started writing assembler language programs. To learn more about VSE, we recommend our book called *DOS/VSE JCL* by Steve Eckols.

Terminology

operating system
multiprogramming
supervisor program
supervisor
priority
task selection
partition
background partition
foreground partition
address space
Shared Virtual Area
SVA
virtual storage
real storage
label
volume
external label
internal label
volume label
standard label
VOL1 label
volume serial number
volser
file
single-file volume

multi-file volume
multi-volume file
file label
VTOC
volume table of contents
extent
file organization
sequential organization
sequential processing
indexed sequential organization
random processing
direct organization
transformation algorithm
access method
native access method
SAM
Sequential Access Method
ISAM
Indexed Sequential Access Method
DAM
Direct Access Method
VSAM
Virtual Storage Access Method
library
member

directory
source statement library
SSL
book
relocatable library
RL
object module
phase
core image library
CIL
procedure library
PL
procedure
job control language
JCL
system library
system residence file
SYSRES
private library
POWER
spooling
language translator
assembler
linkage editor
catalog
VSE Librarian
utility program
utility

Objectives

1. Describe how VSE implements multiprogramming.

2. Describe the purpose of the SVA.

3. Explain the function of volume and file labels.

4. Describe the three file organizations available under VSE.

5. List the VSE access methods that can be used for each type of file organization supported by VSE.

6. List the four types of VSE libraries (when classified by contents) and describe how they fit in the sequence of program development for a typical application.

7. Differentiate between a system library and a private library.

8. Describe the function of POWER.

Chapter 3

An introduction to program
development in assembler language

If you've already written programs for a VSE system in another language and if you already know how to use VSE JCL, you won't learn much from this chapter. I suggest, then, that you skim this chapter just trying to pick up any specific information related to assembler language and the assembly process. You can probably do this most easily by reviewing the figures in this chapter.

On the other hand, if you're new to programming and to VSE JCL, you should realize right now that there's more to writing a program in assembler language than just coding the program. To give you some idea of what's involved, topic 1 of this chapter describes the tasks of a student's procedure for developing assembler language programs. Then, topic 2 teaches you how to write the job control procedures that you will need when you compile and test your first assembler language programs on a VSE system. When you finish this chapter, you will be ready to learn assembler language itself.

TOPIC 1   A student's development procedure

When you write a program in assembler language, you should follow a standard development procedure. To some extent, this procedure will vary from one company or school to another. As a starting point, though, figure 3-1 lists the six tasks of a student's procedure for developing assembler language programs. In most training environments, you'll use a procedure like this when you develop case study programs like the one in appendix B.

Task 1: Get complete program specifications

As a programmer, it is your responsibility to make sure you know exactly what a program is supposed to do before you start to develop it. You must know not only what the inputs and outputs are, but also what processing is required to derive the desired output from the input. If you are assigned a programming problem that isn't adequately defined, be sure to question the person that assigned the program until you're confident that you know what the program is supposed to do.

Most companies have standards for what a complete program specification must include. In general, a complete program specification should include at least three items: (1) some sort of program overview, (2) record layouts for all files used by the program, and (3) print charts for all printed output prepared by the program. Other documents may be required for specific programs, but these are the most common ones.

The program overview   *Program overviews* can be prepared in many different forms. Most companies have their own standards. What's important is that a program overview must present a complete picture of what the program is supposed to do.

Figure 3-2 presents the kind of program overview we use in our shop. You will work with a program overview like this if you do the case study for this course. As you can see, the form is divided into three parts. The top section is for identification. It gives the name and number of the program as specified by the system documentation. The middle part of the form lists and describes all of the files that the program requires. In addition, it tells what the program will do with each of those files: use them only for input, use them only for output, or use them for update.

The last section of the form is for processing specifications. It's this section, of course, that is the most critical. Here, you must make sure that all of the information you need to develop the program has been provided. If it isn't all there, you must develop it yourself.

Record layouts   For each file used by a program, your specification should include a *record layout*. Figure 3-3 shows a typical record-layout

Analysis

1. Get complete program specifications.

Design

2. Design the program (chapters 3, 8, and 19).

Implementation

3. Code the program and enter it into the system (chapters 5 through 16).
4. Compile the program and correct diagnostics (chapter 17).
5. Test and debug the program (chapter 18).
6. Document the program.

Figure 3-1   A student's procedure for developing assembler language programs

form. In general, a record layout shows what fields the record contains, what the format of each field is, and where each field is located in the record. In figure 3-3, for example, you can see that the item description is 20 characters long and that it occupies positions 6-25 of the inventory master record. In the characteristics portion of the form, CL20 means that the field contains character (C) data and that it has a length (L) of 20.

Print charts   A *print chart*, such as the one in figure 3-4, shows the layout of a printed report or other document. It indicates the print positions to be used for each item on the report. For example, on the print chart in figure 3-4, the heading INVESTMENT REPORT is to be printed in print positions 15-31 of the first line of the report; the column heading ITEM NUMBER is to be printed in print positions 2-7 of the second and third lines following the heading line; and so on. Similarly, the item-number field for each detail line (as opposed to a heading line) is to be printed in print positions 2-6 and the amount invested is to be printed in positions 38-46. At the end of the report, two lines are to be skipped and then a total of the amount invested is to be printed. This total is to be indicated by two asterisks printed in positions 48 and 50.

Program: INVRPT PRODUCE INVESTMENT REPORT	Page: 1
Designer: Anne Prince	Date: 06-07-85

Input/output specifications

File	Description	Use
INVMAST	Inventory master file	Input
INVRPT	Investment report	Output

Process specifications

This program prepares an investment report from a file of inventory records. The records are in sequence by item number and the report should be printed in the same sequence. If a record is found to be out of sequence, the program should end and an appropriate message should be printed.

The basic processing requirements follow:

For each inventory record

1. Read the inventory record.
2. Calculate the investment amount.
   (Investment amount = on-hand balance x unit cost.)
3. Add the investment amount to the investment total.
4. Format and print a detail line.

After all records have been processed, prepare and print a total line.

Figure 3-2   A program overview

File name INVMAST		Record name Inventory Master Record Date 6/7/85					
Application			Designer				
Comments							

Field Name	Item number	Item description	Unit cost	Unit price	Reorder point	On hand	On order	
Characteristics	CL5	CL20	CL5	CL5	CL5	CL5	CL5	
Usage								
Position	1-5	6-25	26-30	31-35	36-40	41-45	46-50	

Figure 3-3   A record-layout form

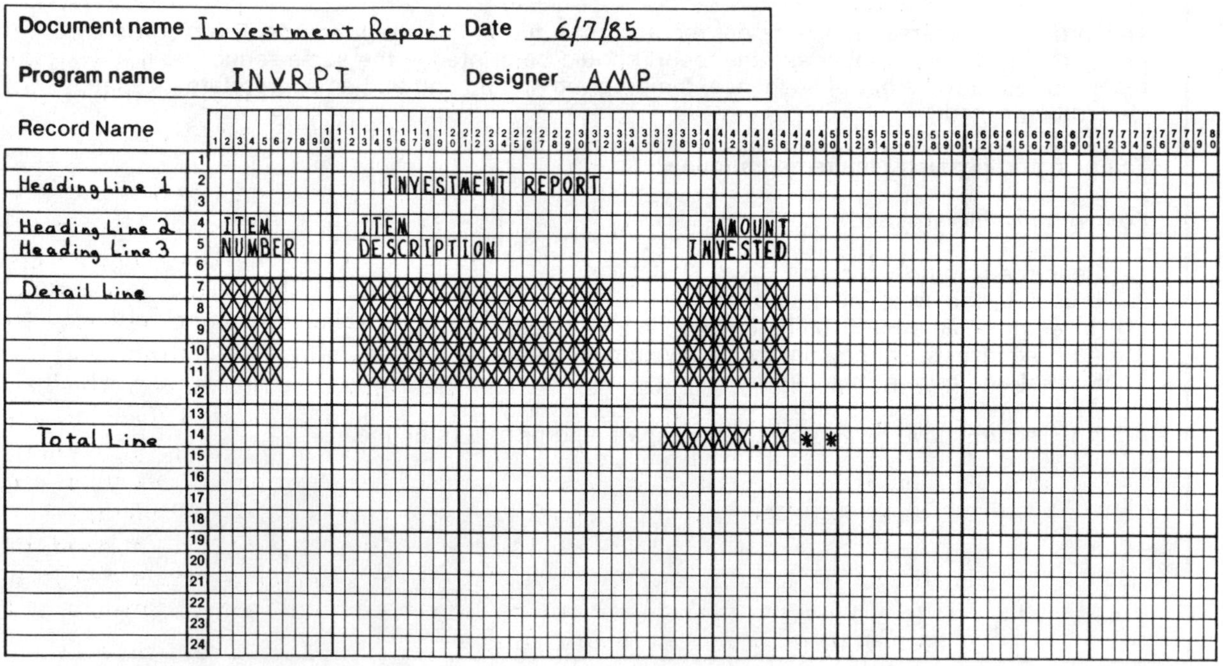

Figure 3-4   A print chart

Task 2: Design the program

The traditional design document for an assembler language program has been the *program flowchart*. It shows the logic required to derive the intended output from the input, and it shows the sequence of the instructions to be used. As a result, it directly corresponds to the coding of the program.

Figure 3-5, for example, is a program flowchart for an inventory program that prepares a report like the one specified by the print chart in figure 3-4 from a file of inventory records that have the format given in figure 3-3. Can you see how the flowchart corresponds to the process specifications given in the program overview in figure 3-2?

In case you're not familiar with flowcharting, figure 3-6 summarizes the five most commonly-used flowcharting symbols. These symbols conform to the flowcharting standards approved by the American National Standards Institute. The most important symbols are the I/O symbol, the process symbol, and the decision symbol.

To read a flowchart, you start at the top and read down and to the right, unless arrows indicate otherwise. When you come to a connector circle with a number in it, you continue at the connector circle with the same number in it. For example, after printing a detail line, the flowchart in figure 3-5 reaches a connector circle with a 1 in it. As a result, processing continues at the connector circle leading into the I/O symbol near the top of the flowchart.

In general, to draw a flowchart, you start at the top and try to show the main functions of the program in a continuous sequence of symbols, from top to bottom. You put functions that are done infrequently, like printing the total line and printing heading lines in figure 3-5, to the right of the mainline functions or on separate pages of the flowchart. Your main concern when drawing a flowchart is to show all of the major functions and all of the branching required by the program.

If the words you use on your flowcharts clearly indicate the functions to be done and the decisions to be made, they are acceptable. However, you may want to use words that correspond to assembler language coding so your flowchart will correspond more closely to the resulting program.

Frankly, we no longer believe that flowcharting is the best way to design a program. Flowcharting is time-consuming, error-prone, and the more complex a program is, the less useful flowcharting is. Nevertheless, because flowcharts are still used in many companies and because they are the traditional design document, we use them occasionally in this book to show the design of a program. Because the programs in this book are short, we think you'll find that our use of flowcharts is satisfactory.

In chapter 8, you'll be introduced to an improved method of flowcharting called *modular flowcharting*, or *modular program design*. It helps you divide a program into manageable modules so you can code and test your programs more efficiently.

Then, in chapter 19, we'll show you another way to design your programs. This design method is based on the theory of structured program-

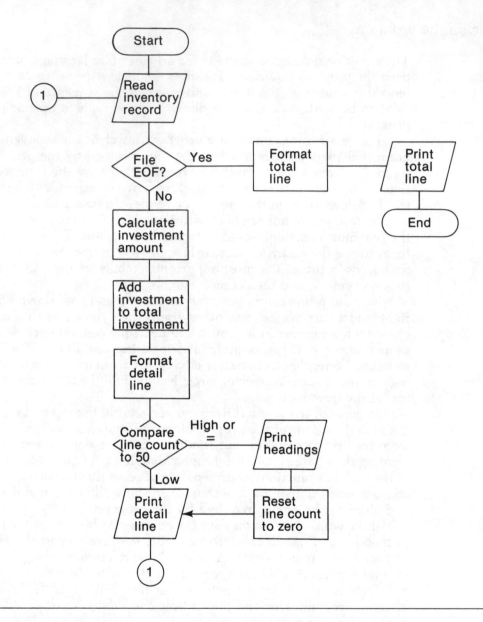

Figure 3-5 A program flowchart

ming, and it is called *structured*, or *top-down*, *design*. When you develop programs of 200 lines or more, we think you'll find structured design far more effective than flowcharting. You can read chapter 19 any time after you finish the first eight chapters of this book, but we recommend that you read it sooner rather than later. You may even want to use structured design when you do the case studies for this course.

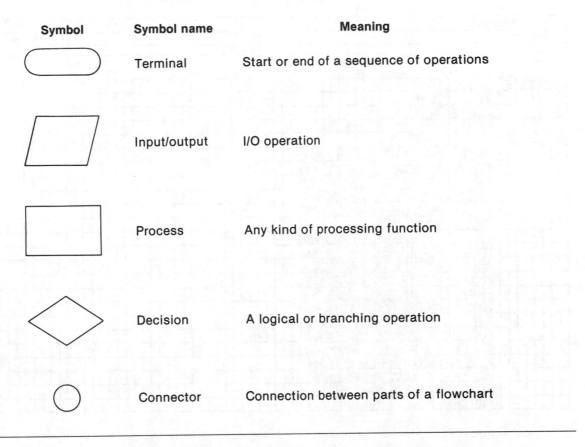

Symbol	Symbol name	Meaning
	Terminal	Start or end of a sequence of operations
	Input/output	I/O operation
	Process	Any kind of processing function
	Decision	A logical or branching operation
	Connector	Connection between parts of a flowchart

Figure 3-6   The most commonly-used ANSI symbols for program flowcharting

Task 3: Code the program and enter it into the system

When you code a program in assembler language, you write the code that gets translated into an object program. Before this code can be translated, though, it must be entered into the computer system. Since the major purpose of this book is to teach you how to code in assembler language, I won't try to introduce coding at this time. However, I will give you some idea of how you will enter your code into the system. Then, chapters 5 through 16 will teach you how to code in assembler language.

In the past, when you coded an assembler language program, you coded it on a special coding form like the one in figure 3-7. Then, when you were finished, you keypunched one 80-column *source card* for each line on the coding form. After the cards were punched, they could be read into the computer system and stored in a source statement library.

Today, punched cards are nearly obsolete, so you will probably enter your source programs directly into the computer system on an interactive basis. In the system, the lines of code will be stored as 80-character records that you can think of as card images.

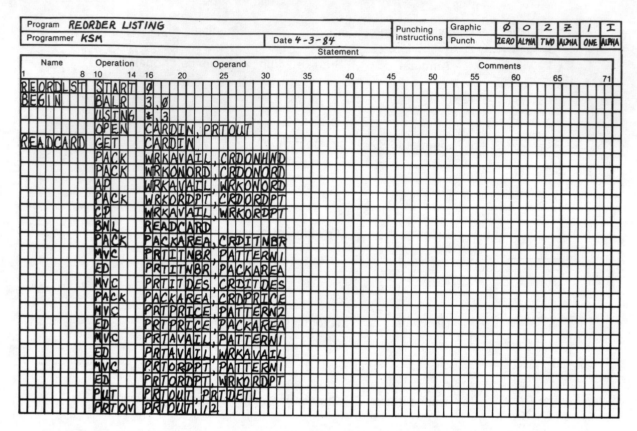

Figure 3-7   The start of an assembler language program coded on a coding form

Although you may be asked to handcode your program on a coding form before you enter it into the system, this isn't really necessary. Instead, you can code your program as you enter it into the system using your flowchart or other design document as a guide for your entries. In fact, with a little practice, you'll find that you can enter your program directly into the system much faster than you can handcode your program and then enter it into the system.

When you enter a program into a system, you do it under the control of an interactive editor program. Although several different editors are available on a VSE system, chances are that you'll be using the editor that comes with ICCF. In case you aren't familiar with ICCF, I will briefly describe its editor at this time. Keep in mind, though, that this book doesn't attempt to teach you how to use ICCF or any other program development system. That's beyond the scope of this book. The material that follows is designed only to introduce you to the idea of interactive program entry.

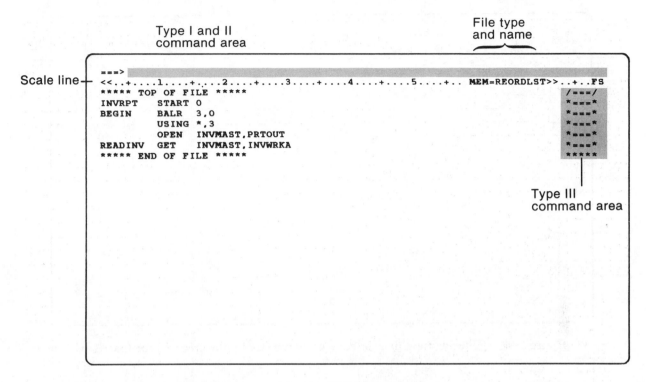

Figure 3-8   Command areas used by the ICCF full-screen editor

An introduction to ICCF   *ICCF*, which stands for *Interactive Computing and Control Facility*, is a comprehensive time-sharing system that allows a VSE system to operate without card input and output devices. Under ICCF, terminal users can create, maintain, and store card-image files that contain procedures, source programs, or data. ICCF stores those card-image files on DASD.

When you use ICCF to enter source code, you invoke a program called the *full-screen editor*. The full-screen editor lets you enter source code and store it in a library member. In addition, it lets you retrieve source code from a library member and make changes to it.

Figure 3-8 presents the screen ICCF displays when you invoke the full-screen editor to edit an existing file. The two areas shaded on the screen are command entry areas. You use the *Type I and II command area* to enter editor commands that manage library members, scroll the text, search for text, end the editing session, and so on.

To illustrate, suppose you want to add new lines to the end of the five lines of source code that are shown in figure 3-8. First, you enter the BOTTOM command in the Type I and II command area. This takes you to the end of your file as illustrated in part 1 of figure 3-9. Then, you enter the INPUT command which allows you to enter source code on the remaining lines of the screen as illustrated in part 2 of figure 3-9. If you want to

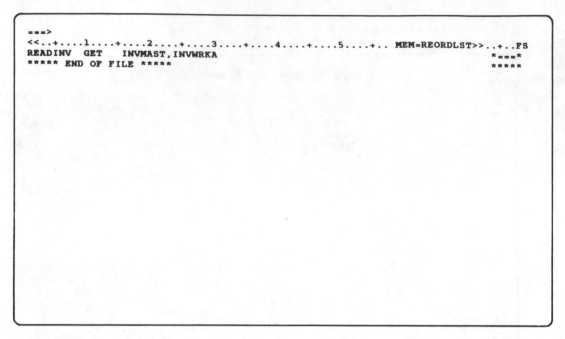

```
===>
<<..+....1....+....2....+....3....+....4....+....5....+.. MEM=REORDLST>>..+..FS
READINV  GET    INVMAST,INVWRKA                                        *===*
***** END OF FILE *****                                               *****
```

Figure 3-9   Entering new lines of code using the ICCF full-screen editor (part 1 of 2)

change any of the text you've entered, you just type the new text right over the old text.

You use the *Type III command area* to enter special full-screen editor commands. These commands are used to manipulate lines within the text. They include commands that let you insert blank lines, move or copy lines from one area of the file to another, and delete lines.

Needless to say, there is a lot more to the full-screen editor of ICCF than this brief introduction indicates. And there's a lot more to ICCF than just the full-screen editor. Most program development facilities, including ICCF, provide tools that help you compile, test, and debug a program as well as enter and edit it. To become a proficient assembler language programmer, you must learn how to make effective use of the program development facility that is available on your system.

Task 4: Assemble the program and correct the diagnostics

Assembling an assembler language source program means converting the source program into an object program. This translation of an assembler language *source program* into an *object program* is called an *assembly*. This is done by the computer under control of a translator program called the *assembler*.

In order to invoke the assembler, you must submit a *job control pro-*

```
==->
<<..+....1....+....2....+....3....+....4....+....5....+.. MEM=REORDLST>>..+..FS
READINV   GET     INVMAST,INVWRKA                                        /===/*
          AP      COUNT=P'1'                                             *INPUT
          MVC     PRINTNBR,INVITNBR                                      *INPUT
          PACK    WRKITCST,INVITCST                                      *INPUT
          MVC     PRTITCST,PATTERN1                                      *INPUT
          ED      PRTITCST,WRKITCST                                      *INPUT
          PACK    WRKBOH,INVBOH                                          *INPUT
          MVC     PRTBOH,PATTERN2                                        *INPUT
          ED      PRTBOH,WRKBOH                                          *INPUT
          PACK    WRKITVAL,INVITCST                                      *INPUT
          MP      WRKITVAL,WRKBOH                                        *INPUT
          AP      TOTVALUE,WRKITVAL                                      *INPUT
          MVC     PRTITVAL,PATTERN3                                      *INPUT
          ED      PRTITVAL,WRKITVAL                                      *INPUT
                                                                         *INPUT
                                                                         *INPUT
                                                                         *INPUT
                                                                         *INPUT
                                                                         *INPUT
                                                                         *INPUT
                                                                         *INPUT
                                                                         *INPUT
```

Figure 3-9   Entering new lines of code using the ICCF full-screen editor (part 2 of 2)

cedure to the operating system. The statements within this procedure tell VSE to execute the assembler. They also tell VSE where to find the source program, where to store the object program, and what options should be in effect during the assembly. You will learn how to create some basic job control procedures in topic 2 of this chapter.

During the assembly, an *assembly listing* is printed by the computer. The assembly listing is a listing of the source program as well as a listing of various reference tables. If any errors are caught by the assembler during the assembly (as is usually the case the first time you assemble a program), one or more *diagnostic messages* (or *diagnostics*) are printed as part of the assembly listing and the object program isn't created. Each diagnostic calls attention to one error in the source code.

If there are diagnostics, you make the necessary corrections to the source code; then, you reassemble the program. You repeat this process until there are no more diagnostics in the assembly listing. At this point, the program is ready to be tested.

Chapter 17 will show you how to correct the diagnostics you en counter. It will also show you some of the optional output that can be part of the assembly listing. You can read chapter 17 any time after you've completed chapter 5. But you will certainly want to read this chapter when you complete your first assembly and receive your first diagnostic messages.

Task 5: Test and debug the program

Before you can test a program, it must be *link edited* by a program called the *linkage editor*. The linkage editor is invoked by your job control procedure for assembly and testing as you'll learn in the next topic. The linkage editor converts the object module created during the assembly into an executable module called a *phase*.

After executing the linkage editor, your assemble-and-test procedure causes your program to be executed. The statements in the procedure tell VSE where to find the test files your program is going to process and where to put the files your program creates.

The test data in your test files should be designed to try all of the conditions that may occur when your program is used. After your program has been executed, you compare the actual output you got with the output you expected to get. If they agree, you can assume that the program does what you intended it to do.

More likely, however, the actual output and the intended output will not agree the first time the program is executed. If this is the case, you must *debug* the program. You must find the errors (*bugs*), make the necessary corrections to the source code using your interactive editor, reassemble the source program, and make another test run. This process is continued until the program executes as intended.

In some cases, your program may not even run to completion the first few times you test it. When a program terminates like this, it is referred to as an *abnormal termination*. An abnormal termination indicates that the program tried to do something invalid like trying to add two alphabetic fields. When an abnormal termination occurs, you use some special debugging techniques to find and correct the bug.

In actual practice, rather than making just one test run on a new program, you make a series of test runs using different sets of test data. The test data for the first test run is usually low in volume, perhaps only a half-dozen records, and may be designed to test only the main processing functions of the program. After you have debugged the program using this data, you may test it on data that tries the exceptional conditions that may come up during the execution of the program. Finally, you may test your program for conditions that depend upon larger volumes of data such as the page overflow condition when printing reports and other documents.

In chapter 18, you will learn how to test and debug your assembler language programs. You will learn how to debug programs that run to normal terminations as well as programs that terminate abnormally. You can read chapter 18 any time after you complete chapter 5 of this book. But you will certainly want to read this chapter when you get your first test run output or experience your first abnormal termination.

As you will see, chapter 18 doesn't try to teach you how to create the test data for your test runs. This book assumes, in fact, that you will be given the test files you need to test your case study programs. As a result, you won't need to create your own test data until you start writing production programs. At that time, you should find out what your shop's standards are for planning test runs and creating test data.

Task 6: Document the program

Documentation in data processing terminology refers to the collection of records that specifies what is being done and what is going to be done within a data processing system. For each program in an installation, there should be a collection of documents referred to as *program documentation*. As a programmer, one of your jobs is to provide this documentation for each program you write.

Program documentation is important because it is almost inevitable that changes will be made to a production program. Sometimes, the users of the program will discover that it doesn't work quite the way it was supposed to. Sometimes, the users will want the program to do more than they originally specified. Sometimes, a company will change the way it does some function, so the related programs have to be changed. No matter what the reason for the modifications, though, it is difficult indeed to modify or enhance a program that isn't adequately documented.

Fortunately, some of the most important components of program documentation are by-products of the program development process: the program overview, the record layouts, the print chart, and the design document. In addition, you should include the final assembly listing since it is the only document that shows the actual programming details. And, you may be asked to include your listings of test data and test run output.

For production programs, your shop standards should specify what's required for program documentation. For your case study programs, you should provide (1) your design document, (2) your final assembly listing, and (3) listings of your test run output, plus any additional items your instructor may request.

Discussion

This topic is designed to give you a better idea of what you must do to develop an assembler language program in a training environment. If you follow the procedure shown in figure 3-1, you should be able to do your case study assignments with relative efficiency.

In contrast to the procedure in figure 3-1, figure 3-10 presents a typical procedure for developing assembler language programs in a production environment. Here, you can see that the programmer should get related source books and subprograms as a task in the analysis phase. You'll learn more about this in chapters 6 and 8. Then, task 3 in the design phase suggests the use of structured design and pseudocode as described in chapter 19. This is logical because production programs are generally longer and more complicated than case study programs so program design is more important. Finally, in the implementation phase, you can see that the procedure suggests that you plan the testing, code the procedures for the test runs, and create the test data for the test runs before any coding is done. Then, the program can be coded and tested, a few modules at a time, using a technique called top-down testing. These tasks show how important it is to test a program in a carefully-controlled manner.

Analysis

1. Get complete program specifications.
2. Get related source books and subprograms.

Design

3. Design the program using a structure chart for the entire program and pseudocode for the modules of the program.

Implementation

4. Plan the testing of the program by creating a test plan.
5. Code the job control procedures for the test runs.
6. If necessary, create the test data for the test runs.
7. Code and test the program using top-down testing.
8. Document the program.

Figure 3-10   A professional procedure for developing assembler language programs

Terminology

program overview	diagnostic
record layout	link editing
print chart	linkage editor
program flowchart	phase
modular flowcharting	debugging
modular program design	bug
structured design	abnormal termination
top-down design	documentation
source card	program documentation
ICCF	
Interactive Computing and Control Facility	
full-screen editor	
Type I and II command area	
Type III command area	
source program	
object program	
assembly	
assembler	
job control procedure	
assembly listing	
diagnostic message	

Objective   List and describe the six tasks of the student's development procedure presented in this topic.

TOPIC 2   VSE JCL for assembling and testing disk-to-printer programs

To assemble and test a program, you have to create the required job control procedures. These job control procedures consist of *job control statements* that are in a sense a language of their own. As a result, the code used in job control statements is often referred to as *job control language*, or *JCL*. A series of job control statements, possibly combined with some data to be processed, is called a *job stream*.

In case you aren't familiar with JCL, this topic presents the JCL you'll need to assemble and test disk-to-printer programs. If you are familiar with JCL, you can go through this topic quickly just to pick up any JCL considerations that apply to the assembly process. As you proceed through this book, you will be shown more advanced job streams so you'll always see how your assembler language program and its JCL are related.

HOW TO CODE JCL STATEMENTS

If you're not familiar with JCL at all, you first need to learn the general format of JCL statements. To start, these statements are 80 characters long because they were originally in the form of 80-column punched cards. Figure 3-11 shows how these 80 characters can be divided into seven fields. In practice, though, most JCL statements require only the name, operation, and operands fields, so that's all I'll present in this book.

The name field   The *name field* (positions 1-3) identifies a statement as a job control statement. This field contains two slashes followed by a space in all JCL statements except four (/*, /&, *, and / +). Frankly, calling the first three positions of a job control statement the "name field" is confusing, but that's how the IBM literature refers to them. In the statements you use for this course, you will always have //, /*, or /& in the first two positions of the name field and a blank in the third position.

The operation field   The *operation field* (positions 4-11) follows the name field. In it, you code a VSE operation code that specifies the statement's function. In figure 3-11, for example, the operation code is JOB. You don't have to start the operation code in position 4, but I think your JCL will be more readable if you do.

The operands field   The *operands field* begins at least one space after the operation code and can extend up through position 71. However, I recommend that you always code the operands starting in position 12. In this field, you code whatever operands a statement requires. If a statement requires more than one operand, you separate the operands with commas.

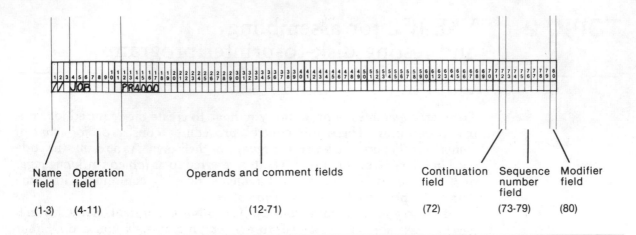

Figure 3-11   The format of a VSE job control statement

Since VSE assumes that the operands are complete when it encounters a blank, make sure that you don't put a blank between two operands by accident.

JOBS AND JOB STEPS

A *job* is submitted as a single unit of work to VSE. A job consists of one or more *job steps* (programs). VSE identifies a new job when it encounters a JOB statement. Within a job, it identifies a new job step when it encounters an EXEC statement. And it identifies the end of a job when it encounters the end-of-job statement (/&) or, if /& is missing, another JOB statement.

The JOB statement   Because up to 12 jobs can be running at the same time in VSE's partitions, it's useful to be able to refer to a job by job name. So, on the JOB statement, you code a one- to eight-character *job name* in the operands field. Then, when VSE issues messages to the system operator, it uses your JOB name. Also, listings produced by the job are labelled with your job name.

Because a typical VSE installation has hundreds of jobs, their names need to be standardized. As a result, your shop or school probably has rules for creating job names. If so, find out what they are and use them.

The second operand of the JOB statement is optional. You use it only if the VSE job accounting interface is installed on your system. If you do code this accounting information, it must begin one space after the job name. Just what you'll code for this operand depends on your shop's or school's standards. So find out if you should use this accounting operand and, if so, what you should code in it.

```
// JOB      MCQUILLN
// EXEC     ASSEMBLY
    .
    .   SOURCE PROGRAM
    .
/*
/&
```

Figure 3-12   An assemble-only job stream

The EXEC statement   The EXEC statement specifies the name of the program to be executed as you'll see in a moment. As a result, the EXEC statement marks the start of one job step and the end of the previous job step.

The end-of-job (/&) statement   At the end of each job, you should code the end-of-job statement. Obviously, this is one of the four JCL statements that doesn't begin with //. If VSE encounters a JOB statement without a preceding /&, it assumes the /& was present. Nevertheless, it's a good practice to end each job with /&.

JCL FOR AN ASSEMBLE-ONLY JOB

Sometimes, when you first test a new program, you will want to assemble it without link editing or executing it. The reason for this is that you will most likely have diagnostics the first couple of times you assemble a program. Figure 3-12 illustrates the job control statements you need to assemble your source program. As you can see, it is a job that contains only one job step.

The first statement in this job gives the job name MCQUILLN to the job. This is simply an eight-character shortening of the programmer's name. The second statement causes the assembler to be loaded into storage and executed. In other words, ASSEMBLY is the phase name of the assembler in the core image library of the system. When the assembler is executed, it reads the source program and prints the assembly listing along with diagnostic messages and other assembly output.

The end-of-data (/*) statement   At the end of the source program, you can see another JCL statement that doesn't start with //. It is called the end-of-data statement. It tells VSE that there are no more data records in the job stream. In this job, the source program is data to the assembler, so the /* statement marks the end of the data.

The OPTION statement   If you want to control the printed output of the assembly, you can use an OPTION statement. For instance, figure

List output	LIST RLD $\begin{Bmatrix} \text{XREF} \\ \text{SXREF} \end{Bmatrix}$	(NOLIST) (NORLD) (NOXREF)	Produce a source code listing. Print the relocation dictionary. Print a cross-reference listing of instructions and data names (SXREF produces a sorted cross-reference listing).
Object module output	$\begin{Bmatrix} \text{LINK} \\ \text{CATAL} \end{Bmatrix}$ DECK ALIGN	(NOLINK) (NODECK) (NOALIGN)	Write the object module on SYSLNK and have the linkage editor convert it into a temporary phase. Write the object module on SYSLNK and have the linkage editor convert it into a permanent (cataloged) phase. Write the object module on SYSPCH. Align all binary fields on the proper boundaries in the object module.
Assembler copy book and edited macro Input	$\begin{Bmatrix} \text{SUBLIB} = \text{AE} \\ \text{SUBLIB} = \text{DF} \end{Bmatrix}$		Use sublibraries A and E for copy books and edited macros. Use sublibraries D and F for copy books and edited macros.

Figure 3-13   OPTION statement operands that control assembler and linkage editor functions

3-13 shows four options that can be set that affect the list output for the assembly process. It also shows four options that affect object module output, which you'll learn about in a moment, and two options that affect the use of copy books. To turn an option on, you code the operand in the left-hand column of figure 3-13 like LIST or ERRS. To turn an option off, you code the operand in the righthand column like NOLIST or NOERRS.

Before you turn any options on or off, though, you should realize that *default values* are in effect if you don't use an OPTION statement. In most cases, the default options will be the list options you will want for your assembly. In general, then, you won't need to use OPTION statements for your assemble-only jobs. If you want to find out what the default options are, just run an assemble-only job like the one in figure 3-12. Near the end of your job output, you'll find a listing of the options in effect (the default options).

If you do want to change the list output options, you code an OPTION statement for the assembly as in the job stream in figure 3-14. Here, the job stream says that the assembler should *not* print a relocation dictionary (NORLD) or a cross-reference listing (NOXREF). When you code the operands of an OPTION statement, you only need to code the

```
// JOB      MCQUILLN
// OPTION   NORLD,NOXREF
// EXEC     ASSEMBLY
   .
   .     SOURCE PROGRAM
   .
/*
/&
```

Figure 3-14   An assemble-only job stream with option changes

ones you want to change. Then, when the job ends, all options are reset to their default values.

JCL FOR AN ASSEMBLE-LINK-AND-TEST JOB

A job to assemble and test a program actually consists of three job steps as shown in figure 3-15. In the first step, the assembler is executed, thus preparing the object program. During this step, the assembler may take some source code from copy books as you'll learn in chapter 6. And, it will usually print an assembly listing along with related list output.

In the second step, the linkage editor is executed. During this step, the object program is combined with any other object modules required by the program. The result is an executable phase. The linkage editor also produces list output that shows which object modules were combined.

In the third step, the phase that was created in the second step is executed. When it is executed, the operations you specified in your assembler language program are performed. As a result, the phase will read whatever old files you specified, create whatever new files you specified, and print whatever printed output you specified. In a simple disk-to-printer program, the phase will read the disk file and print the output you specified.

Figure 3-16 gives a complete job stream for an assemble-link-and-test job. If you study it, you can see how it relates to the flowchart in figure 3-15.

Job step 1: Assembling the source program

The statements for the first job step are these:

```
// JOB      MCQUILLN
// OPTION   LINK
// EXEC     ASSEMBLY
   (source program)
/*
```

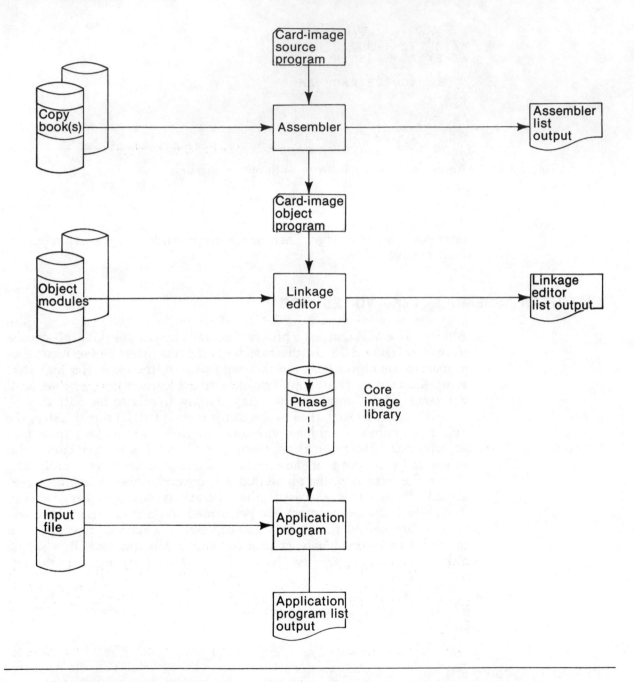

Figure 3-15   The steps in an assemble-link-and-test job for a disk-to-printer program

```
// JOB       MCQUILLN
// OPTION    LINK
// EXEC      ASSEMBLY
   .
   .   SOURCE PROGRAM
   .
/*
// LIBDEF    CL,TO=USRCL2
// EXEC      LNKEDT
// ASSGN     SYS008,240
// DLBL      INVMAST,'INVENTORY.MASTER.FILE'
// EXEC
/&
```

Figure 3-16   An assemble-link-and-test job stream for a disk-to-printer program

Here, you can see that the OPTION statement is used to change an option related to object module output. The LINK option indicates that the resulting object program will be link edited so the object code created during the assembly is saved on disk. Usually, the default option is NOLINK so you'll need to code this OPTION statement in your assemble-link-and-test jobs.

Job step 2: Link editing the object program

The second job step executes the linkage editor program. The JCL for this step is this:

```
// LIBDEF    CL,TO=USRCL2
// EXEC      LNKEDT
```

Here, LNKEDT is the name for the linkage editor program that is stored in the system's core image library. When the linkage editor is executed, it combines the required object modules into a phase and stores the resulting phase in a core image library.

The LIBDEF statement   When you run the linkage editor, you have to specify the core image library in which the linkage editor should store the phase it produces. That's necessary whether the linkage editor is producing a temporary (LINK) or permanent (CATAL) phase. In this example, the statement

```
// LIBDEF    CL,TO=USRCL2
```

causes the linkage editor to store the phase it produces in the core image library (CL) called USRCL2 (USeR Core image Library 2).

Job step 3: Testing the program

The third job step executes your assembler language program. Its JCL is this:

```
// ASSGN    SYS008,240
// DLBL     INVMAST,'INVENTORY.MASTER.FILE'
// EXEC
```

Here, the EXEC statement doesn't specify a program name so the system executes the temporary phase that was stored in the core image library in the second job step. This is consistent with the LINK option because this option specifies a temporary phase.

Before your application program can be executed, though, your JCL must tell VSE what files and devices your program uses. To do this for a simple sequential file, you use the ASSGN and DLBL statements. At this time, then, I will discuss these statements briefly, just enough to get you started writing disk-to-printer programs. Then, in chapters 13 through 16, you'll learn more about the JCL for disk files.

The ASSGN statement   The ASSGN statement is used to assign the files defined in your program to physical I/O devices. The basic format of the ASSGN statement is this:

```
// ASSGN    SYSxxx,cuu
```

where SYSxxx is the logical unit name and cuu is the address of the device you want to associate with that logical unit. Here, the logical unit name refers to the name given for the file in your assembler language program. You'll learn how to code the logical unit name in your program in chapter 5.

All *logical unit names* are six characters long and begin with SYS. The logical unit names you're most likely to use in ASSGN statements for application programs are called *programmer logical units*. They have numbers between 000 and 255 in the xxx position of the name. However, you may occasionally need to assign a *system logical unit*. These unit names have letters in the xxx positions as in the name SYSLST, which refers to the system printer.

The device address (cuu) is the standard VSE address that I described in chapter 1, where the first hex digit (c) is the device's channel address and the second and third hex digits (uu) are its unit address. So, in figure 3-16, the ASSGN statement

```
// ASSGN    SYS008,240
```

relates the logical unit SYS008 to the device at address 240.

Since many programmer logical units have *permanent assignments*, you won't need to code an ASSGN statement for a file if the permanent assignment is the one you want. In other words, if the permanent assignment for SYS008 is device address 240, you don't need the ASSGN statement in figure 3-16. Similarly, since most system logical units have permanent assignments, you usually don't have to code ASSGN statements for them.

The DLBL statement   The DLBL statement names a file and describes its characteristics. Although it can have more than two operands, its basic format is this:

```
// DLBL     file-name,'file-id'
```

Here, the file-name operand refers to the name given for the file in your assembler language program. In contrast, the file-id operand gives the name in the file's physical label. So, the DLBL statement in figure 3-16

```
// DLBL     INVMAST,'INVENTORY.MASTER.FILE'
```

says that the file identified in the program as INVMAST is supposed to be the physical file identified in its label as INVENTORY.MASTER.FILE.

USING JCL ON AN INTERACTIVE BASIS

When you develop assembler language programs on a VSE system, you need to know job control language so you can assemble and test your programs. But how you use your job streams will depend on the program development software you're using.

Traditionally, of course, a job stream like the one in figure 3-16 would have been punched in cards and submitted to the system by way of a card reader. Today, however, it's far more likely that you'll create your job streams interactively. Then, you can submit your jobs to VSE using a *submit-to-batch facility*.

To illustrate, suppose you're using ICCF as introduced in topic 1 of this chapter to develop the program for the case study in appendix B. After you've created your source program and you're ready to assemble or test it, you add job statements before and after your source program as shown in figures 3-12 and 3-16. Next, you store your job in a file named something like CS1 (for case study 1). Then, to submit the job for batch processing, you invoke ICCF's submit-to-batch facility with a command like this:

```
SUBMIT CS1 DIRECTBG
```

Once this command is executed, your job is placed in a queue of batch jobs and a message is returned to your screen indicating that the job was successfully submitted. As a result, you can continue with another ICCF job. Meanwhile, your batch job will be executed by VSE when its turn comes up and its printed output will be printed by one of the system's printers.

As I mentioned in topic 1, you may not use ICCF in your shop. Also, ICCF provides other ways in which you can assemble and test your programs. Since this book is about assembler language, not interactive program development, I only wanted to give you an idea of how you might be using your JCL at this time. It's your job to find out how you will actually use it in your shop.

DISCUSSION

When preparing assembler language programs, the job streams in figures 3-12, 3-14, and 3-16 are all that you will need for sequential disk-to-printer programs. Normally, the assemble-only stream in figure 3-12 is used until all diagnostics have been corrected. Then, the assemble-link-and-test stream in figure 3-16 is used for a series of test runs. Each time an error is debugged, the source program is changed, and the program is reassembled and tested again.

In figures 3-12, 3-14, and 3-16, the shading indicates elements in the job streams that you may have to change to suit your circumstances. For example, you will want to code a job name in the JOB statement that conforms to the standards of your shop or school. Then, in the job stream in figure 3-16, you'll want to specify the proper core image library in the LIBDEF statement in the link-edit step. And, you'll want to give the proper specifications for the input file your program will be using in the ASSGN and DLBL statements.

Needless to say, this topic is only the briefest of introductions to VSE JCL. So I hope you realize that most of the statements I've shown have other operands and that VSE offers many other JCL statements. Also, you should realize that you must know both assembler language and the related JCL if you want to become an effective programmer. As you go through this book, you'll be introduced to the JCL for using copy books, subprograms, and disk files. But if you want to become proficient at using VSE JCL, by all means get our *DOS/VSE JCL* book by Steve Eckols.

Terminology

job control statement
job control language
JCL
job stream
name field
operation field
operands field
job

job step
job name
default value
logical unit name
programmer logical unit
system logical unit
permanent assignment
submit-to-batch facility

Objective

Create job streams for assembling and for assembling and testing an assembler language program that requires disk input and printer output. You will be given the logical unit name and the file-id for each disk file used by the application program.

Section 2

A professional subset of assembler language

The five chapters in this section present a professional subset of assembler language. Once you have mastered it, you will be able to write assembler language programs and subprograms the way professional programmers write them.

Whether or not you ever write assembler language programs as a professional, we believe the material in this section will be useful to you if you work with an IBM mainframe under DOS/VSE. As you will see, a knowledge of assembler language helps you understand both IBM mainframes and DOS/VSE. That's why we think the material in this section is "the least you should know about assembler language."

Once you complete this section, the rest of the material in this book should be relatively easy for you to master. For instance, it should be easy for you to learn how to use the elements for table handling, the elements for writing macros, the elements for VSAM file access, and so on. As a result, you should be prepared to put more effort into this section than any of the other sections.

Chapter 4

CPU Concepts for IBM mainframes

To program in assembler language, you need considerable knowledge of the internal organization and operation of the System/370. This chapter is designed to provide that knowledge. First, it describes how data and instructions are stored in the System/370. Then, it explains how some commonly used instructions operate.

Throughout this chapter and the rest of this book, please keep in mind that a reference to the System/370 includes any of the other mainframes in the System/370 family of mainframes. Although these mainframes differ in terms of price and performance, their instructions all operate the same way from a conceptual point of view.

MAIN STORAGE   When a program is loaded into a computer, it is placed in the main storage of the CPU. In terms of VSE, a program must be loaded into a partition that is large enough to store the complete object program. For instance, a 64K partition can be used to store programs that require up to 65,536 *storage positions*, or *bytes*. (Remember that K is used to refer to approximately 1,000 storage positions, but one K is actually 1024 storage positions.)

Associated with each of the storage positions of main memory is a number that identifies it; this number is called the *address* of the storage position. A computer with 1M of storage, for instance, has addresses ranging from 0 to 1,048,575. As a result, you can talk about the contents of the storage position at address 180, the contents of byte 4,482, and so on.

In a System/370, data can be stored in four different forms. In one form, one character is stored in each byte of storage. To illustrate this form, suppose the following boxes represent the twenty storage positions from 480 through 499:

Contents: | G | E | O | R | G | E | 3 | 4 | 3 | 9 | 9 | 8 | 2 | | * | 1 | 1 | 2 | 1 | 4 |

Addresses: 480   485   490   495

In this case, you can say that storage position 480 contains the letter G, storage position 487 contains the number 4, storage position 494 contains an asterisk, and position 493 contains a blank. Or you can say that there is a 2 at address 497 and the number 343 is stored in bytes 486 through 488. This is simply the way programmers talk about storage and its contents.

Several consecutive storage positions that contain one item of data such as item number or unit price are commonly referred to as a *field*. For example, bytes 486-490 (this is read as 486 through 490) might represent a balance-on-hand field, while positions 495-499 might represent an item-number field. To address a field, a System/370 instruction specifies the address of the leftmost storage position as well as the number of storage positions in the field. Thus, address 486 with a length of 5 would address the field in positions 486-490, while address 1024 with a length of 20 would address the field in positions 1024-1043.

Of course, a byte of storage isn't really a small box with a character of data in it. Instead, each storage position consists of electronic components that are called *binary components* because they can be switched to either of two conditions. These two conditions are commonly referred to as "on" and "off" and are represented by 0 and 1. In this case, 0 and 1 are called *binary digits*, or *bits*, and 0 represents an "off" bit while 1 represents an "on" bit.

In order to represent data, the bits at a storage position are turned on or off in selected combinations. Each combination represents a digit or digits, a letter, or a special character. On the System/370, for example, 11000010, 11110010, and 11111001 can be used to represent the characters B, 2, and 9. In other words, eight bits represent one storage position. You can also say that eight bits make up one byte of storage.

Although you rarely need to know it, each byte on the System/370 is actually made up of nine bits: eight data bits plus one *parity bit*. The parity bit is used as a check on operations that take place within the CPU. Each time a byte of data is moved into or out of storage during the execution of a program, the byte is *parity checked*. That is, the number of on-bits in the byte is checked to make sure that it is an odd number. If the number of on-bits is even, as in the code 011110011, an error is indicated.

Fortunately, parity errors on a modern computer system are extremely rare, and the parity checking that goes on is completely transparent to the programmer. As a result, the parity bit is usually ignored when discussing specific codes or storage forms, and the System/370 is usually

Decimal	Binary	Hexadecimal
0	0000	0
1	0001	1
2	0010	2
3	0011	3
4	0100	4
5	0101	5
6	0110	6
7	0111	7
8	1000	8
9	1001	9
10	1010	A
11	1011	B
12	1100	C
13	1101	D
14	1110	E
15	1111	F
16	10000	10

Figure 4-1   Hexadecimal conversion chart

said to have an eight-bit, rather than a nine-bit, byte. For this reason, no further mention of parity checking will be made. After all, parity checking is simply an electronic check on the accuracy of internal operations.

DATA STORAGE

Because it is awkward to work with binary codes, *hexadecimal* notation is commonly used to represent the contents of System/370 storage. The intent of hexadecimal notation is to provide a method of shorthand in which one group of four binary digits is replaced with one hexadecimal character. Figure 4-1 shows the relationship between binary, decimal, and hexadecimal notation. Thus, the binary 1111 is written as F in hexadecimal (or *hex*); the binary 1001 is a hex 9; and binary 0110 is a hex 6.

As I mentioned before, data can be stored in four forms in the System/370. Three of these are covered in this chapter. They are *EBCDIC*, *packed decimal*, and *fixed-point binary* (or just *binary*). The fourth form is called *floating-point binary*; it is presented in chapter 12.

EBCDIC

In *EBCDIC* code (pronounced ee'-bee-dick or ib'-si-dick), each byte of storage contains one character of data. Because eight bits can be arranged in 256 different combinations, EBCDIC can be used to represent the letters of the alphabet (both upper and lower case), the decimal digits, and many special characters. However, not all of the 256 combinations are used.

Figure 4-2 gives the EBCDIC codes for the more commonly used characters. It shows the binary code for each character as well as the hexadecimal code. As indicated in the figure, it is common to divide an EBCDIC code into two halves. The leftmost four bits represent the *zone bits*; the rightmost four bits represent the *digit bits*.

Character	EBCDIC		Hexadecimal code
	Zone bits	Digit bits	
blank	0100	0000	40
.	0100	1011	4B
(	0100	1101	4D
+	0100	1110	4E
&	0101	0000	50
$	0101	1011	5B
*	0101	1100	5C
)	0101	1101	5D
;	0101	1110	5E
-	0110	0000	60
/	0110	0001	61
,	0110	1011	6B
%	0110	1100	6C
?	0110	1111	6F
#	0111	1011	7B
'	0111	1101	7D
=	0111	1110	7E
"	0111	1111	7F
A	1100	0001	C1
B	1100	0010	C2
C	1100	0011	C3
D	1100	0100	C4
E	1100	0101	C5
F	1100	0110	C6
G	1100	0111	C7
H	1100	1000	C8
I	1100	1001	C9
J	1101	0001	D1
K	1101	0010	D2
L	1101	0011	D3
M	1101	0100	D4
N	1101	0101	D5
O	1101	0110	D6
P	1101	0111	D7
Q	1101	1000	D8
R	1101	1001	D9
S	1110	0010	E2
T	1110	0011	E3
U	1110	0100	E4
V	1110	0101	E5
W	1110	0110	E6
X	1110	0111	E7
Y	1110	1000	E8
Z	1110	1001	E9
0	1111	0000	F0
1	1111	0001	F1
2	1111	0010	F2
3	1111	0011	F3
4	1111	0100	F4
5	1111	0101	F5
6	1111	0110	F6
7	1111	0111	F7
8	1111	1000	F8
9	1111	1001	F9

Figure 4-2   EBCDIC coding chart

If you review the codes in figure 4-2, you can see that the zone bits for the letters A-I are 1100 (hex C); the zone bits for the letters J-R are 1101 (hex D); the zone bits for the letters S-Z are 1110 (hex E); and the zone bits for the digits 0-9 are 1111 (hex F). For special characters, other zone bit combinations are used. Thus, 01011011 is used for the dollar sign, 01001101 is used for the left parenthesis, and 01000000 is used for a blank (yes, a blank is considered to be a character). Although it is sometimes handy for a programmer to know the EBCDIC codes for numbers and letters, decoding special characters is usually unnecessary. If it is required, the codes can easily be looked up in reference tables.

To represent EBCDIC data in storage, hex can be used as in this example:

```
E2 C1 D4 40 40 40 40 40 40 40
```

Here, the name SAM is stored in ten bytes (hex 40 represents a blank). Similarly, a six-byte numeric EBCDIC field containing 1234 can be shown as:

```
F0 F0 F1 F2 F3 F4
```

This EBCDIC form of representing numbers is referred to as *zoned decimal*. You should notice from these two examples that an alphanumeric field is normally left-justified with blanks filling out the unused bytes to the right of the data. A numeric field is normally right-justified with zeros filling out the unused bytes in the left of the field.

To represent the sign of a zoned-decimal field, the zone portion of the rightmost byte of the field is used. If the zone portion is hex F or hex C, the number is positive; if the zone portion is hex D, the number is negative. Thus, a positive 1234 in four storage positions can be shown as:

```
F1 F2 F3 C4
```

A negative 1234 can be shown as:

```
F1 F2 F3 D4
```

Packed decimal

Packed decimal, in contrast to zoned decimal, is a more compact form of System/370 storage. Except for the rightmost byte of a packed-decimal field, two decimal digits are stored in each eight-bit byte. The rightmost byte of the field contains a decimal digit in its zone half and the sign of the field in its digit half. Using hex notation, the number +12345, stored in three bytes, is shown as follows:

```
12 34 5C
```

(Remember that either C or F is a valid sign for a positive field.) If the number -12345 is stored in four bytes, it can be shown as:

```
00 12 34 5D
```

This illustrates that leading zeros must fill out the positions of a packed-decimal number if the number has fewer digits than the field allows.

Packed-decimal fields in hex are relatively easy to decode because the decimal digits 0 through 9 are also 0 through 9 in hex. The only problem, then, is determining the sign of the field by analyzing the digit portion of the rightmost byte of the field.

Binary

On the System/370, two or four consecutive bytes are used for a *binary* field. Thus, 16 or 32 bits are used to represent a binary number. A two-byte binary field is referred to as a *halfword* and a four-byte binary field as a *fullword*. For some conversion operations, an eight-byte field known as a *doubleword* is also used.

If a binary number is represented by binary digits, it can be converted by assigning a *place value* to each bit. The place values start at the rightmost bit position with a value of 1 and double for each position to the left. Thus, the place values for a 32-bit binary number are from right to left 1, 2, 4, 8, 16, 32, 64, and so on, until the next to the leftmost bit, the 31st bit, has a value of 1,073,741,824. The leftmost bit is used to indicate the sign of the number. If the leftmost bit is 0, the number is positive; if it is 1, the number is negative. In a 16-bit binary number, 15 bits are used for the number, while the leftmost bit indicates the sign.

To illustrate binary coding, consider the following binary number: 0010010000011011. Since the leftmost bit is 0, the number is positive. By adding the place values of the on-bits, you can determine that the decimal equivalent is 9243. The decoding process is illustrated in figure 4-3. The maximum value of a 16-bit binary number is a positive 32,767; the maximum value of a 32-bit number is a positive 2,147,483,647.

Using hex, the binary storage of decimal 9243 in a halfword can be shown as:

24 1B

If 9243 is stored in a fullword, it can be shown as:

00 00 24 1B

To convert the hex representation of a positive binary number to decimal, you can use a calculator that provides hex-to-decimal and decimal-to-hex conversion functions. If you don't have a calculator like this, you can use a chart such as the one in figure 4-4. By looking up the decimal value of each hex digit in the corresponding column in the chart and then adding the decimal values, the decimal number can be derived. Thus, hex A in the rightmost four bits of a binary number has a value of 10; hex 4 in the next four bits has a value of 64; and so on. When these decimal values are added, the decimal number 15,178 is derived from hex 3B4A. (Incidentally, the hex chart simply reflects the place values of a hex number. The rightmost hex digit has a place value of 1; the next hex digit to its left has a place value of 16; the hex digit to its left has a place value of 256; and so on.)

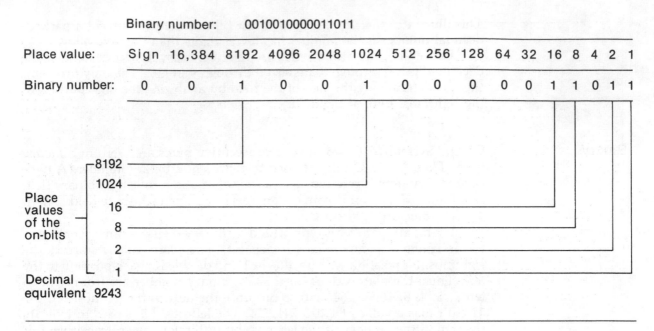

Figure 4-3   Converting a binary number to its decimal equivalent

Because negative binary numbers are not simply binary numbers with a 1-bit preceding them, you will not be able to decode negative hex numbers by using this technique. Fortunately, though, you rarely (if ever) have to. For the most part, it is enough to know that any hex representation of a binary number in which the leftmost hex digit is 8 or greater is a negative number. More about negative binary numbers in chapter 7.

Data storage summary

With three different types of data representation, the number of storage positions required for a numeric field on the System/370 is determined by the number of digits in the field and the data format used. If, for example, a field is supposed to contain the number +205,597,474, it requires nine bytes of storage using zoned decimal, five bytes using packed decimal, and a fullword (four bytes) using binary. If a field consists of only one decimal digit such as the number +7, one byte is required using zoned decimal, one byte using packed decimal, and a halfword (two bytes) using binary. Figure 4-5 summarizes these examples.

FULLWORD															
HALFWORD								HALFWORD							
Byte 1				Byte 2				Byte 3				Byte 4			
Zone		Digit		Zone		Digit		Zone		Digit		Zone		Digit	
Hex	Decimal	Hex	Decimal	Hex	Decimal	Hex	Decimal	Hex	Decimal	Hex	Decimal	Hex	Decimal	Hex	Decimal
0	0	0	0	0	0	0	0	0	0	0	0	0	0	0	0
1	268,435,456	1	16,777,216	1	1,048,576	1	65,536	1	4,096	1	256	1	16	1	1
2	536,870,912	2	33,554,432	2	2,097,152	2	131,072	2	8,192	2	512	2	32	2	2
3	805,306,368	3	50,331,648	3	3,145,728	3	196,608	3	12,228	3	768	3	48	3	3
4	1,073,741,824	4	67,108,864	4	4,194,304	4	262,144	4	16,384	4	1,024	4	64	4	4
5	1,342,177,280	5	83,886,080	5	5,242,880	5	327,680	5	20,480	5	1,280	5	80	5	5
6	1,610,612,736	6	100,663,296	6	6,291,456	6	393,216	6	24,576	6	1,536	6	96	6	6
7	1,879,048,192	7	117,440,512	7	7,340,032	7	458,752	7	28,672	7	1,792	7	112	7	7
8	2,147,483,648	8	134,217,728	8	8,388,608	8	524,288	8	32,768	8	2,048	8	128	8	8
9	2,415,919,104	9	150,994,944	9	9,437,184	9	589,824	9	36,864	9	2,304	9	144	9	9
A	2,684,354,560	A	167,772,160	A	10,485,760	A	655,360	A	40,960	A	2,560	A	160	A	10
B	2,952,790,016	B	184,549,376	B	11,534,336	B	720,896	B	45,056	B	2,816	B	176	B	11
C	3,221,225,472	C	201,326,592	C	12,582,912	C	786,432	C	49,152	C	3,072	C	192	C	12
D	3,489,660,928	D	218,103,808	D	13,631,488	D	851,968	D	53,248	D	3,328	D	208	D	13
E	3,758,096,384	E	234,881,024	E	14,680,064	E	917,504	E	57,344	E	3,584	E	224	E	14
F	4,026,531,840	F	251,658,240	F	15,728,640	F	983,040	F	61,440	F	3,840	F	240	F	15
8		7		6		5		4		3		2		1	

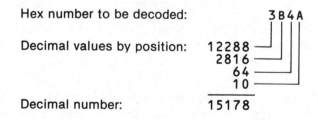

Hex number to be decoded: 3 B 4 A

Decimal values by position: 12288
                                  2816
                                    64
                                    10

Decimal number: 15178

Figure 4-4   Converting a hex number to its decimal equivalent

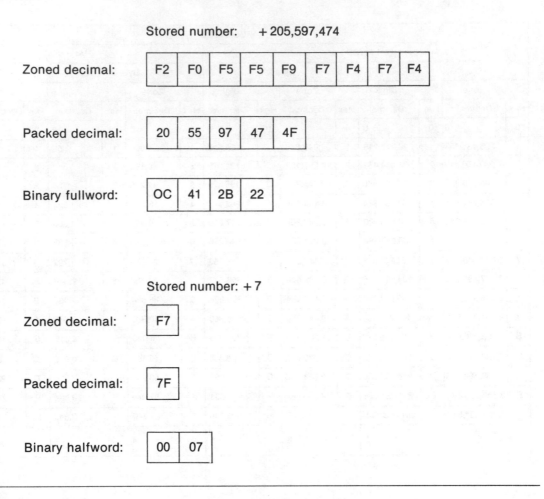

Figure 4-5   Three forms of numerical representation on the System/370

INSTRUCTION FORMATS

While a program is being executed, both the instructions of the program and the data being processed are contained in storage. The instructions, in coded form, indicate both the operations that are to be performed and the addresses and lengths of the fields that are to be operated upon. In the System/370, instructions are two, four, or six storage positions in length, depending on the function of the instruction.

A six-byte instruction format

To illustrate the parts of a typical System/370 instruction, consider one of its basic move instructions called the *move characters instruction*. This instruction causes the data from one field in storage to be moved unchanged to another field. If, for example, a move characters instruction specifies that an EBCDIC field in bytes 1551-1555 should be moved to bytes 1701-1705, the execution of the instruction can be shown in hex notation as:

	Receiving field	Sending field
Before:	F0 F4 F3 F9 F9	F0 F0 F7 F0 F1
After:	F0 F0 F7 F0 F1	F0 F0 F7 F0 F1

The effect is that data in one field, called the *sending field,* is duplicated in the second field, called the *receiving field.* In this case, a zoned-decimal value of 701 replaces the previous contents of the receiving field.

The format of this move characters instruction is:

Op Code	Length Factor	Address-1	Address-2
0 7	8 15	16 31	32 47

The first byte (bits 0-7) of this six-byte instruction contains the *operation code.* There is a unique operation code for each of the System/370 instructions, and, in the case of the move characters instruction, the operation code is 11010010, or hex D2. The second byte of the instruction (bits 8-15) is a *length factor,* an eight-bit binary number from 0-255 that indicates how many storage positions should be moved. A length factor of 0 indicates one byte is to be moved; a length factor of 1 indicates two bytes are to be moved; and so on. In other words, length factor plus one is the number of bytes to be moved.

The last four bytes of the instruction represent two addresses that specify the starting locations of the fields involved in the instruction. If the length factor is a binary 9 (indicating that ten bytes should be moved), the ten bytes of data starting at the location specified as address-2 are moved to the ten bytes of storage starting at the location specified as address-1. In this instruction, as in most System/370 instructions, the address-2 field is the sending field, while the address-1 field is the receiving field.

An address in a System/370 instruction is actually made up of two parts: four bits that specify a *base register* and 12 bits that represent a *displacement factor.* The base register can be any one of the 16 *general purpose registers* that are components of the System/370's CPU. These general purpose registers consist of 32 bit positions, the equivalent of a fullword in storage. When a *register* is used as a base register, the rightmost 24 bit positions are used to represent a *base address,* which is always a positive number. To get the actual address, the base address is added to the displacement factor specified in the instruction. This is referred to as *base-plus-displacement addressing.*

To be more specific, then, the format of the move characters instruction is:

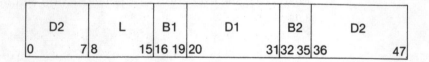

D2		L	B1	D1		B2	D2
0	7	8 15	16 19	20 31		32 35	36 47

Here, D2 is the actual operation code in hex, L is the length factor, B1 and B2 are four-bit binary numbers that specify one of the 16 registers (numbered 0 through 15 or hex 0 through F), and D1 and D2 are 12-bit binary numbers that represent displacement factors.

With this as background, you should be able to understand that the instruction described above (moving bytes 1551-1555 to 1701-1705) might be represented in hex as:

```
D20432A5320F
```

By breaking this down, you can determine that the operation code is D2; the number of bytes to be moved is 5 (hex 4+1); address-1 consists of a base address in register 3 plus a displacement of hex 2A5 (decimal 677); and address-2 consists of a base address in register 3 plus hex 20F (decimal 527). If register 3 contains hex 400 (decimal 1024) at the time the instruction is executed, bytes 1551-1555 will be moved to bytes 1701-1705. It is this type of decoding of the parts of an instruction that is done by the CPU at the time that an instruction is executed.

Two four-byte instruction formats

A second form of the move instruction, often called the *move immediate instruction*, illustrates a four-byte instruction format. When it is executed, one byte of data is moved from the instruction itself to a receiving field. This instruction's format is:

92		12	B1	D1
0	7	8 15	16 19	20 31

Here, the operation code is hex 92. There is no length code since the move immediate always involves only one byte, and there is only one address since the data to be moved is stored in the second byte of the instruction (bits 8-15). Bits 16-31 give the base register and displacement of the receiving field.

Suppose, for example, that the move immediate instruction in hex is:

```
92C1B100
```

This moves the letter A (hex C1) into the byte at the address computed by adding the contents of register 11 (hex B) to hex 100. If register 11 contains hex 1000, A is moved into the byte at address hex 1100, or decimal 4352. (By using the chart in figure 4-4, you can see that hex 1000 is 4096; hex 100 is 256; 4096 + 256 = 4352.)

Another four-byte instruction format is illustrated by the binary add instruction. This instruction adds the binary number in one fullword of storage to the contents of a general purpose register. If, for example, an instruction indicates that the fullword at address 8000 should be added to the contents of register 7, the instruction execution might be shown in hex as:

	Register 7	Fullword
Before:	00 00 00 10	00 00 00 0A
After:	00 00 00 1A	00 00 00 0A

Thus, the register is the receiving field because it receives the result (hex 1A), which is the sum of register 7's initial contents (hex 10) plus the fullword value (hex 0A).

The format of the fullword add instruction follows:

5A	R1	X2	B2	D2
0　　　7	8　11	12 15	16 19	20　　　31

Here, the operation code is 5A, the receiving register is specified in bits 8-11, and the address of the fullword is given in bits 16-31. No length factor is needed because this instruction always operates on a fullword.

Bits 12-15 in the format of the fullword add instruction can be used to specify an *index register*, signified by X2 in the format, which can be used for a function called *indexing*. When indexing is used, an address is derived by adding the base address, the displacement, and the contents of the index register. When bits 12-15 are zero, they are ignored.

A two-byte instruction format

A two-byte System/370 instruction is illustrated by the register-to-register add instruction. In this case, a binary number in one register is added to a binary number in another register as in this example:

	Register 1	Register 2
Before:	00 00 04 01	00 00 00 83
After:	00 00 04 84	00 00 00 83

Here, the contents of register 2 are added to the contents of register 1, and the result is stored in register 1.

The format of this register-to-register instruction is:

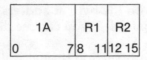

Quite simply, the register numbers of the two fields are given along with the operation code, hex 1A.

Instruction format summary

You have now seen examples of six-, four-, and two-byte instructions of the System/370. In order of presentation, they are often referred to as SS format (storage-to-storage), SI format (immediate-to-storage), RX format (storage-to-register), and RR format (register-to-register). These formats as well as RS format (another form of storage-to-register instructions) and a variation of SS format are presented in figure 4-6.

As you proceed through this book, you will learn how to use all of these types of instructions. By referring to the formats in figure 4-6, you will be able to understand how the assembler language code relates to the machine language. You will also be able to appreciate the value of assembler language when you see how the language frees the programmer from dealing with actual instruction formats.

INSTRUCTION SET

The term *instruction set* applies to the collection of machine instructions that a computer can execute. Of the 180 or more instructions in the System/370 instruction set, most assembler language programmers use only about 60 of them. The rest are used for specialized functions that are rarely needed for application programming.

In general, a computer's instruction set can be broken down into these functional groups:

1 Data movement instructions
2 Arithmetic instructions
3 Logical instructions
4 Input/output instructions

At this time, I'm going to present examples of System/370 instructions in each of these four groups. Because there is a close relationship between machine language instructions and assembler language instructions, this material will help you learn assembler language more easily later on.

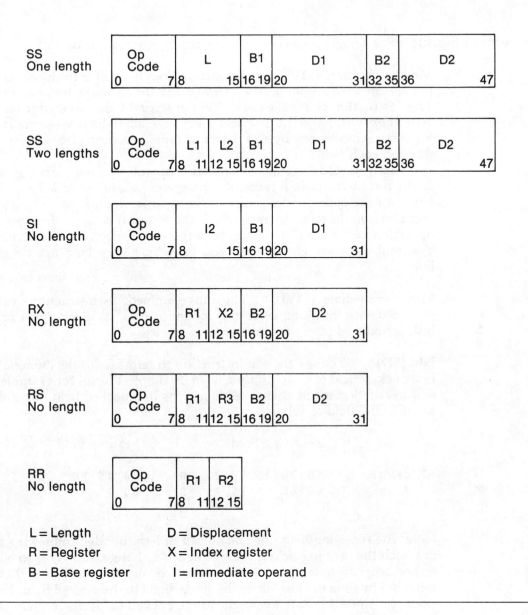

Figure 4-6   System/370 instruction formats

Data movement instructions

Move characters (MVC)   You have already been introduced to *data movement instructions* in the form of the move characters instruction. This instruction places the data from the second field specified (called the second *operand*) into the first field specified (called the first operand). The instruction moves one byte of data at a time, processing from left to right through each field.

    MVC is the assembler language operation code for the move characters instruction. It is called a *mnemonic operation code* because the letters of the code are designed to aid memorization of the code, and the word *mnemonic* refers to memory. In the rest of this topic, the mnemonic operation codes are given along with the descriptions of the instruction. You will use these codes when you code assembler language programs later on.

Move immediate (MVI)   The move immediate instruction was introduced with the examples of instruction formats. It takes a byte from the instruction and places it into a byte of storage.

Edit (ED)   You use the edit instruction to refine (*edit*) the numeric data in a packed field prior to printing it. In its simplest form, for example, the edit instruction might change leading zeros in a packed field to blanks in an EBCDIC field as follows:

	Receiving field	Sending field
Before:	40 20 20 20 20 20	00 15 8C
After:	40 40 40 F1 F5 F8	00 15 8C

Here, the receiving field must be an *edit pattern* that determines the form in which the sending field is to be edited. To change lead zeros to blanks (called *zero suppression*), the pattern must consist of a lead blank (hex 40) followed by as many hex 20s as there are digits in the packed field. In this example, since there are five digits in the packed field, the receiving field consists of five hex 20s preceded by a blank. When used in an edit pattern, hex 20 is called a *digit selector*. Incidentally, hex 20 is one of the 256 EBCDIC combinations that does not have a character to represent it.

    You can use a more complex edit pattern with the edit instruction to insert a decimal point or commas into a number. For example, the packed decimal number 0512389 can be edited as follows:

	Receiving field	Sending field
Before:	40 20 20 6B 20 20 21 4B 20 20	05 12 38 9C
After:	40 40 F5 6B F1 F2 F3 4B F8 F9	05 12 38 9C

Because hex 6B is a comma and hex 4B is a decimal point, the receiving field after the editing operation would print as: 5,123.89.

Figure 4-7 gives several examples of the edit patterns required for suppressing lead zeros and inserting commas and decimal points into a number. In all cases, the leftmost character in the pattern, called the *fill character*, is a blank so that lead zeros are changed to blanks. Also, either a digit selector (hex 20) or a *significance starter* (hex 21) must be used wherever a digit from the sending field is to be placed. The significance starter is used for the same purpose as a digit selector except that it also indicates where lead zeros should start printing. In group 2, for example, the pattern 40 20 20 20 21 20 causes a packed-decimal field containing zero to be converted into a form that prints as 0. In other words, lead zeros aren't zero suppressed if they come to the right of the significance starter.

In group 3, commas and decimal points are used in edit patterns as *message characters*. As instruction execution proceeds from left to right through the sending and receiving fields, the message characters are unchanged if a *significant digit* (a non-zero digit) or the significance starter has been encountered. Thus, the commas and decimal points are inserted into the edited result. On the other hand, if significance hasn't been started by either a significant digit or the significance starter, a message character is changed to a blank (the fill character). Although message characters can be any hex code other than hex 20, 21, or 22, hex 6B (the comma) and hex 4B (the decimal point) are most commonly used.

In group 4, a minus sign (hex 60) is used as a message character to indicate that a field has a negative value. When a message character is coded to the right of all digit selectors, it is unchanged if the field that is edited is negative. However, the message character is replaced by the fill character if the field is zero or positive. As a result, the edited fields in figure 4-7 are followed by minus signs if they are negative; by blanks, if they aren't negative.

With these examples as guides, you should now be able to create a pattern that will do simple editing on any packed field. Then, in chapter 10, you will learn how to use more sophisticated edit patterns. The main point to remember now is that each pattern must consist of a leftmost fill character as well as one digit selector or significance starter for each digit in the packed decimal sending field. Logically, of course, there can only be one significance starter in an edit pattern.

Pack (PACK)   Since all System/370 arithmetic must be done on packed decimal or binary fields, EBCDIC fields must be converted to packed decimal or binary before they can be operated upon. The pack instruction, then, is one of the conversion instructions. It takes an EBCDIC sending field and converts it into packed decimal in the receiving field as in this example:

	Receiving field	Sending field
Before:	99 99 99	F1 F2 F3 F4 F5
After:	12 34 5F	F1 F2 F3 F4 F5

As you can see, the zone and digit halves of the rightmost byte of the sending field are reversed in the rightmost byte of the receiving field. Thereafter, the digit portions of the bytes in the sending field are packed two digits per byte in the receiving field. Another view of the operation of the pack instruction is this:

Sending field: F1 F2 F3 F4 F5
Receiving field: 12 34 5F

The pack instruction, in contrast to the move or edit instruction, proceeds from right to left during execution. It uses the second form of the SS format shown in figure 4-6. This means that both sending and receiving fields have length factors. Therefore, it is possible to *pad* a field as in this example:

Sending field (length 4):   F2 F6 F4 F8
Receiving field (length 4): 00 02 64 8F

In other words, unfilled half-bytes are padded with zeros.

It is also possible to *truncate* a field as in this example:

Sending field (length 5):   F6 F3 F2 F0 F4
Receiving field (length 2): 20 4F

Because the receiving field is too small to receive all digits in the sending field, two significant digits are truncated.

Unpack (UNPK)   The unpack instruction converts a packed decimal field into an EBCDIC field as in this example:

Sending field: 56 43 7F
Receiving field: F5 F6 F4 F3 F7

As in the case of the pack instruction, both operands have length factors, so padding can take place:

Sending field (length 2):   03 4C
Receiving field (length 5): F0 F0 F0 F3 C4

And truncation can take place:

Sending field (length 3):   12 91 2D
Receiving field (length 2): F1 D2

In addition to pack and unpack, there are instructions that convert numbers from packed decimal to binary and vice versa. These data movement instructions are covered in chapter 7.

Group	Sending field	Receiving field pattern	Edited result field	Printed result field
1 Lead zero suppression	12345C 00123F 00000C	4020202020202020 4020202020202020 4020202020202020	40F1F2F3F4F5 4040F1F2F3 4040404040	12345 123
2 Significance starting	00511F 00001C 00000C	4020202021202020 4020202021202020 4020202021202020	404040F5F1F1 4040404040F1 40404040F0	511 1 0
3 Decimal point and comma insertion	123456789C 000123456C 000000123C 000000000C	402020206B2020206B202020 402020206B2020206B202020 402020206B2020206B202020 402020206B2020206B202020	40F1F2F36BF4F5F66BF7F8F9 4040404040F1F2F36BF4F5F6 404040404040404040F1F2F3 4040404040404040404040F0	123,456,789 123,456 123 0
	123456789C 000000123C 000000005C	4020206B2020206B2020204B2020 4020206B2020206B2020204B2020 4020206B2020206B2020204B2020	40F16BF2F3F46BF5F6F74BF8F9 404040404040404040F14BF2F3 4040404040404040404BF0F5	1,234,567.89 1.23 .05
	1234567C 0000123F 0000105C	402020202020204B2020 402020202020204B2020 402020202020204B2020	40F1F2F3F4F54BF6F7 404040404040F14BF2F3 4040404040404BF0F5	12345.67 1.23 1.05
4 Minus sign message character for negative numbers	01234C 01234D 00000C	4020202020202060 4020202020202060 4020202020202060	4040F1F2F3F440 4040F1F2F3F460 404040404040	1234 1234-
	1234567D 0000123D 0000005D	4020206B2020204B202060 4020206B2020204B202060 4020206B2020204B202060	40F1F26BF3F4F54BF6F760 404040404040F14BF2F360 4040404040404BF0F560	12,345.67- 1.23- .05-

Figure 4-7   Some simple editing patterns

Arithmetic instructions

When arithmetic is done on packed decimal fields, it is referred to as *decimal arithmetic*. Because less conversion is required for decimal arithmetic than for binary arithmetic, decimal arithmetic is used for most of the arithmetic done in business programs. The five basic decimal instructions are add, subtract, multiply, divide, and zero-and-add.

Add decimal (AP)   When the add decimal instruction is executed, operand-2 is added to operand-1 and the result replaces operand-1. The second SS format is used for this instruction, so fields of different lengths (up to 16 bytes each) can be added as in this example:

	Operand-1	Operand-2
Before:	10 00 0F	01 0F
After:	10 01 0C	01 0F

Since 10 is added to 10000, the result is 10010. Either positive or negative fields can be added, and the sign of the result field is always hex C for positive or hex D for negative.

One thing to watch for when coding decimal operations is *arithmetic overflow*. This takes place when the receiving field is not large enough for the result. In the following example, arithmetic overflow occurs:

	Operand-1	Operand-2
Before:	87 11 0F	40 00 0F
After:	27 11 0C	40 00 0F

Since the actual result is 127110, the leftmost digit has been truncated due to the overflow. Because arithmetic overflow will cause inaccurate results, you should avoid overflow by making the receiving field large enough for any possible result.

Subtract decimal (SP)   The subtract decimal instruction operates in the same manner as the add instruction except that the operation is subtraction. Once again, the programmer should avoid overflow by making the receiving field large enough for any possible result.

Multiply decimal (MP)   When the multiply decimal instruction is executed, the first operand (the multiplicand) is multiplied by the second operand (the multiplier), and the result replaces the first operand. The multiplicand can be up to 16 bytes long and the multiplier can be up to 8 bytes long. To prevent overflow, the first operand should have at least as many leading bytes of hex zeros as the number of bytes in the second operand as in this example:

	Operand-1	Operand-2
Before:	00 00 8C	50 0F
After:	04 00 0C	50 0F

Here, operand-1 has two leading bytes of zeros and operand-2 is two bytes long, so overflow can't occur.

Divide decimal (DP)   The divide decimal instruction is similar to multiply decimal with one additional complication: the remainder. The first operand (the dividend) can be up to 16 bytes long, and the second operand (the divisor) can be up to 8 bytes long. When executed, the divisor is divided into the dividend, and the resulting quotient *and* the remainder replace the dividend. Here is an example:

	Operand-1	Operand-2
Before:	00 00 00 05 3C	00 7C
After:	00 00 7C 00 4C	00 7C

The remainder portion of the result is always the same number of bytes as the divisor, and it is located in the rightmost bytes of the operand-1 area. The quotient portion of the result, complete with valid sign, occupies the rest of the dividend area. Because of this, you must make sure that operand-1 has at least as many leading bytes filled with zeros as there are bytes in the divisor.

Zero-and-add (ZAP)   The zero-and-add instruction operates in the same manner as an add decimal instruction that adds a packed field to another packed field containing a value of zero. Here's an example of a zero-and-add instruction:

	Operand-1	Operand-2
Before:	12 45 9C	1 C
After:	00 00 1C	1 C

In other words, operand-1 is first changed to zero; then, operand-2 is added to it.

Logical instructions

The basic logical instruction and the basis of logic in the computer is the *branch instruction*. When a program is initially loaded into storage, the supervisor transfers control to its first instruction. Then, when the computer finishes executing one instruction, it continues with the next instruction in storage. After executing the instruction in bytes 1000-1005, for example, the computer executes the instruction starting at address 1006. The only exception to this involves the branch instruction. When the branch instruction is executed, it can cause the computer to break the sequence and continue with the instruction beginning at the address specified in the branch instruction.

When a branch instruction branches every time it is executed, it is called an *unconditional branch*. If, for example, an unconditional branch instruction in positions 4032-4035 specifies a branch to address 801, the computer will continue with the instruction starting in storage position 801.

Conditional branch instructions cause branching only when specified conditions are met. For example, a conditional branch instruction might branch only if the result of an arithmetic instruction is negative. To illustrate, suppose a branch instruction occupies storage positions 2044-2047 and specifies that the computer should branch to address 1000 if the result of the preceding arithmetic instruction is negative. Then, if the result is zero or positive, the computer continues with the instruction starting at address 2048, the next instruction in sequence. But if the result is negative, the computer continues with the instruction starting at address 1000.

One of the most useful conditions to be branched upon is based on the results of a comparison between two fields in storage. This branch instruction is used in conjunction with the other type of logical instruction, the *compare instruction*. The System/370 has compare instructions that compare EBCDIC, packed decimal, and binary fields. In the instruction descriptions that follow, the compare decimal instruction is presented followed by two of the System/370 branch instructions. Other compare and branch instructions are presented in other chapters of this book.

Compare decimal (CP)   The compare decimal instruction specifies that two packed decimal fields are to be compared. When it is executed, the computer determines the relationship between the fields: Are they equal? Is the first field greater in value than the second? Is the first field less in value than the second? Based on this comparison, a *condition code* is set that can be used by subsequent branch instructions.

The condition code can be thought of as four bits that are located in the CPU and that can be tested by a branch instruction. For the compare decimal instruction, if the leftmost bit of the condition code is turned on (bit 0), it indicates that operand-1 and operand-2 are equal. If bit 1 is turned on, it indicates that operand-1 is less than operand-2. If bit 2 is turned on, it indicates that operand-1 is greater than operand-2. The rightmost condition code bit (bit 3) isn't used by the compare decimal instruction.

Branch-on-condition (BC)   The most widely used branch instruction, called the branch-on-condition instruction, has this RX format:

47	M1	X2	B2	D2
0 7	8 11	12 15	16 19	20 31

Condition code bit setting	0	1	2	3
Add decimal	Zero	Minus	Plus	Overflow
Compare decimal (A:B)	Equal	A low	A high	_____
Edit	Zero	Minus	Plus	_____
Subtract decimal	Zero	Minus	Plus	Overflow
Zero-and-add	Zero	Minus	Plus	Overflow

Figure 4-8   Condition code settings for the instructions presented so far

When this instruction is executed, it compares the *mask* bits (bits 8-11) with the condition code. If the on-bit in the condition code has a corresponding on-bit in the instruction mask, the program branches to the address specified in bits 12-31 of the instruction (base register plus displacement plus the contents of an index register if bits 12-15 specify a register number other than zero). If the on-bit in the condition code does not have a corresponding 1-bit in the mask, the program continues with the next instruction in sequence.

To illustrate, suppose that the condition code is 0100 after a compare decimal instruction has been executed. Then, if the mask in the branch-on-condition instruction is 0100 or 0110, the branch takes place. On the other hand, if the mask is 1011 or 0001, the branch will not take place.

The mask bits in an instruction can be used in any of the 16 combinations that are possible with four bits. This makes it possible for a branch-on-condition instruction to branch on multiple conditions. If, for example, the mask is 1010 following a compare decimal instruction, a branch will take place when the operands are equal (condition code is 1000) or when operand-1 is greater than operand-2 (condition code is 0010). If all four mask bits are on, the branch is unconditional (it will take place every time); if all four bits are off, it will never branch.

Figure 4-8 summarizes the condition code settings for the instructions that have been presented thus far that affect the condition code. It shows which bits are set on for each possible result of an instruction. The branch-on-condition instruction can branch based on the results of any of these instructions. You should realize that many instructions, such as move characters or add binary, do not change the condition code in any way.

Branch-and-link-register (BALR)   The branch-and-link-register instruction is a two-byte instruction in RR format. When this instruction is executed, it places the address of the next instruction in storage in the first register specified. Then, it branches to the address that is given by the second register specified. However, if zero is specified for the second register, no branch takes place.

To illustrate the execution of this instruction, suppose it is stored in bytes 5000-5001 and specifies register 8 as operand-1, and register 9, which contains the binary equivalent of 2048, as operand-2. When the branch-and-link-register instruction is executed, address 5002 will be stored in register 8 after which the program will branch to address 2048. In contrast, if zero was specified for register 2, 5002 would be stored in register 8 and no branch would take place. You will see this no-branching use of the branch-and-link-register instruction in chapter 5.

I/O instructions

The System/370 *I/O instructions* are perhaps the most complex instructions in the instruction set. In fact, a computer user's program never executes I/O instructions. Instead, all I/O operations are started by the VSE supervisor program. Then, whenever a user's program requires an I/O operation, it branches to the supervisor which in turn causes the appropriate instructions to be executed by a channel.

The operation of I/O instructions   When an I/O instruction is executed, it either reads a record from an input device into main storage or it writes a record from main storage to an output device. For example, an input instruction like a read-disk instruction might specify that one record is to be read and that its data is to be stored in the storage positions starting at address 5501. Then, if the disk record is 100 bytes long, its data will be stored in positions 5501-5600. In this case, bytes 5501-5600 are called the *input area* of the read instruction.

An output instruction like a print instruction specifies the storage positions from which the output data is to be written. This area of main storage is called the *output area* of the write instruction. If a print instruction specifies that a line should be printed from bytes 6601-6732 of main storage, the content of byte 6601 is printed in print position 1 on the printer (on the far left of the form), the content of byte 6602 is printed in print position 2, and so on.

If the data in an output area is to print properly, it must be in EBCDIC form prior to printing. Furthermore, a numeric field that carries a hex C or D sign must be edited if it is to print properly. To illustrate, suppose a zoned decimal field contains a positive 00557 in this form:

    F0 F0 F5 F5 C7

If it is printed, it will print as 0055G since G is the EBCDIC equivalent of hex C7. However, by packing the field and using the edit instruction prior to printing, the lead zeros can be suppressed and the hex C sign changed to hex F.

A similar problem occurs when printing negative fields. For example, a negative 12 will print as 1K. However, if a negative field is packed and edited using the patterns presented thus far, it can be printed correctly with a minus sign to its right.

Overlap and the need for dual I/O areas   On a modern computer system, an application program *overlaps* CPU operations with I/O operations. It does this by executing the internal processing instructions of a program while channels execute the I/O instructions. If a program is preparing a report from a disk file, for example, it's likely that one channel will be reading a record from a disk while another channel controls the printing of a record while the CPU executes data movement, arithmetic, or logical operations of the program...all at the same time. By overlapping I/O operations with processing, a program can be executed much more quickly than it can be without overlap.

One programming complexity resulting from overlap is that two I/O areas in storage must be used for each I/O operation. If, for example, only one output area were used for a print operation, the data for the second print record would be moved into the output area while the first record was being printed, thus causing errors in the printed data. As a result, for overlap to work, the data for the second record must be moved into a second output area while the first record is being printed from the first output area. Then, the third record can be moved into the first output area, while the second record is being printed from the second output area. And so on. This switching from one output area to the other, which is shown schematically in figure 4-9, must be continued throughout the execution of the program. Similarly, dual I/O areas must be used for all other I/O operations that are overlapped.

To relieve the programmer of the responsibility of switching I/O areas and coping with the other I/O complexities (such as writing channel commands), VSE supplies I/O modules that handle these functions. Although there is a complex relationship between the user's program, the I/O modules, and the supervisor, it is a complexity that the programmer need not be concerned with. As you will see in chapter 5, the programmer codes specifications for each of the files used by the program, and the rest is done by the assembler in combination with the VSE I/O modules and the supervisor. You do need to realize, though, that two I/O areas are required for an overlapped file.

DISCUSSION   The material you have just finished reading may seem to contain an overwhelming amount of detail. Nevertheless, this is the level of machine operation that you must understand if you are to be an effective assembler language programmer. As you will see in chapter 5, the knowledge you gain from this chapter will make your introduction to assembler language quite manageable.

If at this time you have a general understanding of the forms in which data and instructions are stored in a System/370 and if you have an appreciation for what happens when the 13 instructions presented in this chapter are executed, you should be able to continue with no problems. Later on, should you feel the need, you can refer back to the specific details presented in this chapter.

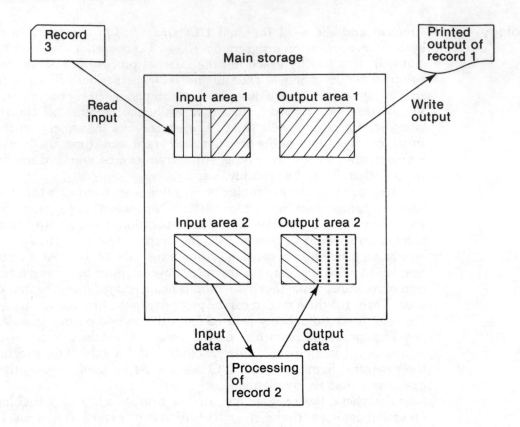

Note: Data is being moved into input area 1 and output area 2

Figure 4-9   A conceptual view of the need for dual I/O areas when CPU and I/O operations are overlapped

Terminology

storage position
byte
address
field
binary component
binary digit
bit
parity bit
parity checking
hexadecimal
hex
fixed-point binary
floating-point binary
EBCDIC
zone bits
digit bits
zoned decimal
packed decimal
binary
halfword
fullword
doubleword
place value
move characters instruction
sending field
receiving field
operation code
length factor
base register
displacement factor
general purpose register
register
base address
base-plus-displacement addressing
move immediate instruction
index register
indexing
instruction set
data movement instruction
operand
mnemonic operation
mnemonic
editing
edit pattern
zero suppression
digit selector
fill character
significance starter

message character
significant digit
padding a field
truncating a field
arithmetic instruction
decimal arithmetic
arithmetic overflow
logical instruction
branch instruction
unconditional branch
conditional branch
compare instruction
condition code
mask
I/O instruction
input area
output area
overlap

Objectives

1. Given the hexadecimal code for an EBCDIC, packed decimal, or binary field, tell what data the field contains. (In the case of a negative binary field, simply indicate that it is negative.)

2. Given all related specifications, codes, and data for any of the 13 instructions described in this chapter, indicate what will happen when the instruction is executed. The 13 instructions described are: move characters, move immediate, edit, pack, unpack, add decimal, subtract decimal, multiply decimal, divide decimal, zero-and-add, compare decimal, branch-on-condition, and branch-and-link-register.

3. Explain what an input or output area is and how one relates to an I/O instruction.

4. Explain why two I/O areas are required for each input or output device if CPU processing and I/O operations are to be overlapped.

Chapter 5

An introductory
subset of assembler language

Officially, IBM's assembler language is known as *Basic Assembler Language*. As a result, you will sometimes see or hear assembler language referred to as *BAL*. In this book, though, we'll just refer to the language as assembler language.

This chapter presents an introductory *subset* of assembler language. In topic 1, you will be introduced to a complete assembler language program that illustrates some of the elements of this subset. Then, in topic 2, you will study an enhanced version of the first program that illustrates the assembler language elements that complete the introductory subset. When you complete this chapter, you should be able to code assembler language programs that require disk input, printer output, and decimal arithmetic. Since the remaining chapters in this book build upon this introductory subset, you should learn quite rapidly once you complete this chapter.

TOPIC 1 An introduction to assembler language

This topic introduces you to assembler language by presenting specifications for a program along with the complete assembler language program that satisfies the specifications. The idea is for you to see the complete picture right away. If you can do that, it should be relatively easy for you to learn the separate elements of assembler language. As a result, when you finish this topic, you shouldn't expect to be able to develop your own assembler language programs. But you should understand the relationships between the elements of an assembler language program.

THE REORDER-LISTING PROGRAM

Figure 5-1 presents the program specifications for a program that we call the reorder-listing program because it reads an inventory master file and prepares a listing of those items in inventory that need to be reordered. Figure 5-2 presents a program flowchart for this program, and figure 5-3 presents the assembler language code for this program.

Because you will be asked to refer to the program specifications, flowchart, and code for the reorder-listing program throughout this chapter, we suggest that you make photocopies of figures 5-1, 5-2, and 5-3 right now. Then, you can spread them out on your desk and study them as you read this topic. This will reduce the amount of page flipping you have to do, so it should improve your learning efficiency.

The program specifications

As you can see in the program overview in figure 5-1, one line should be printed on the reorder listing whenever an item's available stock (on-hand plus on-order) is less than its reorder point. If you check the record layout for the inventory master record, you can see that it is a 50-byte record that contains only seven fields. If you check the print chart for the reorder listing, you can see that neither heading lines nor total lines are required on the report. In other words, we've simplified this program as much as possible to make your introduction to assembler language as manageable as possible.

Program:	REORDLST PREPARE REORDER LISTING	Page: 1
Designer:	Anne Prince	Date: 06-07-85

Input/output specifications

File	Description	Use
INVMAST	Inventory master file	Input
PRTOUT	Print file: Reorder listing	Output

Process specifications

This program prepares a reorder listing from a sequential file of inventory records. The program reads the inventory records in sequence and prints one line on the reorder listing whenever the available stock for an inventory record is less than its reorder point. To simplify this introductory program, no headings or total lines are to be printed on the listing.

The basic processing requirements for each inventory record follow:

1. Read the inventory record.
2. Calculate the available amount.
   (Available = on hand + on order.)
3. If available is less than reorder point, format and print a detail line.

Figure 5-1   Specifications for a reorder-listing program (part 1 of 2)

Record layout for inventory master record

Field Name	Item number	Item description	Unit cost	Unit price	Reorder point	On hand	On order
Characteristics	CL5	CL20	CL5	CL5	CL5	CL5	CL5
Usage							
Position	1-5	6-25	26-30	31-35	36-40	41-45	46-50

Print chart

Figure 5-1   Specifications for a reorder-listing program (part 2 of 2)

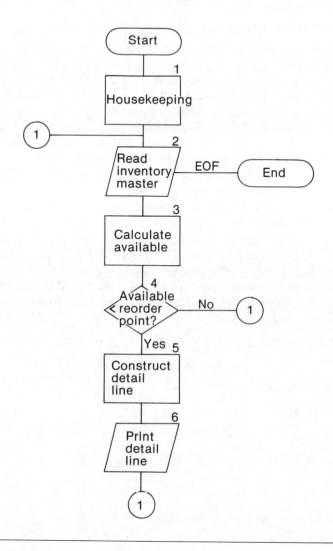

Figure 5-2   A flowchart for the reorder-listing program

The program flowchart

Figure 5-2 is a program flowchart for this program. After doing some setup for the program (housekeeping), the program reads an inventory record, calculates the amount of available stock, and compares it with the reorder point. If the available stock is greater than or equal to the reorder point, the program branches back and reads another record. Otherwise, it constructs and prints the reorder line, then branches back to read another record. When the end-of-file (EOF) condition is reached, the program ends.

**The program
listing**

Take time now to look at the program listing in figure 5-3. It is the complete program for printing a reorder listing from a sequential disk file of inventory records. As you will soon appreciate, any assembler language program can be divided into three types of statements: (1) instructions, (2) file definitions, and (3) data definitions. The file definitions give the characteristics of the input and output files; the data definitions define fields that are operated upon by the program; and the instructions use names defined by the file and data definitions to describe the sequence of operations required by the program. In figure 5-3, lines 100 through 2600 are instructions; lines 2700 through 3000 are file definitions; and lines 3100 through 5800 are data definitions.

To highlight various portions of this program, the programmer has used comment lines. A *comment line* has an asterisk in position 1 and a comment or note written by the programmer in the remaining positions. For example, lines 2700 and 2900 in figure 5-3 are comment lines. During assembly, the contents of the comment lines are printed, but otherwise they are ignored. As a result, they can be used by the programmer to make the program listing easier to follow, but they do not affect the resulting object code.

```
REORDLST  START  0              BLOCK 1:  HOUSEKEEPING              00000100
BEGIN     BALR   3,0                                               00000200
          USING  *,3                                               00000300
          OPEN   INVMAST,PRTOUT                                    00000400
READINV   GET    INVMAST        BLOCK 2:  READ RECORD              00000500
          PACK   WRKAVAIL,INVONHND   BLOCK 3:  CALCULATE AVAILABLE 00000600
          PACK   WRKONORD,INVONORD                                 00000700
          AP     WRKAVAIL,WRKONORD                                 00000800
          PACK   WRKORDPT,INVORDPT   BLOCK 4:  DECISION            00000900
          CP     WRKAVAIL,WRKORDPT                                 00001000
          BNL    READINV                                           00001100
          PACK   PACKAREA,INVITNBR   BLOCK 5:  CONSTRUCT DETAIL LINE 00001200
          MVC    PRTITNBR,PATTERN1                                 00001300
          ED     PRTITNBR,PACKAREA                                 00001400
          MVC    PRTITDES,INVITDES                                 00001500
          PACK   PACKAREA,INVPRICE                                 00001600
          MVC    PRTPRICE,PATTERN2                                 00001700
          ED     PRTPRICE,PACKAREA                                 00001800
          MVC    PRTAVAIL,PATTERN1                                 00001900
          ED     PRTAVAIL,WRKAVAIL                                 00002000
          MVC    PRTORDPT,PATTERN1                                 00002100
          ED     PRTORDPT,WRKORDPT                                 00002200
          PUT    PRTOUT         BLOCK 6:  PRINT LINE               00002300
          B      READINV        UNCONDITIONAL BRANCH               00002400
INVEOF    CLOSE  INVMAST,PRTOUT END-OF-JOB ROUTINE                 00002500
          EOJ                                                      00002600
*  THE INVENTORY FILE DEFINITION                                  00002700
INVMAST  DTFSD BLKSIZE=50,IOAREA1=INVINPA,EOFADDR=INVEOF,DEVADDR=SYS008 00002800
*  THE PRINTER FILE DEFINITION                                    00002900
PRTOUT   DTFPR BLKSIZE=132,IOAREA1=PRTOUTA,DEVADDR=SYSLST         00003000
*  THE DATA DEFINITIONS FOR THE INVENTORY FILE INPUT AREA        00003100
INVINPA  DS     0CL50                                             00003200
INVITNBR DS     CL5                                               00003300
INVITDES DS     CL20                                              00003400
         DS     CL5                                               00003500
INVPRICE DS     CL5                                               00003600
INVORDPT DS     CL5                                               00003700
INVONHND DS     CL5                                               00003800
INVONORD DS     CL5                                               00003900
*  THE DATA DEFINITIONS FOR THE PRINTER OUTPUT AREA              00004000
PRTOUTA  DS     0CL132                                            00004100
PRTITNBR DS     CL6                                               00004200
         DC     5C' '                                             00004300
PRTITDES DS     CL20                                              00004400
         DC     4C' '                                             00004500
PRTPRICE DS     CL7                                               00004600
         DC     4C' '                                             00004700
PRTAVAIL DS     CL6                                               00004800
         DC     4C' '                                             00004900
PRTORDPT DS     CL6                                               00005000
         DC     70C' '                                            00005100
*  THE DATA DEFINITIONS FOR REQUIRED WORK AREAS                  00005200
PATTERN1 DC     X'402020202020'                                   00005300
PATTERN2 DC     X'4020202148202 0'                                00005400
WRKAVAIL DS     PL3                                               00005500
WRKONORD DS     PL3                                               00005600
WRKORDPT DS     PL3                                               00005700
PACKAREA DS     PL3                                               00005800
         END    BEGIN                                             00005900
```

Figure 5-3   The reorder-listing program

THE FORMAT OF AN ASSEMBLER LANGUAGE INSTRUCTION

Figure 5-4 presents the format of a typical line of code in assembler language. As you can see, each line of code can be broken down into six fields. Positions 1-8 contain the *label*, or *name*, field. This field can be used to give a symbolic name to a data field or an instruction. Thus, the instruction in the figure 5-4 has been given the name REORDLST.

Positions 10-14 contain the *operation* field. In this field, you code the mnemonic operation code of an instruction. In figure 5-4, the operation code is START.

Positions 16-71 contain the *operands* and *comments* fields. The operand or operands start in position 16. If there is more than one operand, they are separated by commas with no intervening blanks. In figure 5-4, the operand is 0.

After the operands, the programmer can code a comment in positions 16-71. However, the comment must be separated from the operands by one or more blanks. In figure 5-4, the comment is BLOCK 1: HOUSEKEEPING. Throughout the program in figure 5-3, comments are used to relate the assembler language code to the blocks in the flowchart in figure 5-2.

Column 72 of the coding line is used to indicate that an instruction is continued on the next line. Although most assembler language instructions must be written on one line, in a few cases it is necessary to use multiple lines. You will see how continuation lines are used later in this chapter.

The last eight positions on a line, positions 73-80, can be used to identify and sequence the lines of the source program. Since most interactive program development systems provide automatic numbering capabilities, you don't usually have to sequence your own program. When the program is complete, you simply invoke the proper command and the program is numbered for you. In any case, positions 73-80 do not affect the resulting object program in any way.

FILE DEFINITIONS

For each file used by a program, there must be a *file definition*. These file definitions are referred to as *DTF* (Define The File) *statements*, or just *DTFs*. In the reorder-listing program there is one DTF statement for the inventory master file, and one for the printer file. Although you may not be used to thinking of printer output as a file, you think of it that way in assembler language.

In the name portion of each DTF statement, you code a label that becomes the *filename* for the file. In the reorder-listing program, the inventory master file is named INVMAST; the printer file is named PRTOUT. When you code a filename, it must (1) start with a letter, (2) consist of only letters and numbers, and (3) be seven characters or less in length. As you will see later, this filename is used when coding I/O operations in the instruction portion of the program.

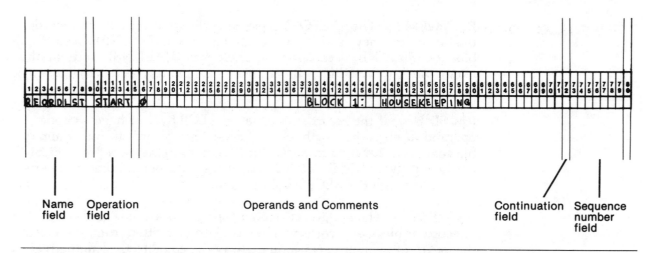

Figure 5-4 Format of an assembler language instruction

Following the label is the operation code that identifies the type of file being defined. In the reorder-listing program, the operation code is DTFSD for the sequential disk file (SD for Sequential Disk). The operation code is DTFPR for the printer file (PR for PRinter). In section 4, you will learn about other types of DTFs, but until then you will only use these two.

After the operation code are the operands that give the specific characteristics of a file. These are called *keyword operands*, because each operand consists of a *keyword* followed by an equals sign followed by programmer-supplied words. As you will see, each type of DTF has different keyword operands.

The DTFSD operands

Figure 5-5 summarizes some of the most commonly used keywords of the DTFSD. Although there are quite a few more operands for the DTFSD, these are all you need to know for now. Some of its other operands will be discussed in chapter 13.

BLKSIZE   In chapter 1, you learned that records in a file are sometimes blocked to increase program and storage efficiency. But whether records are blocked or unblocked, the BLKSIZE operand specifies the length of each block of data. When a file contains unblocked records, the block size is equal to the length of a single record. Since the program in figure 5-3 processes an input file with unblocked records, the block size for the inventory file is 50.

RECFORM   The RECFORM operand tells what format the records in the file are in. They can be fixed-length unblocked (FIXUNB); fixed-length blocked (FIXBLK); variable-length unblocked (VARUNB); and variable-length blocked (VARBLK). If the operand is omitted, as it is in figure 5-3, FIXUNB is assumed.

RECSIZE   If the records in a file are FIXBLK, you have to code this operand. It gives the length of one fixed-length record. If, for example, a file consists of 200-byte records with 10 records to the block, the RECSIZE is 200 and the BLKSIZE is 2000. You'll see this operand used in the next topic along with the RECFORM operand.

IOAREA1   The IOAREA1 operand specifies the name of the area that a record or block of records will be read into or written from. As a result, the length of the input area should always be equal to the length given in the BLKSIZE operand. In the reorder-listing program, the programmer has defined an input area named INVINPA, so this name is given in the IOAREA1 operand.

IOAREA2   In chapter 4, you learned that I/O operations and CPU processing are normally overlapped. To provide for this in an assembler language program, two I/O areas must be used. When two are used, you give the name of the second area in this keyword operand. You will see how this works in the next topic.

WORKA   The WORKA operand can be specified when you want to provide for overlap or blocked records, as you'll see in the next topic. In addition, work areas can be used to define multiple formats of a single record. However, this usage isn't common and we won't illustrate it in this book.

IOREG   If you don't specify the WORKA operand when you want to provide for overlap or blocked records, you must use IOREG. This operand identifies the I/O register that will give the address of the next record to be processed. The use of an I/O register for blocked records is illustrated in topic 3 of chapter 7. Until then, all programs will use work areas for both overlap and blocked records.

EOFADDR   The EOFADDR operand is required for an input file so a branch will take place when the end-of-file (EOF) condition is reached. Then, when the end of the file is reached during the execution of a GET instruction, the program branches to the label given in this operand. In figure 5-3, the program will branch to INVEOF when the end of the disk file is reached.

Priority	Keyword	Programmer code	Remarks
Required	BLKSIZE	Length of I/O area	Block length.
Optional	RECFORM	FIXUNB FIXBLK VARUNB VARBLK	FIXBLK for fixed-length blocked records is most common; FIXUNB is the default.
Optional	RECSIZE	Record length	Use only if RECFORM is FIXBLK.
Required	IOAREA1	Name of first I/O area	Length must equal block length.
Optional	IOAREA2	Name of second I/O area	Must be same length as first I/O area.
Optional	WORKA	YES	When used, records will be read into or written from the area named in the related GET or PUT statement. Don't use if IOREG is specified.
Optional	IOREG	Register number (nn)	When used, the register will give the address of the next record to be processed. Don't use if WORKA = YES is specified. IOREG is illustrated in topic 3 of chapter 7.
Required for input files	EOFADDR	Label of first instruction of EOF routine	
Optional	DEVADDR	Logical unit name in form SYSxxx	Programmer logical units are commonly used.

Figure 5-5   DTFSD operand summary

DEVADDR   The DEVADDR operand is used to specify the logical unit name associated with a file. As I mentioned in chapter 3, the logical unit names you code for disk files will be in the form SYSxxx and will have numbers between 000 and 255. Then, when your program is executed, the logical unit name is assigned to a physical I/O device by an ASSGN statement in your JCL (unless the permanent assignment for the logical unit name is acceptable).

| The DTFPR operands | Figure 5-6 summarizes the keywords for the DTFPR. Here, all of the keyword operands except DEVADDR, CTLCHR, and DEVICE are coded the same as in the DTFSD statement. As a result, I will only describe these three. |

DEVADDR   The DEVADDR operand assigns a logical unit name to the printer file. In the program in figure 5-3, the DEVADDR keyword specifies SYSLST. This is the system logical name for the system printer so its permanent assignment is usually to the printer you want. As a result, you usually won't have to assign SYSLST to the address of a physical device in your JCL. That's why you should code SYSLST for all printer files.

CTLCHR   The CTLCHR operand specifies the type of characters you will use to control the vertical spacing of your printed output. Since the most commonly used characters are the ones standardized by the American National Standards Institute, they are the only ones we'll use in the programs in this book. They are specified by coding ASA for this operand. Although they aren't used in the program in this topic, you'll see how they're used in the next topic.

DEVICE   The DEVICE operand is used to specify the type of physical device that is going to be used for printer output. The default value for this operand is 1403 so you don't need to code it if you're using a 1403 printer. If you're using a 3211 printer or one that is compatible with the 3211, you code PRT1 for this operand.

DATA DEFINITIONS

Data definitions are used to give symbolic names to the fields in storage. The symbolic names can then be used as operands in the instructions of the program. In general, the programmer writes data definitions for the I/O areas and for any other areas or fields required by the program. The latter are called *work areas* or *work fields*, which means that they are not an I/O area or any part of one.

| The disk file's input area | The data definitions for the disk file's input area in figure 5-3 (lines 3200-3900) follow: |

```
INVINPA   DS      0CL50
INVITNBR  DS      CL5
INVITDES  DS      CL20
          DS      CL5
INVPRICE  DS      CL5
INVORDPT  DS      CL5
INVONHND  DS      CL5
INVONORD  DS      CL5
```

For all of the coding lines, the operation code DS (Define Storage) is used. In positions 1-8 of the statements, names are given to the fields. These

Priority	Keyword	Programmer code	Remarks
Optional	BLKSIZE	Length of I/O area	Usually, 133 when ASA control characters are used; default is 121.
Required	IOAREA1	Name of first I/O area	Length must equal block length.
Optional	IOAREA2	Name of second I/O area	Must be same length as first I/O area.
Optional	WORKA	Yes	When used, records will be written from the work area named in the related PUT statement.
Required	DEVADDR	Logical unit name in form SYSxxx	SYSLST is commonly used.
Optional	CTLCHR	ASA or YES	ASA characters are commonly used; YES means System/370 characters are used.
Optional	DEVICE	Device number or PRT1	PRT1 is coded for 3202-4, 3203-5, 3211, 3262, and 3289-4 printers; for other printers, code the device number; 1403 is the default value.

Figure 5-6   DTFPR operand summary

names must (1) start with a letter, (2) consist entirely of letters and numbers, and (3) be eight characters or less in length.

The first coding line assigns the name INVINPA to the entire input area. Then, the next eight coding lines define fields within this 50-byte area. The name for this input area must be the same as the name given as IOAREA1 in the DTFSD for the file.

When creating names, you should try to make them as easy as possible to remember and use. Thus, I have given the name INVINPA to the inventory (INV) input (INP) area (A) and the name INVITNBR to the item-number field in the inventory record.

The operand for each DS statement has three parts: (1) a *duplication factor*, (2) a *type code*, and (3) a *length modifier*. In the statement

```
INVINPA DS     0CL50
```

the duplication factor is 0, the type code is C for EBCDIC (or character) data, and the length modifier is L50 indicating a length of 50 bytes.

A duplication factor of zero simply means that the fields that follow are within the area being defined. Since INVINPA has a length of 50, the zero duplication factor means that the DS statements for the next 50 bytes are within the input area. Thus, INVITNBR, INVITDES, and so on, are within the input area.

When the duplication factor is omitted, it is assumed to be one. Thus,

```
INVITNBR DS      CL5
```

defines a field named INVITNBR that is five bytes long, should receive EBCDIC data, and is bytes 1-5 of the area named INVINPA. Similarly, the remaining fields in the input area are defined so they correspond to the fields in the record layout for the input records. Since characters 26-30 of the record (the unit-cost field) aren't used by the program, bytes 26-30 of the input area aren't named.

The printer output area

The printer output area in the reorder-listing program is defined in lines 4100 through 5100 like this:

```
PRTOUTA  DS      0CL132
PRTITNBR DS      CL6
         DC      5C' '
PRTITDES DS      CL20
         DC      4C' '
PRTPRICE DS      CL7
         DC      4C' '
PRTAVAIL DS      CL6
         DC      4C' '
PRTORDPT DS      CL6
         DC      70C' '
```

Here, the name given to the output area must be the same as the one specified by the IOAREA1 operand in the DTFPR. Since the duplication factor is 0 and the length modifier is L132, the next 132 character positions are within the printer output area.

These definitions use the operation code DS as well as the operation code DC, which stands for Define Constant. The DC statement is coded in the same manner as a DS except that a value is also given to the field. This value is given between apostrophes (or single quotation marks) following the length modifier. This value is called the *nominal value*.

The first five bytes of the output area are defined as:

```
PRTITNBR DS      CL6
```

This field is given a length of 6 bytes rather than the 5 bytes indicated by the print chart because the edit pattern for item number requires 6 bytes. You'll see in a moment how this works.

The five bytes following PRTITNBR are defined by this DC statement:

```
         DC      5C' '
```

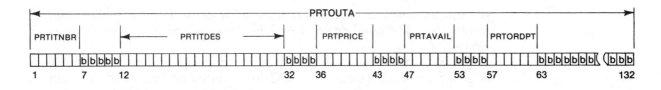

Figure 5-7   Printer output area

Here, no length modifier is given so the length is derived from the nominal value. Since one blank is coded between the apostrophes, the nominal value has a length of one and the length factor is assumed to be one. Since the duplication factor is five, this one-byte blank is duplicated five times. As a result, there will be five blanks between the item-number and item-description fields. This, of course, corresponds to the spacing indicated by the print chart in figure 5-1. An alternate way to code this operand is C'bbbbb' (where b is one blank), which means a duplication factor of one and a length factor of five taken from the nominal value.

The remaining DS and DC statements in the printer work area are defined in a similar manner. Thus, PRTITDES is a 20-byte field followed by four blanks. Then, PRTPRICE is a 7-byte field followed by four blanks; and so on. The PRTPRICE, PRTAVAIL, and PRTORDPT fields are one byte longer than indicated by the print chart so the edit patterns for these fields will fit properly. The last DC for this area has an operand of 70C'b' (where b is one blank), so 70 blanks fill out the area. In figure 5-7, the names assigned to this output area are shown schematically.

Work fields

The last series of data definitions (lines 5300-5800) are for various work fields used by the program. They use the type codes X for hexadecimal and P for packed decimal. For example,

```
PATTERN1 DC      X'402020202020'
```

defines a constant named PATTERN1 with a length of six containing the hex codes

```
    40   20   20   20   20   20
```

When the type code X is used, two hex characters in the nominal value represent one byte of storage.

Similarly,

```
WRKAVAIL DS      PL3
```

defines a three-byte field named WRKAVAIL that should receive five digits of packed-decimal data. When a DC is used for a packed field, the nominal value is a decimal number with or without a leading plus or minus sign. The numeric value is then placed in the field in proper packed decimal format.

One type of code not shown that you may find useful is Z, which stands for zoned decimal. In a DC for a zoned decimal field, you code a decimal number, with or without a sign, as its nominal value. Then, the numeric value is stored in the field in proper zoned decimal format.

Although these examples should give you a good idea of how to code DS and DC statements, there are some other points you should become familiar with. First, you can give an implied length to a DS statement by using a nominal value just as you can with a DC statement. Thus,

```
INVITNBR DS      C'99999'
```

defines a five-byte field named INVITNBR. This is sometimes done deliberately to show how large a number a field can hold, but more often it happens when you code DS instead of DC by mistake. You must realize, then, that the DS statement is assembled, but no value is placed in the field.

Second, you can use a zero duplication factor to define subfields within fields as well as fields within areas. Thus,

```
DATE        DS      0CL6
MONTH       DS      CL2
DAY         DS      CL2
YEAR        DS      CL2
```

defines two-byte month, day, and year fields within a six-byte date field. The date field in turn can be part of an input area, so that as many levels of subdefinitions as are needed can be coded in assembler language. This is explained more fully in chapter 7.

Third, you should be aware that *padding* and *truncation* can occur when you code a DC statement. For zoned, packed, or hex fields, padding occurs to the left with zero values, as in these examples:

Source code		Resulting field in hex			
DC	Z'15'			F1	F5
DC	ZL4'15'	F0	F0	F1	F5
DC	P'15'			01	5C
DC	PL3'315'		00	31	5C
DC	XL3'0F'		00	00	0F

For character fields, padding occurs to the right with blanks, as in these examples:

Source code		Resulting field in hex					
DC	C'A'	C1					
DC	CL3'A'	C1	40	40			
DC	CL6'NAME'	D5	C1	D4	C5	40	40
DC	CL5' '	40	40	40	40	40	

Similarly, truncation occurs on the left for zoned, packed, or hex fields, as in these examples:

Source code   Resulting field in hex

```
DC    ZL2'-132'                        F3  D2
DC    PL1'+12'                             2C
DC    PL3'400382                  00   38  2C
DC    XL2'140FB12C'                    B1  2C
```

And, truncation occurs on the right for character fields, as in these examples:

Source code   Resulting field in hex

```
DC    CL3'NAME'              D5  C1  D4
DC    CL1'YES'               E8
```

Although padding is used intentionally by assembler language programmers, truncation usually results from a programming error. As a result, although you wouldn't intentionally code a DC statement for truncation, you should know what will happen if you do it by error.

Finally, you should know that you can't just code an apostrophe (') or an ampersand (&) in a DS or DC statement. To code a character constant containing one of these characters, you must code two ampersands or two apostrophes in the nominal value for each one you want. For instance,

```
DC     C'A''B'
```

defines a three-byte field containing the characters A'B. The DC statement

```
DC     CL5'S && R'
```

defines a five-byte field containing S & R.

INSTRUCTIONS

The instructions of this program are found in the first 26 lines. They correspond to the program flowchart in figure 5-2. In the comment field for the first instruction of a flowchart block, you'll find a comment that relates the code to the flowchart. When you use a flowchart as a design document, you use the flowchart as a guide for coding the instructions of the program.

The housekeeping routine

All assembler language programs start with some sort of *housekeeping routine* (or *initialization routine*). In the program in figure 5-3, the first four instructions represent the housekeeping block of the flowchart. Not including the comments, these instructions are:

```
REORDLST START 0
BEGIN     BALR  3,0
          USING *,3
          OPEN  INVMAST,PRTOUT
```

START   The first instruction doesn't cause any object code to be assembled. It is one of several *assembler commands* that you use to control the assembly of your program. The START command signals the assembler that the source code is starting and tells the assembler the address at which the object code should start. Since the object program will be link edited to a different starting address than the one specified in the START command, zero is the easiest value to use in the START command.

The name given in the name field for the START instruction becomes the *program name*. In this case, the program name is REORDLST. A name for the START instruction, or any other instruction, is formed by using the same rules as those used for field names: (1) it must start with a letter; (2) it must use only letters and numbers; and (3) it must be eight characters or less in length.

BALR   The branch-and-link-register instruction is the first *machine instruction* of the reorder-listing program. When it is assembled, one machine language instruction will be assembled from it.

The BALR instruction has two operands: 3 and 0. In chapter 4, you learned that the BALR instruction causes the address of the next instruction to be placed in operand-1 (in this case, register 3). Also, if the register specified by operand-2 is 0 (as in this case), no branching takes place and the program continues with the next instruction. If, for example, this program is loaded starting at address 5200, the BALR instruction will occupy bytes 5200-5201. Then, when the BALR is executed, address 5202 will be stored in register 3, and the program will continue with the next instruction in sequence.

The purpose of this BALR instruction is to store a base address in a base register. Thus, register 3 will be used as the base register for this program. If a program is loaded into storage and a proper address is not loaded into the base register used by the program, the program will not execute as intended. As a result, a BALR instruction with zero for operand-2 is normally the first machine instruction of a program.

USING   A USING instruction is another assembler command. As a result, it generates no object code. Instead, it tells the assembler which register is going to be used as the base register. The first operand (in this case, *) tells the assembler at which point in the program the base register should start being used. The second operand (in this case, 3) tells the assembler which register to use as the base register. Since * means "at this point" or "starting now," the USING statement of the reorder-listing program tells the assembler to use register 3 as the base register for all addresses following the USING statement. Since the preceding BALR instruction has already stored the address of the next instruction in register 3, the USING statement and BALR instruction are properly coordinated.

The BALR and USING instructions, coded as shown, are the standard method of loading and specifying the base register. Therefore, you will have similar instructions at the start of each of your programs. Since registers 0, 1, 2, 13, 14, and 15 are used by various programs of VSE, these registers are generally not used as base registers. Instead, registers 3 through 12 are used. More specifically, it is a common practice to use registers 3, 4, and 5 for base registers and registers 6 through 12 for other register operations. That's why we recommend that you use register 3 as the first base register in all your programs.

A single base register can accommodate a program of up to 4096 bytes since the maximum displacement value is 4095 bytes. If a program is larger than this, additional base registers must be loaded and assigned. The coding required to load and specify multiple base registers is explained in the next chapter.

OPEN   The OPEN instruction is a *macro instruction* (or just *macro*), which means that more than one object instruction is assembled from it. Actually, the assembler first converts the macro into two or more source instructions; then, it converts the source instructions into object instructions. In contrast to macro instructions, only *one* object instruction is assembled from each machine instruction.

An OPEN instruction must be executed before an input file can be read or an output file written. You can think of opening a file as checking to be sure the device is ready to operate. For a disk file, the OPEN instruction also checks to make sure the appropriate file is available to the program.

The operands of the OPEN instruction are the filenames given to each file by the DTFs. For the reorder-listing program, the operands are INVMAST for the DTFSD and PRTOUT for the DTFPR. Although this OPEN instruction opens only two files, there is no limit to the number of files that can be opened in a single instruction.

The mainline routine

The *mainline routine* is the part of a program that accomplishes the main processing of the program. It is usually a loop that includes input, processing, and output. In the flowchart in figure 5-2, blocks 2 through 6, including branching back to connector circle 1, make up the mainline routine.

Flowchart block 2   The first instruction of the mainline routine is:

```
READINV   GET   INVMAST
```

The GET instruction is a macro instruction that causes a record to be read into storage. In this case the operand is INVMAST, so one record from the inventory file is read. Since the DTFSD specifies IOAREA1=INVINPA with no work area, the inventory data is read into the 50-byte area named INVINPA.

The GET instruction corresponds to block 2 of the flowchart. Because the DTF for the inventory file specifies EOFADDR=INVEOF, the GET instruction will cause a branch to the instruction named INVEOF when the end-of-file condition is reached. The flowline out of block 2 in the flowchart represents this branching. As you can see in the listing in figure 5-3, INVEOF is the name given to the instruction coded in line 2500.

Flowchart block 3   The coding for block 3 of the flowchart indicates that the available inventory amount should be calculated. The program does this as follows:

```
PACK    WRKAVAIL,INVONHND
PACK    WRKONORD,INVONORD
AP      WRKAVAIL,WRKONORD
```

In other words, the input field named INVONHND is packed into the work field named WRKAVAIL; the input field named INVONORD is packed into the work field named WRKONORD; and WRKONORD is added to WRKAVAIL (which contains the value of the on-hand field). After the three instructions are executed, WRKAVAIL contains the available amount (on-hand plus on-order). You should realize that the names used as operands in these instructions must be identical to the names given in the data definitions.

Flowchart block 4   Block 4 of the flowchart is a decision block that tests whether the available amount is less than the reorder point. Its instructions are:

```
PACK    WRKORDPT,INVORDPT
CP      WRKAVAIL,WRKORDPT
BNL     READINV
```

Because the compare decimal (CP) instruction is used to compare available and reorder point, the reorder-point field (INVORDPT) must be packed before comparison. Then, WRKAVAIL and WRKORDPT are compared, and the condition code is set based on this comparison.

The third instruction of this decision block is a branch instruction. However, the instruction doesn't specify a specific mask for branching as described in chapter 4. Instead, it uses a mnemonic operation code that tells the assembler what the mask should be. These codes are summarized in figure 5-8. For instance, operation code B specifies an unconditional branch; operation code BE, following a compare instruction, specifies a branch when operand-1 equals operand-2; and BP, following an

Type	Code	Meaning
Unconditional	B	Branch unconditionally
After compare instructions	BH	Branch on A high
	BL	Branch on A low
	BE	Branch on A equal B
	BNH	Branch on A not high
	BNL	Branch on A not low
	BNE	Branch on A not equal B
After arithmetic instructions	BO	Branch on overflow
	BP	Branch on plus
	BM	Branch on minus
	BZ	Branch on zero
	BNP	Branch on not plus
	BNM	Branch on not minus
	BNZ	Branch on not zero

Figure 5-8   Mnemonic codes for branch operations

arithmetic operation, specifies a branch if the result is positive. You should realize that all of the operation codes in figure 5-8 cause one branch-on-condition instruction to be assembled, but the mask differs, depending on the operation code.

In the reorder-listing program,

```
BNL     READINV
```

means that the program should branch to the instruction named READINV if WRKAVAIL is not less than WRKORDPT. If WRKAVAIL is less than WRKORDPT, the program continues with the next instruction in sequence.

This branching could also be coded this way:

```
BH      READINV
BE      READINV
```

In this case, if available is greater than reorder point, a branch to READINV takes place. If not, the second branch instruction is executed. Then, if available is equal to reorder point, the branch to READINV takes place. If not, the next instruction in sequence is executed.

Incidentally, the branch-on-condition instruction can also be coded by using a decimal number that represents the mask. For instance, this instruction

```
BC      15,READINV
```

gives a mask of decimal 15 (hex F, or binary 1111) so it is an unconditional branch to the instruction named READINV. Similarly, if operand-1 is an 8 (hex 8, or binary 1000), the branch only takes place if the first bit in the condition code is on. Following a compare decimal instruction,

```
BC      8,READINV
```

has the same effect as

```
BE      READINV
```

By using a decimal number from 0 through 15, any mask can be coded so the instruction can branch on any combination of condition codes. This form of coding is rarely used, however, since codes like BE, BH, and BNL are so much easier to use.

Flowchart block 5   Block 5 in the flowchart says "construct detail line." This means arrange the data in the printer output area in a form suitable for printing. This normally involves moving alphanumeric fields into the output area and editing numeric fields into the output area so that leading zeros are suppressed and commas and decimal points are inserted wherever needed.

Lines 1200-2200 represent this block of processing. For instance, the first three instructions following the branch instruction edit the item-number field into the printer output area:

```
PACK    PACKAREA,INVITNBR
MVC     PRTITNBR,PATTERN1
ED      PRTITNBR,PACKAREA
```

In the first instruction, the five-byte input field is packed into the three-byte work field named PACKAREA. Then, the hex pattern 402020202020 is moved into the first six bytes of the printer output area. Finally, the packed item number is edited into the pattern thus suppressing lead zeros.

The next instruction moves the item-description field, unchanged, into the printer output area. Then, the next seven instructions edit the unit price, available, and reorder point fields. Since available and reorder point are already in packed form, they do not need to be packed before editing. In all cases, an edit pattern is moved into the appropriate output field before the edit instruction is executed.

Flowchart block 6   Block 6 of the flowchart is an output block. It indicates that a line should be printed on the output listing. The instruction representing this block is:

```
PUT    PRTOUT
```

The PUT instruction is a macro instruction that causes output. Because the device is a printer, one line is printed each time the PUT is executed, and single spacing takes place.

The connector circle   The final instruction of the mainline routine is:

```
B       READINV
```

This means an unconditional branch to the instruction named READINV is executed. It corresponds to the flowline leading to the connector circle on the flowchart. As a result, the program repeats the processing for the next record in the inventory file.

The end-of-job routine

An assembler language program normally ends with an an *end-of-job routine*, or *EOJ routine*. At the least, this routine closes the files used by the program and signals the supervisor that the program has completed execution.

The end-of-job routine for the reorder-listing program is:

```
INVEOF    CLOSE INVMAST,PRTOUT
          EOJ
```

Since the name INVEOF is given for the keyword EOFADDR in the DTFSD, these instructions are executed when the end-of-file condition for the inventory master file is reached.

CLOSE   The CLOSE instruction parallels the OPEN instruction. It is a macro instruction that closes the files to further processing. Its operands are the filenames for the input and output files taken from the DTFs.

EOJ   The EOJ instruction has no operands. It simply tells the supervisor that the program has finished so it can load another program into the partition.

The END instruction

The last instruction in an assembler language source program must always be the END instruction. It, like the START instruction, is an assembler command. It tells the assembler that there is no more source code and its operand tells the assembler where program execution should begin. In most cases, the operand is the name of the BALR instruction that loads the base register at the start of the program since this is the first executable instruction of the program.

In figure 5-3, the END instruction for the reorder-listing program specifies BEGIN as the operand since that's the first executable instruction of the program. However, it could also specify REORDLST. Since the START instruction generates no machine instructions, it has the same address as the BALR instruction that follows it.

DISCUSSION

As you can see from this example, you actually write three types of instructions when you code an assembler language program: assembler commands, machine instructions, and macro instructions. In addition, you code file definitions and data definitions. As you code, you give names to all DTFs and to the data fields and instructions that are referred to by other instructions. These names are then used as operands in the instructions that refer to them.

In figure 5-3, the instructions are coded first followed by the file definitions followed by the data definitions. However, you don't have to put them in your program in that sequence because the assembler doesn't require any specific order. As a result, it is also common to code the file definitions first, the instructions second, and the data definitions last. If you don't code the instructions first, though, be sure your END instruction gives the label of the first executable instruction of the program. For the sake of efficiency, we recommend that you use the order shown in the reorder-listing program or the common variation I've just described.

By comparing assembler language code with the machine instructions presented in chapter 4, you can see how assembler language aids the programmer. First, by using symbolic names for files, data, and instructions, the programmer doesn't have to keep track of addresses and length codes. Second, by using mnemonic operation codes, the programmer doesn't have to remember hex operation codes. Third, by using macros, many machine instructions can be assembled from a single line of assembler language coding.

On the other hand, if you've used a higher-level language than assembler language, you can also see the limitations of assembler language. If, for example, you were to compare the program in figure 5-3 with a COBOL program for the same specifications, you would find the differences quite striking. First, operations that require only one statement in COBOL require two or more instructions in assembler language. Second, because you use English verbs like READ and ADD in your COBOL programs and because your data names can be up to 31 characters in length, COBOL is much easier to read than assembler language. Finally, it's obvious that the assembler language programmer has to know far more about the operation of a CPU than the COBOL programmer.

Terminology

Basic Assembler Language
BAL
subset
comment line
label
name
operation
operand
comment
file definition
DTF statement
DTF
filename
keyword operand
keyword
data definition
work area
work field
duplication factor
type code
length modifier
nominal value
padding
truncation
housekeeping routine
initialization routine
assembler command
program name
machine instruction
macro instruction
macro
mainline routine
end-of-job routine
EOJ routine

Objectives

1. Given the program listing in figure 5-3 and samples of input data, describe the execution of any instruction or group of instructions in the program.

2. Given descriptions of storage areas or fields, code acceptable data definitions for them using C, Z, P, or X type codes.

TOPIC 2   Refining the reorder-listing program

The reorder-listing program in topic 1 presented the essential components of an assembler language program. In actual practice, though, even the simplest of programs would be much more complex than that reorder-listing program. As a result, this topic presents an enhanced version of the reorder-listing program. By the time you complete this topic, you will have learned an introductory subset of assembler language. You will then be able to develop simple programs of your own in assembler language.

Figure 5-9 shows an expanded print chart for the reorder-listing program. As you can see, a three-line heading is required at the top of each page of the reorder listing. Also, a count of the number of records in the input file is to be printed at the end of the listing. Otherwise, the specifications for this refined reorder-listing program are like those in figure 5-1.

A flowchart for this refined reorder-listing program is shown in figure 5-10. If you compare this with the flowchart in figure 5-2, you can see that the additional blocks on the enhanced flowchart provide for printing the heading lines and the count line. If more than 50 detail lines are printed on one page of the reorder listing, the form is skipped to the top of the next page and the headings are printed again.

Figure 5-11 shows the complete program for the refined reorder-listing program. This program not only provides for the enhanced printing requirements, but it provides for overlapped I/O and CPU operations and blocked disk records. For efficiency, both overlap and the use of blocked disk records are normally required of production programs. If you review the program in figure 5-11, you can see that comments are used in many of the instructions to describe what the instructions do.

Coding one operand per line in your DTFs

Because it's difficult to read a DTF when several operands are coded in a single line, DTFs are often coded with one operand per line. This is illustrated by the DTFs in the program in figure 5-11. For example, the DTFSD is written like this:

```
INVMAST   DTFSD BLKSIZE=500,                    X
                RECFORM=FIXBLK,                  X
                RECSIZE=50,                      X
                IOAREA1=INVIO1,                  X
                IOAREA2=INVIO2,                  X
                WORKA=YES,                       X
                EOFADDR=INVEOF,                  X
                DEVADDR=SYS008
```

When you code a DTF in this way, you must be sure that (1) the operands are separated only after commas, (2) a continuation character like X is

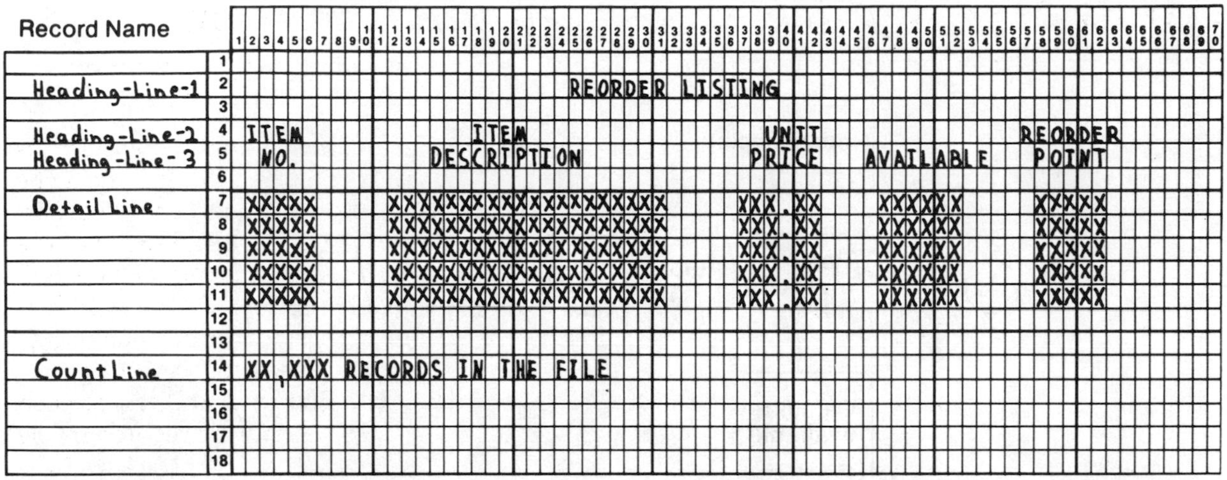

Figure 5-9   The print chart for the refined reorder-listing program

coded in position 72 on every line preceding a continuation line, and (3) all continuation lines start in position 16.

When you code DTFs in this way, it's easier to modify the operands and the code is easier to read so this is a worthwhile coding practice. We also recommend that you code the operands in your DTFs in the same sequence every time since this too makes your code easier to read. In the rest of the programs in this book, we always code the operands in the same basic order with one operand per coding line.

Providing for overlap

To provide for overlap, the program in figure 5-11 specifies two I/O areas in the DTFs for each file. In other words, the keyword operands IOAREA1 and IOAREA2 are used for both disk and printer files. Then, two I/O areas are defined for each file in the data definitions section of the program. For the disk file, they are INVIO1 and INVIO2. For the printer, they are PRTIO1 and PRTIO2.

When disk or print operations are overlapped with processing, a work area is often used. As a result, WORKA=YES is specified for both files. Then, after a record is read into an input area, the data is moved to the work area specified in the GET macro. Similarly, before data is printed from an output area, the data is moved into the appropriate I/O area from the work area specified in the PUT macro.

If you look at the GET and PUT instructions in figure 5-11, you can see that they specify a second operand. This second operand names the work area to be used for the I/O operation. In this program, only one GET instruction is coded for the disk file, but five different PUT instructions are coded for the printer file, and they specify five different work

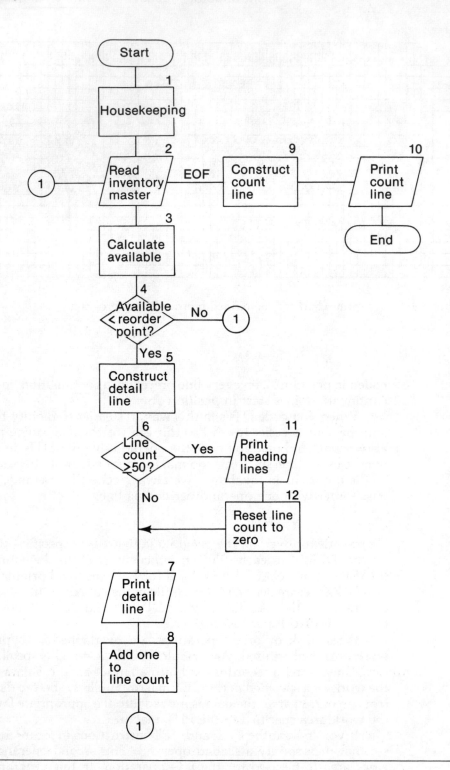

Figure 5-10   The flowchart for the refined reorder-listing program

areas. As you can see, then, you don't have to use the same work area each time you code an I/O macro for a file.

These are the only changes required for overlap to take place in the program. Once you've coded the DTFs, the dual I/O areas, the work areas, and the GET and PUT statements, overlap takes place automatically. In other words, you aren't aware of which I/O area is being used at any given time. All you know, is that the GET instruction moves the next record in sequence into the work area specified, and that the PUT instruction writes the next record from the work area specified.

Providing for blocked records

Look at the operands for the disk file DTF in figure 5-11. The BLKSIZE operand specifies 500 bytes; the RECSIZE operand specifies 50 bytes; and the RECFORM operand specifies fixed-length, blocked records. This means that the 50-byte records are blocked with 10 records to a block. If you look at the I/O area definitions for the disk file, you can see that INVIO1 and INVIO2 are both 500-bytes long.

This coding combined with the use of a work area (WORKA=YES) is the only coding that is required for blocked records. Then, whenever a GET instruction is executed for the disk file, the next record to be processed is moved into the work area specified. As a result, you don't have to keep track of which record in the block in which I/O area is next to be processed. The assembler and its I/O modules take care of that for you. All you have to realize is that the next record is always available in the work area just as though the records weren't blocked and just as though the program weren't overlapping the I/O operation with CPU processing.

Controlling printed forms

When a program prints a document, it normally has to control the skipping and spacing of the printed form. This is referred to as *forms control*. At the least, a program that prints a document must provide for *page overflow*. This means that the form should be skipped from the last printing line of one page to the first line of the next page so the printer doesn't print on the perforation between two forms. In assembler language, you accomplish forms control by using control characters and line counting.

Control characters A *control character* is used as the first character in a print area to specify the spacing or skipping required before printing. When you use control characters, you must use the CTLCHR keyword in the DTF for the printer file. In figure 5-11, the DTFPR for the refined reorder-listing program specifies CTLCHR=ASA. This means that the control characters recommended by the American National Standards Institute are going to be used. Since these characters are the most widely used characters today, they are the only ones we'll present in this book.

When control characters are used, one byte at the start of an output area indicates the skipping or spacing to be performed before the area is printed. Thus, BLKSIZE in the DTFPR specifies 133; that is, one control byte followed by the 132 bytes corresponding to the 132 print positions of

```
REORDLST START  0                                                          00000100
BEGIN     BALR  3,0                     LOAD BASE REGISTER                  00000200
          USING *,3                                                        00000300
          OPEN  INVMAST,PRTOUT                                             00000400
READINV   GET   INVMAST,INVWRKA         READ RECORD INTO WORK AREA         00000500
          AP    COUNT,=P'1'             ADD ONE TO COUNT                   00000600
          PACK  WRKAVAIL,INVONHND                                          00000700
          PACK  WRKONORD,INVONORD                                          00000800
          AP    WRKAVAIL,WRKONORD       ADD ON HAND AND ON ORDER           00000900
          PACK  WRKORDPT,INVORDPT                                          00001000
          CP    WRKAVAIL,WRKORDPT       COMPARE AVAILABLE, REORDER POINT   00001100
          BNL   READINV                                                    00001200
          PACK  PACKAREA,INVITNBR                                          00001300
          MVC   PRTITNBR,PATTERN1                                          00001400
          ED    PRTITNBR,PACKAREA       EDIT ITEM NUMBER                   00001500
          MVC   PRTITDES,INVITDES       MOVE ITEM DESCRIPTION              00001600
          PACK  PACKAREA,INVPRICE                                          00001700
          MVC   PRTPRICE,PATTERN2                                          00001800
          ED    PRTPRICE,PACKAREA       EDIT UNIT PRICE                    00001900
          MVC   PRTAVAIL,PATTERN1                                          00002000
          ED    PRTAVAIL,WRKAVAIL       EDIT AVAILABLE                     00002100
          MVC   PRTORDPT,PATTERN1                                          00002200
          ED    PRTORDPT,WRKORDPT       EDIT ORDER POINT                   00002300
          CP    LINECNT,=P'50'          COMPARE LINE COUNT TO 50           00002400
          BL    PRTDET                  BRANCH ON LOW TO PRTDET            00002500
          PUT   PRTOUT,HDGLINE1         PRINT FIRST HEADING LINE           00002600
          PUT   PRTOUT,HDGLINE2         PRINT SECOND HEADING LINE          00002700
          PUT   PRTOUT,HDGLINE3         PRINT THIRD HEADING LINE           00002800
          ZAP   LINECNT,=P'0'           RESET LINE COUNT TO ZERO           00002900
          MVI   PRTDCTL,C'0'            MOVE ZERO TO ASA CONTROL BYTE      00003000
PRTDET    PUT   PRTOUT,PRTDETL          PRINT DETAIL LINE                  00003100
          AP    LINECNT,=P'1'           ADD ONE TO LINE COUNT              00003200
          MVI   PRTDCTL,C' '            MOVE BLANK TO ASA CONTROL BYTE     00003300
          B     READINV                                                    00003400
INVEOF    ED    CNTPATRN,COUNT          EDIT COUNT                         00003500
          PUT   PRTOUT,CNTLINE          PRINT COUNT LINE                   00003600
          CLOSE INVMAST,PRTOUT                                             00003700
          EOJ                                                              00003800
*   THE INVENTORY FILE DEFINITION                                         00003900
INVMAST   DTFSD BLKSIZE=500,                                             X00004000
                RECFORM=FIXBLK,                                         X00004100
                RECSIZE=50,                                             X00004200
                IOAREA1=INVIO1,                                         X00004300
                IOAREA2=INVIO2,                                         X00004400
                WORKA=YES,                                             X00004500
                EOFADDR=INVEOF,                                         X00004600
                DEVADDR=SYS008                                           00004700
*   THE PRINTER FILE DEFINITION                                           00004800
PRTOUT    DTFPR BLKSIZE=133,                                            X00004900
                IOAREA1=PRTIO1,                                         X00005000
                IOAREA2=PRTIO2,                                         X00005100
                WORKA=YES,                                             X00005200
                DEVADDR=SYSLST,                                         X00005300
                CTLCHR=ASA                                               00005400
*   THE DATA DEFINITIONS FOR THE TWO INVENTORY FILE I/O AREAS             00005500
INVIO1    DS    CL500                                                     00005600
INVIO2    DS    CL500                                                     00005700
*   THE DATA DEFINITIONS FOR THE TWO PRINTER OUTPUT AREAS                 00005800
PRTIO1    DS    CL133                                                     00005900
PRTIO2    DS    CL133                                                     00006000
```

Figure 5-11   The refined reorder-listing program (part 1 of 2)

```
*   THE DATA DEFINITIONS FOR THE INVENTORY FILE WORK AREA            00006100
INVWRKA  DS     0CL50                                                00006200
INVITNBR DS     CL5                                                  00006300
INVITDES DS     CL20                                                 00006400
         DS     CL5                                                  00006500
INVPRICE DS     CL5                                                  00006600
INVORDPT DS     CL5                                                  00006700
INVONHND DS     CL5                                                  00006800
INVONORD DS     CL5                                                  00006900
*   THE DATA DEFINITIONS FOR THE PRINTER HEADING LINES               00007000
HDGLINE1 DS     0CL133                                               00007100
         DC     C'1'                                                 00007200
         DC     24C' '                                               00007300
         DC     C'REORDER LISTING'                                   00007400
         DC     93C' '                                               00007500
HDGLINE2 DS     0CL133                                               00007600
         DC     C'0'                                                 00007700
         DC     C' ITEM             ITEM              UNIT     X00007800
                REORDER'                                             00007900
         DC     69C' '                                               00008000
HDGLINE3 DS     0CL133                                               00008100
         DC     C' '                                                 00008200
         DC     C' NO.          DESCRIPTION        PRICE   AVAILABLEX00008300
                POINT'                                               00008400
         DC     70C' '                                               00008500
*   THE DATA DEFINITIONS FOR THE PRINTER DETAIL LINE                 00008600
PRTDETL  DS     0CL133                                               00008700
PRTDCTL  DS     CL1                                                  00008800
PRTITNBR DS     CL6                                                  00008900
         DC     5C' '                                                00009000
PRTITDES DS     CL20                                                 00009100
         DC     4C' '                                                00009200
PRTPRICE DS     CL7                                                  00009300
         DC     4C' '                                                00009400
PRTAVAIL DS     CL6                                                  00009500
         DC     4C' '                                                00009600
PRTORDPT DS     CL6                                                  00009700
         DC     70C' '                                               00009800
*   THE DATA DEFINITIONS FOR THE COUNT LINE                          00009900
CNTLINE  DS     0CL133                                               00010000
         DC     C'-'                                                 00010100
CNTPATRN DC     X'40202068202020'                                    00010200
         DC     C' RECORDS IN THE INPUT FILE'                        00010300
         DC     99C' '                                               00010400
*   THE DATA DEFINITIONS FOR THE WORK FIELDS                         00010500
PATTERN1 DC     X'402020202020'                                      00010600
PATTERN2 DC     X'4020202148202 0'                                   00010700
WRKAVAIL DS     PL3                                                  00010800
WRKONORD DS     PL3                                                  00010900
WRKORDPT DS     PL3                                                  00011000
PACKAREA DS     PL3                                                  00011100
CCOUNT   DC     PL3'0'                                               00011200
LINECNT  DC     P'50'                                                00011300
         END    BEGIN                                                00011400
```

Figure 5-11   The refined reorder-listing program (part 2 of 2)

the printer. If you look at the data definitions for the printer output and work areas, you will see that this control byte is provided for in each of these areas.

The four most commonly used ASA control characters are:

Character	Meaning
blank	Space one line before printing
0	Space two lines before printing
-	Space three lines before printing
1	Skip to the top of the next page before printing

If you check the code in figure 5-11, then, you can see that the work area for HDGLINE1 has a control character of 1. This means that the form will be advanced to the top of the next page before HDGLINE1 is printed. Similarly, the form will be advanced two lines before HDGLINE2 is printed, and one line before HDGLINE3 is printed. If you're interested, you can find the complete range of ASA control characters and their uses in Appendix A of IBM's *VSE/Advanced Functions Macro User's Guide*, ST24-5210.

Line counting and literals   The technique of *line counting* is used to determine when a page is full and the form should be advanced to the next page. If you look at the flowchart in figure 5-10, you can see that the logic for line counting is simple. The line-counting routine first checks to see whether 50 lines have been printed on a page. If yes, the program skips to the next page, prints headings, resets a field (called the line-count field) to zero, and continues. If no, the program prints a detail line, adds one to the line-count field, and continues.

To count the number of lines printed on a page, the program in figure 5-11 uses a field named LINECNT. It is defined in line 11300. This is a two-byte packed field with a starting value of 50. You'll see why it has this starting value in a moment. You'll also see that it is set to a value of zero each time the heading lines are printed for a page.

After a detail line is printed by the program, the value 1 is added to LINECNT using the AP instruction with a *literal* as an operand:

```
AP      LINECNT,=P'1'
```

A literal is identified by an equals sign. After the equals sign, the literal gives a value just as you give a value in a DC definition. In this case, the literal gives a value of one in a packed decimal form. As a result, the AP instruction just shown is the equivalent of the instruction

```
AP      LINECNT,PCON1
```

and the data definition

```
PCON1    DC      P'1'
```

By using the literal, though, the amount of coding is reduced.

To code a literal operand, use an equals sign followed by a type code and a nominal value enclosed in single quotes. All of the DC type codes are valid, so any of the following are acceptable literals:

```
=P'-15'
=Z'+5000'
=X'40'
=C'ABC'
```

As you might guess, a literal can be used as the sending field in an instruction, but it cannot be used as the receiving field.

The line counting logic is given in lines 2400-3200 of the program in figure 5-11. The first two lines correspond to block 6 of the flowchart in figure 5-10:

```
CP      LINECNT,=P'50'
BL      PRTDET
```

First, LINECNT is compared to a packed value of 50. If LINECNT is less than 50, a branch to PRTDET takes place and a detail line is printed. But if LINECNT is equal to or greater than 50, no branch takes place. Since LINECNT has a starting value of 50, as defined in its DC, no branching takes place the first time through the program so the PUT instructions that follow are executed to print the heading lines of the reorder listing.

The instructions that follow the PUT instructions are these:

```
ZAP     LINECNT,=P'0'
MVI     PRTDCTL,C'0'
```

The ZAP instruction first changes the value of LINECNT from 50 to 0; then, it adds the literal value zero to LINECNT. As a result, the ZAP instruction has the effect of resetting LINECNT to a value of zero.

The MVI instruction moves the control character 0 into the first byte of the work area for the detail print line. Note, however, that the second operand in this instruction isn't a literal because it doesn't start with an equals sign. Instead, the second operand of an immediate instruction (the SI format) is an *immediate operand*. It is specified using a type code and nominal value in the same manner as for a DC statement, but without the equals sign used in a literal operand.

The next three lines of code are:

```
PRTDET    PUT     PRTOUT,PRTDETL
          AP      LINECNT,=P'1'
          MVI     PRTDCTL,C' '
```

Since the control character in the PRTDETL area is set to zero after the heading lines are printed, the printer is spaced twice before printing the first detail line on a page. Then, after a detail line is printed, the AP instruction adds one to LINECNT and the MVI instruction changes the control character of the detail line back to blank for single spacing.

Printing headings

To print headings, work areas that contain the required heading data must be defined. Thus, the three heading lines needed for the reorder listing are defined in the work areas named HDGLINE1, HDGLINE2, and HDGLINE3 (lines 7100-8500 of figure 5-11). The data to be printed is defined using DCs, and continuation lines for the DCs are used whenever needed.

Continuation lines for DCs   When a DC line is continued, the coding in the line continues through position 71. Next, a continuation character like X must be coded in position 72 of the line. Then, the instruction is continued starting in position 16 of the next coding line. Although you can code as many continuation lines as you need for macro instructions like DTFs, you can code a maximum of only two continuation lines for instructions like DCs.

PUT macros that specify work areas   When a PUT macro is issued to print a heading line, the appropriate work area is given as the second operand. To illustrate, consider the heading routine in figure 5-11:

```
        PUT     PRTOUT,HDGLINE1
        PUT     PRTOUT,HDGLINE2
        PUT     PRTOUT,HDGLINE3
```

Here, three different work areas are specified as the operands of three successive PUT macros.

Printing the count line

In figure 5-11, right after the GET instruction for the inventory master file, an AP instruction is used to add one to a field named COUNT. As a result, COUNT, which was defined with a starting value of zero, keeps an accurate count of the number of records read by the program.

When the end-of-file condition is reached, the GET instruction causes a branch to INVEOF. The count is then printed using this code:

```
INVEOF  ED      CNTPATRN,COUNT
        PUT     PRTOUT,CNTLINE
```

Here, COUNT is first edited into an edit pattern that is part of the printer work area named CNTLINE. Then, the PUT macro causes the count line to be printed. Since the control character for CNTLINE is a minus sign, the form will be advanced three spaces before the line is printed.

Using comments

Comments have been used extensively in the program in figure 5-11 with the hope that they will help you understand the program. In practice, however, it isn't usually necessary to go to this level of detail when coding comments. Instead, you'll want to use comment lines to document blocks of code as illustrated in the other programs of this book. When coding comments, be sure that they start one or more spaces after your operands and that they don't go beyond position 71 of your source lines.

Discussion

If you understand this refined reorder-listing program, you should be able to start coding programs of your own. Although I haven't illustrated the use of the SP, MP, and DP instructions yet, you should be able to use them because their coding is analogous to the coding for the AP instruction. Similarly, you should be able to code the UNPK instruction because it is the reverse of the PACK instruction. As you code your programs, though, you may want to refer back to chapter 4 to check the operational details of these instructions.

Terminology

forms control
page overflow
control character
line counting
literal
immediate operand

Objective

Given program specifications, code an assembler language program that meets the specifications. The specifications will require disk input, printer output, forms control, and decimal arithmetic.

Chapter 6

A basic subset of assembler language

In this chapter, you will be shown some instructions and techniques that will complete a basic subset of assembler language. Topic 1 is a collection of instructions and techniques that you need to know in order to clear I/O and work areas, round numeric results, and so on. Topic 2 presents some standard macros that let you access the current date and time of your system and that let you print the contents of storage when you encounter problems during program testing. Topic 3 presents some assembler commands that let you assign more than one base register to your program, copy source code from source libraries into your program, and control the way your assembly listing prints.

TOPIC 1   Other elements of the basic subset

Thus far, you have been introduced to the basic instructions and coding techniques of an assembler language program. In this topic, you will learn some additional techniques and instructions that complete a basic subset of assembler language. You will learn how to use relative addressing and explicit lengths, how to use overlapped operands, how to round your arithmetic results, and so on.

Relative addressing and explicit lengths

Figure 6-1 illustrates the use of relative addressing and explicit lengths. If the data definitions in this figure define a printer work area, the instructions set all the bytes of PRTDETL to blanks as follows:

```
MVI     PRTDETL,X'40'
MVC     PRTDETL+1(132),PRTDETL
```

Here, the MVI instruction moves one blank into the first byte of this area. Although PRTDETL has a length of 133 bytes, only one byte is affected because the MVI instruction has an implied length of only one byte. Since this first byte of the work area is the control character of the detail line, this instruction prepares the area for single spacing.

The second instruction, the MVC, uses a *relative address* and an *explicit length* for the first operand, PRTDETL+1(132). The relative address (PRTDETL+1) means that the address used in the instruction should be one greater than the address assigned to PRTDETL. The relative length in the instruction (132) means that the length used should be 132 rather than the 133 associated with the area named PRTDETL.

In other words, if address 8000 is assigned to PRTDETL when the program is executed, the first operand in the MVC instruction above refers to the 132 bytes beginning at address 8001. Since the second operand is PRTDETL and since the MVC instruction moves from left to right during execution, this means that blanks will be moved into the remaining 132-bytes of PRTDETL. First, the blank in byte 8000 will be moved to byte 8001; then, the blank in 8001 will be moved to byte 8002; and so on, until 132 blanks have been moved.

In many programs, this blanking technique is used to set a print area to blanks before moving data into the area. This sets any data left over from previous print lines to blanks. As a result, you don't have to define any of the fields in the work area with blank values. That's why all of the fields in figure 6-1 are defined with DS instructions. This contrasts the way in which PRTDETL is defined in the reorder-listing program in chapter 5.

To code a relative address, you use a plus or minus sign followed by a decimal number. Thus, PRTPRICE+11 has the same address as

```
PRTDETL   DS    0CL133
          DS    CL1
PRTITNBR  DS    CL6
          DS    CL5
PRTITDES  DS    CL20
          DS    CL4
PRTPRICE  DS    CL7
          DS    CL4
PRTAVAIL  DS    CL6
          DS    CL4
PRTORDPT  DS    CL6
          DS    CL70
          .
          .
          .
          MVI   PRTDETL,X'40'
          MVC   PRTDETL+1(132),PRTDETL
```

Figure 6-1   Using relative addressing, an explicit length, and overlapped operands to set a
work area to blanks

PRTAVAIL in figure 6-1. And PRTPRICE-24 addresses the first byte of
the PRTITDES field.

An explicit length shows as a decimal number in parentheses following a data name or relative address. Thus, PRTPRICE(4) refers to the first
four bytes of the 7-byte PRTPRICE field while PRTPRICE+5(2) refers to
the last two bytes of the field. When you use relative addressing, you often
code an explicit length. If you don't, the length is taken from the data
definitions of the fields being operated upon. As a result, PRTPRICE+3
refers to seven bytes starting with the fourth byte of the PRTPRICE field.
Since this would take three bytes from the field defined after PRTPRICE in
figure 6-1, you would probably code an explicit length of four or less in a
case like this. As a rule, you should code an explicit length whenever you
require an operand length other than the one given in the data definition
for the field. You'll see this illustrated more clearly in just a moment.

You can use an explicit length on any operand that has a length factor
in its instruction format. If, for example, you refer to the formats given in
figure 6-2, you can see that the MVC instruction can have an explicit
length only on the first operand, but the AP instruction can have an explicit length on both operands as in this example:

```
AP    FIELDA+1(4),FIELDB+3(2)
```

**Overlapped
operands**

The blanking technique in figure 6-1 also illustrates *overlapped operands*.
This means that it is possible to have the same field specified in both
operands for some of the data movement instructions. To blank the
printer work area, for example, PRTDETL is given for both operands.

Instruction	Mnemonic operation	Implicit operand format
Compare logical characters	CLC	S1,S2 or S1(L),S2
Compare logical immediate	CLI	S1,I2
Edit	ED	S1,S2 or S1(L),S2
Move characters	MVC	S1,S2 or S1(L),S2
Move immediate	MVI	S1,I2
Move numerics	MVN	S1,S2 or S1(L),S2
Move with offset	MVO	S1,S2 or S1(L1),S2(L2)
Move zones	MVZ	S1,S2 or S1(L),S2
Pack	PACK	S1,S2 or S1(L1),S2(L2)
Unpack	UNPK	S1,S2 or S1(L1),S2(L2)
Branch and link register	BALR	R1,R2
Branch on condition	BC	M1,S2
Add decimal	AP	S1,S2 or S1(L1),S2(L2)
Compare decimal	CP	S1,S2 or S1(L1),S2(L2)
Divide decimal	DP	S1,S2 or S1(L1),S2(L2)
Multiply decimal	MP	S1,S2 or S1(L1),S2(L2)
Subtract decimal	SP	S1,S2 or S1(L1),S2(L2)
Zero and add decimal	ZAP	S1,S2 or S1(L1),S2(L2)
Shift and round decimal	SRP	S1,S2,I3 or S1(L1),S2(L2),I3

Figure 6-2   The implicit operand formats with explicit lengths for the instructions presented in chapters 1 through 6

Then, when the operation is executed, the bytes of the area are operated upon in overlapped fashion.

Similarly, you can pack a field in its own area. Thus, this code is valid:

```
PACK   INVPRICE,INVPRICE
```

Then, if INVPRICE is a five-byte field, the instruction is executed as in this example:

INVPRICE

Before:	F0	F0	F4	F4	F0
After:	00	00	00	44	0F

In other words, when the instruction is executed, the five zoned decimal digits are packed into the rightmost three bytes of INVPRICE; the other two bytes are padded out with hex zeros.

Instructions for character comparisons

Thus far, you know how to compare packed decimal fields, but you don't know how to compare EBCDIC fields. To compare these fields, you use the CLC (compare logical characters) and the CLI (compare logical immediate) instructions. If the fields to be compared are over 256 bytes, you can also use the CLCL (compare logical long) instruction, but it isn't presented until the next chapter.

These instructions are called *logical* since they compare bit patterns rather than numeric values. Although the operands should normally be in EBCDIC format, a logical comparison will take place regardless of data format. In contrast to a logical comparison, the compare decimal instruction bases its comparison on the numeric values of the operands.

Compare logical characters (CLC)   The CLC instruction can be used to compare two areas of storage up to 256 bytes in length. Like the MVC instruction, the length code is taken from the first operand as in this example:

```
CLC    FIELDA,FIELDB
```

Here, FIELDA will be compared to a field of equal length beginning at the address represented by the label FIELDB. After a compare logical characters instruction, you normally code a branch instruction to test the result of the comparison.

Compare logical immediate (CLI)   The CLI instruction operates in the same manner as the CLC, except that only one byte of data is used in the comparison. The data in the field specified by the first operand is compared with the immediate operand given in the instruction. For example, when this instruction is executed,

```
CLI    FIELDZ,C'0'
```

the first byte of FIELDZ is compared to the character constant zero given in the instruction. If FIELDZ contained four bytes and you wanted to compare the rightmost byte with a hex F0, you could code it this way using a relative address:

```
CLI    FIELDZ+3,X'F0'
```

Remember that you code an immediate operand using type code X, Z, P, or C followed by a one-byte nominal value enclosed in single quotes. As a result, X'F0', C'0', and Z'0' are equivalent.

Collating sequence   When two fields are compared logically, they are considered equal if the bit patterns in both fields are identical. But what if they aren't? Is X-12-13 lower or higher than X12345? The answer depends on the binary values of the bytes being compared. In this case, since the CLC instruction operates from left to right, the leftmost bytes would be compared first and would be found to be equal. Then, the bit pattern for the hyphen (-) would be compared with the bit pattern for 1, or 01100000 would be compared with 11110000. Since 01100000 is less than 11110000 in terms of binary values, X-12-13 is considered less than X12345 by the System/370.

The sequence from lowest to highest of the characters within a coding system is called the *collating sequence*. The collating sequence of some commonly used EBCDIC characters from lowest to highest follows:

the blank

.

(

&

)

-

/

,

#

'

"

the letters A-Z
the numbers 0-9

Therefore, T/X is less than TOM, H&R is less than H-R, and T2S is less than T29.

Once you understand the notion of collating sequence, you can see why it is usually an error to compare logically two fields with different formats. For instance, if a CLC instruction compares an EBCDIC field containing 123 (hex F1F2F3) with a packed decimal field containing 58234 (hex 58234C), the EBCDIC field will be considered higher (the leftmost four bits are 1111 as compared with 0101). Data formats, then, are critical when using compare instructions, and the operands for a compare logical instruction should normally be in EBCDIC format.

Instructions for rounding packed-decimal fields

The System/370 decimal instructions operate only on whole numbers. For instance, a unit price of $4.49 is treated as 449 when arithmetic operations are performed on it. As a result, the programmer is responsible for keeping track of the location of decimal points and, if necessary, for rounding the results of calculations.

To code rounding operations, you often use relative addressing and explicit length codes along with two new move instructions, the move numerics (MVN) and the move-with-offset (MVO). After I show you how to round using these instructions, I'll show you an easier way using the shift-and-round-decimal (SRP) instruction. Since the SRP instruction is the easiest way to code rounding operations, you'll probably use it most of the time. Nevertheless, it's worth knowing how to use the MVN and MVO instructions too.

Move numerics (MVN)   The move numerics instruction operates in the same way as an MVC instruction, but only the digit (numeric) halves of the fields are moved. To illustrate, the instruction

```
MVN     RECEIVE,SEND
```

executes as in this example:

	Before				After			
SEND:	12	34	56	78	12	34	56	78
RECEIVE:	AA	BB	CC	DD	A2	B4	C6	D8

As you can see, the zone portions of the bytes in the receiving field are unchanged.

The MVN instruction is useful in rounding numbers as illustrated in figures 6-3 and 6-4. In figure 6-3, the problem is to multiply an amount field with two decimal positions by a percent field with two decimal positions and obtain a rounded result with two decimal positions. Two ways to do this are shown in figure 6-3.

Using the first technique, RESULT4 contains an unrounded result with four decimal positions after the multiply instruction has been executed. Then, 50 is added to this result by using a literal in the AP instruction. The effect of this is to increase the second decimal position by one if the third decimal position is 5 or over. In the example in figure 6-3, the third and fourth decimal positions contain 41 so when 50 is added to them the result is 91 and the second decimal position is unchanged. On the other hand, if the third and fourth positions had contained 71, the addition of 50 would have carried a one over to the second decimal position so the result would have been rounded up by one.

The next two instructions complete the rounding by dropping the rightmost two digits of RESULT4 as the result is moved to RNDRSLT2:

```
MVC     RNDRSLT2,RESULT4+1
MVN     RNDRSLT2+3(1),RESULT4+5
```

When the MVC instruction is executed, the second through fifth bytes of RESULT4 are moved into the four-byte RNDRSLT2 field. (Because the length is taken from operand-1 and RNDRSLT2 is defined as PL4, four bytes are moved; otherwise, explicit lengths could be used to move the appropriate number of bytes.) Then, when the MVN instruction is executed, the sign of RESULT4 is moved to RNDRSLT2 so RDNRSLT2 holds the rounded result field with two decimal positions.

Source Code

Source Code	Field values after instruction execution			
	AMOUNT2	PERCENT2	RESULT4	RNDRSLT2

Technique 1

```
ZAP   RESULT4,AMOUNT2
MP    RESULT4,PERCENT2
AP    RESULT4,=P'50'
MVC   RNDRSLT2,RESULT4+1
MVN   RNDRSLT2+3(1),RESULT4+5
```

	AMOUNT2	PERCENT2	RESULT4	RNDRSLT2
	12 34 56 7C	02 3F	00 00 12 34 56 7C	99 99 99 99
			00 00 02 83 95 04 1C	02 83 95 09
			00 00 02 83 95 09 1C	02 83 95 0C

Technique 2

```
ZAP   RESULT4,AMOUNT2
MP    RESULT4,PERCENT2
AP    RESULT4,=P'50'
MVN   RESULT4+4(1),RESULT4+5
ZAP   RNDRSLT2,RESULT4(5)
```

	AMOUNT2	PERCENT2	RESULT4	RNDRSLT2
	12 34 56 7C	02 3F	00 00 12 34 56 7C	99 99 99 99
			00 00 02 83 95 04 1C	02 83 95 0C
			00 00 02 83 95 09 1C	
			00 00 02 83 95 0C 1C	

Problem

```
 12345.67
       23
 2839.5041

Rounded:  2839.50
```

Data definitions

```
AMOUNT2   DS   PL4
PERCENT   DS   PL2
RESULT4   DS   PL6
RNDRSLT2  DS   PL4
```

Figure 6-3   Rounding an even number of decimal places using the MVN instruction

The second technique in figure 6-3 is similar. After the literal 50 is added to the result field, the sign of RESULT4 is moved one byte to the left with this instruction:

```
MVN     RESULT4+4(1),RESULT4+5
```

Here, an explicit length is needed, so only one byte is operated upon. After the instruction is executed, the leftmost five bytes of RESULT4 have the rounded result value. These bytes are then moved to RNDRSLT2 by this ZAP instruction:

```
ZAP     RNDRSLT2,RESULT4(5)
```

Because the sending field has an explicit length of five, the rightmost byte of RESULT4 isn't added to RNDRSLT2. Because the receiving field is only four bytes long, the leftmost byte of RESULT4 is truncated. Thus, RNDRSLT2 holds the rounded result field with two decimal positions.

Move-with-offset (MVO)   The move-with-offset instruction has the unique attribute of offsetting the data one half-byte to the left during the move. As a result, this instruction

```
MVO     RECEIVE,SEND
```

executes as in this example:

	Before			After			
SEND:	12	34	56		12	34	56
RECEIVE:	FF	FF	FF	FF	01	23	45	6F

As you can see, the data from the sending field is placed in the receiving field, but it is offset one half-byte to the left. Meanwhile, the rightmost half-byte of the receiving field isn't changed. Also, the leftmost half-bytes that are not filled by the sending field are padded to hex zeros.

Truncation can also occur. For example, if the field RECEIVE is only three bytes, the leftmost half-byte is truncated as in this example:

	Before			After		
SEND:	12	34	56	12	34	56
RECEIVE:	FF	FF	FF	23	45	6F

truncated

The operation of the MVO instruction, then, is similar to that of the packed decimal instructions, not to the operations of the other move instructions. The MVO instruction uses length factors on both operands, and execution moves from right to left. Padding with hex zeros and truncation can both occur.

The common use of the MVO instruction is in rounding packed-decimal numbers to an odd number of digits. In figure 6-4, the first technique illustrates a result with five decimal positions being rounded to two decimal positions. Since three positions must be dropped, the constant that is added to the result is 500 rather than 50 as in figure 6-3. In this example, the second decimal position is increased by one (from 6 to 7) when the AP instruction is executed.

Next, the MVO instruction moves the digits from the leftmost four bytes of RESULT5 to RNDRSLT2:

```
MVO    RNDRSLT2,RESULT5(4)
```

The explicit length of four is used so that three decimal positions are dropped during the move. Because the move is offset, the digit half of the rightmost byte of RNDRSLT2 is not changed by the move. Instead, this MVN instruction moves the sign from RESULT5 to RNDRSLT2:

```
MVN    RNDRSLT2+3(1),RESULT5+5
```

The second technique in figure 6-4 shows how overlapped fields can be used with the MVO instruction. When this MVO instruction is executed,

```
MVO    RESULT5,RESULT5(4)
```

it moves one byte at a time from right to left like this:

RESULT5

Before:	00	28	02	47	20	9C
After Byte 1:	00	28	02	47	24	7C
After Byte 2:	00	28	02	40	24	7C
After Byte 3:	00	28	02	80	24	7C
After Byte 4:	00	20	02	80	24	7C
Padding:	00	00	02	80	24	7C

Of course, this technique for rounding can't be used if all the decimal positions in the field are needed in subsequent calculations. Obviously, when a result is rounded in its own field, the truncated decimal positions are not available for later processing.

Source Code		Field values after instruction execution			
		AMOUNT2	PERCENT3	RESULT5	RNDRSLT2
Technique 1		12 34 56 7C	22 7C	00 00 12 34 56 7C	99 99 99 99
ZAP	RESULT5,AMOUNT2			00 28 02 46 70 9C	
MP	RESULT5,PERCENT3			00 28 02 47 20 9C	02 80 24 79
AP	RESULT5,=P'500'				02 80 24 7C
MVO	RNDRSLT2,RESULT5(4)				
MVN	RNDRSLT2+3(1),RESULT5+5				
Technique 2		12 34 56 7C	22 7C	00 00 12 34 56 7C	
ZAP	RESULT5,AMOUNT2			00 28 02 46 70 9C	
MP	RESULT5,PERCENT3			00 28 02 47 20 9C	
AP	RESULT5,=P'500'			00 00 02 80 24 7C	
MVO	RESULT5,RESULT5(4)				
Data definitions		**Problem**			
AMOUNT2 DS PL4		12345.67			
PERCENT DS PL2		.227			
RESULT5 DS PL6		2802.46709			
RNDRSLT2 DS PL4		Rounded: 2802.47			

Figure 6-4 Rounding an odd number of decimal places using the MVO and MVN instructions

	———————Values of FIELD———————	
Instruction	**Before**	**After**
SRP FIELD,2,0	00 12 34 56 7C	12 34 56 70 0C
SRP FIELD,5,0	00 12 34 56 7C	45 67 00 00 0C
SRP FIELD,63,5	00 12 34 56 7C	00 01 23 45 7C
SRP FIELD,62,5	00 12 34 56 7C	00 00 12 34 6C
SRP FIELD,59,5	00 12 34 56 7C	00 00 00 01 2C
SRP FIELD,63,0	00 12 34 56 7C	00 01 23 45 6C
SRP FIELD,62,0	00 12 34 56 7C	00 00 12 34 5C
SRP FIELD,59,0	00 12 34 56 7C	00 00 00 01 2C

Figure 6-5   Shifting and rounding fields using the SRP instruction

Shift-and-round-decimal (SRP)   Shifting and rounding of packed decimal fields can also be accomplished by using the shift-and-round-decimal instruction. With it, you can shift the packed data in a field to the left or right any number of digit positions and round when required. Figure 6-5 gives some examples of how this instruction operates. In an instruction like

```
SRP    FIELD,3,0
```

the first operand specifies the packed-decimal field to be operated upon; the second operand indicates the shift direction and the number of digit positions to be shifted; and the third operand specifies the rounding factor.

Specifying the second operand can be the tricky part of using this instruction. This operand is actually interpreted as a 32-bit storage address. When the instruction is executed, bits 0 through 25 are ignored and bits 26 through 31 are treated as a 6-bit signed binary value. Positive values indicate left shifts and negative values indicate right shifts. Fortunately, though, you can code the second operand quite easily by using the values shown in figure 6-6. (In the next chapter, you will learn that these values for the second operand of the SRP instructions are actually explicit addresses, but you don't need to know that now.)

To shift a field 2 digit positions to the left, for example, you code:

```
SRP    FIELD,2,0
```

To round a field and shift it 3 digit positions to the right, you code:

```
SRP    FIELD,61,5
```

This example illustrates the most common rounding factor, 5, which is ad-

Operand-2 code	Number of shift-left positions
1	1
2	2
3	3
4	4
5	5

Operand-2 code	Number of shift-right positions
63	1
62	2
61	3
60	4
59	5

Figure 6-6   Operand-2 codes for the shift-and-round-decimal (SRP) instruction

ded to the digit position to the right of the one being rounded to. The rounding factor is applied only to right shifts and must be in the range 0 through 9. When a field is shifted left, the rightmost digit positions are padded with zeros, so rounding doesn't apply. Note in figure 6-5 that no rounding takes place on a right shift when the rounding factor is zero.

Move zones (MVZ)

One other instruction that can be handy for manipulating numeric data is the move zones instruction. When it is executed, the zone halves of the bytes in the sending field are moved to the zone halves of the bytes in the receiving field. For example,

```
MVZ     FIELDA(3),=X'D0D0D0'
```

moves hex Ds into the zone portions of the first three bytes of FIELDA. You won't use this instruction for rounding packed decimal fields, but I wanted to cover it in this topic because it's so closely related to the MVN instruction.

Terminology

relative address
explicit length
overlapped operands
logical comparison
collating sequence

Objective

Apply the instructions and techniques of this topic to your programs.

TOPIC 2   Standard macros

There are several different kinds of standard macros that are provided with VSE. One kind you are already familiar with is the *I/O macro*. For example, the DTF, OPEN, CLOSE, GET, and PUT macros are I/O macros. In chapter 8, you will learn how to use *program-linkage macros*. In addition, VSE provides *system-generation macros* and *multitasking macros*, but these are beyond the scope of this book.

One type of macro that almost all assembler language programmers use is *supervisor-communication macros*. This type allows you to get information from the supervisor, give information to it, or request a service from it. Some of the most widely used macros in this group are: COMRG, GETIME, CANCEL, DUMP, and PDUMP.

COMRG   Within the VSE supervisor, there is a special area called the *communication region*. In this area, the date and various other items of information are stored. Figure 6-7 is a map of the 46 bytes of the communication region that are of interest to the assembler language programmer. For instance, bytes 24-31 contain the jobname of the job being run, and bytes 12-22 can be used to pass data from a program in one job step to a program in a job step that follows. Note in this figure that the date is an 8-byte field in the form MM/DD/YY or DD/MM/YY where MM is a two-character month, DD is a two-character day, and YY is a two character year (like 85 for 1985). The format of the date depends on the system default. The third and sixth bytes of this field contain slashes (/).

In actual practice, one of the main uses of the COMRG macro is to get the date from the communication region so it's available to your program. The COMRG macro has no operands, but it can have a label if you need to refer to it. When this macro is executed, the address of the communication region is placed in register 1.

Figure 6-8 shows a short routine that uses the COMRG macro to get the current date and put it into a field named PDATE. Once you have the date stored in a field within your own program area, you can use it as needed. In the MVC instruction in figure 6-8, an explicit address is used to access the date after COMRG puts the address of the date in register 1. Although you won't learn about explicit addresses until the next chapter, you should still be able to access the date for your program by coding your routine as shown.

GETIME   The VSE supervisor also maintains the time of day in an internal clock. To retrieve the current time from the supervisor, you use the GETIME macro.

When the GETIME macro is executed, the time itself is stored in register 1, not the address of the time. The format of this value is deter-

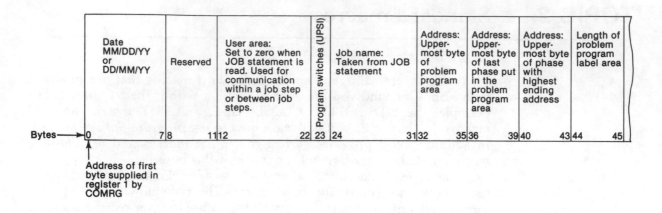

Bytes——▶

Address of first
byte supplied in
register 1 by
COMRG

Figure 6-7   The format of the communication region

mined by the operand of the macro. The three valid forms of the operand
are:

```
GETIME STANDARD
GETIME BINARY
GETIME TU
```

If the operand is omitted, STANDARD is assumed.

When STANDARD is coded or the operand is omitted, the time is
returned as a packed decimal number in the format HHMMSS where HH
is hours, MM is minutes, and SS is seconds. If, for example, the time is
08:32:48, the four bytes of register 1 will contain hex 0083248C. Here, the
rightmost half-byte contains a valid positive sign.

Figure 6-9 illustrates a routine that gets the current time and edits it into a field named PTIME. In its edited form, the seconds are dropped so a
time of 14:22:49 will be stored in PTIME as 14:22 with two leading blanks.
After the GETIME macro is executed, the ST instruction moves the time
from register 1 to a four-byte field named TIME. In the next chapter,
you'll learn how the ST instruction works in more detail, but for now it's
enough to know that it stores the contents of a register in a four-byte field.
Since registers are the equivalent of four bytes, this is logical enough.
After the MVC instruction moves an edit pattern into PTIME, the ED instruction edits TIME into PTIME. Since the pattern only provides for five
decimal digits, the seconds are dropped when the time is edited. And,
since hex 7A in the edit pattern is the code for a colon, PTIME ends up in
the form HH:SS with two leading blanks.

Although you'll normally use the STANDARD form of time, you
may occasionally need one of the other forms. When BINARY is coded as

```
PROGC6F8  START  0
          BALR   3,0
          USING  *,3
          COMRG
          MVC    PDATE,0(1)
          .
          .
PDATE     DS     CL8
```

NOTE: 0(1) in this routine is an explicit address that means base register 1 with a displacement of 0. After the COMRG instruction, 0(1) refers to the first byte of the date field in the communication region.

Figure 6-8   A routine for getting the current date from the communication region and storing it in a field named PDATE

```
          .
          .
          .
          GETIME STANDARD
          ST     1,TIME
          MVC    PTIME,PATTERN
          ED     PTIME,TIME
          .
          .
          .
TIME      DS     CL4
PATTERN   DC     X'402021207A2020'
PTIME     DS     CL7
```

NOTE: The GETIME STANDARD macro stores the time in register 1 as a 7-digit packed-decimal number in the form HHMMSS with one leading zero.

Figure 6-9   A routine for storing the current time in a field named PTIME in the form HH:MM

the operand, the time placed in register 1 is a binary number. It represents the number of seconds that have elapsed since midnight. The operand TU also causes a binary value to be placed in register 1, but this value is in units of 1/300 of a second. As a result, it is 300 times the value returned when the operand is BINARY.

CANCEL, DUMP, and PDUMP   As your programs become more complex and the number of possible error situations increases, you will find cases in which you'll want a storage dump to help you figure out what caused the problem. If you've already read chapter 18, you know that a *storage dump* is a printout of the contents of the general registers and storage in both hex and character formats. If you haven't read chapter 18, you'll learn more about storage dumps when you do. But right now, I want you to learn how to use the three standard macros that let you control storage dumps.

For the most catastrophic error conditions, you can code a CANCEL macro. This macro can have a label but no operands. It causes a program to be cancelled. It also causes a storage dump to be printed if the dump option is in effect. You can turn this option on using an OPTION statement with the DUMP option in your JCL for the program. The storage dump that results from a CANCEL macro includes the general registers and all of main storage including the partitions you aren't using. Since this is a tremendous amount of printout, most of which you won't be able to use for debugging your own program, you shouldn't use this option unless you have a definite need for it. And you shouldn't have a need for it unless you're developing a program that affects more than one partition of the system, not an application program.

The DUMP macro provides a similar capability, but a dump will occur whether or not the DUMP option is in effect. The DUMP will print the contents of the general registers, the supervisor area, and the program area (that is, the partition of your application program). It won't print the contents of the other partitions of main storage. Since the amount of printout is limited to what you need for your program, this macro is more practical for most purposes than the CANCEL macro.

For less critical errors, you may want to use the PDUMP (partial dump) macro. A PDUMP provides a dump of the general registers and the program area between two addresses that you supply as operands. For example, this instruction

```
PDUMP SYMBOL1,SYMBOL2
```

dumps the area between the two labels, SYMBOL1 and SYMBOL2, wherever they are defined in your program. Of course, SYMBOL1 should precede SYMBOL2. Similarly, this instruction

```
PDUMP (6),(8)
```

dumps the area between the address given in registers 6 and 8. (This second instruction uses explicit addressing, which you'll learn about in the next chapter.) After the dump has been printed, processing continues with the next instruction in sequence.

PDUMP thus provides a "snapshot" dump capability. You can code it in certain parts of a new program to dump record areas, count fields, total fields, and so on, in order to track the processing of a program. Then, when the program has been debugged, you can remove the PDUMP macros and reassemble.

You may also want to include PDUMP as a permanent part of some error routines. This will allow you to get a snapshot dump of the troublesome data and then continue to process the rest of the data. In chapter 8, you'll see how a PDUMP function can be useful as an assembler language subprogram that is used by programs written in other languages.

Terminology	I/O macro
	program-linkage macro
	system-generation macro
	multitasking macro
	supervisor-communication macro
	communication region
	storage dump
Objective	Apply the macros in this topic to your programs.

Topic 3   Assembler commands

You are already familiar with a few assembler commands. For instance, START, USING, and END are all assembler commands. This topic will present several more assembler commands. First, this topic shows you how to code the USING command to specify more than one base register for a large program. Next, it shows you how to use the COPY command to copy source code into a program from a source library. Then, it presents two commands for controlling the assembly process: LTORG and EQU. Finally, it presents a few commands that control the appearance of the assembly listing.

How to specify more than one base register for a program with the USING command

In chapter 5, you learned that a single base register can serve a maximum program segment of 4096 bytes. This means that another base register must be assigned and loaded for each additional program segment of 4096 bytes. If, for example, a program requires three base registers, the base registers can be assigned and loaded as shown in figure 6-10.

In figure 6-10, after the BALR instruction loads the first base register as usual, the USING statement assigns register 3 as the first base register, but it also assigns registers 4 and 5 as succeeding base registers. As a result, the assembler will use register 3 as the base register until 4096 bytes have been defined. Then, for references to bytes 4097 to 8192, it will use register 4 as the base register. And, for references to bytes 8193 to 12288, it will use register 5.

To load the proper base addresses in registers 4 and 5, you can use the load multiple register (LM) instruction with *address constants* (or *adcons*). An address constant (type code A) causes the address or addresses of one or more locations in storage to be stored in one or more fullwords of storage. In figure 6-10, these address constants are used:

```
BASEADR   DC      A(START+4096)
          DC      A(START+8192)
```

Thus, the address of START+4096 is placed in the first fullword; the address of START+8192 is placed in the second fullword. You can get this same result by coding two addresses in one adcon like this:

```
BASEADR   DC      A(START+4096,START+8192)
```

When the LM instruction in figure 6-10 is executed,

```
START     LM      4,5,BASEADR
```

```
PROGC6FA  START  0
          BALR   3,0
          USING  *,3,4,5
START     LM     4,5,BASEADR
          B      EXEC
BASEADR   DC     A(START+4096)
          DC     A(START+8192)
EXEC      .
          .
          .
```

Figure 6-10   Using more than one base register in a program

the addresses in BASEADR are loaded into registers 4 and 5. When you code the LM instruction, operand-1 specifies the first register to be loaded, operand-2 specifies the last register in sequence to be loaded, and operand-3 specifies the storage location of the first address to be loaded. As a result, this instruction

```
START     LM     4,7,BASEADR
```

causes registers 4, 5, 6, and 7 to be loaded with the addresses that start at BASEADR. In this case, of course, you would have to make sure that BASEADR was the start of four valid addresses.

In figure 6-10, you should notice that the unconditional branch instruction branches over the address constants to the next instruction of the program. If it didn't, the program wouldn't run properly since an address constant isn't an instruction. Although the address constants can be defined anywhere within the first 4096-byte segment of the program, it is most common to find them in the housekeeping routine as shown in figure 6-10.

To determine the number of base registers required by your program, you can estimate the number of bytes that the program will require. To do this, use 100 bytes for each DTF statement and 5 bytes for each instruction. Then, add the DTF bytes, the instruction bytes, and the number of bytes for I/O areas. This rough estimate should help you determine the number of registers needed. But if you assign too few, a diagnostic will call attention to your error.

The COPY command

The COPY command is used to copy source code from a source statement library into your program. It is commonly used to copy code that is going to be used in one or more programs of a system, such as a file description or a standard report heading. By using the COPY command, you can save the time it would take to enter the code and you can be sure that the code will be free of errors.

Copy member INVMAST in library USRSL1

```
INVMAST   DTFSD BLKSIZE=500,                              X
                RECFORM=FIXBLK,                           X
                RECSIZE=50,                               X
                IOAREA1=INVIO1,                           X
                IOAREA2=INVIO2,                           X
                WORKA=YES,                                X
                EOFADDR=INVEOF,                           X
                DEVADDR=SYS008
```

COPY command in source program

```
        COPY   INVMAST
```

LIBDEF statement in JCL for the assembly job

```
// LIBDEF SL,SEARCH=(USRSL1)
```

Figure 6-11   Using the COPY command to insert a copy book into a source program

Figure 6-11 shows how the source statement library, the COPY command, and the LIBDEF JCL statement are related. To insert a copy book named INVMAST into a source program, you use this command:

```
        COPY   INVMAST
```

The code in the source book is then copied into your program right after the COPY command, just as if you had entered it yourself.

Since a system can have many different source statement libraries, you must make sure that VSE knows which libraries to use when it runs your assembly job. You can specify the libraries to be used with a LIBDEF statement like

```
    // LIBDEF   SL,SEARCH=(USRSL1,USRSL2)
```

This says that the first library to be searched is USRSL1, the second is USRSL2. However, if the right libraries are already specified in the permanent search chain, you don't need a LIBDEF JCL statement when you run your assembly job.

Similarly, you must make sure that the assembler looks for the specified book in the right sublibrary of the right library. The default is sublibrary A and the copy books you use will probably be in this sublibrary, so you shouldn't have any problem here. But if the copy books are in sublibrary D, you'll have to use an OPTION statement in your JCL as described in chapter 3 of this book. Both library search chains and options are covered in detail in our *VSE JCL* book, and it will also show you how to store copy books in a source statement library.

```
                    .
                    .
             AP     QTYWORK,=P'1'
                    .
                    .
QTYWORK      DC     PL4'0'
             LTORG
PRTWK1       DS     CL133
INAREA1      DS     CL400
             END    BEGIN
```

Figure 6-12   Using LTORG

The LTORG command

The assembler program normally places literal constants coded as instruction operands at the end of your program. By using the LTORG command, though, you can force placement of these literal constants at some other position in your program. You may want to do this as part of a debugging operation if your literals are being overlaid by data movement instructions that incorrectly address the fields before the literals.

In figure 6-12, for example, the LTORG instruction causes the literal constant =P'1' to be defined after the field QTYWORK and before the area named PRTWK1. If the LTORG command was omitted, the literal constant would have been defined after INAREA1. You can code any number of LTORG statements in a program. Each time the assembler encounters a LTORG instruction, it places all the literals defined in operands since the last LTORG statement immediately following the new LTORG.

The EQU command

The EQU command lets you assign the attributes of one label to another label as:

```
FIELD1       DS     CL8
FIELD2       EQU    FIELD1
```

Here, the label FIELD2 is assigned the address and length attribute of FIELD1. Both labels then address the same 8-byte field.

One of the most common uses of the EQU command assigns labels to register numbers. Since labels are included in a cross-reference listing but registers aren't, using the EQU command allows you to get a trace of register usage that wouldn't normally be available. If, for example, the register numbers are equated with labels as shown in figure 6-13, you can substitute the equivalent labels whenever you require a register number as in these examples:

```
LM       R4,R5,BASEADR
BALR     R14,R15
```

Equating the numbers 0 through 15 to the labels R0 through R15

```
R0          EQU      0
R1          EQU      1
R2          EQU      2
             .
             .
             .
R14         EQU      14
R15         EQU      15
```

Instructions in the source program that use the equivalent labels

```
      LM      R4,R5,BASEADR
      BALR    R14,R15
```

Figure 6-13   Using the EQU command to assign labels to register numbers

Then, the statement numbers of the instructions that use the register equivalents will be included in the cross-reference listing that is prepared during assembly. This coding technique can be especially useful when you debug large programs.

Commands for controlling the assembly listing

You can use several different assembler commands to control the appearance of an assembly listing. These include PRINT, TITLE, EJECT, and SPACE.

The PRINT command   The PRINT command has three operands that can be in any order and in any combination. To start, you can code the ON or OFF operand as follows:

```
      PRINT ON
      PRINT OFF
```

This operand determines whether or not the listing will be printed at all. If you code ON or if you omit the operand, the listing is printed. If you code OFF, no assembly listing is printed. When you code OFF, the other operands and any other assembler commands that control the listing are ignored. The OFF operand is rarely used, but it can be used if you have made no changes to a source program since the last assembly and you need to assemble and test again.

A second operand controls the printing of the instructions generated by macros. If you code NOGEN, none of the generated instructions are

```
PROGC6FE  START  0
BEGIN     BALR   3,0
          USING  *,3
          B      PROCESS
          PRINT  NOGEN
DISKIN    DTF    BLKSIZE=500,IOAREA1=DIO1,....
PRTOUT    DTF    BLKSIZE=133,IOAREA1=PIO1,....
          PRINT  GEN
PROCESS   OPEN   DISKIN,PRTOUT
            .
            .
            .
```

Figure 6-14   Using the NOGEN option of the PRINT command to suppress the printing of the instructions generated by the DTFs

printed. If you omit the operand or code GEN, all of the generated instructions are printed on the assembly listing and denoted with a plus sign to the right of the statement number.

Figure 6-14 illustrates a typical use of the PRINT instruction with the GEN/NOGEN operand. Here, the printing of macro-generated statements is turned off before the DTFs so the many statements generated by the DTFs will not be listed. After the DTFs, the printing of macro-generated statements is turned back on so the code generated by the other macros, such as the OPEN macro, will be printed on the listing.

The last PRINT operand controls the printing of the data generated by DC instructions and literals. If you code the operand DATA, each byte of generated data is printed in the object code column of the assembly listing, eight bytes per line. If you omit the operand or code NODATA, only the first eight bytes of the defined data appear on the listing.

You won't use the DATA operand often, because you generally don't need to see all of the data generated by DC instructions and literals. Sometimes, though, you'll want to use the DATA option so you can see the generated data. In figure 6-15, for example, you can see the use of the DATA option to print just the data in a table definition. The first PRINT turns the option on so all the data in the table will print. The last PRINT instruction turns the option off again. You can then use the assembly listing to proofread the table definition. The listing can also serve as documentation for the contents of the table.

The TITLE command   The TITLE command causes a heading to be printed at the top of each page of an assembly listing as in this example:

```
          TITLE  'PROG86 BILLING PROGRAM'
```

The TITLE instruction commonly appears as the first statement of a program, and the heading that prints is taken from its operand (the data

```
                   .
                   .
                   .
              PRINT DATA
   TABLE      DS    0CL176
              DC    18CL4'10AA'
              DC    C'11AB'
              DC    C'12AC'
              DC    4C'16DD'
              DC    20C'20XX'
              PRINT NODATA
                   .
                   .
                   .
```

Figure 6-15   Using the DATA option of the PRINT command to print table definitions

enclosed in single quotation marks). The maximum length of the title is 100 characters.

The EJECT command   The EJECT command causes the assembler to skip to the top of a new page before printing the next line of the assembly listing. EJECT has no operand, and labels are ignored.

The SPACE command   The SPACE command causes one or more lines to be skipped in the assembly listing. The operand must be a decimal number that specifies the number of lines to be skipped. If no value is coded, one line is skipped. If the number of lines to be skipped is more than the number of lines remaining on the page, the effect of SPACE is equal to EJECT.

Terminology

address constant
adcon

Objectives

1. Code the instructions and commands required when your program requires more than one base register. To do this, you will have to code the USING command, the LM instruction, and address constants.

2. Apply the commands presented in this topic to your programs.

Chapter 7

Register operations, binary arithmetic, and storage definition techniques

This chapter expands the assembler language subset presented in chapters 5 and 6 by presenting some instructions and techniques commonly used by professional programmers. Topic 1 presents instructions and techniques that involve the use of registers. Topic 2 shows you how to perform arithmetic operations using binary rather than packed decimal data. And topic 3 presents some advanced techniques for defining fields and areas in storage. When you complete this chapter, you should be able to code your programs more efficiently. Also, the material in this chapter will help you understand assembler language programs and subprograms written by professional programmers.

TOPIC 1   Register operations

On an IBM mainframe, there are more than 60 instructions that involve registers. This topic, though, presents only those that are most widely used by professional programmers. In addition, this topic shows you how to use explicit base registers and displacements to address fields and how to define the fields that are used by the register instructions.

EXPLICIT BASE REGISTERS AND DISPLACEMENTS

In chapter 6, you were introduced to explicit lengths; that is, the numbers in parentheses following labels or relative addresses that indicate the length of an operand. In addition, though, the assembler language programmer can code *explicit addresses* by coding *explicit base registers* and *explicit displacements*. This is illustrated by this instruction:

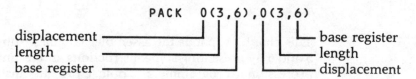

In other words, this PACK instruction uses overlapped operands to pack the three-byte field at the address in base register 6 to the three-byte field at the address in base register 6. In this example, the displacement values are zero.

Here's another instruction that illustrates explicit addressing:

```
AP      WKLYHRS,3(3,6)
```

This instruction adds the three-byte field that is explicitly addressed to the field labelled WKLYHRS. The address of operand-2 is calculated by adding the displacement 3 to the contents of base register 6.

Figure 7-1 gives the explicit instruction formats for all of the instructions presented in chapters 1 through 6 of this book, and figure 7-2 gives the explicit formats for the instructions presented in this chapter. The explicit formats for all of the instructions presented in this book are given in appendix A. In general, an operand in storage can be expressed as a displacement (D), length (L), and base register (B) in this form:

```
D(L,B)
```

That is, a number representing a displacement is followed by two numbers in parentheses: first, the number of bytes to be operated upon in decimal; second, the number of the base register in decimal.

Other codes used in the explicit formats in figures 7-1 and 7-2 are I for an immediate operand, X for an index register, and M for a mask. In an instruction that provides for an index register, you will normally code a zero

Instruction	Mnemonic operation	Type	Explicit operand format
Compare logical characters	CLC	SS	D1(L,B1),D2(B2)
Compare logical immediate	CLI	SI	D1(B1),I2
Edit	ED	SS	D1(L,B1),D2(B2)
Move characters	MVC	SS	D1(L,B1),D2(B2)
Move immediate	MVI	SI	D1(B1),I2
Move numerics	MVN	SS	D1(L,B1),D2(B2)
Move with offset	MVO	SS	D1(L1,B1),D2(L2,B2)
Move zones	MVZ	SS	D1(L,B1),D2(B2)
Pack	PACK	SS	D1(L1,B1),D2(L2,B2)
Unpack	UNPK	SS	D1(L1,B1),D2(L2,B2)
Branch and link register	BALR	RR	R1,R2
Branch on condition	BC	RX	M1,D2(X2,B2)
Add decimal	AP	SS	D1(L1,B1),D2(L2,B2)
Compare decimal	CP	SS	D1(L1,B1),D2(L2,B2)
Divide decimal	DP	SS	D1(L1,B1),D2(L2,B2)
Multiply decimal	MP	SS	D1(L1,B1),D2(L2,B2)
Subtract decimal	SP	SS	D1(L1,B1),D2(L2,B2)
Zero and add decimal	ZAP	SS	D1(L1,B1),D2(L2,B2)
Shift and round decimal	SRP	SS	D1(L1,B1),D2(B2),I3

Figure 7-1   The explicit operand formats for the instructions presented in chapters 1 through 6

for the index register. Thus, an explicit address in the first add instruction in figure 7-2 can be coded in either of these two ways:

```
A       4,8(0,5)
A       4,8(,5)
```

Here, the second operand specifies the address calculated by adding the displacement 8 to the contents of register 5.

As an alternative, you can specify an index register instead of a base register when using this add instruction. Then, the add instruction can be written as:

```
A       4,8(5)
```

Here, the second operand points to the address calculated by adding the displacement 8 to the contents of index register 5. Note that you don't have to code a comma after the index register when you omit the base register.

When coding explicit operands, you must remember that the formats for different instructions have different parts. For instance, the register instructions in figure 7-2 don't have lengths. Neither do the immediate instructions in figure 7-1, and the MVC instruction only has a length for

Instruction	Mnemonic operation	Type	Explicit operand format
Add	A	RX	R1,D2(X2,B2)
Add halfword	AH	RX	R1,D2(X2,B2)
Add register	AR	RR	R1,R2
Branch on count	BCT	RX	R1,D2(X2,B2)
Branch on count register	BCTR	RR	R1,R2
Compare	C	RX	R1,D2(X2,B2)
Compare halfword	CH	RX	R1,D2(X2,B2)
Compare register	CR	RR	R1,R2
Convert to binary	CVB	RX	R1,D2(X2,B2)
Convert to decimal	CVD	RX	R1,D2(X2,B2)
Divide	D	RX	R1,D2(X2,B2)
Divide register	DR	RR	R1,R2
Load	L	RX	R1,D2(X2,B2)
Load address	LA	RX	R1,D2(X2,B2)
Load halfword	LH	RX	R1,D2(X2,B2)
Load multiple	LM	RS	R1,R3,D2(B2)
Load register	LR	RR	R1,R2
Multiply	M	RX	R1,D2(X2,B2)
Multiply halfword	MH	RX	R1,D2(X2,B2)
Multiply register	MR	RR	R1,R2
Store	ST	RX	R1,D2(X2,B2)
Store halfword	STH	RX	R1,D2(X2,B2)
Store multiple	STM	RS	R1,R3,D2(B2)
Subtract	S	RX	R1,D2(X2,B2)
Subtract halfword	SH	RX	R1,D2(X2,B2)
Subtract register	SR	RR	R1,R2

Figure 7-2 The instructions for register operations that are presented in this chapter

operand-1. Because each explicit value is critical to the resulting object code, you must check the formats to be sure each explicit value means what you think it means.

INSTRUCTIONS THAT DEFINE HALFWORDS, FULLWORDS, DOUBLEWORDS, AND ADDRESS CONSTANTS

Most register instructions operate on fullwords. However, some operate on halfwords and doublewords of storage. As a result, you must know how to define these fields. In addition, you should know how to define address constants, because they are often useful when coding register operations.

Fullwords, halfwords, and doublewords

The type codes for fullwords, halfwords, and doublewords are F, H, and D as in these examples:

```
FWEX1     DC      F'1'
FWEX2     DS      4F
FWEX3     DC      F'-125'

HWEX1     DC      H'123'
HWEX2     DS      3H

DWEX1     DS      D
DWEX2     DS      3D
```

Because the length is always four bytes for a fullword, two for a halfword, and eight for a doubleword, no length factor is required. Duplication factors can be used as required, and the nominal value is a signed or unsigned decimal number. Thus, FWEX1 will have a starting binary value of +1; and FWEX3 will have a starting value of minus 125.

Note, however, that a nominal value cannot be used with type code D. If one is specified, it will cause a floating-point constant to be assembled. This will be explained in more detail in chapter 12.

Address constants

In the last chapter, you were introduced to *address constants*, or *adcons*. But I'll present them again here for completeness since they are often used in routines that involve registers. An address constant defines a fullword that gives the address of a label as in this example:

```
ADCON1    DC      A(START)
```

In this case, ADCON1 will be generated with a value equal to the address of the field or instruction named START. Because an adcon is a fullword, it can be loaded into a register. Then, the register can be used in an explicit address to refer to the field. You'll see this illustrated later on in this topic.

You can also define an address constant with a relative address as in this example:

```
DC      A(START+4096)
```

Here, the address that is stored in the constant is the sum of the address of START plus 4096. Beyond this, you can code more than one address constant in a single DC as in this example:

```
DC      A(START,START+4096,START+8192)
```

In this case, three consecutive fullwords of storage are defined, one word for each of the three addresses specified.

INSTRUCTIONS THAT USE REGISTERS

Figure 7-2 lists the instructions that are presented in this topic. In general, the first operand in one of these instructions is the number of a register. The second operand is either a label representing a fullword or halfword of storage or a register number. A few of the register instructions have three operands, in which case the second operand is a register number and the third operand is a label for a fullword of storage.

Instructions for loading registers

When you use registers, the first step is to get some data into one of them. Here are five instructions used for that purpose.

Load (L)   You can use the load instruction to load data from any fullword into any one of the 16 registers as in this example:

```
L       4,FWORD
```

This instruction places the contents of the fullword named FWORD into register 4. The first operand can be any register number from 0 through 15; the second operand can be the name of any fullword.

Load register (LR)   You can also load a register from another register as in this instruction:

```
LR      4,7
```

Here, the second operand is the number of one of the 16 registers. The effect of this instruction is to duplicate the contents of register 7 in register 4.

Load halfword (LH)   The load halfword instruction operates just like the load instruction (L). However, only two bytes of data are loaded into the register. All four bytes of the register, though, are set to the two-byte value that is loaded into it. For a positive value, that means that the first two bytes of the register will contain binary zeros.

Load multiple (LM)   You can load two or more consecutive registers from an equal number of consecutive words of storage using the load multiple instruction. This is illustrated in figure 7-3. Here, registers 4, 5, and 6 are loaded with the data in the 12-byte area beginning with the byte referred to by the name WORD1. As a result, register 4 is loaded with bytes 1 through 4, register 5 with bytes 5 through 8, and register 6 with bytes 9 through 12.

In any instruction that refers to multiple registers, the *wrap-around concept* applies. Wrap-around means that the register numbers form an endless sequence with register 0 following register 15. As a result, a load

Assembler language code

```
        LM      4,6,WORD1
                .
                .
                .
WORD1   DC      F'1'
WORD2   DC      F'2'
WORD3   DC      F'3'
```

Contents of registers 4, 5, and 6 in hex

	Before				After			
Register 4:	00	56	0A	71	00	00	00	01
Register 5:	00	00	0B	AA	00	00	00	02
Register 6:	34	B1	CC	00	00	00	00	03

Figure 7-3   The operation of the load multiple instruction

multiple instruction can be coded like this:

```
        LM      14,1,FOURWORD
```

Then, register 14 will be loaded with the first fullword of storage beginning at FOURWORD, register 15 with the second word, register 0 with the third, and register 1 with the fourth.

Load address (LA)   The last of the five load instructions is the load address instruction. You can use it to load the address of a field into a register as in this example:

```
        LA      6,FIELDA
```

Here, register 6 is loaded with the address of FIELDA, not the data stored there. If, for example, FIELDA refers to a two-byte field containing hex C1C2 at location 004B60, 004B60 is loaded into register 6 when the instruction is executed.

Instructions for storing registers

After you code a program's register operations, you often code instructions to store the contents of the registers used. To do this, you use the store, store multiple, and store halfword instructions.

Store (ST)   The store instruction stores the contents of one register into a fullword of storage. In this and the other store instructions, the first operand is the sending operand and the second operand is the receiving operand. For instance, this store instruction places the contents of register 14 in the fullword named SAVE14:

```
ST      14,SAVE14
```

Store multiple (STM)   In a store multiple instruction, the contents of consecutive registers are stored in consecutive words as in this example:

```
STM     7,10,SAVE7
```

Here, the contents of registers 7, 8, 9, and 10 are stored in the four fullwords beginning at the byte addressed by the label SAVE7.

The wrap-around concept applies to the store multiple instruction just as it does to the load multiple. For instance, this instruction is commonly used to save all the general registers except register 13:

```
STM     14,12,SAVEAREA
```

In this case, 15 registers are stored in this sequence: 14, 15, 0, 1, 2, 3, 4, 5, 6, 7, 8, 9, 10, 11, 12.

Store halfword (STH)   The store halfword instruction stores the contents of the rightmost two-bytes of a register into a halfword of storage. Otherwise, it operates like the store (ST) instruction.

Instructions for register addition and subtraction

You can code add, subtract, multiply, and divide operations when using register instructions. In most cases, though, you only need addition and subtraction to manipulate explicit addresses. As a result, this topic only describes the add and subtract instructions. The multiply and divide instructions are covered in topic 2.

Add (A), add halfword (AH), and add register (AR)   The add and subtract instructions are available in the register-to-storage and the register-to-register forms. In each case, the first operand is a number that specifies the register that will receive the result. The second operand can be a fullword, a halfword, or another register.

Here are some examples of add instructions:

```
A       6,FW1
AH      7,HW1
AR      8,6
```

In the first instruction, the contents of the fullword named FW1 are added to the contents of register 6. In the second instruction, the contents of the halfword named HW1 are added to the contents of register 7. In the third instruction, the contents of register 6 are added to the contents of register 8. In each case, the result replaces the original contents of the register specified in the first operand.

Subtract (S), subtract halfword (SH), and subtract register (SR)   The subtract instructions are analagous to the add instructions only the operation is subtraction. Here are some examples of subtract instructions:

```
S      10,FW1
SH     11,HW1
SR     12,9
```

In the first instruction, a fullword is subtracted from register 10. In the second instruction, a halfword is subtracted from register 11. In the third instruction, the contents of register 9 are subtracted from the contents of register 12.

Instructions for comparison

Compare instructions allow you to compare the contents of a register with the contents of a fullword, halfword, or another register. Here, are some examples:

```
C      3,FW1
CH     4,HW1
CR     5,12
```

As in the case of the compare decimal or compare logical instructions, you would expect to find these compare instructions followed by a conditional branch instruction.

The branch-on-count instructions

Sometimes, you will want to use a register to count the number of times a routine is executed. Then, when the routine has been executed the right number of times, you will want your program to branch out of the loop. When you want to use registers in this way, you can take advantage of the branch-on-count instructions.

The branch-on-count instructions are coded like this:

```
BCT    4,LOOP
BCTR   4,9
```

In the first example, the second operand is the label of an instruction. In the second example, the second operand is a register that should contain the address of an instruction.

Field Name	Employee code	Hours worked day-1	Hours worked day-2	Hours worked day-3	Hours worked day-4	Hours worked day-5	Hours worked day-6	Hours worked day-7	
Characteristics	CL5	CL3	CL3	CL3	CL3	CL3	CL3	CL3	
Usage									
Position	1-5	6-8	9-11	12-14	15-17	18-20	21-23	24-26	

Figure 7-4   A record layout for a payroll transaction

Each time the branch-on-count instruction is executed, the value in the register specified as the first operand is reduced by one. Then, when the resulting value in this register becomes zero, control falls through to the next instruction in sequence. Otherwise, a branch is made to the address given by the second operand. You'll see this instruction illustrated in just a moment.

SOME EXAMPLES OF REGISTER OPERATIONS

To illustrate the use of register operations for repetitive processing, consider this problem. A payroll program reads an input record that has the record layout given in figure 7-4. To calculate the number of hours an employee worked during the week, one of the routines of the program must add the seven daily hours-worked fields. Although this routine could be coded using the basic subset of chapters 5 and 6, figures 7-5, 7-6, and 7-7 show routines that add these fields using register operations.

Example 1: A payroll routine using register operations

Figure 7-5 shows a routine that adds the seven fields using explicit addressing. For each input record, the first two instructions of the routine set up registers 4 and 6 for repetitive processing. The third instruction sets TOTHRS to zero. As you will see, TOTHRS is used to accumulate the total number of hours worked for each employee, register 6 is used as a temporary base register for the daily hours-worked fields, and register 4 is used to control the number of times the ADDLOOP routine is repeated.

The first instruction, the SR instruction, sets register 4 to zero by subtracting the contents of register 4 from itself. The second instruction, the LA instruction, places the address of the first daily hours-worked field in register 6; it uses a relative address: PAYREC+5. The third instruction, the ZAP instruction, sets TOTHRS to zero.

The next two instructions pack one hours-worked field and add it to TOTHRS. Both use an explicit address for the hours-worked field. These instructions will be repeated seven times, once for each hours-worked field

```
            .
            .
            .
            SR       4,4
            LA       6,PAYREC+5
            ZAP      TOTHRS,=P'0'
ADDLOOP     PACK     0(3,6),0(3,6)
            AP       TOTHRS,0(3,6)
            A        4,=F'1'
            A        6,=F'3'
            C        4,=F'7'
            BL       ADDLOOP
            .
            .
            .
PAYREC      DS       CL26
TOTHRS      DS       PL3
```

Figure 7-5   A payroll routine using register operations

in the input record. Because the instructions use explicit addresses, the same instructions will refer to all seven hours-worked fields. The explicit address consists of an explicit base register, 6, which is the one that has been loaded with the address of PAYREC+5. As a result, the explicit address refers to the first hours-worked field the first time through the loop.

The next four instructions cause the loop starting with ADDLOOP to be executed six more times:

```
            A        4,=F'1'
            A        6,=F'3'
            C        4,=F'7'
            BL       ADDLOOP
```

First, the binary constant 1 is added to the counter, which is register 4. Second, 3 is added to the base register, which is register 6. Third, register 4 is compared with a value of 7. Fourth, a branch to ADDLOOP takes place if the contents of register 4 are less than the value 7.

Since register 4 starts with a value of zero, the branch to ADDLOOP will take place six times for each input record. Since the contents of register 6 are increased by three each time through the loop, the PACK and AP instructions operate on successive hours-worked fields in the input record. If, for example, the base address is 6000 the first time the PACK instruction is executed, it will be 6003 the next time through.

```
                    .
                    .
                    .
                L       4,=F'7'
                LA      6,PAYREC+5
                ZAP     TOTHRS,=P'0'
ADDLOOP         PACK    0(3,6),0(3,6)
                AP      TOTHRS,0(3,6)
                A       6,=F'3'
                BCT     4,ADDLOOP
                    .
                    .
                    .
PAYREC          DS      CL26
TOTHRS          DS      PL3
```

Figure 7-6   The payroll routine with a branch-on-count refinement

Example 2: The payroll routine using the BCT instruction

Figure 7-6 shows the same payroll routine, but this time it uses the branch-on-count instruction to control the program flow. In effect, the BCT instruction takes the place of the add, compare, and branch-low instructions of the routine in figure 7-5. The first time through the loop, register 4 is decreased from its initial value of seven to six. Since the value is not yet zero, the branch to ADDLOOP takes place. On the seventh time through the loop, the BCT instruction will again reduce register 4 by one. But this time the result will be zero so the branch to ADDLOOP will not occur and control will pass to the next instruction in sequence.

Example 3: The payroll routine using a load-address refinement

Figure 7-7 shows how you can simplify the payroll routine one more step by using the load address instruction to load an initial value into register 4. This technique eliminates the need to use literals. For example, to load the initial value of seven into register 4, you can code this load address instruction:

```
                LA      4,7
```

This loads the value 7, as though it were an address, into register 4. If you check the explicit operand formats in figure 7-2, you will see that the 7 is treated as though it were the displacement for an operand with no index and no base register.

```
             .
             .
             .
             LA      4,7
             LA      6,PAYREC+5
             ZAP     TOTHRS,=P'0'
ADDLOOP      PACK    0(3,6),0(3,6)
             AP      TOTHRS,0(3,6)
             LA      6,3(6)
             BCT     4,ADDLOOP
             .
             .
             .
PAYREC       DS      CL26
TOTHRS       DS      PL3
```

Figure 7-7   The payroll routine with a load-address refinemant

In figure 7-7, the load address instruction is also used to increase the value in a register by a positive value:

```
             LA      6,3(6)
```

If you look at the formats in figure 7-2 again, you will see that this instruction means that the address in index register 6 plus a displacement of 3 is to be placed in register 6. This has the effect of increasing the contents of register 6 by 3. You can increase the value in a register by any fixed amount with a load address instruction coded in this way.

SOME SYSTEM/370 INSTRUCTIONS

The MVC and CLC instructions that you learned about in chapters 5 and 6 operate on fields that are a maximum of 256 bytes long. But sometimes that can be a serious limitation. To remove these limitations, the System/370 designers put several instructions into its instruction set that weren't in the instruction set of the System/360 mainframes. Two of these instructions are the move long and the compare long instructions. Two others that you may find useful are the insert-characters-under-mask and the store-characters-under-mask instructions. These instructions are included in this topic because they all require the use of registers.

```
          .
          .
    LA    8,RECVFLD
    LA    9,800
    LA    4,SENDFLD
    LA    5,800
    MVCL  8,4
          .
          .
```

Figure 7-8   Moving one 800-byte field to another with the MVCL instruction

---

**Move long
(MVCL)**

The move long instruction is coded in register-to-register format as in this example:

```
    MVCL  6,10
```

Each operand, which must be an even-numbered register, represents an even-odd register pair. The even register of the first operand pair must contain the address of the first byte of the receiving field. The odd register of this pair, register 7 in the instruction above, must contain the length of the receiving field as a binary value.

Similarly, the even register of the second operand pair must contain the address of the sending field. The odd register of this pair must contain two values: (1) the length of the sending field in the second, third, and fourth bytes, and (2) a pad character which must be stored in the first, or leftmost, byte.

When the MVCL instruction is executed, the data from the sending field is moved to the receiving field, byte by byte from left to right. If the receiving field is shorter than or as long as the sending field, it executes just like the MVC instruction without the 256-byte limit. But, if the receiving field is longer than the sending field, the pad character is used to fill the extra bytes of the receiving field.

Figure 7-8 shows a typical use of the MVCL instruction. Here, the sending and receiving fields are the same length, and the load-address instruction is used to place the appropriate addresses and lengths into the four registers used by the instruction. The pad character in this case is hex 00 since it will be loaded into the leftmost byte of register 5 by the LA instruction. In this case, though, because both fields are the same length, the pad character won't be used.

Figure 7-9 shows how you can use the MVCL instruction to clear a storage area to blanks. In this case, the length of the sending field is intentionally set to zero and the pad character is set to blank (hex 40). As a result, pad characters fill in all 2000 bytes of the receiving field.

```
         .
         .
         .
         LA      10,TABLE
         LA      11,2000
         LM      6,7,BLANK
         MVCL    10,6
         .
         .
BLANK    DC      X'00000000'
         DC      X'40000000'
         .
         .
         .
```

Figure 7-9   Clearing a 2000-byte area to blanks with the MVCL instruction

Compare long (CLCL)

The compare long instruction is coded in register-to-register format as in this example:

```
    CLCL   4,8
```

Each operand, which must be an even-numbered register, represents an even-odd register pair. The even register of the first operand pair (register 4 in the example above) must contain the address of the first byte of the first field to be compared. The odd register of the pair (register 5 in the example) must contain the length of the first field as a binary value. Similarly, the even register of the second operand pair (register 8 above) must contain the address of the second field to be compared. The odd register must contain two values: (1) the length of the second field which must be stored in the second, third, and fourth bytes, and (2) a pad character which must be stored in the first, or leftmost, byte. Then, the shorter of the two fields is considered to be extended with the pad character so that both fields are of equal length.

This instruction compares the bytes of the fields one at a time, from left to right, bumping the address registers by one and decrementing the length values by one as each byte is compared. If all the bytes are equal, the condition code is set to indicate an equal compare. But, if an unequal pair of bytes is found, the condition code is set to indicate whether operand A is low or high, and the contents of the address and length registers are left at their current settings. At that time, the address registers contain the addresses of the unequal bytes, and the length registers contain the number of bytes remaining to be compared. These addresses can then be used to locate the unequal bytes.

To illustrate, the routine in figure 7-10 uses CLCL to compare two 2000-byte records. If they are equal, a branch is made to NEXT so the next two records can be processed. But, if a mismatched pair of bytes is found,

```
          .
          .
          LA    4,INREC1
          LA    5,2000
          LA    8,INREC2
          LA    9,2000
COMP      CLCL  4,8
          BE    NEXT
          MVC   ERRBYTE1(1),0(4)
          MVC   ERRBYTE2(2),0(8)
          BALR  11,12
          LA    4,1(4)
          LA    8,1(8)
          S     5,=F'1'
          S     9,=F'1'
          B     COMP
          .
          .
```

Figure 7-10   Comparing two 2000-byte records with the CLCL instruction

the unequal bytes are moved to fields named ERRBYTE1 and ERRBYTE2 using the addresses left in registers 4 and 8 by the compare instruction. Then, the BALR instruction branches to the routine that is addressed by the contents of register 12. After this routine returns to the next instruction in figure 7-10 (the one addressed by register 11), registers 4 and 8 are increased by one so they point to the first byte in each field that is after the unequal one. Also, the remaining length of each field is decreased by one. Then, the CLCL instruction is executed again so comparison of the two records continues.

If another unequal pair of bytes is found, they are stored in ERRBYTE1 and ERRBYTE2, the branch to the address in register 12 takes place, and, after the return to the next instruction, the addresses and lengths are adjusted and the CLCL is executed again. This procedure continues until all of the bytes of the two blocks have been compared and the branch to NEXT takes place.

If the lengths of the fields to be compared are not equal, the shorter of the two is considered to be extended with the pad character. The routine in figure 7-11 shows how this feature of CLCL can be used to find the first nonblank character in an area. Here, the odd register of the second operand pair (register 11) is loaded with the pad character and a zero length value. Each byte of the first operand is then compared with the pad character. When the first character that doesn't match the pad character is found, the instruction will stop and the address of the nonblank character will be left in the even register of the first operand pair, register 8.

```
                    .
                    .
          NEWREC    LM      8,11,START
                    CLCL    8,10
                    BE      NODATA
                    ST      8,ADDR1
                    .
                    .
          ADDR1     DS      F
          START     DC      A(RECORD)
                    DC      F'80'
                    DC      F'0'
                    DC      X'40000000'
                    .
                    .
```

Figure 7-11   Searching for blanks with the CLCL instruction

Insert-characters-under-mask (ICM)

The insert-characters-under-mask instruction is a register instruction that operates much like a load instruction. However, it allows you to load data into selected bytes of the register instead of always filling all four bytes. Here's an example:

```
          ICM     6,12,SOURCE
```

When executed, bytes from the third operand are loaded into the register specified as the first operand. However, the second operand is treated as a four-bit mask that governs which of the register bytes are to be filled.

Figure 7-12 shows several examples of the insert-characters-under-mask instruction. When executed, each bit of the mask corresponds to a byte of the register: the first mask bit to the first byte of the register; the second mask bit to the second byte of the register; and so on. If a mask bit is on, the corresponding byte of the register is loaded. If a mask bit is off, the corresponding byte is left unchanged. The selected register bytes are loaded from consecutive bytes of storage, beginning with the one addressed by operand three.

The last example in figure 7-12 shows how the instruction can be used to insert a pad character into the leftmost byte of a register. Since the move long and compare long instructions require a pad character in this byte of an odd register, the ICM and MVCL and CLCL instructions can be coded so they work together.

Instruction		Mask	Register before	Storage	Register after
ICM	4,4,STOR	0100	00000000	FFFFFFFF	00FF0000
ICM	7,15,STOR	1111	00000000	804B36AD	804B36AD
ICM	10,10,STOR	1010	FFA33629	8000FFFF	80A30029
ICM	12,3,STOR	0011	00000000	F1F2F3F4	0000F1F2
ICM	11,8,PAD	1000	00007B36	40FFFFFF	40007B36

Figure 7-12 Some examples of the insert-characters-under-mask instruction

Instruction		Mask	Register contents	Stored bytes
STCM	6,15,FLD	1111	00006A4C	00006A4C
STCM	12,4,FLD	0100	00367FA2	36
STCM	4,10,FLD	1010	80003D68	803D

Figure 7-13 Some examples of the store-characters-under-mask instruction

Store-characters-under-mask (STCM)

The store-characters-under-mask instruction is the converse of the insert-characters-under-mask instruction. That is, bytes selected from the register coded as the first operand are stored in consecutive bytes of storage beginning at the address of the third operand. The second operand in the instruction is the mask that determines which bytes are to be stored. Figure 7-13 shows three examples of this instruction.

Terminology

explicit address
explicit base register
explicit displacement
address constant
adcon
wrap-around concept

Objective

Apply the register techniques and instructions presented in this topic to your programs.

TOPIC 2   Binary arithmetic

As I mentioned in chapter 4, there are two forms of binary data storage: fixed-point and floating-point. When arithmetic operations are performed using either binary form, the operations are faster than decimal arithmetic operations. Nevertheless, decimal instructions are used for most mathematical routines that are written in assembler language. You'll learn why by the time you complete this topic.

This topic shows you how to perform arithmetic operations using the fixed-point binary instructions. Then, in chapter 12, you'll learn how to use the floating-point instructions. Although there are times when you're likely to do arithmetic operations using the fixed-point instructions, you may never find the need for the floating-point instructions. In the remainder of this topic, whenever I refer to binary data or binary arithmetic instructions, please keep in mind that I'm referring to fixed-point binary, not floating-point binary.

In topic 1 of this chapter, you were introduced to many of the instructions that are used for binary arithmetic. There, you learned how to define halfwords, fullwords, and doublewords, how to load registers, how to code binary addition and subtraction instructions, how to compare binary operands, and how to store the contents of registers in storage fields. In this topic, then, all you need to learn is how to code the binary multiplication and division instructions and how to code the instructions for converting binary data to and from packed decimal format. In addition, you should learn more about the way negative numbers are stored in binary format.

Instructions for multiplication and division

Multiply (M), multiply halfword (MH), and multiply register (MR)   In a fullword instruction (M or MR), the multiplicand must be placed in the odd register of a pair of even-odd registers, such as registers 6 and 7 or registers 10 and 11, before the instruction is executed. The even register of the even-odd pair is specified as the first operand and the product (or result) is placed in the even-odd pair as a doubleword value. The sign of the product is developed according to the rules of algebra: like signs produce positive products, unlike signs produce negative products. To illustrate, figure 7-14 shows a routine that multiplies two fields, then stores the answer from registers 6 and 7 in a doubleword of storage.

Often, though, the range of values you deal with causes all significant bits in the product to be contained in the odd register of the even-odd pair. If this is the case, you can ignore the even register and just store the contents of the odd register as the product:

```
M     6,FIELDB
ST    7,FWORD
```

```
        L       7,FIELDA
        M       6,FIELDB
        STM     6,7,DOUBLE
```

Figure 7-14   A binary multiplication routine

```
        SR      8,8
        L       9,DIVIDEND
        D       8,DIVISOR
        ST      9,QUOTNT
        ST      8,REMNDER
```

Figure 7-15   A binary division routine

In the multiply halfword (MH) instruction, only one register is required and any register, odd or even, can be used. The product is a fullword value that replaces the contents of the register specified:

```
        LH      9,FACTOR1
        MH      9,FACTOR2
        ST      9,FWORD
```

In any binary multiply instruction, arithmetic overflow isn't possible.

Divide (D) and divide register (DR)   The divide instruction also requires an even-odd pair of registers as the first operand. The dividend must occupy the pair as a doubleword value and the divisor must be a fullword or a register as in these examples:

```
        D       6,FWORD1
        DR      4,9
```

The quotient that results is stored as a fullword value in the odd register with its sign determined by the normal algebraic rules. The remainder is stored in the even register with its sign the same as the dividend's. If the values of the dividend and divisor are such that the quotient won't fit in the odd register, an abnormal program termination occurs due to a fixed-point divide exception.

Figure 7-15 illustrates a binary division routine that assumes that DIVIDEND will be a positive number since the SR register instruction will cause register 8 to contain a value of binary zero. As you'll see in a moment, binary zeros would *not* be an acceptable value for register 8 if DIVIDEND were a negative number.

Negative value: 0000000001011101

1. Reverse the bits: 1111111110100010
2. Add 1:   + 1

Two's complement: 1111111110100011

Figure 7-16   Deriving the two's complement of a number

Fullword hex notation: FFE4

1. Convert to binary: 1111 1111 1110 0100
2. Subtract 1:   -1
                          1111 1111 1110 0011
3. Reverse the bits: 0000 0000 0001 1100

4. Convert to decimal: -28

Figure 7-17   Converting a negative hex value to decimal

Two's complement form for negative binary numbers

Using binary data format, a negative number is indicated by a binary 1 in the leftmost bit of the word. The rest of the word contains the binary number but in *two's complement form*. To get the two's complement of a binary number, you reverse the bits and add 1 to the rightmost bit as shown in figure 7-16. Here, the two's complement of decimal 93 is derived. Thus, negative 93 is stored in one fullword as this series of bits:

    1111   1111   1010   0011

Then, if you wanted to load this value as a dividend in registers 8 and 9, you would have to load this value in register 9 and hex FFFF in register 8.

Occasionally, when debugging, you may want to find the decimal value of a fixed-point field or register whose value is given in hex. If the value is positive as indicated by a hex value of seven or less in the leftmost half-byte of the word, you can convert to decimal as described in chapter 4. But, if the value is negative, you must determine the decimal value by using a technique like the one in figure 7-17.

Instructions for binary data conversion

The pack and unpack instructions let you convert numeric data from EBC-DIC format to packed decimal format, and vice versa. Then, to convert from packed decimal to binary, and vice versa, you use the convert-to-binary and the convert-to-decimal instructions. Note that there isn't any instruction that directly converts data from EBCDIC to binary, and back again.

Convert to binary (CVB)   The convert-to-binary instruction converts a packed decimal value into a binary value. The packed decimal number must be stored in a doubleword area; the resulting binary value is stored in a register. Here's an example:

```
CVB    12,DBLEPACK
```

When this instruction is executed, the packed decimal value stored in the doubleword named DBLEPACK is converted to binary and loaded into register 12.

As in all packed decimal instructions, the data in the doubleword must have a valid sign in the rightmost half-byte and decimal digits in all other half-bytes. Since packed decimal fields aren't normally defined as doubleword areas, you can use the zero-and-add (ZAP) instruction to insert your packed decimal value into a doubleword work area.

Convert to decimal (CVD)   The convert-to-decimal instruction is the opposite of the convert-to-binary. It converts a binary value in a register to packed decimal format and stores it in a doubleword area as in this example:

```
CVD    10,DBLEAREA
```

Here, the binary value in register 10 is packed into the doubleword named DBLEAREA.

A payroll routine that uses binary arithmetic

Just for illustration, figure 7-18 shows the payroll routine you last saw in figure 7-7 in another form. This time the arithmetic is done in binary. After each hours-worked field has been packed into the doubleword area, it is converted to binary in register 7 and then added to the weekly-hours total in register 5. When the hours for all seven days have been accumulated, control falls through the BCT instruction and the total hours in register 5 is converted back to packed decimal. The CVD instruction makes use of the same doubleword that had been used in the CVB instruction.

```
                    .
                    .
            SR      5,5
            LA      4,7
            LA      6,PAYREC+5
ADDLOOP     PACK    DBLEWRK,0(3,6)
            CVB     7,DBLEWRK
            AR      5,7
            LA      6,3(6)
            BCT     4,ADDLOOP
            CVD     5,DBLEWRK
            ZAP     TOTHRS,DBLEWRK
                    .
                    .
PAYREC      DS      CL26
DBLEWRK     DS      D
TOTHRS      DS      PL3
```

Figure 7-18   The payroll routine using binary arithmetic

Discussion   As the routine in figure 7-18 demonstrates, binary arithmetic requires
                 some extra conversion instructions that aren't required when you use
                 decimal arithmetic. That's why decimal arithmetic is normally used in
                 business programs. On the other hand, the binary instructions execute
                 more rapidly than the decimal instructions. As a result, binary arithmetic
                 can be useful when arithmetic speed is critical and data conversions are
                 minimal.

Terminology   two's complement form

Objective   Apply the binary arithmetic instructions to appropriate arithmetic
                 routines in your programs.

TOPIC 3   Storage definition techniques

Chapters 5 and 6 presented the basic methods of defining I/O areas, work areas, and work fields. You should realize, though, that you can use other elements and techniques to define and process storage areas. In particular, this chapter reviews the use of zero duplication factors and introduces you to the ORG instruction and to dummy sections.

How to use zero duplication factors to define fields within fields

Figure 7-19 shows you how zero duplication factors can be used to define a record area for an accounts receivable record. This illustrates that fields can be defined within fields within areas. In fact, any number of levels within levels can be defined.

Whenever a zero duplication factor is used, the assembler doesn't increase the value of its *location counter* during an assembly. The location counter keeps track of the next address to be used for an instruction or data element during an assembly. If its value isn't increased, two or more data elements can be assigned the same address.

In figure 7-19, for example, note that both ARBALFWD and ARDATE have a zero duplication factor. As a result, ARBALFWD refers to the 13 bytes that hold data from record positions 58-70; ARDATE refers to the 6 bytes that hold data from record positions 58-63; and ARMONTH refers to the 2 bytes that hold data for record positions 58 and 59. In other words, ARBALFWD, ARDATE, and ARMONTH all have the same address in the program. However, their lengths differ.

How to use the ORG instruction to redefine storage areas

Sometimes, a file will contain several types of records. For example, a transaction file for a billing program could contain a set of records for each shipment made. The first record of each set could contain the customer name and billing address and have a 1 in byte 1. The second record could specify the date of shipment and the shipping address and have a 2 in byte 1. And for each item of a shipment, there could be a third type of record that gives the identification number and quantity for one item of the shipment.

Rather than use three separate work areas for these records, though, you could use the ORG command to define all three formats in a single area. This is illustrated in figure 7-20. As you can see, three ORG commands are used to define all three record types in a single area. The ORG command is an assembler command that tells the assembler to change the value of its location counter.

Record layout

Field Name	Customer number	Customer name	Customer address				Balance forward			
			Street address	City	State	Zip code	Date			Amount
							Mo	Day	Yr	
Characteristics	CL5	CL15	CL15	CL15	CL2	CL5	CL2	CL2	CL2	ZL7
Usage										
Position	1-5	6-20	21-35	36-50	51-52	53-57	58-59	60-61	62-63	64-70

Record definition

```
        .
        .
        .
ARREC     DS    0CL80
ARCUSTID  DS    0CL20
ARCUSTNO  DS    CL5
ARNAME    DS    CL15
ARADDR    DS    0CL37
ARSTREET  DS    CL15
ARCITY    DS    CL15
ARSTATE   DS    CL2
ARZIP     DS    CL5
ARBALFWD  DS    0CL13
ARDATE    DS    0CL6
ARMONTH   DS    CL2
ARDAY     DS    CL2
ARYEAR    DS    CL2
ARBALAMT  DS    ZL7
```

Figure 7-19   Using zero duplication factors to define fields within fields

When the ORG command is specified with an operand, it tells the assembler to set the location counter to the location of its operand. Thus, in figure 7-20, RECORD2 is given a location counter value that is the same as RECORD1's. As a result, the fields in RECORD2 are given location values that are in the RECORD1 area. Similarly, RECORD3 and its fields are given location values in the RECORD1 area. The final ORG command, without an operand, tells the assembler to set the location counter to the location value that represents the next available storage location. In figure 7-20, the next available location is the first byte following the 67-byte area defined and redefined as RECORD1, RECORD2, and RECORD3.

The operand for the ORG command can consist of names, decimal values, or the asterisk (which stands for the current location counter value) and can be combined in arithmetic expressions also. Thus, the first ORG command in figure 7-20 would have the same effect if coded as:

```
ORG     *-67
```

This means the current location counter value minus 67. Similarly, the

```
LOC CTR VALUE            STATEMENT

02A0            RECORD1    DS      0CL67
02A0            R1TYPE     DS      CL1
02A1            R1IDNUM    DS      CL4
02A5            R1NAME     DS      CL25
02BE            R1STRT     DS      CL15
02CD            R1CITY     DS      CL15
02DC            R1STATE    DS      CL2
02DE            R1ZIP      DS      CL5
02A0                       ORG     RECORD1
02A0            RECORD2    DS      0CL67
02A0            R2TYPE     DS      CL1
02A1            R2IDNUM    DS      CL4
02A5            R2DATE     DS      CL6
02AB                       DS      CL19
02BE            R2STRT     DS      CL15
02CD            R2CITY     DS      CL15
02DC            R2STATE    DS      CL2
02DE            R2ZIP      DS      CL5
02A0                       ORG     RECORD1
02A0            RECORD3    DS      0CL67
02A0            R3TYPE     DS      CL1
02A1            R3IDNUM    DS      CL4
02A5            R3DATE     DS      CL6
02AB            R3ITEM     DS      CL8
02B3            R3QTY      DS      CL6
02B9                       DS      CL42
02E3                       ORG
```

Figure 7-20   Using the ORG command to redefine a work area

second ORG command would have the same effect if coded as any one of the following:

```
ORG    RECORD2
ORG    *-67
ORG    R1TYPE
ORG    R2TYPE
ORG    R2DATE-5
```

Dummy sections   When you code an assembler language program or subprogram, it is a *control section*, or CSECT, in assembler language terms. For instance, the reorder-listing program of chapter 5 represented one control section. After assembly, a control section becomes a relocatable module that can be link edited and executed.

In contrast, a *dummy section*, or DSECT, doesn't become a relocatable module. When you use a dummy section, it's similar to using explicit addresses as discussed in topic 1. However, a dummy section lets you code labels instead of explicit addresses. This helps prevent coding errors and makes it easier for you to come back to a program later on and change it. As a result, DSECTs are commonly used by professional programmers.

How to use a DSECT for repetitive processing   Figure 7-21 gives an example of the use of a DSECT to control the processing of 25 warehouse-location segments within an inventory master record. The inventory master record (INVMSTR in figure 7-21) is a 430-byte record that ends with a 400-byte area that contains 25 repetitions of a 16-byte warehouse-location segment. Each 16-byte segment contains the warehouse number, bin number, quantity stored in the bin, and date it was stored in this format:

Bytes	Field
1-2	Warehouse number
3-5	Bin number
6-10	Quantity stored
11-16	Date stored (MMDDYY)

In figure 7-21, a DSECT is used for each location segment so each of the 25 groups can be processed using the same labels. The DSECT is coded after the definitions for the 430-byte record area. When a DSECT is coded, no storage area is reserved for it (that's why it's called a dummy section). Instead, the location counter values for the fields within the DSECT are relative to the start of the DSECT. The CSECT instruction at the end of the dummy section restores the location counter value for the program so TOTQTY in figure 7-21 begins at the first location after the 430-byte area reserved for INVMSTR.

When you code a DSECT, you must also code a USING statement to tell the assembler what register to use as the base register for the DSECT fields. If you remember that the DSECT itself reserves no storage positions, you can see that the USING statement must relate the DSECT to some actual storage positions. In figure 7-21, this USING statement relates the DSECT to register 8:

```
      USING INVLOC,8
```

Then, this instruction later on in the program puts the address of INVSTOR in register 8:

```
      LA    8,INVSTOR
```

As a result, the first time the routine goes through the ADDLOC loop, the field names in the DSECT refer to the first of the 25 segments of the input

```
INVPROG   START 0
          BALR  3,0
          USING *,3
          USING INVLOC,8
          .
          .
          LA    8,INVSTOR
          LA    9,25
          ZAP   TOTQTY,=P'0'
ADDLOC    AP    TOTQTY,INVQTY
          LA    8,16(8)
          BCT   9,ADDLOC
          CP    INVONHND,TOTQTY
          BNE   ERROR
          .
          .
INVMSTR   DS    0CL430
INVITNBR  DS    CL10
INVITDES  DS    CL15
INVONHND  DS    PL5
INVSTOR   DS    CL400
INVLOC    DSECT
INVWHSE   DS    CL2
INVBIN    DS    CL3
INVQTY    DS    PL5
INVDATE   DS    0CL6
INVMONTH  DS    CL2
INVDAY    DS    CL2
INVYEAR   DS    CL2
INVPROG   CSECT
TOTQTY    DS    PL5
          .
          .
```

Figure 7-21   Using a DSECT to process 25 location segments

record that are located in the 400-byte area named INVSTOR. After the first INVQTY is added to TOTQTY, this instruction increases the address in register 8 by 16:

```
LA    8,16(8)
```

So, the next time through the ADDLOC loop, INVQTY will refer to the second location segment in the 400-byte area. And so on. After the loop has been executed 25 times, the sum of the warehouse quantities is compared with the on-hand balance for the item. If they aren't equal, a branch to an error routine takes place.

The CSECT (Control Section) instruction at the end of the dummy section restores the original base register and location counter value for the continuation of the assembly. The label field of the CSECT instruction must be the program name taken from the label field of the START instruction for the control section. A DSECT should always end with either a CSECT or the DSECT of another dummy section.

```
REORDLST  START   0
          BALR    3,0
          USING   *,3
          USING   IMDSECT,4
            .
READINV   GET     INVMAST
          AP      COUNT,=P'1'
          PACK    WRKAVAIL,INVONHND
          PACK    WRKONORD,INVONORD
            .
INVMAST   DTFSD   BLKSIZE=500,                          X
                  RECFORM=FIXBLK,                        X
                  RECSIZE=50,                            X
                  IOAREA1=INVIO1,                        X
                  IOAREA2=INVIO2,                        X
                  IOREG=(4),                             X
                  EOFADDR=INVEOF                         X
                  DEVADDR=SYS008
            .
            .
IMDSECT   DSECT
INVITNBR  DS      CL5
INVITDES  DS      CL20
INVCOST   DS      CL5
INVPRICE  DS      CL5
INVORDPT  DS      CL5
INVONHND  DS      CL5
INVONORD  DS      CL5
REORDLST  CSECT
            .
            .
```

Figure 7-22   Using a DSECT and an IOREG to deblock records

How to use a DSECT for blocking and deblocking   When you use blocked records for a tape or DASD file, you can use a DSECT for blocking and deblocking records. If you do, you don't need to specify a work area for the file. Instead, you specify an I/O register in the DTF for the file. If, for example, the reorder-listing program of chapter 5 used two I/O areas, no work area, and a DSECT for deblocking the input records, it would be coded as shown in figure 7-22. Since blocking and deblocking are just forms of repetitive processing, this code is similar to the code in figure 7-21. As a result, I'll just point out the differences, which are shaded in figure 7-22.

First, note in figure 7-22 that the keyword operand IOREG is used in the DTF for INVMAST. This operand specifies a register that is used by the blocking and deblocking routines associated with the file. Second, note that the USING statement for INVMAST specifies the same register that is given in the IOREG operand (register 4). Finally, note that no address is ever loaded into register 4 by the machine instructions of the program. Instead, deblocking is handled automatically. After each input record is read, the address in register 4 is adjusted so it contains the address of the next record to be processed. In other words, it goes through all the records in the first I/O area, next goes through all the records in the second I/O area, then starts over with the records in the first I/O area. For this to happen, all the programmer has to do is to code the USING command and the IOREG operand correctly.

In section 4, you'll see other examples of DSECTs used for blocking and deblocking. For now, you should simply realize that you can provide for blocking and deblocking by using a work area (WORKA=YES). You can also provide for it by using a DSECT and an I/O register.

Terminology

location counter
control section
dummy section

Objective

Apply zero duplication factors, the ORG instruction, and dummy sections to your programs.

Chapter   8

How to use
subroutines and subprograms

This chapter is divided into three topics. The first shows you how to use subroutines; the second shows you how to use subprograms; the third shows you how to code the VSE JCL that you will need when you use subprograms.

TOPIC 1   How to use subroutines

A *subroutine* is a group of instructions that is used within a larger routine or within a complete program. Subroutines are important for two main reasons.

First, subroutines can help you reduce coding duplication when the same routine is required in two or more portions of a program. By coding the routine as a subroutine, you only have to code it once. This can shorten the time you take to code a program, and it reduces the amount of storage required by the program.

Second, the use of subroutines lets you divide a program into smaller, more manageable modules. This in turn lets you develop a program one module (or subroutine) at a time, so both coding and testing become more manageable. Normally, though, when you develop a program as a series of subroutines, you must use a program design technique that is consistent with their use. So let's start this topic with some thoughts on program design.

Modular program design

Program flowcharts like the ones we've used so far in this book are okay...as long as the programs you're developing are short and simple. But as your programs increase in size and complexity, traditional flowcharts become less and less effective. In particular, these flowcharts don't encourage you to think of your programs as a collection of modules that fit together in an organized way. Instead, they treat a program, no matter how large, as a series of steps and logical branches.

In contrast, the idea behind *modular program design* is to divide a program into a number of separate modules: one mainline module and one or more subroutine modules. Then, each module can be designed so it will print on a single page or less of an assembly listing. And each page will have a limited amount of logic, or branching. This, in turn, makes it easier to code, test, and maintain the program.

When you use modular program design, you normally draw *modular flowcharts* to represent your design. To illustrate, figure 8-1 represents a modular flowchart for the mainline module of the refined reorder-listing program of chapter 5. If you compare figure 8-1 with the complete flowchart in figure 5-10, you can see that the modular flowchart for the mainline module is much simpler, with only four processing boxes and one decision symbol.

Each of the boxes in figure 8-1 that has a stripe across the top represents another module, or subroutine, of the program. Thus, the mainline module uses three subroutines named READREC, PROCESS, and PRTCOUNT. When one module uses a lower-level module, it is referred to as *calling a module*, or *calling a subroutine*. Then, the higher-level subroutine is the *calling module*. And the lower-level subroutine is the *called module*, or *called subroutine*. In figure 8-1, three subroutines are called by the mainline module.

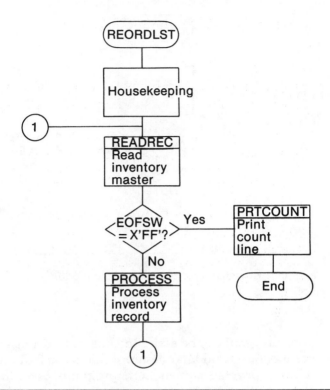

Figure 8-1 A modular flowchart for the mainline module of the refined reorder-listing program

Figure 8-2 presents the modular flowcharts for the subroutines called by the module in figure 8-1. Here again, the striped boxes refer to lower-level modules. So, the PROCESS module calls the PRTDET module, and the PRTCOUNT module calls the PRINT module.

Figure 8-3 presents the modular flowcharts for the subroutines called by the modules in figure 8-2. Note, here, that PRTDET calls the PRINT module, which was also called by PRTCOUNT. In other words, the PRINT module is called from two modules, rather than one.

When you use modular program design, you'll often find that one module is called by two or more other modules. And this usually means that you have simplified your code by using modular program design. In contrast, using traditional flowcharting techniques, you may not even realize that you could use the same code in more than one place in your program.

Although the reorder-listing program is so simple that you can code it without designing it at all, I hope it serves to illustrate the value of modular flowcharting. When you use modular flowcharting, you can design your program so each module can easily be charted on a single page. This, in turn, means that you can code each module of the flowchart so it will print on a single page of the assembly listing. And that means

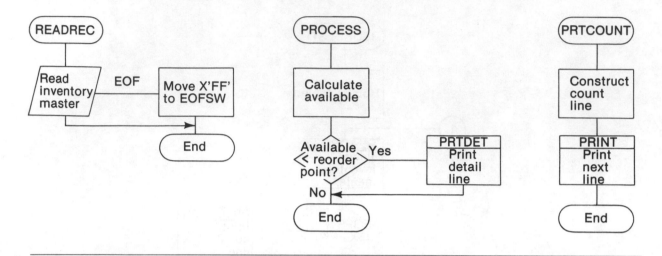

Figure 8-2   Modular flowcharts for the subroutine modules called by the mainline module in figure 8-1

your program will be easier to code, test, debug, and maintain. If you experiment with modular design, I think you'll discover how it can help you develop programs, even short programs. And the larger your programs are, the more modular design can help you.

How to code a modular program using subroutines

Figure 8-4 gives the coding for the program that is charted in figures 8-1, 8-2, and 8-3. However, this figure doesn't include the DTFs and data definitions that were used in the original version of the program shown in figure 5-11 since that coding is the same as in figure 5-11. Shading is used in figure 8-4 to show the statements that have been added to the program to provide for the linkage between the six modules of the program.

To understand this version of the program and to code one like it, you need to know how to code the instructions used for linkage (BAL and BR). You also need to know how to provide the extra coding required when nested subroutines are used. Finally, you should know how many entry and exit points you should allow for each subroutine.

The BAL and BALR instructions   To call a subroutine, the mainline module in figure 8-4 uses a branch-and-link (BAL) instruction like this one:

```
BAL    11,READREC
```

When this instruction is executed, the address of the first instruction after the BAL instruction is placed in the register specified as operand-1. Then,

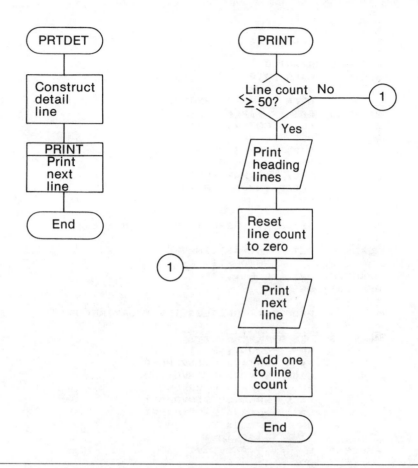

Figure 8-3   Modular flowcharts for the subroutine modules called by the subroutine modules in figure 8-2

the BAL instruction causes a branch to the instruction named as operand-2. In the program in figure 8-4, this instruction causes the address of the CLI instruction to be placed in register 11; then, the program branches to READREC.

You could also code this call to READREC using a BALR instruction as follows:

```
LA    10,READREC
BALR  11,10
```

Here, the BALR instruction first places the address of the next instruction in register 11; then, it branches to the address in register 10. Since register 10 has been loaded with the address of READREC, these instructions work the same as the one BAL instruction.

You can use any register for linking to a subroutine, but remember that most I/O operations use registers 14, 15, 0, and 1. As a result, if you were to use register 14 as a link register to a subroutine that does some in-

```
*
*              REORDLST:   THE MAINLINE MODULE
*
REORDLST START 0
BEGIN    BALR  3,0
         USING *,3
         OPEN  INVMAST,PRTOUT
MAINLOOP BAL   11,READREC
         CLI   EOFSW,X'FF'
         BE    EOJRT
         BAL   11,PROCESS
         B     MAINLOOP
EOJRT    BAL   11,PRTCOUNT
         CLOSE INVMAST,PRTOUT
         EOJ
*
*              READREC:  READ INVENTORY MASTER
*
READREC  GET   INVMAST,INVWRKA
         B     READEXIT
READEOF  MVI   EOFSW,X'FF'
READEXIT BR    11
*
*              PROCESS:   PROCESS INVENTORY RECORD
*
PROCESS  ST    11,PROCSAVE
         AP    COUNT,=P'1'
         PACK  WRKAVAIL,INVONHND
         PACK  WRKONORD,INVONORD
         AP    WRKAVAIL,WRKONORD
         PACK  WRKORDPT,INVORDPT
         CP    WRKAVAIL,WRKORDPT
         BNL   PROCEXIT
         BAL   11,PRTDET
PROCEXIT L     11,PROCSAVE
         BR    11
PROCSAVE DS    F
*
*              PRTCOUNT:  PRINT COUNT LINE
*
PRTCOUNT ST    11,PCNTSAVE
         ED    CNTPATRN,COUNT
         MVC   PRTNEXT,CNTLINE
         BAL   11,PRINT
         L     11,PCNTSAVE
         BR    11
PCNTSAVE DS    F
```

Figure 8-4 Modular coding for the refined reorder-listing program (part 1 of 2)

put or output operation that uses register 14, the address in register 14 would be destroyed. However, you can use registers 14, 15, 0, and 1 if you save their contents as the first step of the subroutine and restore them just before exiting the subroutine. This save and restore technique is illustrated later in this topic.

```
*
*           PRTDET:    PRINT DETAIL LINE
*
PRTDET     ST        11,PRTDSAVE
           PACK      PACKAREA,INVITNBR
           MVC       PRTITNBR,PATTERN1
           ED        PRTITNBR,PACKAREA
           MVC       PRTITDES,INVITDES
           PACK      PACKAREA,INVPRICE
           MVC       PRTPRICE,PATTERN2
           ED        PRTPRICE,PACKAREA
           MVC       PRTAVAIL,PATTERN1
           ED        PRTAVAIL,WRKAVAIL
           MVC       PRTORDPT,PATTERN1
           ED        PRTORDPT,WRKORDPT
           MVI       PRTDCTL,C' '
           MVC       PRTNEXT,PRTDETL
           BAL       11,PRINT
           L         11,PRTDSAVE
           BR        11
PRTDSAVE   DS        F
*
*           PRINT:    PRINT NEXT LINE
*
PRINT      CP        LINECNT,=P'50'
           BL        PRTNLINE
           PUT       PRTOUT,HDGLINE1
           PUT       PRTOUT,HDGLINE2
           PUT       PRTOUT,HDGLINE3
           ZAP       LINECNT,=P'0'
           MVI       PRTNEXT,C'0'
PRTNLINE   PUT       PRTOUT,PRTNEXT
           AP        LINECNT,=P'1'
           BR        11
```

Figure 8-4   Modular coding for the refined reorder-listing program (part 2 of 2)

The BR instruction   To return to a calling module from a subroutine, you code a branch register (BR) instruction like this:

    BR   11

This instruction branches unconditionally to the address given in the register specified. In the READREC module in figure 8-4, this instruction branches back to the CLI instruction in the REORDLST module since the address of the CLI instruction was loaded into register 11 before the branch to READREC took place. In figure 8-4, all subroutines are called using register 11 in a BAL instruction. So, all subroutines return to the calling module using register 11 in a BR instruction.

Nested subroutines   When a mainline module calls a subroutine that calls another subroutine, the subroutines can be referred to as *nested subroutines*. In figure 8-4, REORDLST calls PROCESS, which calls PRTDET, which calls PRINT, so these modules are nested four deep. Similarly, REORDLST calls PRTCOUNT, which calls PRINT, so these modules are nested three deep. When you design a modular program, it usually results in nested subroutines. And there's no limit to how deeply you can nest your modules.

When you code a subroutine in the middle of a nest, you must realize that you have to save the value of the register you're using for linkage or you can destroy the linkage chain. This is illustrated in figure 8-5, which shows just the coding of figure 8-4 that affects the *linkage* between REORDLST, PROCESS, PRTDET, and PRINT. Here, REORDLST is the top-level module in the nest of subroutines, PRINT is the lowest-level module, and PROCESS and PRTDET are in the middle of the linkage chain.

Note, then, that both PROCESS and PRTDET start by storing the contents of register 11 in a fullword save area. Then, they use register 11 as the linkage register in their calls to lower-level modules. After their subroutines return to them and they complete their processing, they load the contents of their save areas back into register 11 and use BR instructions to branch back to the module that called them.

Can you see why PROCESS and PRTDET must save the contents of register 11 before calling their subroutines? If they didn't, the *linkage chain* would be destroyed. If, for example, PROCESS didn't save register 11, the contents of register 11 would be replaced by the address of the instruction after its own BAL instruction when this BAL instruction is executed. Then, the BR instruction at the end of PROCESS would branch to one of its own instructions and an endless loop would be started. To keep the linkage chain intact, a subroutine in the middle of a nest must store and reload the address sent to it in the linkage register.

Incidentally, this saving and restoring of linkage registers can be useful during debugging. When a program terminates abnormally, the save area for the link register in each subroutine provides a trace back to the calling routine. As a result, you can recreate the series of links that took place before program termination by analyzing the storage dump.

Entry and exit points   When a BAL or BALR instruction is used to call a subroutine, the address in the operand-1 register is called the *return address*, and the operand-2 address is called the *entry point* of the subroutine. Similarly, the instruction of the subroutine that returns to the calling module is referred to as the subprogram's *exit point*.

In figure 8-5, then, register 11 always contains the return address for the subroutine that is being executed. The first instruction of each subroutine is always the entry point of the subroutine. And the last instruction of each subroutine is its exit point. In other words, each subroutine has only one entry point and only one exit point. As you will learn in chapter 19, this is consistent with modern program development

```
*
*           REORDLST:   THE MAINLINE MODULE
*
REORDLST START   0
            .
            .
            BAL    11,PROCESS
            .
            .
*
*           PROCESS:   PROCESS INVENTORY RECORD
*
PROCESS  ST      11,PROCSAVE
            .
            .
            BAL    11,PRTDET
            L      11,PROCSAVE
            BR     11
PROCSAVE DS      F
*
*           PRTDET:   PRINT DETAIL LINE
*
PRTDET   ST      11,PRTDSAVE
            .
            .
            BAL    11,PRINT
            L      11,PRTDSAVE
            BR     11
PRTDSAVE DS      F
*
*           PRINT:   PRINT NEXT LINE
*
PRINT       .
            .
            .
            BR     11
```

Figure 8-5   The linkage for one set of nested subroutines in the reorder-listing program in figure 8-4

methods. So, when coding subroutines, we recommend that you follow the rule of only one entry and exit point in each subroutine.

You should realize, though, that it is possible to code a subroutine with more than one entry or exit point. In fact, if you review the subroutines used in your shop, particularly, the older ones, you may find that many have multiple entry or exit points. For instance, completion of normal processing by a subroutine might have one exit point while some error routine within the subroutine might use a different exit point. Keep in mind, then, that modern programming practices dictate against this, and that it's always possible to code a subroutine so it only has one exit point.

How to code a generalized subroutine

Usually, when you write a subroutine, it will only be used in one program, your own. Sometimes, though, a *generalized subroutine* is valuable. A generalized subroutine is one that is written in a general way so it can be used in any program, not just one program. If, for example, the PRINT subroutine of figure 8-4 were generalized, it could be used in any program that requires page overflow and the printing of a three-line heading at the top of each printed page.

No matter how much you generalize a subroutine, though, the calling program has to know what the subroutine requires. For instance, to call a generalized version of the PRINT module, you must know what fields PRINT is going to operate on and how it's going to know where those fields are in your calling module.

To illustrate, figure 8-6 shows just a slightly generalized version of the PRINT module of figure 8-4 along with the linkage instructions in the two modules that call it. In this case, to use the PRINT subroutine, you must know that it expects the address of your print line in register 10 and it expects the return address in register 11. Also, PRTOUT must be the label of your printer DTF, the DTF must be coded with WORKA=YES, and the names of your heading line definitions must be HDGLINE1, HDGLINE2, and HDGLINE3.

The instructions in the PRINT subroutine that relate to its generalization are shaded in figure 8-6. In other words, register 10 is used as an explicit base address for the next line to be printed by the program. Also, the control character in the line addressed by register 10 is saved in PCTLSAVE when the heading lines are printed so the control character can be changed to provide for double spacing after the heading lines. Then, after the heading lines are printed, the control character in the line is restored to the value in PCTLSAVE so the subroutine won't affect the forms-control logic of the calling module.

Figure 8-7 presents a more generalized version of the PRINT subroutine. In this case, the calling module must place the address of an address list in register 9, the address of the next line to be printed in register 10, and the return address in register 11. The address list must contain three addresses that point to the heading lines to be printed at the top of each page. Then, the PRINT subroutine uses the three addresses in the address list and the one address in register 10 as it prints the next line of output. So the subroutine can store the three addresses in the list in registers 6, 7, and 8, the contents of these registers are stored at the start of the subroutine and reloaded at the end of the routine. If you have any trouble understanding the coding in figure 8-7, you may want to review the material on register operations in topic 1 of chapter 7.

Whether a subroutine is only slightly generalized as in figure 8-6 or more heavily generalized as in figure 8-7, you still need to know what the subroutine expects before you can use it. As a result, there's a limit to how much effort you should put forth to generalize a subroutine. There's also a limit as to how useful a generalized subroutine can be. As a result, you may not use generalized subroutines in your shop at all.

```
          LA       10,CNTLINE
          BAL      11,PRINT
          .
          .
          .
          LA       10,PRTDETL
          BAL      11,PRINT
          .
          .
          .
*
*         PRINT:   GENERALIZED ROUTINE TO PRINT NEXT  LINE AND
*                     PROVIDE FOR PAGE OVERFLOW
*
*         ADDRESS OF NEXT LINE MUST BE IN REGISTER 10
*         RETURN ADDRESS MUST BE IN REGISTER 11
*         PRTOUT MUST BE LABEL OF PRINTER DTF
*         WORKA=YES MUST BE CODED FOR PRINTER DTF
*         HEADING LINES MUST BE NAMED HDGLINE1, HDGLINE2, & HDGLINE3
*
          CP       LINECNT,=P'50'
          BL       PRTNLINE
          PUT      PRTOUT,HDGLINE1
          PUT      PRTOUT,HDGLINE2
          PUT      PRTOUT,HDGLINE3
          ZAP      LINECNT,=P'0'
          MVC      PCTLSAVE,0(10)
          MVI      0(10),C'0'
PRTNLINE  PUT      PRTOUT,0(10)
          MVC      0(1,10),PCTLSAVE
          AP       LINECNT,=P'1'
          BR       11
LINECNT   DC       P'99'
PCTLSAVE  DS       CL1
```

Figure 8-6   A generalized PRINT subroutine

Using COPY statements for generalized subroutines   If you do use generalized subroutines, you will probably get them into your source programs with COPY commands. If, for example, you're using the PRINT subroutine in figure 8-7, you can get it into your program using an instruction like this:

```
          COPY     PRINT
```

This assumes, of course, that PRINT is the name of the book that contains the PRINT subroutine in the source statement library. This also assumes that the library has been established in the search chain for the job as described in chapter 6. Then, when the assembler encounters the COPY instruction, it will insert the book into your source program. This can reduce the amount of code you have to enter into the system for your program, so generalized subroutines like this do have their purpose.

```
          LA      9,ADDRLIST
          LA      10,PRTDETL
          BAL     11,PRINT
          .
          .
ADDRLIST  DC      A(HDGLINE1)
          DC      A(HDGLINE2)
          DC      A(HDGLINE3)
          .
          .
*
*         PRINT:  GENERALIZED ROUTINE TO PRINT NEXT LINE
*                 AND PROVIDE FOR PAGE OVERFLOW
*
*         ADDRESS OF ADDRESS LIST FOR 3 HEADING LINES MUST BE IN REG 9
*         ADDRESS OF NEXT DETAIL LINE MUST BE IN REGISTER 10
*         RETURN ADDRESS MUST BE IN REGISTER 11
*         PRTOUT MUST BE LABEL OF PRINTER DTF
*         WORKA=YES MUST BE CODED FOR PRINTER DTF
*
          STM     6,8,REGSAVE
          LM      6,8,0(9)
          CP      LINECNT,=P'50'
          BL      PRTNLINE
          PUT     PRTOUT,0(6)
          PUT     PRTOUT,0(7)
          PUT     PRTOUT,0(8)
          ZAP     LINECNT,=P'0'
          MVC     PCTLSAVE,0(10)
          MVI     0(10),C'0'
PRTNLINE  PUT     PRTOUT,0(10)
          MVC     0(1,10),PCTLSAVE
          AP      LINECNT,=P'1'
          LM      6,8,REGSAVE
          BR      11
REGSAVE   DS      3F
LINECNT   DC      P'99'
PCTLSAVE  DS      CL1
```

Figure 8-7   A more generalized version of a PRINT subroutine

Discussion   Subroutines are useful primarily because they provide a means of im-
                            plementing a modular program design. However, subroutines are also
                            useful when they help reduce the amount of coding required by a pro-
                            gram. As a result, you may find a number of generalized subroutines in
                            common use in your shop.
                                  Since modular program design is a significant improvement over
                            traditional flowcharting techniques, you may find it useful when you
                            develop programs. However, you should realize that it's not the most cur-
                            rent method of program design. Structured program design is. As a result,
                            chapter 19 shows you how to develop structured programs in assembler
                            language. When you read that chapter, you will see that structured pro-
                            grams require the use of subroutines in much the same way that modular
                            programs do.

Terminology   subroutine
                            modular program design
                            modular flowchart
                            calling a module
                            calling module
                            called module
                            called subroutine
                            nested subroutines
                            linkage
                            linkage chain
                            return address
                            entry point
                            exit point
                            generalized subroutine

Objectives

                            1. Describe the benefits of modular program design.

                            2. Given a set of modular flowcharts, code the linkage between the pro-
                                gram modules.

TOPIC 2   How to use subprograms

Like a subroutine, a *subprogram* represents one module of a program. Unlike a subroutine, though, a subprogram is assembled by itself. Then, it is combined with the other modules of the program by the linkage editor.

Subprograms are useful for two main reasons. First, some routines are repeated in many different types of programs. As a result, by treating them as subprograms, they only need to be coded and assembled once. This reduces coding duplication, and thus programming effort.

Second, some routines can be written more efficiently in one language than in another. For instance, some functions can't be coded at all in COBOL. In a case like this, a COBOL main program can call an assembler language subprogram to perform the function. Since all of a computer's functions can be coded in assembler language, writing special-purpose subprograms is one of the main uses of assembler language.

SUBPROGRAM LINKAGE

When a higher-level module transfers control to a subprogram, it is referred to as *calling the subprogram*. Then, the higher-level module is the *calling module* and the subprogram is the *called module*. The coding that provides for the transfer of control between calling and called module is referred to as the *subprogram linkage*. This terminology, of course, is like the terminology related to subroutines.

Similarly, the calling module provides a *return address* to the subprogram, and it enters the subprogram at its *entry point*. When the subprogram returns to the calling module, it leaves at its *exit point*.

Adcon resolution

When you use subprograms, the calling module and the called module are assembled separately. As a result, the assembler can't determine the address of the called module during the assembly. Instead, the programmer uses assembler commands and adcons to tell the assembler that certain addresses can't be assembled correctly. Then, the linkage editor will resolve the addressing problems in a process called *adcon resolution* that is a part of linkage editing.

Figure 8-8 shows one way to provide for adcon resolution in the calling and called modules. This method uses EXTRN and ENTRY instructions. Once you understand this method of providing for adcon resolution, I'll show you two standard forms of subprogram linkage.

The EXTRN command in the calling module   Since the calling module doesn't know that RATESUB is the entry point of the subprogram, it can't be used as an operand in a BAL instruction that links to the subprogram. Instead, the name of the entry point in the subprogram must appear in an address constant like this:

```
ADDRSUB   DC      A(RATESUB)
```

Calling module			Subprogram		
	.		SUBPROG	START	0
	.			ENTRY	RATESUB
	L	12,ADDRSUB	RATESUB	BALR	10,0
	BALR	11,12		USING	*,10
	.			.	
	.			.	
	.			.	
	EXTRN	RATESUB		BR	11
ADDRSUB	DC	A(RATESUB)		END	

Figure 8-8   Using EXTRN and ENTRY instructions to provide for adcon resolution

Also, because RATESUB isn't defined in the calling module, this address constant must be preceded by an EXTRN command with RATESUB as the operand:

```
EXTRN RATESUB
```

The EXTRN command is a message to the assembler that the symbol appearing as an operand is external to this program. That is, it isn't defined within this program.

The EXTRN command causes the assembler to allow the address constant to be assembled as hex zeros (X'00000000'). It also causes the adcon to be put into a list for resolution by the linkage-editor program. Later on, the linkage editor will fill the adcon area with the proper address when it link edits the calling module and the subprogram.

An EXTRN command can have more than one operand. Also, you can code as many EXTRN commands as you need in a single program. For instance, a program that calls five subprograms might have these EXTRN statements:

```
EXTRN SUB1,SUB2,SUB3
EXTRN SUB4,SUB5
```

Since EXTRN statements don't generate any object code and therefore occupy no storage, they can be placed anywhere in a program. However, they must precede the use of the symbols that they define as external.

The ENTRY command in the subprogram   The ENTRY command in the subprogram in figure 8-8 tells the assembler to make the entry-point address available for resolution by the linkage editor. In other words, the ENTRY command is a counterpart to the EXTRN command. The ENTRY command also follows the same coding form as the EXTRN. You can use more than one operand in an ENTRY command and more than one command in a program.

In figure 8-8, an ENTRY command isn't actually needed because the subprogram only has one entry point. Instead, the subprogram could start with this instruction:

```
RATESUB   START 0
```

Since the address of the label on the START instruction is always available for adcon resolution, you don't have to code an ENTRY command if the entry point is the same as the address of the START instruction. In figure 8-8, both SUBPROG and RATESUB have the same address since the BALR instruction at RATESUB is the first machine instruction of the subprogram.

Multiple entry and exit points

In the last topic, I recommended that you write your subroutines with only one entry and exit point. In general, that's true for subprograms also. Subprograms are easiest to manage when they have only one entry and one exit point. Since it's relatively easy to make sure each subprogram has only one exit point, there's usually no problem there. But sometimes, it makes sense to write a subprogram that has more than one entry point.

To illustrate, consider the PRINT subroutine in the last topic that printed one detail line and provided for headings and page overflow. Now, think what it would take to make that subroutine into a subprogram. So the subprogram can be assembled separately, the DTF statement for the print file has to be in the subprogram along with the definitions for the I/O areas. No problem there, but remember that a print file has to be opened before it can print a record and it must be closed when a program ends. That means that the OPEN and CLOSE statements must also be in the subprogram.

If you're writing the subprogram, this leaves you with a design problem. Do you open and close the file each time the subprogram is called? That would be inefficient in terms of computer time. Or, do you provide three entry points for the subprogram: one for the opening of the file, one for the processing function of the subprogram, and one for the closing of the file? In many cases, this second alternative is the right solution for the problem.

If you code the subprogram with three entry points, the calling module must call the subprogram once at the start of the program using the first entry point to open the print file. It must call the subprogram repeatedly during the execution of the program to print the detail lines using the second entry point. And it must call the subprogram once at the end of the program using the third entry point to close the file. In a case like this, of course, the calling module must specify three entry points for adcon resolution. And the subprogram must specify three entry points too.

STANDARD LINKAGE

Figure 8-9 illustrates a form of subprogram linkage that is considered an informal standard within most IBM-supplied programs. As a result, it is often referred to as *standard linkage*.

Although figure 8-9 doesn't show the processing instructions of the subprogram, you should know that the subprogram finds an employee's pay rate (PAYRATE) when it is given the employee's pay class (PAYCLASS). In other words, the calling module sends the subprogram the PAYCLASS field and the subprogram returns the PAYRATE field. Both fields, however, are defined in the calling module. In this example, if the subprogram can't find the pay rate in the table, it returns a pay rate of 999.

The calling module

There are three important points to be noted in the calling module in figure 8-9. You should see how the PAYCLASS and PAYRATE fields are sent to the subprogram using an address list. You should learn how to code a Vcon. And you should make sure you understand the use of the BALR instruction.

Loading the address of the address list in register 1   In figure 8-9, the calling module starts by loading an address into register 1:

```
        LA    1,ADDRLIST
```

Here, ADDRLIST is the starting address of two adcons that contain the addresses of PAYCLASS and PAYRATE, the two fields to be passed to the subprogram. In other words, these adcons make up the *address list* that is going to be passed to the subprogram. In standard linkage, the address of this address list must always be loaded into register 1.

The Vcon that identifies the subprogram's entry point   Near the bottom of the calling module, a V-type address constant is coded for the subprogram's entry point. The effect of a *Vcon* is equal to the combination of an A-type adcon and an EXTRN for the symbol. As a result, the last two lines in the calling module in figure 8-8 could be coded with the single Vcon in figure 8-9:

```
    ADDRSUB   DC    V(RATESUB)
```

This Vcon causes a four-byte address constant (initially filled with hex zeros) to be defined, and the adcon is placed in the external symbol list for adcon resolution by the linkage editor.

The BALR instruction that calls the subprogram   To transfer control to the subprogram, the calling module in figure 8-9 uses this code:

```
        L     15,ADDRSUB
        BALR  14,15
```

The first instruction loads the address constant for the subprogram into register 15. Then, a BALR instruction puts the address of the next instruction in register 14, after which it branches to the address in register 15. In standard linkage, register 15 always contains the entry point of the subprogram that is being called, and register 14 always contains the return address.

The subprogram

The subprogram in figure 8-9 is, of course, coded to be compatible with the calling routine. Here, the ENTRY statement is omitted because the subprogram's only entry point, RATESUB, appears as the program name on the START instruction. There are several points to note in this subprogram related to the subprogram linkage so let's take them from the top.

The base register Since subprograms are assembled separately, they are not addressed by the calling module's base register. As a result, in the subprogram in figure 8-8, register 10 is loaded and assigned as the base register with the standard BALR and USING technique. The previous contents of register 10 are thus destroyed.

In figure 8-9, though, the USING instruction says that register 15 should be used as the base register in the subprogram. This is a commonly-used technique when writing subprograms, because it avoids the possibility of destroying the contents of some other register that may be used by the calling module. Note that a BALR instruction to load register 15 isn't necessary because the calling routine has already loaded the subprogram's starting address into it.

Storing and reloading the registers used by the subprogram In the subprogram in figure 8-9, the first machine instruction stores the contents of registers 6, 7, and 8:

```
STM    6,8,SAVE
```

It does this, because these are the registers that are going to be used by the subprogram. When the subprogram is ready to return to the calling module, it uses this instruction to reload the registers:

```
LM     6,8,SAVE
```

As a result, if the calling module is using registers 6, 7, or 8, the subprogram won't destroy the calling module's data.

Loading the address constants in the address list into registers After the subprogram in figure 8-9 stores registers 6 through 8, it loads the addresses in the address list into registers 6 and 7 using this instruction:

```
LM     6,7,0(1)
```

Here, register 1 is used in an explicit address in the load multiple instruction. Remember that register 1 was loaded with the starting address of the address list by the calling module.

After this instruction is executed, register 6 addresses the PAYCLASS

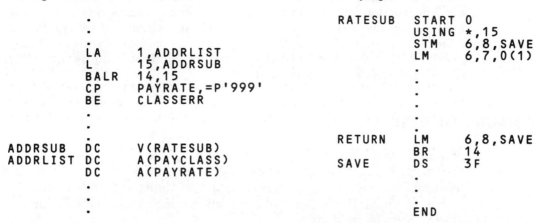

Calling module

```
             .
             .
             .
             LA      1,ADDRLIST
             L       15,ADDRSUB
             BALR    14,15
             CP      PAYRATE,=P'999'
             BE      CLASSERR
             .
             .
             .
ADDRSUB   DC        V(RATESUB)
ADDRLIST  DC        A(PAYCLASS)
          DC        A(PAYRATE)
             .
             .
             .
```

Subprogram

```
RATESUB   START   0
          USING   *,15
          STM     6,8,SAVE
          LM      6,7,0(1)
             .
             .
             .
             .
             .
RETURN    LM      6,8,SAVE
          BR      14
SAVE      DS      3F
             .
             .
          END
```

Notes:

1. Register 1 points to an address list.

2. Register 15 contains the subprogram entry point.

3. Register 14 contains the return address.

4. The subprogram entry point is defined with a Vcon.

Notes:

1. The entry point is the name given on the START command.

2. Register 15, loaded by the calling module, is used as the base register.

Figure 8-9   Standard subprogram linkage

---

field in the calling module; and register 7 addresses the PAYRATE field in the calling module. Registers 6 and 7 can then be used in instructions with explicit addresses to operate upon the PAYCLASS and PAYRATE fields.

The BR instruction that returns to the calling module   Just as in a subroutine, the BR instruction is used in a subprogram to return to the calling module. In figure 8-9, this instruction is used:

```
BR      14
```

As I said, register 14 is always used for the return address when using standard linkage.

The END instruction Note in the subprogram in figure 8-9 that the END instruction doesn't have an operand. That's because this module isn't going to be the first module in a phase that's assembled by the linkage editor. As a result, you should only specify an operand in your END statement when it won't be called by another module. You should never specify an operand in a subprogram.

STANDARD MACRO LINKAGE

Standard macro linkage is like standard linkage but it uses macro instructions to facilitate the linkage. It also uses a standard method of storing and reloading registers so that register data isn't destroyed and so there's a traceable chain from one subprogram to the next. This linkage is illustrated in figure 8-10.

The calling module

Loading the address of the save area into register 13 The first linkage instruction in the calling module in figure 8-10 is this:

```
LA      13,SAVE
```

This loads register 13 with the address of an 18-word save area defined in the calling module. As you will see in a moment, this address is used by the subprogram to save the contents of all 16 registers. In other words, the register contents are saved in the calling module's area.

The CALL macro In figure 8-10, the calling module uses this CALL macro to link to the subprogram:

```
CALL      RATESUB,(PAYCLASS,PAYRATE)
```

The code generated by this CALL macro is much like the standard linkage code used in figure 8-9. The first operand of the CALL macro is used in the definition of a V-type address constant; its address is loaded into register 15. The data names that appear in the second operand of the CALL macro (PAYCLASS and PAYRATE) are used to construct an address list; the address of this list is loaded into register 1. Finally, a BALR instruction is generated that uses register 14 for the return address and register 15 for the entry-point address. This causes the branch to the subprogram.

The subprogram

The SAVE macro The first executable code in the subprogram in figure 8-10 is generated by this SAVE macro:

```
SAVE    (14,12)
```

This macro generates a store multiple instruction that saves the contents of the register group specified within parentheses. In this case, registers 14 through 12 are stored. Using the wrap-around concept, this means that all of the registers except register 13 are stored.

The macro stores these registers in the 18-word save area addressed by register 13. As a result, for the standard macro linkage to work right, the address of the area to be used must have been placed in register 13 by the calling program. That means that the 18-word area is in the calling program, not the subprogram.

The 18-word save area has the fixed format that is given in figure 8-11. When the SAVE macro is assembled, it generates code so the registers will always be stored in the same locations within the save area. For instance, if register 3 has been included in the range specified in the SAVE macro, it is always stored in the ninth word. Although the programmer can use any register range in the SAVE macro, the range 14 through 12 is the most common way to code the macro.

Once the SAVE macro has been executed, the subprogram can use any registers except 13 without disrupting the operations of the calling program after its return. As a result, the subprogram in figure 8-10 uses a normal BALR/USING combination to load and assign register 3 as the base register for the subprogram. And it can use any register but 3 or 13 for other register functions.

Loading the address of the subprogram's save area into register 13   The two instructions that follow the USING statement prepare this subprogram so it can CALL other subprograms if required:

```
ST    13,SUBSAVE+4
LA    13,SUBSAVE
```

First, the address of the calling program's save area in register 13 is stored in the second word of the subprogram's own 18-word save area, SUBSAVE+4. Second, register 13 is loaded with the address of its own 18-word save area, SUBSAVE. When this has been done, the subprogram can link to another subprogram in which a SAVE macro is coded. I'll explain this "chaining" of save areas in more detail in a moment.

Loading the address constants into registers   The next instruction of the subprogram loads the addresses of PAYCLASS and PAYRATE into registers 6 and 7:

```
LM    6,7,0(1)
```

Because the CALL macro put the address of the address list in register 1, this LM instruction loads the registers starting with the word addressed by register 1. From this point on, the subprogram can operate upon the PAYCLASS and PAYRATE fields by referring to them using registers 6 and 7 as explicit base registers.

Calling module

```
         .
         .
         LA     13,SAVE
         CALL   RATESUB,(PAYCLASS,PAYRATE)
         CP     PAYRATE,=P'999'
         BE     CLASSERR
         .
         .
SAVE     DS     18F
         .
         .
```

Notes:

1. Register 13 is loaded with the address of an
    18-word save area.

2. The CALL macro does four things:
    a. it contructs the adcon list and places
        the list address in register 1;
    b. it loads register 15 with a Vcon literal
        that contains the address of the
        subprogram entry point;
    c. it loads register 14 with the return
        address; and
    d. it generates a BALR to the subprogram.

Figure 8-10   Standard macro linkage (part 1 of 2)

Reloading register 13   After the subprogram completes its lookup function, it can return to the calling module. But first, it must restore the original contents of the registers. To reload register 13, the subprogram uses this instruction:

```
         L       13,SUBSAVE+4
```

This loads the contents of the second word of the subprogram's save area into register 13. Since the address of the calling module's save area was stored in SUBSAVE+4 at the start of the subprogram, register 13 addresses the calling module's save area after this instruction is executed.

The RETURN macro   This RETURN macro is coded at the end of the subprogram in figure 8-10:

```
         RETURN  (14,12)
```

It generates instructions that do two things. First, registers 14 through 12

Subprogram

```
RATESUB    START   0
           SAVE    (14,12)
           BALR    3,0
           USING   *,3
           ST      13,SUBSAVE+4
           LA      13,SUBSAVE
           LM      6,7,0(1)
           .
           .
RETURN     L       13,SUBSAVE+4
           RETURN  (14,12)
SUBSAVE    DS      18F
           .
           .
           END
```

Notes:

1. The SAVE macro stores registers 14 through 12 in the calling module's save area.

2. Standard base register assignment is used.

3. Register 13 is stored in the second word of the subprogram save area.

4. Register 13 is loaded with the address of the subprogram save area.

5. Register 13 is reloaded with the address of the calling module's save area prior to return.

6. The RETURN macro reloads registers 14 through 12 and returns to the calling module.

Figure 8-10   Standard macro linkage (part 2 of 2)

are reloaded from the calling module's save area. Second, the subprogram branches back to the calling program by using the return address in register 14.

When you code the RETURN macro, you should make sure that its operands are identical to the operands of the SAVE macro with which it is paired so the proper registers are restored. You might notice that the RETURN macro has a six-character operation code, so you must start its operands in position 17, not 16, of the source statement.

Word	Displacement	Contents
1	0	Used by PL/I
2	4	Address of previous save area in calling program
3	8	Address of next save area
4	12	Contents of register 14
5	16	Contents of register 15
6	20	Contents of register 0
7	24	Contents of register 1
8	28	Contents of register 2
9	32	Contents of register 3
10	36	Contents of register 4
11	40	Contents of register 5
12	44	Contents of register 6
13	48	Contents of register 7
14	52	Contents of register 8
15	56	Contents of register 9
16	60	Contents of register 10
17	64	Contents of register 11
18	68	Contents of register 12

Figure 8-11   Assignments for a standard save area

NESTED SUBPROGRAMS

When one subprogram calls another subprogram, they are referred to as *nested subprograms*. And subprograms are frequently nested. In fact, you can think of VSE itself as a large nest of subprograms. A program of the operating system calls an application program that calls a subprogram and so on. That's why the chain that is provided by the standard macro linkage can be so useful.

Figure 8-12 shows the linkage for three levels of nested subprograms. If you follow the flow from the CALL of the first module to the second, you can see that the coding in this subprogram is the same as that illustrated in figure 8-10. Note, however, that the save area in all three modules is named SAVE. This is okay because the modules are assembled separately. Because the relationship between the calling module and the

Main program

```
          .
          .
          LA      13,SAVE
          .
          .
          CALL    SUB1,(.....)
          .
          .
          .
          .
          .
          .
SAVE      DS      18F
```

Word 1: Not used

Word 2: Not used

Word 3: Not used

Word 4: Register 14, return address

Word 5: Register 15, SUB1 address

Words 6-18: Registers 0-12

First subprogram

```
SUB1      START   0
          SAVE    (14,12)
          BALR    .....
          USING   .....
          ST      13,SAVE+4
          LA      13,SAVE
          .
          .
          CALL    SUB2,(.....)
          .
          L       13,SAVE+4
          RETURN  (14,12)
SAVE      18F
          END
```

Word 1: Not used

Word 2: Save address in calling module

Word 3: Not used

Word 4: Register 14, return address

Word 5: Register 15, SUB2 address

Words 6-18: Registers 0-12

Second subprogram

```
SUB2      START   0
          SAVE    (14,12)
          BALR    .....
          USING   .....
          ST      13,SAVE+4
          LA      13,SAVE
          .
          .
          .
          .
          L       13,SAVE+4
          RETURN  (14,12)
SAVE      DS      18F
          END
```

Word 1: Not used

Word 2: Save address in calling module

Words 3-18: Not used

Figure 8-12   Nested subprogram linkage using standard macros

called module is the same at any level, this nesting of subprograms can extend to any number of levels.

When you save and restore the registers using the SAVE and RETURN macros, you receive a special debugging benefit. Because the second word of each program's save area contains the address of the calling program's save area, a chain through each level of the structure exists. As a result, if the phase ends abnormally, the storage dump can be used to trace through each save area and figure out the path that was followed just before the abnormal termination.

LINKING A COBOL PROGRAM WITH AN ASSEMBLER LANGUAGE SUBPROGRAM

So far, I have only shown you the linkage from an assembler language calling module to an assembler language subprogram. But, as I've already mentioned, subprograms can be useful for performing tasks that are difficult or impossible to write in a higher-level language. At this time, then, I would like to present the linkage from a COBOL main program to an assembler language subprogram.

You will recall from topic 2 of chapter 6 that the PDUMP macro provides a dump of the general registers and the program area between two addresses that you supply as operands. Since you can't force a snapshot dump like this from a COBOL program, it is sometimes useful to call an assembler language subprogram for this function. Figure 8-13 shows the complete assembler language subprogram for this function along with the linkage for the COBOL program.

As you can see, the COBOL main program provides the starting and ending addresses for the dump by referring to its own data names in its link to the subprogram. Like the CALL macro in assembler language, the CALL statement in COBOL does several things. First, it constructs an address list from the data names identified in the USING portion of the statement, and it places the address of this list in register 1. Then, it loads the address of the subprogram into register 15, and it executes a BALR that branches to the address in register 15 and uses register 14 as the return address.

In the assembler language subprogram in figure 8-13, standard linkage is used, but either standard linkage or standard macro linkage can be used for a subprogram like this. Note in figure 8-13 that register 15 is used as the base register for the subprogram. Since it contains the address of the entry point of the subprogram, it doesn't have to be loaded because it already has the right value for the base register.

From this example, I think you can realize that it doesn't matter what language the calling program or subprogram are written in on an IBM mainframe. As long as you use standard linkage, you shouldn't have any linkage problems. Register 1 is always used as the address of the address list for the fields that are passed to the subprogram. Register 15 is always used for the address of the entry point in the subprogram. And register 14 is always used for the return address.

COBOL calling program

```
 DATA DIVISION.
*
 FILE SECTION.
         .
         .
 01  WORK-FIELDS.
*
     05   PDUMP-START          PIC X(11)      VALUE 'PDUMP START'.
     05   WORK-FIELD-1         PIC S9(5).
     05   WORK-FIELD-2         PIC S9(7).
         .
         .
     05   PDUMP-END            PIC X(9)       VALUE 'PDUMP END'.
         .
 PROCEDURE DIVISION.
*
         .
         .
     CALL 'PDUMP' USING PDUMP-START, PDUMP-END.
         .
         .
```

Assembler language subprogram

```
PDUMP      START 0
           USING *,15
           STM   6,7,SAVE
           LM    6,7,0(1)
           PDUMP (6),(7)
           LM    6,7,SAVE
           BR    14
SAVE       DS    2F
           END
```

Figure 8-13   An assembler language subprogram for a snapshot dump that is called by a COBOL program

Terminology

subprogram
calling a subprogram
calling module
called module
subprogram linkage
return address
entry point
exit point
adcon resolution
standard linkage
address list
Vcon
standard macro linkage
nested subprograms

Objectives

1. Given the description of a subprogram and its calling program, write the calling program in assembler language.

2. Given the description of a subprogram and its calling program, write the subprogram in assembler language.

TOPIC 3   VSE JCL for using subprograms

When you develop a program that calls one or more subprograms or when you develop a subprogram, you must provide JCL that assembles your program or subprogram, links the appropriate modules, and tests the resulting phase. When using subprograms, you're likely to encounter three combinations of calling modules and subprograms. In this topic, then, you'll learn how to code the job streams for these combinations.

VSE JCL for assembling and testing a program that calls one or more subprograms that are stored in a relocatable library

Many of the assembler language programs you write will call one or more existing subprograms. After you code this type of program, you assemble it just as you do any other program. Then, once the program has assembled without errors, you link edit it with the called subprograms in order to test it.

Figure 8-14 shows the JCL you need for this type of job. It's just like the job stream for assembling and testing a program that doesn't call subprograms except for the extra LIBDEF statement. In this example, the first LIBDEF statement uses the SEARCH format to set up a search chain for the relocatable libraries in which the called subprograms can be found. This information, of course, is used by the linkage editor. In this case, the linkage editor will look first in the library named USRRL2 for the subprograms called by the main program, then in USRRL3. If it can't find a subprogram in either of these libraries, it will search the system relocatable library.

You can specify more than one relocatable library in the LIBDEF statement as shown in figure 8-14. Also, if the search chain for your partition specifies the appropriate libraries, you don't need a LIBDEF statement for the relocatable libraries at all.

VSE JCL for assembling both calling program and subprogram, link editing them, and testing the resulting phase

Sometimes, you will develop both the calling program and the subprogram. In this case, you can assemble both modules at the same time, link edit them, and test them using the JCL in figure 8-15. This is just like the JCL for a simple assemble-and-test job, except that two job steps in a row are assembly steps. Note, then, that it doesn't use a LIBDEF statement for the relocatable library because neither main program nor subprogram are in that library.

```
// JOB      TEST
// OPTION   LINK,DUMP
// EXEC     ASSEMBLY
         .
         .  SOURCE CODE FOR MAIN PROGRAM
         .
/*
// LIBDEF   RL,SEARCH=(USRRL2,USRRL3)
// LIBDEF   CL,TO=USRCL2
// EXEC     LNKEDT
         .
         .  ASSGN AND DLBL STATEMENTS FOR DISK FILES
         .
// EXEC
/&
```

Figure 8-14   VSE JCL for assembling a program, linking it with a subprogram that's in a relocatable library, and testing the resulting phase

```
// JOB      TEST
// OPTION   LINK,DUMP
// EXEC     ASSEMBLY
         .
         .  SOURCE CODE FOR MAIN PROGRAM
         .
/*
// EXEC     ASSEMBLY
         .
         .  SOURCE CODE FOR SUBPROGRAM
         .
/*
// LIBDEF   CL,TO=USRCL2
// EXEC     LNKEDT
         .
         .  ASSGN AND DLBL STATEMENTS FOR DISK FILES
         .
// EXEC
/&
```

Figure 8-15   VSE JCL for assembling a program and a subprogram, linking the modules into one phase, and testing the phase

```
// JOB       TEST
// OPTION    LINK,DUMP
   INCLUDE   program-name
// EXEC      ASSEMBLY
   .
   .  SOURCE CODE FOR SUBPROGRAM
   .
/*
// LIBDEF    RL,SEARCH=(USRRL2)
// LIBDEF    CL,TO=USRCL2
// EXEC      LNKEDT
   .
   .  ASSGN AND DLBL STATEMENTS FOR DISK FILES
   .
// EXEC
/&
```

Figure 8-16   VSE JCL for assembling a subprogram, linking it with a main program that's in a relocatable library, and testing the resulting phase

VSE JCL for assembling a subprogram, link editing it with a calling program that's in a relocatable library, and testing the resulting phase

Occasionally, you will have to test a subprogram that is called by a main program that's already tested and stored in a relocatable library. Long after a subprogram has been put into production, for example, someone may discover a bug in it. Then, you have to modify the subprogram and test it to make sure that it works, even though the main program is assumed to work correctly.

Figure 8-16 shows the JCL you can use in this situation. This is like the code in figure 8-14 except for the INCLUDE statement. The INCLUDE statement tells the linkage editor that it should include a module from the relocatable library that isn't called by the module that's being assembled. In figures 8-14 and 8-15, an INCLUDE statement wasn't necessary because the calling programs identified the subprograms. But in figure 8-16, the subprogram doesn't identify the calling program so the INCLUDE statement is needed. Note in this figure that only one relocatable library is identified in the LIBDEF statement.

Discussion   Although this topic shows you the JCL that you're likely to need when you use subprograms, there's more to subprogram JCL than what's shown. As a professional programmer, for example, you need to know how to add modules to a relocatable library and how to maintain the ones that are already in the library. Also, you should know how to use the LISTLIB statement to find out what search chains are in effect. To learn how to use JCL like this, we strongly recommend our *VSE JCL* book by Steve Eckols.

Now that you know how to provide for the link editing of two or more object modules, you may want to consider what happens during link editing. Because base registers are used for addressing on an IBM mainframe, an object module can be loaded into any storage positions. Then, when the base registers are loaded during program execution, all operand addresses will address the appropriate fields or instructions. That, in fact, is one major reason for using base-plus-displacement addressing: the object modules can be easily relocated.

The only addresses that aren't base-plus-displacement addresses in an assembler language program are the address constants. During link-editing, then, the linkage editor has to put the proper addresses in the adcons of a program in the process called adcon resolution. The editor does this after it assigns storage locations to each object module to be linked.

Terminology   None

Objective   Given a testing job in one of the three forms presented in this topic, code VSE job streams for assembling, link editing, and testing the specified modules.

Section 3

Assembler language capabilities by function

Once you complete section 2, you can study any of the chapters in this section. In other words, you don't have to read chapters 9 through 12 in sequence. Each of the chapters in this section shows you how to use one or more of the assembler language functions such as table handling, bit manipulation, or macro writing.

Chapter   9

Table handling

Tables are used in many data processing applications. For example, a tax table may be used to look up the amount of income tax to be withheld from paychecks. To find the premium to be charged for an insurance policy, rating tables are often used. And in many statistical analyses, tables are printed to show how data breaks down into categories.

This chapter is divided into two topics. The first topic describes the coding and lookup techniques for simple tables, called single-level tables. The second topic describes the coding and techniques for more advanced tables, called multilevel tables.

TOPIC 1   Single-level tables

A *single-level table* is a table that tabulates data for one variable factor. For instance, the rate table in figure 9-1 is a single-level table in which the pay class is the variable. There are two standard methods for defining a table and looking up values in it. These two methods, called factor matching and positional lookup, are illustrated in this topic.

FACTOR MATCHING

Factor matching can be used for any table. In brief, the technique consists of searching through a table sequentially to find an entry that matches the variable factor you're looking for. But, before you can code the search routine, you must know how the table is defined.

How to define a table for factor matching

Suppose you want to store the rate table in figure 9-1 and use it to look up an employee's pay rate. Figure 9-2 shows two ways the table can be defined in assembler language. Both provide for the factor-matching method of lookup.

The first table consists of ten entries with each entry consisting of one pay class and one pay rate. Each pay class is two-bytes long in EBCDIC form. Each pay rate is two-bytes long in packed-decimal form.

The second table defines each entry in hex. In this case, the resulting object code for the entries is identical to that resulting from the first table definition. However, this second table ends with an entry containing hex FFFFFFFF. This entry will be used to indicate the end of the table in storage.

Although you can use either of the table definitions presented in figure 9-2, we recommend the second one. Since the second table ends with hex Fs, you don't have to know how many entries there are in the table so its processing routine can be more flexible than a routine using the first table definition. Since the second table definition uses only one line for each table entry, we think it is more readable than the first table definition.

In many cases, particularly if a table needs frequent changes, you won't define the values of the table in your program. Instead, you will read the table values into storage from a file at the start of the program using the register techniques described in chapter 7. Then, you only reserve the storage for the table in your program. If, for example, you were loading the first pay-rate table in figure 9-2 into your program from a table file, you could define the table area in your program like this:

```
PAYTABLE DS    10CL4
```

Pay Class	Pay Rate
1	4.21
2	4.39
3	4.58
4	4.77
5	4.97
6	5.17
7	5.38
8	5.60
9	5.81
10	6.03

Figure 9-1   A single-level table

When a table's values are loaded from a file, you can change the table values without changing the programs that use the table. Since that's an important benefit, the values for most tables are stored in table files. Then, any program that uses the table has to first read the file and load the table values. If you learn how to look up the rates in the tables defined in figure 9-2, you shouldn't have any trouble coding a routine that loads a table's values so I won't take the time to illustrate a loading routine.

How to use factor matching

When you use factor matching, you search a table sequentially. To show you how this is done, I will use the second table definition in figure 9-2. Starting at the first entry, you compare the input pay class with the pay-class value in the table. If the pay classes match, you use the corresponding pay rate to calculate the worker's pay. If the pay-class values don't match, you compare the input pay class with the next entry in the table. If you reach the end of the table without finding a match, you can assume that the input pay class is invalid.

This sequential search technique is illustrated by the routine in figure 9-3. This routine uses register 8 as a substitute base register so the search can be done in a loop. To start, register 8 is loaded with the address of the table by using the LA instruction. Then, the CLC instruction compares the pay-class field in the input record, EMPPAYCL, to the first two bytes of the first table entry. If they are equal, the BE instruction transfers control to the instruction named PAYFOUND, which is the first instruction of the routine that calculates the worker's pay. Since the pay rate to be used is two bytes beyond the address in register 8, the following instruction is the first one in the PAYFOUND routine:

```
PAYFOUND ZAP    PAYWORK,2(2,8)
```

It places the pay rate from the table (the two-byte field addressed by register 8 plus a displacement of 2) into the field named PAYWORK.

If EMPPAYCL and the pay class in the table don't match, control falls

Method 1

```
PAYTABLE DS      0CL40
         DC      C'01'
         DC      PL2'421'
         DC      C'02'
         DC      PL2'439'
         DC      C'03'
         DC      PL2'458'
         DC      C'04'
         DC      PL2'477'
         DC      C'05'
         DC      PL2'497'
         DC      C'06'
         DC      PL2'517'
         DC      C'07'
         DC      PL2'538'
         DC      C'08'
         DC      PL2'560'
         DC      C'09'
         DC      PL2'581'
         DC      C'10'
         DC      PL2'603'
```

Method 2

```
PAYTABLE DS      0CL44
         DC      X'F0F1421C'
         DC      X'F0F2439C'
         .
         .
         .
         DC      X'F1F0603C'
         DC      X'FFFFFFFF'
```

Figure 9-2   Two table definitions for the factor-matching technique

through the branch to the next instruction. Then, the CLI instruction checks to see if the end of the table has been reached. If the table entry is hex FF, indicating the end of the table, the BE instruction that follows will branch to an error routine named NOTFOUND. If neither a match nor end-of-table is found, the program must go through the loop again to examine the next table entry. To do this, the LA instruction increases register 8 by four so it contains the address of the next table entry, and the program branches to the beginning of the loop, CMPCLASS.

Factor matching can be used for many kinds of tables because the variable factors don't have to form a continuous sequence. If, for example, some old pay classes are deleted from the table and some new ones are added to it, the lookup routine in figure 9-3 will still work. Also, it doesn't matter what order the table entries are in. If the table entries are in reverse order or completely out of order, the proper pay rate will still be found by matching with the pay class.

The sequence of entries can, however, affect the efficiency of the lookup routine in terms of processing time. Since the table is always searched from the first to the last entry, the most-used entry should be the first one in the table and the least-used entry should be the last. If, for example, 65 of the 100 jobs in a factory are for pay class 4, why compare pay class to classes 1, 2, and 3 before getting to class 4? Instead, class 4 should be the first entry in the table. Similarly, the rest of the table should be sequenced according to frequency of use. You can imagine what a difference this could make for the pay-rate lookup if class 10 were the most frequently used class.

```
                          .
                          .
                          .
                   LA     8,PAYTABLE
          CMPCLASS CLC    EMPPAYCL,0(8)
                   BE     PAYFOUND
                   CLI    0(8),X'FF'
                   BE     NOTFOUND
                   LA     8,4(8)
                   B      CMPCLASS
                          .
                          .
                          .
          PAYFOUND ZAP    PAYWORK,2(2,8)
                          .
                          .
                          .
          PAYTABLE DS     0CL44
                   DC     X'F0F1421C'
                   DC     X'F0F2439C'
                   DC     X'F0F3458C'
                   DC     X'F0F4477C'
                   DC     X'F0F5497C'
                   DC     X'F0F6517C'
                   DC     X'F0F7538C'
                   DC     X'F0F8560C'
                   DC     X'F0F9581C'
                   DC     X'F1F0603C'
                   DC     X'FFFFFFFF'
          PAYWORK  DS     PL2
                          .
                          .
                          .
```

Figure 9-3   A table lookup routine that uses factor matching

POSITIONAL LOOKUP

When you use a *positional lookup* technique, you locate a table entry by its position in the table rather than by matching factors. To use this technique, the variable factors must form an unbroken sequence. Then, when you define the table, you don't have to include the variable factors.

How to define a table for positional lookup

To illustrate the table definition for a positional lookup, I will again use the rate table presented in figure 9-1. Since the variable factor in this table, pay class, forms an unbroken sequence, the positional lookup method can be used. Figure 9-4 shows a table definition that can be used with this method. Here, only the pay rates are defined in the table. The pay classes can be determined by the position of each entry in the table.

```
                         .
                         .
                         .
              PACK    PAYCLASS,EMPPAYCL
              CP      PAYCLASS,LOWLIMIT
              BL      CLASSERR
              CP      PAYCLASS,HILIMIT
              BH      CLASSERR
              LA      12,PAYTABLE
              ZAP     TABCOUNT,LOWLIMIT
   COMPLOOP   CP      TABCOUNT,PAYCLASS
              BE      RATEFND
              AP      TABCOUNT,=P'1'
              LA      12,2(12)
              B       COMPLOOP
   RATEFND    ZAP     WRATE,0(2,12)
                         .
                         .
                         .
   TABCOUNT   DS      PL2
   HILIMIT    DC      P'10'
   LOWLIMIT   DC      P'1'
   PAYCLASS   DS      PL2
   WRATE      DS      PL2
   PAYTABLE   DS      0CL20
              DC      PL2'421'
              DC      PL2'439'
              DC      PL2'458'
              DC      PL2'477'
              DC      PL2'497'
              DC      PL2'517'
              DC      PL2'538'
              DC      PL2'560'
              DC      PL2'581'
              DC      PL2'603'
```

Figure 9-4   A positional table lookup routine that uses the counting technique

How to use positional lookup

To look up a pay rate in this table, you must use the input pay class as some sort of index. There are two techniques for doing this. One is to start at the beginning of the table and count through the entries until the count is equal to the input pay class. The other is to convert the input pay class to a displacement value.

The counting technique   The first of these techniques, known as the *counting technique*, is illustrated in figure 9-4. The first five instructions of this routine check to see that the input pay class (EMPPAYCL) is a value from one through ten. If the value is less than one or more than ten, the program branches to a routine named CLASSERR and the lookup is *not* performed. If the pay class is a valid number, the address of the table is loaded into register 12 and a value of one is placed in the count field. The program then enters the table-lookup loop.

In the lookup loop, the counter field, TABCOUNT, is compared with the packed input pay-class field, PAYCLASS. If they are equal, register 12 points to the proper pay rate and the program branches to RATEFND. If they're not equal, TABCOUNT is increased by one, register 12 is increased by two so it points to the next pay-rate entry, and the program repeats the loop. Since the program has already checked to see that the input pay class is in the proper range, there should always be a match. In the RATEFND instruction (the first instruction of the pay-calculation routine), the table value addressed by register 12 is placed in the field named WRATE.

The direct-addressing technique   Figure 9-5 illustrates a second way to use the input pay class as an index to the positional pay-rate table. This is known as the *direct-addressing technique*. Here, the input pay class is converted to a displacement value. Then, by adding this displacement value to the starting address of the table, the proper pay rate can be addressed directly.

The first five instructions of this routine perform the range check of the input pay-class value. First, the pay class is packed into a doubleword work area so it will be ready to convert to binary. If the pay class is within the proper range (from one through ten), the lookup continues. If not, the routine branches to CLASSERR and the lookup isn't performed.

The next five instructions determine the address of the proper pay rate. First, the input pay class is converted to binary in register 7. Second, the value in register 7 is reduced by one. Third, the value in register 7 is multiplied by two. (Since the multiply instruction, described in chapter 7, requires an even-odd pair of registers as the first operand, the first operand is registers 6 and 7. When the multiply instruction is executed, the product is placed in both registers. In this case, since the product will be between zero and 18, all significant bits in the answer are in register 7.) Fourth, the address of the table is loaded into register 8. Fifth, the address in register 8 is added to the displacement in register 7 so register 7 contains the address of the appropriate table value. The next instruction

```
ZAP     WRATE,0(2,7)
```

stores this rate in a work field named WRATE and the pay calculation begins.

Note that if a sequence of variable factors starts at a value other than one, this direct-addressing technique can still be used. In a case like this, you subtract an appropriate value from the variable factor at the start of the routine. If, for example, the pay classes started at 11, you would subtract 11 from pay class at the start of the routine. Similarly, the multiplication factor is determined by the length of the table entries. If the pay classes were four bytes long, the multiplication factor would be four.

```
                         .
                         .
                         PACK    DBLEWORK,EMPPAYCL
                         CP      DBLEWORK,LOWLIMIT
                         BL      CLASSERR
                         CP      DBLEWORK,HILIMIT
                         BH      CLASSERR
                         CVB     7,DBLEWORK
                         S       7,=F'1'
                         M       6,=F'2'
                         LA      8,PAYTABLE
                         AR      7,8
                         ZAP     WRATE,0(2,7)
                         .
                         .
                         .
        DBLEWORK  DS     D
        HILIMIT   DC     P'10'
        LOWLIMIT  DC     P'1'
        PAYTABLE  DS     0CL20
                  DC     PL2'421'
                  DC     PL2'439'
                  DC     PL2'458'
                  DC     PL2'477'
                  DC     PL2'497'
                  DC     PL2'517'
                  DC     PL2'538'
                  DC     PL2'560'
                  DC     PL2'581'
                  DC     PL2'603'
        WRATE     DS     PL2
                         .
                         .
                         .
```

Figure 9-5   A positional table lookup routine that uses the direct-addressing technique

The direct-addressing technique, like the counting technique, works best if the variable factors form an unbroken sequence. If there are only a few "holes" in the sequence as in 1, 2, 3, 5, 6, 7, 9, 10, 11, and 12, you can fill them with dummy entries. However, if there are many holes in the table, the technique becomes inefficient.

Discussion   As you have seen, handling single-level tables in assembler language is quite easy once you know how to code register operations. In general, you search tables with simple loops by using explicit operands and manipulating the entry addresses in a substitute base register. Whenever you must design a table and the search routine that goes with it, your objectives should be (1) to cover all possible conditions and (2) to maximize processing efficiency.

Terminology   single-level table
                factor matching
                positional lookup
                counting technique
                direct-addressing technique

Objective   Given program specifications involving a single-level table, code the required assembler language routine.

TOPIC 2   Multilevel tables

For many table-lookup problems, single-level tables can't do the job. Then, *multilevel tables* must be used. Income tax withholding tables, for instance, vary based on two factors: amount of pay and number of dependents. Because two variables are involved, an income tax table can be referred to as a *two-level table*.

Three-level tables are also relatively common. Figure 9-6, for example, is a three-level insurance table. The three variable factors (age, sex, and job class) determine the premium to be charged for accident insurance.

How to define a multilevel table

A two- or three-level table can be designed as a factor-matching table, a positional table, or a combination of the two. For the table in figure 9-6, I would use factor matching for the age variable, and positional lookup for the sex and job class variables. I would choose factor matching for the age variable for two reasons: (1) because each table entry serves a range of ages, not just one age, and (2) because the size and range of the age brackets are likely to change. If the age factor were to be treated in positional terms, a change in the number of age brackets would cause a change in the table search routine. On the other hand, the number of sex and job class categories are fixed. These factors can therefore be handled most efficiently by using a positional lookup technique.

If the values in this table weren't ever going to change, I would define this three-level table as shown in figure 9-7. Here, there are six entries for each age bracket. The last entry has nines as the low and high age limit to indicate the end of the table.

In practice, though, the values in an insurance table like this are likely to change. As a result, the table values would probably be stored in a table file. Then, any program that uses the table has to first read the file and load the table values. If you learn how to look up the rates in the table defined in figure 9-7, though, you shouldn't have any trouble coding a routine that loads the table values so I won't take the time to illustrate one.

How to search a multilevel table

Figure 9-8 shows a lookup routine for the table defined in figure 9-7. This routine will find the proper insurance rate when age, sex code (M or F), and job-class code (1 or 2) are input fields. First, the address of the table is loaded into register 7, the input age (INPAGE) is packed, and its value is compared with the lower limit of the first age-bracket entry:

```
CP      AGEWRK,0(2,7)
```

	Men		Women	
Age	Class 1	Class 2	Class 1	Class 2
18-34	$23.50	$27.05	$24.75	$28.45
35-39	24.00	27.55	25.80	29.50
40-44	24.60	28.15	27.10	30.80
45-49	25.30	28.85	29.10	32.80
50-54	26.30	29.85	31.55	35.25
55-59	28.00	31.55	35.00	38.70

Figure 9-6   A three-level insurance table

```
RATETAB    DS    0CL112
           DC    PL2'18'          Low age limit
           DC    PL2'34'          High age limit
Age        DC    PL3'2350'        Rate for men, class 1
Segment    DC    PL3'2705'        Rate for men, class 2
1          DC    PL3'2475'        Rate for women, class 1
           DC    PL3'2845'        Rate for women, class 2
                  .
                  .
                  .
           DC    PL2'55'          Low age limit
           DC    PL2'59'          High age limit
Age        DC    PL3'2800'        Rate for men, class 1
Segment    DC    PL3'3155'        Rate for men, class 2
6          DC    PL3'3500'        Rate for women, class 1
           DC    PL3'3870'        Rate for women, class 2

End of     DC    PL2'99'
Table      DC    PL2'99'
Entry      DC    4PL3'99999'
```

Figure 9-7   A three-level table definition

If the input age is lower than this lower limit of the table, a branch to AGEERR takes place and the table lookup isn't performed.

Next, the program enters a factor-matching loop for the proper age bracket. In this loop, a lower limit of 99 indicates that the end-of-table has been reached and a branch to AGEERR takes place. To find the proper bracket, the input age is compared with the higher limit of each age segment. If the age is lower than or equal to this higher limit, the proper bracket has been found. Otherwise, 16 is added to register 7 (the size of each age segment) and the loop is repeated.

When the age bracket is found, four is added to register 7. Then, the sex code is compared to M. If they are equal, the program goes to MALE

```
                   .
                   .
                   .
            LA     7,RATETAB
            PACK   AGEWRK,INPAGE
            CP     AGEWRK,0(2,7)
            BL     AGEERR
AGELOOP     CP     0(2,7),=P'99'
            BE     AGEERR
            CP     AGEWRK,2(2,7)
            BNH    AGEFOUND
            LA     7,16(7)
            B      AGELOOP
AGEFOUND    LA     7,4(7)
            CLI    INPSEX,C'M'
            BE     MALE
            LA     7,6(7)
MALE        CLI    INPJOBCL,C'1'
            BE     RATEFND
            LA     7,3(7)
RATEFND     ZAP    RATEWRK,0(3,7)
                   .
                   .
                   .
AGEWRK      DS     PL2
RATEWRK     DS     PL3
RATETAB     DS     0CL112
            DC     PL2'18'
            DC     PL2'34'
            DC     PL3'2350'
            DC     PL3'2705'
            DC     PL3'2475'
            DC     PL3'2845'
                   .
                   .
                   .
            DC     PL2'55'
            DC     PL2'59'
            DC     PL3'2800'
            DC     PL3'3155'
            DC     PL3'3500'
            DC     PL3'3870'
            DC     PL2'99'
            DC     PL2'99'
            DC     4PL3'9999'
```

Figure 9-8   A three-level lookup routine that uses both factor matching and positional lookup techniques

and register 7 is left unchanged. If they are unequal, indicating a female, the program adds six to the address in register 7 so it points to the first of the women's rates instead of the men's.

Finally, a comparison of the input job class is made. If the job class is equal to one, the register is pointing at the proper rate-table entry. If it isn't one, the input pay class must be two. Then, three is added to the address in register 7 so it points to the rate that should be used.

As you should realize by now, this table-lookup routine is actually three single-level table lookups combined. The age-group lookup picks a table segment rather than an individual table entry. Then, within an age segment, the sex code picks a smaller segment composed of two individual rate entries. Finally, the job class is used to select one of the two rate entries.

This same type of table structure can be used for more than three levels. Then, each level of the structure corresponds to one input factor and you can use either factor-matching or positional lookup techniques for it. In practice, though, you will rarely come across tables that require more than three levels.

Discussion   Most tables are stored in files so they can be updated without making changes to the programs that use them. As a result, you must keep future changes in mind when you design multilevel tables and be sure to reserve space for these changes in your table definitions. You must also code your processing routines so they are adaptable to table changes. In figure 9-8, for example, you should note that the routine will work whether the number of age brackets is increased or decreased, whether the lower limit of the first age bracket is lowered, or whether any of the other age limits are changed.

Terminology   multilevel table
two-level table
three-level table

Objective   Given program specifications involving a multilevel table, code the required assembler language routine.

Chapter 10

Editing, bit manipulation, and translation

This chapter starts by presenting some new patterns that can be used with the edit instruction along with a new instruction, the edit-and-mark instruction. Next, it presents some instructions that let you manipulate the bits within bytes of data. Finally, it presents some instructions that let you translate data from one form to another or to manipulate the bytes within fields.

EDITING

In chapters 4 and 5 you were introduced to some simple editing patterns for the edit instruction. For completeness, figure 10-1 presents those patterns along with some new patterns. The patterns you already are familiar with are in groups 1 through 3.

In group 4, you can see patterns that use nonblank fill characters. If, for example, you use a dollar sign or an asterisk as the fill character, a string of those characters is made to precede the first significant digit in the edited result. This feature is commonly used when printing checks so the amount of the check cannot easily be tampered with.

In group 5, you can see how message characters can be used to indicate negative values. In the first three examples, you can see the minus sign used as the message charater. In the next three, the message characters are a blank followed by CR. When you use message characters to the right of the rightmost digit position in an edit pattern, the characters are left unchanged if the value being edited is negative. But, if the value is positive, these rightmost message characters are replaced by the fill character. As a result, you can print one or more message characters after a negative number. You can use any message characters to indicate a negative field, but the most common ones are CR, DB, and the minus sign.

In group 6, you can see date-field editing. Here, the message characters are inserted into a seven-digit date field. As the examples show, slashes, hyphens, or blanks are commonly used when editing a date.

Finally, in group 7, you can see patterns that cause an edit instruction to edit two or more fields. For this to work, the fields to be edited must be located in successive bytes of storage and the receiving field must have one or more *field separators* (hex 22s) between the individual edit patterns. As you can see in figure 10-1, you use only one fill character in the receiving field no matter how many fields are going to be edited by a single edit instruction. This fill character is used for all fields to be edited, and it replaces all field separators during editing.

Edit-and-mark (EDMK)

The edit-and-mark instruction is used primarily in programs that print money values. The EDMK instruction operates in exactly the same manner as the edit instruction except that it also stores the address of the first significant digit in register 1. You can then use this register 1 to place a dollar sign to the left of the first digit of the edited value. This is often referred to as using a *floating dollar sign*.

Figure 10-2 presents a routine that uses the edit-and-mark instruction. If the value is 1.23, the edited result will print as $1.23. If the value is .05, the edited result will print as $.05. Note that you must subtract one from register 1 to address the proper byte for the dollar sign in the edited result.

Did you notice this LA instruction at the start of the routine in figure 10-2?

```
LA      1,PRTVALUE+4
```

This instruction loads the address that corresponds to the decimal point in the edited result field into register 1. This is required because the EDMK instruction doesn't load any value into register 1 if the sending field contains no significant digits until after the significance starter in the receiving field has been reached. As a result, a value like .05 doesn't cause a proper address to be loaded into register 1 by the EDMK instruction. If this routine didn't start with the LA instruction, the MVI instruction wouldn't put the floating dollar sign in the right place for a value like .05. But with the LA instruction, this routine works correctly whether significance is started by a significant digit or by a significance starter in the edit pattern.

BIT MANIPULATION

Bit manipulation instructions are often called "bit twiddlers" because you use them to test or change selected bits in an eight-bit byte. The three most important instructions in this group are the OR, the AND, and the test-under-mask instruction.

Group	Sending field	Receiving field pattern	Edited result field	Printed result field
1 Lead zero suppression	12345C	40202020202020	40F1F2F3F4F5	12345
	00123F	40202020202020	40404F1F2F3	123
	00000C	40202020202020	404040404040	
2 Significance starting	00511F	40202020212020	404040F5F1F1	511
	00001C	40202020212020	4040404040F1	1
	00000C	40202020212020	4040404040F0	0
3 Decimal point and comma insertion	123456789C	402020206B2020206B202120	40F1F2F36BF4F5F66BF7F8F9	123,456,789
	000123456C	402020206B2020206B202120	404040404040F1F2F36BF4F5F6	123,456
	000000123C	402020206B2020206B202120	40404040404040404040F1F2F3	123
	1234567C	402020202020214B2020	40F1F2F3F4F54BF6F7	12345.67
	0000123F	402020202020214B2020	4040404040F14BF2F3	1.23
	0000005D	402020202020214B2020	4040404040404BF0F5	.05
4 Non-blank fill character	12345C	5C202020202020	5CF1F2F3F4F5	*12345
	00123F	5C202020202020	5C5C5CF1F2F3	***123
	00000C	5C202020202020	5C5C5C5C5C5C	******
	123456789C	5B206B2020206B2020214B2020	5BF16BF2F3F46BF5F6F74BF8F9	$1,234,567.89
	000000123C	5B206B2020206B2020214B2020	5B5B5B5B5B5B5BF14BF2F3	$$$$$$$1.23
	000000005C	5B206B2020206B2020214B2020	5B5B5B5B5B5B5B5B4BF0F5	$$$$$$$$.05
5 Message characters for negative fields	01234C	40202020202060	4040F1F2F3F44040	1234
	01234D	40202020202060	4040F1F2F3F460	1234-
	00000C	40202020202060	404040404040 40	
	00123C	40202020214B202040C3D9	404040F14BF2F3404040	1.23
	00001D	40202020214B202040C3D9	40404040404BF0F14040C3D9	.01 CR
	00000C	40202020214B202040C3D9	404040404040 4BF0F0404040	.00
6 Date editing	0020485F	40202021612020612020	404040F261F0F461F8F5	2/04/85
	0121985F	40202021602020602020	4040F1F260F1F960F8F5	12-19-85
	0120285F	40202021402020402020	4040F1F240F0F240F8F5	12 02 85
7 Field separators	123C123C123F	40202120222022202120	40F1F2F34040F1F2F34040F1F2F3	123 123 123
	100C000C001C	40202120222022202120	40F1F0F04040404040F14040404040F1	100 0 1
	123C12345C	402021202222202021204B2020	404040F1F2F34040F1F2F34BF4F5	123 123.45
	001C000000C	402121202222202021204B2020	40404040F14040404040404BF0F0	1 .00

Figure 10-1   Editing patterns

```
            LA      1,PRTVALUE+4
            MVC     PRTVALUE,PATTERN
            EDMK    PRTVALUE,VALUE
            S       1,=F'1'
            MVI     0(1),C'$'
            .
            .
            .
PRTVALUE    DS      CL7
VALUE       DS      PL3
PATTERN     DC      XL7'402020214B2020'
```

Figure 10-2   A routine that uses the edit-and-mark instruction to place a floating dollar sign

OR
(OI, OC, O, OR)

When an OR instruction is executed, the bits in the sending field (operand-2) are used to modify the bits in the receiving field (operand-1) according to the table in figure 10-3. If, for example, the leftmost bit is 1 in the sending field and 0 in the receiving field, it is changed to 1 in the receiving field. You should be able to see from the table why this instruction is named OR. A bit in the receiving field is on after the execution of the OR instruction if the bit is on initially *or* if the associated bit in the sending field is on.

Figure 10-3 also illustrates the execution of an OR instruction on a one-byte field. As you can see, if both bits in a bit position are off, the result bit is off; otherwise, the result bit is on. By constructing a sending pattern of on-bits, you can force selected bits in the receiving field to be turned on, while leaving others unchanged. In this example, the zone bits are unchanged, while all of the digit bits are turned on.

The OR instruction is used in four forms. These are the immediate, storage-to-storage, register-to-storage, and register-to-register forms. They are illustrated in figure 10-4. The immediate and storage-to-storage forms are used most often.

How to use the immediate form of the OR instruction   The immediate form of the OR instruction offers an easy way to change the zone bits of a sign byte from hex C to hex F after unpacking a decimal field. This is illustrated in the first example in figure 10-4. Here, the type code B for binary is used in the immediate operand. Then, the binary digits 1 and 0 are used in the nominal value. This type code can also be used in DS and DC statements. Because any immediate operand with the same bit pattern, 11110000, can also be used, the following instructions have the same effect:

```
OI      PRTVALUE+4,X'F0'
OI      PRTVALUE+4,C'0'
```

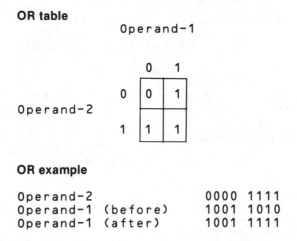

Figure 10-3   The execution of the OR instruction

The OR-immediate can also be used to turn bits on as program switches. For instance, the instruction

```
OI     PRGSWTCH,B'00000001'
```

sets the rightmost bit in the one-byte PRGSWTCH field to on. This bit might be used to indicate that the eighth field in an input record is invalid. The test-under-mask instruction can then be used to test this bit setting and set an appropriate condition code, as you'll learn in a minute.

How to use the storage-to-storage form of the OR instruction   The storage-to-storage version of the OR instruction is often used to change blanks in numeric input fields to zeros as shown in the example in figure 10-4. This is done to prevent abnormal program terminations due to invalid numeric data (blanks). If the input field does contain numeric data, the OR doesn't change it at all because the digit bits in the second operand are all zeros. However, if a byte in the field contains a blank, it will be changed to hex F0.

Note in the example in figure 10-4 that an invalid character like the letter D will also be changed to a valid numeric value when this technique is used. If, for example, INPQTY contains a character D (hex C4) in its third byte, the byte will have a numeric value of 4 after the OR operation. Although it's sometimes okay to convert blanks to zeros in an editing routine, it usually isn't okay to convert letters and special characters to numbers. As a result, you must know what type of input data your program might encounter before you can code your editing routines properly.

The immediate form

```
        OI      PRTVALUE+4,B'11110000'
```

	Before	After
PRTVALUE	F0 F0 F6 F4 C3	F0 F0 F6 F4 F3

The storage-to-storage form

```
        OC      INPQTY,ORPATRN
        .
        .
        .
INPQTY  DS      CL4
ORPATRN DC      4X'F0'
```

	Before	After
INPQTY	40 40 C4 40	F0 F0 F4 F0

The register-to-storage form

```
        O       6,FULLWORD
        .
        .
        .
FULLWORD DC     F'1'
```

	Before	After
Register 6	00 00 03 02	00 00 03 03

The register-to-register form

```
        L       7,WORD1
        OR      6,7
        .
        .
        .
WORD1   DC      F'1'
```

	Before	After
Register 6	00 00 04 02	00 00 04 03

Figure 10-4   The four forms of the OR instruction

AND table

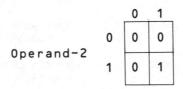

AND example

```
Operand-2              1111 0000
Operand-1 (before)     1011 0101
Operand-1 (after)      1011 0000
```

Figure 10-5   The execution of the AND instruction

```
NI      PRGSWTCH,B'11111110'
NC      FIELDA,ANDPATRN
N       6,FULLWORD
NR      9,3
```

Figure 10-6   The four forms of the AND instruction

AND
(NI, NC, N, NR)

The AND instructions are used to turn off selected bits in a receiving field. This is shown in figure 10-5. When an AND instruction is executed, the resulting bit is on only if both operands have an on-bit in the same position. You can see from the AND table why this instruction is named AND. A bit in the receiving field is on after the execution of an AND instruction only if the bit is on initially *and* if the related bit in the sending field is on.

The most widely used form of the AND instruction is the AND immediate, as illustrated in the first example in figure 10-6. In this case, the first seven bits of PRGSWTCH will be left unchanged. However, the eighth bit will be set to off no matter what its previous setting was.

When coding AND patterns, code a zero in all bit positions you want to set to off and a one in the positions you want to stay as they are. Although the storage-to-storage (NC), register-to-storage (N), and register-to-register (NR) forms of the AND instruction are available, they aren't commonly used.

Operation code	Meaning	Remarks
BO	Branch if ones	The branch is taken if all the tested bits are on.
BM	Branch if mixed	The branch is taken if some of the tested bits are on, some off.
BZ	Branch if zeros	The branch is taken if all the tested bits are off, or zero.
BNO	Branch if not ones	The branch is taken if one, some, or all of the tested bits are off.

Figure 10-7   The branch instructions used with the test-under-mask instruction

Test-under-mask (TM)   The test-under-mask instruction allows you to check the status of one or more bits in a byte. This is an immediate instruction with the second operand used as a mask for selecting the bits to be tested. For example, the following test-under-mask instruction tests the condition of the one-byte field named PRGSWTCH:

```
TM      PRGSWTCH,B'00000001'
```

Since the mask only has a one-bit in the rightmost position, only that bit in PRGSWTCH will be tested. If you wanted to test both the seventh and eighth bits, you would code this instruction:

```
TM      PRGSWTCH,B'00000011'
```

When executed, the TM instruction sets a condition code based on the results it finds in the bit positions indicated by the mask. The resulting condition code can be used to alter the processing sequence of the program by using one of the mnemonic branch instructions in figure 10-7.

How to use the test-under-mask instruction to check program switches   The most common use of the test-under-mask instruction is to check the setting of program switches. To illustrate, suppose you are coding a portion of a program to check the validity of input data in four fields. If one of the four fields is invalid, the corresponding bit in a byte named ERRBYTE is turned on. Then, if one of these bits is on, your program must execute a routine that prints an error message. If they are all off, your program must continue with the processing of the input data.

Figure 10-8 shows how you can check ERRBYTE using the test-under-mask instruction. After each of the data fields is examined and the appropriate bits are turned on in the program switch, the test-under-mask instruction is used to test the bits. If all of the bits tested are off, the program

Bit meanings for ERRSWTCH

Bit 1:   Error in FIELD1
Bit 2:   Error in FIELD2
Bit 3:   Error in FIELD3
Bit 4:   Error in FIELD4

Code to test the error bits

```
      .
      .
      TM       ERRSWTCH,B'11110000'
      BZ       PROCESS
      .
      .
```

Figure 10-8   Code that uses the test-under-mask instruction to test the bits of an error switch

branches to the routine labeled PROCESS. Otherwise, control falls through the branch to the next instruction, which should be the first instruction of the error print routine.

TRANSLATION

Most high-level languages are limited when it comes to translating data from one code to another. They are also limited when it comes to handling free-form input data, the kind that is often used in teleprocessing applications. As a result, assembler language programs and subprograms are often used for functions like these. When you code these functions, you use the translate, the translate-and-test, and the execute instructions.

Translate (TR)

The translate instruction can translate the bit pattern of each byte in a field to any other bit pattern. This instruction works in conjunction with a table that gives the bit patterns of the replacement codes. Since there are 256 different patterns for an eight-bit byte, the maximum size of the translation table is 256 bytes, but, as you will see, it is sometimes possible to use a smaller table.

To code this instruction, you use the name of the field to be translated as the first operand and the name of the table as the second operand as in this instruction:

```
      TR     FIELDA,TABLE
```

When the instruction is executed, the field is translated from left to right, one byte at a time. To find the appropriate code in the table, the code in the operand-1 field is treated as a binary value that is added to the address of the table. Then, the byte at the resulting address replaces the byte in the operand-1 field.

```
              TR       FIELDA,TABLE
              .
              .
              .
FIELDA   DC      CL5'MOD14'
TABLE    DS      0CL256
         DC      192X'00'
         DC      X'010203040506070809'
         DC      7X'00'
         DC      X'0A0B0C0D0E0F101112'
         DC      8X'00'
         DC      X'131415161718191A'
         DC      23X'00'
```

Figure 10-9   A translation routine that uses the translate instruction

To illustrate, look at the translation routine in figure 10-9. Here, FIELDA is defined with a value of MOD14. Although it's unrealistic to define the value of a field to be translated with a DC, this routine is only intended to show you how the TR instruction works.

When the TR instruction is executed, the binary value of M (the first byte in the operand-1 field) is added to the address of TABLE. Since M is hex D4, or binary 11010100, it has a value of 212. As a result, the 213th byte in the table is substituted for the letter M. Since this byte contains hex 0E, the first byte of FIELDA will contain hex 0E after execution.

The TR instruction continues the translation with the remaining bytes in FIELDA on a left to right basis. Since the letter O has a binary value of 214, the 215th table value, hex 10, is substituted for it. Since the letter D has a binary value of 196, the 197th table value, hex 05, is substituted for it. Since the numbers 1 (hex F1) and 4 (hex F4) have binary values of 241 and 244, hex 00 is substituted for each of them. When the instruction finishes its execution, FIELDA contains this data:

    0E   10   05   00   00

How to use the translate instruction to translate a specific range of characters   In practice, you can usually avoid defining a table of 256 bytes because the input data is normally restricted to a smaller range. For example, if you are translating the alphabetic characters of the EBCDIC code to some other bit patterns, the input range is from hex C1 (A) to hex E9 (Z). As a result, the translation table used to cover the range need be only 41 bytes long. (Hex C1 through hex E9 equals binary values 193 through 233.)

To refer to this table in the translate instruction, you adjust the beginning address of the second operand so the lowest binary value in the input range results in a displacement of zero. Since the low end of the range in this example is hex C1, the translate instruction should be coded as:

              TR   DATA,TABLE-193

```
                    .
                    .
                    .
            GET     TAPEFLE,TAPEREC
            TR      TAPEREC,TRANSTAB
                    .
                    .

TRANSTAB    DC      X'F0F1F2F3F4F5F6F7F8F9'
            DC      X'7D7E7A406E50F0'
            DC      X'C1C2C3C4C5C6C7C8C9'
            DC      X'5E4B5D4D5DF0'
            DC      X'D0D1D2D3D4D5D6D7D8D9'
            DC      X'7B5B5C7D5ED04C61'
            DC      X'E2E3E4E5E6E7E8E9'
            DC      X'7C6B4D605D4A'
TAPEREC     DS      CL200
                    .
                    .
```

Figure 10-10   A routine that translates octal code to hexadecimal code

The effect is that an input character A will be translated into the first byte of the table:

```
(TABLE-193) + X'C1' = (TABLE-193) + 193
                    = TABLE + 0
```

Note, however, that a bit pattern that isn't between hex C1 and hex E9 will not be translated properly.

How to use the translate instruction to translate from one data code to another   Though the need for it is rare, the translate instruction is ideal for translating a file from one data code to another. For instance, I once wrote a program to translate a group of magnetic tape files written by a Honeywell 200 computer to IBM System/360 format. The Honeywell tapes were written in *octal code*. Each character was made up of six bits treated as two groups of three. The program I wrote had to read the tape records into storage, allowing the System/360 hardware to add two high-order zero bits to each six-bit character. Then, my program had to translate the resulting bit patterns to EBCDIC.

This translation routine and table are illustrated in figure 10-10. Of course, I had to know what EBCDIC characters each of the six-bit octal codes represented so I could make up an appropriate translation table for the program. But once you create the table, the translate instruction does all the work.

In this example, the translation table didn't have to be 256 bytes long since each input byte had only six significant bits with two high-order zero bits added by the hardware. As a result, the maximum hex input value was B'00111111', or X'3F.' Since the range X'00' to X'3F' represents 64 combinations, my table only had to be 64 bytes long.

```
                        TRT     INPAREA,TRTTABLE
                        .
                        .
                        .
              INPAREA   DS      CL80
              TRTTABLE  DS      0CL256
                        DC      64X'00'
                        DC      X'40'
                        DC      191X'00'
```

Figure 10-11   A routine to find the first blank in a record using the translate-and-test instruction

Translate-and-test (TRT)

The translate-and-test instruction operates somewhat like the translate instruction. That is, the data bytes of the first operand are used as displacements from the second operand address, which is the address of a table. Instead of replacing the data byte with the corresponding byte in the table, though, the TRT instruction only checks to see if the byte in the table is hex 00. If so, processing continues with the next byte in the first operand field. If not, execution of the translate-and test instruction is halted, the address of the byte in the first operand is put in register 1, and the nonzero byte from the table is inserted into the rightmost byte of register 2.

One use of the translate-and-test instruction is to find certain characters in an input stream. For example, you might use this instruction to find the first blank in an input record as illustrated in figure 10-11. When the translate-and-test instruction is executed, each of the bytes in the input area (processing from left to right) will be used as a displacement from the start of the table, TRTTABLE. Since all of the table bytes except the 65th byte (displacement of 64) are hex zeros, only a blank in the input field (hex 40) will cause the instruction to stop. Then, the address of the blank is put in register 1, and the nonzero table character, also a blank in this case, is put into the rightmost byte of register 2. If necessary, then, you can use the address in register 1 to calculate the length of the nonblank field in the input area.

When the translate-and-test instruction is executed, three conditions can result, as summarized in figure 10-12. Then, you can use the branch-on-condition instruction to alter the processing sequence based on the resulting condition code. For instance,

```
              BC      8,NOCHAR
```

will branch if only zero values are found for a field, while

```
              BC      2,LSTBYTE
```

will branch if a nonzero value has been found for the last byte in the operand-1 field.

Condition code on-bit	Condition
Bit 0	All bytes in the input field have corresponding hex zeros in the table.
Bit 1	A nonzero table byte has been found.
Bit 2	The last byte in the input field has a corresponding nonzero byte in the table.

Figure 10-12   The conditions resulting from the translate-and-test instruction

Execute (EX)

The execute instruction is one of the more complex System/370 instructions. When it is executed, it does two things. First, it ORs the rightmost byte of the register that is specified as its first operand with the second byte (bits 8-15) of the instruction specified as the second operand. Second, it executes the operand-2 instruction using the results of the OR as the second byte of this instruction without actually changing the byte in the instruction. That is complicated, isn't it?

The execution instruction is often used in conjunction with the translate-and-test instruction. This is illustrated in figure 10-13. Once you understand this routine, you should understand more fully how the execute instruction works.

As you study figure 10-13, suppose that WRKAREA has this data in bytes 1-16:

```
THIS IS THE LAST
```

Suppose also that the address of WRKAREA is decimal 8000. Then, when the LA instruction at the start of the routine is executed, 8000 is loaded into register 4.

When the translate-and-test instruction that follows is executed, it will stop only when it encounters a blank in WRKAREA because TRTTABLE is all hex zeros except for the 65th table entry. Since the first blank in WRKAREA is the fifth byte of the field, the TRT instruction will load address 8004 into register 1 and place hex 40 in the rightmost byte of register 2 when it stops. Then, the routine subtracts the contents of register 4 from register 1, leaving a value of 4, which is the length of the first input word. Because the length stored in an instruction is one less than the number of bytes operated upon, the program next subtracts one from register 1 leaving a value of 3. At this point, register 1 contains a proper length factor for the MVC instruction labelled MOVEWORD, so it's time for this EX instruction:

```
EX    1,MOVEWORD
```

As I described before, the execute instruction does its work in two phases. In the first phase, it ORs the rightmost byte in register 1 with the second byte of the MVC instruction named MOVEWORD. You will

```
                         .
                         .
                 LA      4,INPAREA
                 TRT     INPAREA,TRTTABLE
                 SR      1,4
                 S       1,=F'1'
                 EX      1,MOVEWORD
                         .
                         .
        WRKAREA  DS      CL80
        TRTTABLE DS      0CL256
                 DC      64X'00'
                 DC      X'40'
                 DC      191X'00'
        MOVEWORD MVC     0(0,5),0(4)
                         .
                         .
```

Figure 10-13   A routine that uses the TRT and EX instructions to locate the first words in an input area

remember from chapter 4 that the second byte of the MVC instruction is a length factor. So, since this move instruction specifies a length of zero, its second byte is hex 00, and the result of the OR operation is hex 03. Then, in the second phase, the execute instruction causes this MVC instruction to be executed using the length factor of hex 03. The result is that the word addressed by register 4 with a length factor of hex 3 (the input word THIS) is moved to the four bytes starting at the address given by register 5. Note, then, that the execute instruction wouldn't work as intended if the length specified in the MVC instruction wasn't hex zeros because the desired length wouldn't be ORed properly.

A program that uses the execute instruction   Since the routine in figure 10-13 only gets the first word in the input area, I thought you might want to see a more complete routine. As a result, figure 10-14 illustrates an entire program that processes free-form input. Here, the input file contains address records with one complete address in each record. The output is a number of two-, three-, or four-line mailing labels.

The difficult part of the program is determining where the data for one address line ends and the next one begins, because a single slash is used to separate the address lines in an input record. Furthermore, the final address line in a record may or may not be ended by a slash. Before a label is printed, the program skips to the top of the next label using ASA control characters.

At the start of the program, the address of the input area is loaded into register 4; the length of the input area minus one (the length factor) is loaded into register 5; and a record is read. Then, this execute instruction is executed:

```
                 EX      5,TRTINST
```

```
LABELS    START  0
BEGIN     BALR   3,0
          USING  *,3
          OPEN   ADDREC,PRINT
NEWREC    LA     4,ADDRIO
          LA     5,79
          GET    ADDREC
NXTFLD    EX     5,TRTINST
          BC     8,LASTFLD
          BC     2,LASTSLSH
          SR     1,4
          S      1,=F'1'
          EX     1,MOVEFLD
          AR     4,1
          A      4,=F'2'
          SR     5,1
          S      5,=F'2'
          PUT    PRINT
          MVI    PRTIO,C' '
          MVC    PRTIO+1(132),PRTIO
          B      NXTFLD
LASTFLD   LA     1,ADDRIO+79
PRTLSTLN  SR     1,4
          EX     1,MOVEFLD
          PUT    PRINT
          MVC    PRTIO+1(132),PRTIO
          MVI    PRTIO,C'1'
          B      NEWREC
LASTSLSH  LA     1,ADDRIO+78
          B      PRTLSTLN
ADDREOF   CLOSE  ADDREC,PRINT
          EOJ
ADDREC    DTFSD  BLKSIZE=80,                X
                 IOAREA1=ADDRIO,            X
                 EOFADDR=ADDREOF,           X
                 DEVADDR=SYS008
PRINT     DTFPR  BLKSIZE=133,               X
                 IOAREA1=PRTIO,             X
                 DEVADDR=SYSLST,            X
                 CTLCHR=ASA
ADDRIO    DS     CL80
PRTIO     DC     CL133'1'
TRTTABLE  DS     0CL256
          DC     97X'00'
          DC     X'61'
          DC     158X'00'
TRTINST   TRT    0(0,4),TRTTABLE
MOVEFLD   MVC    PRTIO+1(0),0(4)
          END    BEGIN
```

Figure 10-14   A program that prepares address labels from free-form input

Since register 5 contains the length of the input area minus one, this instruction is executed with a length equivalent to 80:

```
TRTINST   TRT    0(0,4),TRTTABLE
```

Since this instruction uses register 4 as the base register, the field that is operated upon is the 80-byte input area for the address record.

The two BC instructions after the execute instruction branch if only zero values are found by the TRT instruction or if the nonzero value is for the last byte of the input area. Since either of these conditions indicates the end of the last address line in a record, the program branches to appropriate last-line routines.

Otherwise, the program continues with the next instructions:

```
SR      1,4
S       1,=F'1'
EX      1,MOVEFLD
```

First, the length of the address field minus one is calculated in register 1. Then, register 1 is used in the execute instruction to modify the length factor in the MVC instruction named MOVEFLD:

```
MOVEFLD  MVC    PRTIO+1(0),0(4)
```

When its execution is complete, one address line has been moved to the printer output area.

Next, register 4 is adjusted so it addresses the first byte of the next address field and register 5 is adjusted so it contains the length minus one of the remaining bytes in the input area. Then, after the print line in the output area is printed by the PUT instruction, the print area including the control character is cleared to blanks. Since address lines of different lengths are being printed, data from a long line would overlap data from a shorter line and print again if the area were not cleared. Finally, the program branches back to the first execute instruction so the loop is repeated for the next address line.

If the last address field is indicated, an appropriate length is developed in register 1, and the MVC instruction is executed via the execute instruction. Next, a line is printed, the print area is cleared, and the line-control character is set to 1 to indicate a skip to the top of the next label before the next line is printed. The program then returns to NEWREC to set up registers 4 and 5 and read another record.

DISCUSSION

The elements presented in this chapter illustrate some of the power of assembler language. By using the bit manipulation, translation, and execute instructions, the assembler language programmer can code complex routines for input validation, translation, or free-form input manipulation. In contrast, routines like this can be difficult or impossible to code in a high-level language.

Terminology

field separator
floating dollar sign

Objective

Apply any of the instructions in this chapter to your programs.

Chapter 11

Writing macro definitions

The use of standard macros is a basic part of assembler language programming. For instance, GET and PUT macros, in combination with DTF macros, are used to perform most I/O operations. In addition, standard macros such as SAVE and RETURN for subprogram linkage and COMRG for supervisor communication provide special processing capabilities.

During assembly, each macro instruction is replaced by the instructions that are generated by the *macro definition*. This is referred to as *macro expansion*. For example, the GET macro (when a work area isn't used) is expanded into two load instructions and a branch-and-link instruction that branches to an I/O module.

Usually, the macro definitions are stored in a source statement library. Then, each time the assembler finds a macro instruction in the source program, it looks up the macro definition in the source statement library. Based on the macro definition, the assembler generates instructions for the macro instruction and inserts them into the source program immediately following the macro instruction.

As an assembler language programmer, you can write macro definitions of your own. Why would you want to? For the same reason that the standard macros were written: to provide an easy way to code a frequently used series of assembler language instructions. Once your macro definition has been written and stored in the source statement library, you can use it just as you use any of the standard macros.

One reason some programmers don't write macro definitions is the difficulty involved in writing them. In truth, writing a macro like the DTFSD (which consists of more than 900 coding lines) can be an extremely complex task. On the other hand, writing simple macro definitions is a manageable task, one that can improve the efficiency of a company's programming efforts.

This chapter is divided into two topics. Topic 1 presents the more straightforward forms of macro writing. These techniques are relevant to the needs of the typical assembler language programmer. Then, topic 2 presents advanced techniques for macro writing. These techniques are more relevant to the needs of the software specialist. Because of the complexity of the subject, you are probably better off if you study this chapter only after you have become quite proficient in assembler language coding.

TOPIC 1   Basic macro writing

Figure 11-1 presents a simple macro definition. This macro adds three binary fields to a register, subtracts one field from it, and adds the literal value 50 to it. The figure shows the macro definition, an example of its use in a macro instruction, and the expansion of the instruction.

THE MACRO DEFINITION

There are four parts in every macro definition. The *header statement* always has MACRO as the operation code; the *trailer statement* always has MEND as the operation code. Following the header statement is the *prototype statement* that gives the form in which the macro instruction must be written. After the prototype statement are the *model statements* that define the code that is to be inserted into the assembler language source program when the macro instruction is expanded.

The prototype statement

Depending on the function of the macro, the prototype statement can consist of just a macro operation code or it can consist of a macro operation code plus one or more *variable symbols*. The macro operation code can be from one to eight letters or numbers in length starting with a letter, but it cannot duplicate an assembler language operation code or another macro name. When variable symbols are used, they can be coded as positional operands or keyword operands, as you'll see in a moment.

How to use variable symbols in the prototype statement   A variable symbol consists of the & sign followed by from one to seven letters or numbers, the first of which must be a letter. Thus, in figure 11-1, &LABEL, &R1, and so on, are variable symbols.

The variable symbols in the prototype statement indicate the operands (or parameters) that can be used when coding the macro instruction. For instance, the SUMWDS macro in figure 11-1 has places for five operands. The SUMWDS macro also provides for a label, &LABEL, which isn't required, but which you can use if the program must branch to the macro instruction. If you do code a label, the value assigned to it is the label of the macro instruction in the source program. You will see how this works in a minute.

How to code variable symbols as positional operands   When you code operands in the prototype statement as in figure 11-1, they are referred to as *positional operands*. This means that the position of each operand indicates its use in the macro expansion. If, for example, the SUMWDS macro were coded

```
SUMWDS WORDA,5,WORDB,WORDC,BCON
```

Macro definition

```
Header statement                        MACRO
Prototype statement        &LABEL       SUMWDS    &R1,&W1,&W2,&W3,&CON
Model statements           &LABEL       SR    &R1,&R1
                                        A     &R1,&W1
                                        A     &R1,&W2
                                        A     &R1,&W3
                                        S     &R1,&CON
                                        A     &R1,=F'50'
Trailer statement                       MEND
```

Macro instruction

```
                           ROUT1        SUMWDS    5,WORDA,WORDB,WORDC,BCON
```

Macro expansion

```
                           ROUT1        SR    5,5
                                        A     5,WORDA
                                        A     5,WORDB
                                        A     5,WORDC
                                        S     5,BCON
                                        A     5,=F'50'
```

Figure 11-1   The SUMWDS macro definition with positional operands

WORDA would be substituted for &R1, which would result in faulty source code because &R1 is supposed to be a register number.

If you aren't going to use one of the positional operands when you code a macro, you omit it. If, for example, you wanted to omit operands 2 and 5 in the SUMWDS macro, you would code the macro instruction as:

```
SUMWDS 5,,WORDB,WORDC
```

Because all of the SUMWDS operands are required, however, this statement would result in faulty code.

How to code variable symbols as keyword operands   The other way to specify operands is to use *keyword operands* in the prototype statement. These are the type of operands used in the DTF statements. If, for example, SUMWDS had been written using keyword operands, it would look like the macro definition in figure 11-2. Here, the parameters in the prototype statement, minus the leading & sign, are the keywords you must use in the macro instruction. Unlike positional operands, you can code keyword operands in any sequence.

Macro definition

```
           MACRO
&NAME      SUMWDS     &REG1=,&WORD1=,&WORD2=,&WORD3=,&CON=
&NAME      SR         &REG1,&REG1
           A          &REG1,&WORD1
           A          &REG1,&WORD2
           A          &REG1,&WORD3
           S          &REG1,&CON
           A          &REG1,=F'50'
           MEND
```

Macro instruction

```
SUMWDS     WORD1=W1,WORD2=W2,WORD3=W3,REG1=7,CON=C1
```

Macro expansion

```
SR         7,7
A          7,W1
A          7,W2
A          7,W3
S          7,C1
A          7,=F'50'
```

Figure 11-2   The SUMWDS macro definition with keyword operands

If a keyword operand is to have a default value, the value is coded in the prototype statement after the equals sign. If, for example, you want the keyword &REG1 to have a default value of 5 in the SUMWDS macro, you code it as &REG1=5 in the prototype statement. Then, should this parameter be omitted when the macro is used, register 5 will be assigned to it during the macro expansion. If a keyword is omitted that doesn't have a default value, no value is assigned to that parameter in the macro expansion.

How to code a combination of positional and keyword operands   It is legal, though rare, to define a combination of positional and keyword operands. In this case, you must define the positional operands first in the prototype statement and code them first when you use the macro. Here, then, is an example of a prototype statement that defines both positional and keyword operands:

```
&NAME      SMPLE &P1,&P2.,&P3,&KEY1=&,KEY2=NO
```

When you code the SMPLE macro, the first three operands must be treated as positional operands, the last two as keyword operands.

```
              MACRO
              ITMSTR
ITMRCD        DS      0CL70         INV MSTR RCD LAYOUT
IITEM         DS      CL6           ITEM NUMBER
IDESC         DS      CL20          ITEM DESCRIPTION
IUM           DS      CL4           UNIT OF MEASURE
IOPOL         DS      CL2           ORDER POLICY CODE
IOQTY         DS      PL4           ORDER QTY
IOPNT         DS      PL4           ORDER POINT
ISS           DS      PL4           SAFETY STOCK
IBOH          DS      PL4           BALANCE ON HAND
IOOQTY        DS      PL4           ON ORDER QTY
IALLOC        DS      PL4           ALLOCATED QTY
              DS      CL14          AVAIL FOR EXPANSION
              MEND
```

Figure 11-3   An ITMSTR macro definition with ordinary symbols

The model statements

The model statements represent the instructions to be used in the expansion of the macro. During expansion, the operands given in the macro instruction are substituted for the corresponding variable symbols in the prototype statement. In figure 11-1, for example, 5 is substituted for &R1 wherever &R1 appears in the model statements. Similarly, WORDC is substituted for &W3 wherever it appears in the model statements. The expanded instructions are then placed in the source program and the assembly continues.

How to use ordinary symbols in the model statements   Although the SUMWDS macro uses variable symbols in the model statements, you can also use *ordinary symbols* in the model statements. Ordinary symbols are those you normally code in a program. If, for example, you code this model statement

```
        MVC     FLD1,FLD2
```

it will be generated unchanged whenever you use the macro instruction. You can define the ordinary symbols within the model statements or in the assembler language program itself.

Figure 11-3 gives an example of a macro that uses only ordinary symbols. It shows an easy way to code the record layout of an inventory master record that is used in several programs. To get the record definitions inserted into the program, you code:

```
        ITMSTR
```

Of course, since the macro expansion defines fields, you can code the macro only once in a program. Otherwise, the fields will be defined more than once, which will result in diagnostics. Note that this use of a macro definition is similar to the use of a COPY statement.

Symbol coded in model statement	Values assigned to variable symbols	Generated symbol
&FLD.A	&FLD=SUM	SUMA
FIELD&A	&A=1	FIELD1
NAME.&Z	&Z=ZZZ	NAMEZZZ
&D1.X.&L1	&D1=B4	B4X32
	&L1=32	
&DISP.(&BASE)	&DISP=84	84(9)
	&BASE=9	
&F1+5*&F2	&F1=6	6+5*FACT
	&F2=FACT	

Figure 11-4   Some symbol combinations that can be used in model statements

How to combine ordinary and variable symbols   The symbols you use for labels and operands in model statements can also be combinations of ordinary and variable symbols. If, for example, an MVC instruction in a macro definition is coded like this

```
MVC    FLD&A,FLD&B
```

the operands of the generated MVC instruction will be the characters FLD plus the values assigned to &A and &B. For instance, if &A equals 1 and &B equals 2, the generated instruction will be:

```
MVC    FLD1,FLD2
```

You can also combine ordinary and variable symbols in reverse order. For example,

```
MVC    &A.FLD,&B.FLD
```

will generate

```
MVC    OUTFLD,INFLD
```

if &A equals OUT and &B equals IN. In this case, the period (.) in &A.FLD and &B.FLD is called a *concatenation character*. It is used to separate a variable symbol from an ordinary symbol so the assembler can tell which is which.

There are many ways in which you can combine variable and ordinary symbols in your model statements. Some of them are illustrated in figure 11-4. Note that a concatenation character is used whenever the assembler might be confused by two operand parts in succession.

Figure 11-5 is a version of the ITMSTR macro that uses symbol combinations. This time the prototype statement shows that a single operand

Macro definition

```
            MACRO
&LABEL      ITMSTR   &PF
&LABEL      DS       OCL70          INV MSTR RCD LAYOUT
&PF.ITEM    DS       CL6            ITEM NUMBER
&PF.DESC    DS       CL20           ITEM DESCRIPTION
&PF.UM      DS       CL4            UNIT OF MEASURE
&PF.OPOL    DS       CL2            ORDER POLICY CODE
&PF.OQTY    DS       PL4            ORDER QTY
&PF.OPNT    DS       PL4            ORDER POINT
&PF.SS      DS       PL4            SAFETY STOCK
&PF.BOH     DS       PL4            BALANCE ON HAND
&PF.OOQTY   DS       PL4            ON ORDER QTY
&PF.ALLOC   DS       PL4            ALLOCATED QTY
            DS       CL14           AVAIL FOR EXPANSION
            MEND
```

Macro instruction

```
MSTRWORK ITMSTR IM
```

Macro expansion

```
MSTRWORK    DS       OCL70          INV MSTR RCD LAYOUT
IMITEM      DS       CL6            ITEM NUMBER
IMDESC      DS       CL20           ITEM DESCRIPTION
IMUM        DS       CL4            UNIT OF MEASURE
IMOPOL      DS       CL2            ORDER POLICY CODE
IMOQTY      DS       PL4            ORDER QTY
IMOPNT      DS       PL4            ORDER POINT
IMSS        DS       PL4            SAFETY STOCK
IMBOH       DS       PL4            BALANCE ON HAND
IMOOQTY     DS       PL4            ON ORDER QTY
IMALLOC     DS       PL4            ALLOCATED QTY
            DS       CL14           AVAILABLE FOR EXPANSION
```

Figure 11-5   The ITMSTR macro with combined symbols

is expected. The label of the macro instruction in the source program will be assigned to the first model statement through the variable symbol &LABEL, and the operand is used as a prefix for the field labels. Notice that the operand for the macro should start with a letter and be three characters or fewer, otherwise invalid labels for the fields will result. (In topic 2, you'll see how you can use conditional assembly instructions to check a macro instruction for valid operands during its expansion.)

```
          MACRO
&LABEL    GETDATE &FLD
*  THE OPERAND FIELD SHOULD BE AT LEAST 8 BYTES
&LABEL    COMRG
          MVC    &FLD.(8),0(1)
          MEND
```

Figure 11-6   A macro that gets the system date

TWO USEFUL MACROS

With this as background, you should be able to write some useful macros. But, to help you along, I'm going to present two additional macros that you should find useful. The first one is a macro to get the system date. The second one is a macro that uses a switch to provide for special processing the first time through a program.

A macro to get the system date

Since getting the date from the supervisor is a function that is done in many programs, the GETDATE macro in figure 11-6 is one that can be useful. This macro illustrates the use of a macro (COMRG) within a macro definition. The COMRG macro, which is described in chapter 6, places the address of the current date in register 1. Then, the GETDATE macro moves the date into the operand given in the macro instruction. As the comment in the macro definition indicates, the date field should be at least eight bytes long since the date is in the form of MM/DD/YY.

Once this macro has been stored in the source statement library, you can store the date in a field named DATEFLD by coding this statement:

```
INITRT    GETDATE DATEFLD
```

Then, the macro expansion will generate these instructions:

```
INITRT    COMRG
          MVC    DATEFLD(8),0(1)
```

When a macro is used within a macro, the inner macro doesn't appear as one of the generated instructions on the assembly listing. As a result, the COMRG macro will not be shown on the assembly listing, but its generated instructions will be shown.

A first-time-switch macro

The purpose of a first-time-switch macro is to let a series of statements be executed the first time through a routine, but to branch around those statements on subsequent passes through the routine. Figure 11-7 shows one version of a first-time-switch macro definition.

```
                    MACRO
        &LABEL      FRSTSW    &BRCH
        &LABEL      BC        0,&BRCH
                    MVZ       *-3,=X'F0'
                    MEND
```

Figure 11-7   A first-time-switch macro

Source code

```
        PRINT       FRSTSW    OTHER
                    MVI       PRTAREA,X'40'
                    MVC       PRTAREA+1(132),PRTAREA
        OTHER       .
                    .
                    .
```

Source code with macro expansion

```
        PRINT       FRSTSW    OTHER
    +   PRINT       BC        0,OTHER
    +               MVZ       *-3,=X'F0'
                    MVI       PRTAREA,X'40'
                    MVC       PRTAREA+1(132),PRTAREA
        OTHER       .
                    .
                    .
```

Figure 11-8   A routine that uses the first-time-switch macro

To use this macro, you code the label of the instruction to be branched to after the first time through the program. For instance, you might code the routine in figure 11-8 in order to clear a print area the first time through a program and to leave it untouched on successive loops through the program. The generated instructions will then look like the second part of figure 11-8.

Because the branch-on-condition (BC) instruction has a mask of zero, the branch to OTHER won't take place the first time through the program. (Remember from chapter 4 that a mask of hex zero means "never branch;" a mask of hex F means "always branch.") However, the MVZ instruction that follows the branch modifies the branch instruction's mask. Since the BC instruction is four bytes long, *-3 in the MVZ instruction refers to the second byte of the branch instruction. (Remember that * indicates the present location counter value.) Then, when the MVZ is executed, the mask in the BC instruction is changed from hex zero to hex F. As a result, the BC instruction will branch to OTHER on all subsequent passes through the routine.

MAKING THE MACRO DEFINITIONS AVAILABLE TO THE ASSEMBLER

Once you have defined a macro, you must make the definition available to your programs in order to test it. The normal way to do this is to put the macro definitions at the start of a source program that uses the macros. You can then use the macros in the program.

After you have successfully tested a macro definition, you normally catalog it in a source statement library. In addition, macros are usually catalogued in standard sublibraries. As a result, you should check your shop's standards to see which libraries and sublibraries you should use. Although this book doesn't show you how to add members to a sublibrary within a source statement library, our VSE JCL book shows you how to do this in detail.

Macros can be catalogued in a source statement library in two forms. When they are catalogued in source form, they must be assembled along with each program they are used in. The standard sublibraries used for source macros are A and D.

To save the time of assembling a macro each time it is used, it can be catalogued as an *edited macro*. An edited macro has already been partially processed by the assembler so there is no need to assemble it each time it is used. To create an edited macro, you simply assemble it and catalog the output in the proper library. The standard sublibraries used for edited macros are E and F. You can find a complete description of the process of cataloging edited macros in IBM manual GC33-4024, *Guide to the DOS/VSE Assembler*.

Although using edited macros can save you assembly time, they can't be modified directly. For this reason, macros are generally catalogued in both source and edited form. Then, if you need to make a change to a macro, you change the source code, assemble it, and replace the old edited macro with the new one. If you don't save a macro in source form, an edited macro can be converted back to source form by a procedure called *de-editing*. However, it is usually more convenient to keep the macro in both source and edited forms.

Terminology		
macro definition	positional operand
macro expansion	keyword operand
header statement	ordinary symbol
trailer statement	concatenation character
prototype statement	edited macro
model statement	de-editing
variable symbol	

Objective	
	Given specifications for a macro, code its macro definition using the elements presented in this topic.

TOPIC 2   Advanced macro writing

The macros in topic 1 accomplish two types of macro expansion. The first, called *text insertion*, simply inserts the model statements into the source program. For example, the first ITMSTR macro and the standard COMRG macro accomplish text insertion only.

The second level of macro expansion is called *text insertion with modification*. The macros with operands in topic 1 are examples at this level since they cause the model statements to be modified based on the operands given. Nevertheless, these macros still involve a fixed series of model statements that are to be inserted into the source program.

The highest level of macro writing involves *text manipulation*. This means that the operands of the macro determine which instructions are inserted into the source program as well as the form those instructions are to take. A GET macro, for example, can be coded with filename as its only operand or it can have a work-area name as its second operand. When the macro is expanded, the generated instructions vary depending on whether the work-area operand is present.

In order to write text-manipulation macros, you need to know how to define and use *SET symbols*. These symbols can have their values changed during macro expansion. In addition, you need to know how to write *conditional assembly statements*. These statements can alter the sequence in which the assembler expands a macro. In fact, these instructions can direct the assembler to loop through the model statements in a macro definition, generating several source statements from a single model statement.

Quite frankly, writing macro definitions for text manipulation is a skill that cannot be mastered by all programmers. On the programming staff of a large company, for instance, perhaps only one programmer will be capable of writing a macro for a specialized I/O function. Nevertheless, the macro writing facilities of assembler language are important because they let you create a macro language within assembler language. That's why macro writing is of interest to computer scientists and software specialists.

Because SET symbols and conditional assembly statements work together, you must know something about both before you can understand text-manipulation macros. As a result, this topic presents the macro writing facilities in this sequence: (1) SET symbols, (2) symbol attributes, (3) assigning values to SET symbols, and (4) conditional assembly statements. After you become familiar with these elements, you'll be introduced to a few text-manipulation macros.

SET symbols   SET symbols are variable symbols that are defined in a macro definition. They can be defined as one of three types and in one of two ranges. First, I

```
GBLA      &NBR1
GBLB      &B1,&B2,&SWITCH
GBLC      &STR,&X37
LCLA      &VAR1,&TIP
LCLB      &OFF
LCLC      &NAME,&FIELD
```

Figure 11-9   SET symbols that use the six valid operation codes

will discuss these types and ranges. Then, I will show you how these symbols are defined. You will see later how values are assigned to these symbols.

Types of SET symbols   The three types of SET symbols are arithmetic (A), binary (B), and character (C). An arithmetic SET symbol can be assigned any numeric value between -2^{31} and $+2^{31}-1$. This is the same range that a binary fullword has. In contrast, a binary SET symbol can be assigned only two values: 0 and 1. A character SET symbol can be assigned a string of up to eight characters.

Ranges of SET symbols   A SET symbol is either *local* or *global* depending on its range within a program. If the value assigned to a SET symbol is effective within only one macro expansion, it is called local. In this case, if the same SET symbol is defined in two different macros, it is two different symbols. In contrast, a global SET symbol that is defined in two different macros is treated as one symbol. In other words, a global SET symbol is common to an entire assembly and is available for use by other macros. Nevertheless, it must still be defined in each macro it is used in. In this book, you won't see examples of macro definitions that use global SET symbols.

How to define SET symbols   All SET symbols used in a macro definition must be defined (or declared) immediately after the prototype statement with globals first, then locals. This is referred to as *symbol declaration*. In a statement that defines symbols, the label area must be blank.

The six operation codes for symbol declaration are shown in the examples of SET statements in figure 11-9. The operation code starts with either GBL (global) or LCL (local), which is followed by the type code of the SET symbols that are going to be defined by the statement. Since SET symbols are a type of variable symbol, the first character of each SET symbol name must be &. Notice that multiple SET symbols can be declared in one statement by separating the names with commas.

When a SET symbol is declared, it is assigned an initial value of zero for A and B types and null for C types. A null value means literally nothing: zero length and no data. To illustrate SET symbol declarations, figure 11-10 shows the prototype statement from the standard CALL macro followed by its declarations. Here, &N, &KAP1, and &KAP2 are all assigned an initial value of zero when the macro is expanded.

```
&NAME     CALL    &P1,&P2
          LCLA    &N
          LCLA    &KAP1,&KAP2
```

Figure 11-10   The prototype statement and symbol declarations of the CALL macro

Type codes for symbols defined in DS and DC statements

A   A-type address constant
B   Binary
C   Character
D   Long floating-point
E   Short floating-point
F   Fullword fixed-point
H   Halfword fixed-point
P   Packed decimal
V   V-type address constant
Z   Zoned decimal

Type codes for symbols defined as instruction labels

I   Machine instruction
M   Macro instruction

Type codes for symbols defined as macro operands

N   A self-defining term (number)
O   An omitted term

Figure 11-11   Type codes for symbols

Symbol attributes

All symbols (ordinary, variable, and SET symbols) have attributes. Two attributes you are familiar with are *length* and *type*. For instance, an ordinary symbol defined as PL3 has a length attribute of 3 and a type code of P. In addition to the normal type codes used in DS and DC statements, though, there are others.

Figure 11-11 summarizes the common type codes for symbols. If, for example, a macro operand is omitted, its type attribute is O. If it is a number, its type attribute is N (a number is a self-defining value).

In addition to length and type, macro symbols also have number, count, scaling, and integer attributes. Since scaling and integer attributes are rarely used, they aren't covered in this book. But the number and count attributes can be important.

How to use the number attribute   The *number attribute* applies only to symbolic parameters that have *sublists*. The term sublist refers to the fact that one symbolic parameter can have several values. The parameter must then have a *subscript* added to identify an individual value in the sublist. The subscript is a number in parentheses following the symbol name. For instance, &P(2) refers to the second item in the sublist for the symbol &P; &P(5) refers to the fifth item in the sublist.

For an operand with a sublist, the prototype statement can indicate the maximum number of values within the sublist as illustrated in figure 11-12. Here, the prototype statement indicates that the symbolic parameter &P2 may have five sublist values. Although you don't have to indicate the maximum number of values for a sublist parameter in a prototype statement, it makes the macro definition easier to understand.

When a macro instruction with one or more sublist parameters is coded in a program, the sublist operands must be separated by commas and enclosed in parentheses as in this example:

```
SAMP    SUM,(X,Y,,AZ)
```

If the macro definition is the one shown in figure 11-12, parameter &P2 will have the values indicated assigned to it. Since the third and fifth names in the sublist are omitted, they are considered to be undefined.

The number attribute of a symbol is equal to the number of sublist positions coded in the macro instruction. More specifically, the number attribute is one more than the number of commas in the parentheses. For &P2 in the macro statement in figure 11-12, the number attribute is 4 because three commas are used. When the sublist operand is omitted, the number attribute is 0. For most parameters (those with no sublist), the number attribute is 1.

How to use the count attribute   The *count attribute* is equal to the number of characters in the operand of an instruction. To illustrate, suppose a prototype statement is coded as:

```
&LABEL    GSPLX &OP1,&OP2
```

Then, if the macro statement is coded as

```
PICT       GSPLX FIELD1,X
```

the count attribute of &LABEL is 4. Similarly, the count attribute of &OP1 is 6 and of &OP2 is 1. As you can see, then, the count attributes of the operands may differ each time the macro instruction is coded.

Assigning values to SET symbols

You assign values to SET symbols during macro expansion by using the SETA (arithmetic), SETB (binary), and SETC (character) statements.

Prototype statement

```
&LABEL    SAMP    &P1,&P2(5)
```

Macro instruction

```
SAMP      SUM,(X,Y,,AZ)
```

Values assigned to the parameters

Parameter	Value
&P1	SUM
&P2(1)	X
&P2(2)	Y
&P2(3)	Undefined
&P2(4)	AZ
&P2(5)	Undefined

Figure 11-12   Symbolic parameters including one with a sublist

The SETA statement   The label of the SETA statement must be the variable symbol to which a value is to be assigned. The operand of the statement is an *arithmetic expression* that represents the value to be assigned. For instance, the following SETA statement assigns a value of 46 to the SET symbol named &A1:

```
&A1       SETA    46
```

In this case, the arithmetic expression is a *self-defining term*, the number 46.

The arithmetic expression can range from a self-defining term to a complex expression involving many variables and the *arithmetic operators*: + for plus, - for minus, * for multiply, and / for divide. Here's a more involved arithmetic expression used as the operand of a SETA statement:

```
&DELTA    SETA    &X1+10/&X2
```

In an expression like this, the evaluation proceeds from left to right with multiplication and division done first, followed by addition and subtraction. If, for example, &X1 has a value of 10 and &X2 has a value of 2, &DELTA will be assigned a value of 15.

If parentheses are used in an arithmetic expression, the expressions

Operator	Meaning
EQ	Equal to
NE	Not equal to
LT	Less than
LE	Less than or equal to
GT	Greater than
GE	Greater than or equal to

Figure 11-13   The logical operators that can be used in the operand of a SETB statement

within the innermost sets of parentheses are evaluated first. If, for example, the statement above is coded as

```
&DELTA    SETA    (&X1+10)/&X2
```

&DELTA is assigned a value of 10 if &X1 equals 10 and &X2 equals 2. Within parentheses, evaluation proceeds as before, with multiplication and division first.

An attribute can also be assigned to a SET symbol by using the SETA statement, provided the attribute is numeric. For example, the following code assigns a value equal to the length attribute of &A1 to &LA1:

```
&LA1      SETA    L'&A1
```

In other words, if the length of the operand that is coded in the macro instruction for &A1 is 8, &LA1 is assigned a value of 8. To indicate an attribute, you use L' (for length), T' (for type), K' (for count), or N' (for number). Since L', N', and K' are numeric, they can be used in SETA expressions.

The SETB statement   The SETB statement can assign a value to a binary SET symbol in much the same way that a SETA statement assigns a value to an arithmetic SET symbol. This is illustrated by this statement:

```
&SW1      SETB    0
```

Here, a value of zero is assigned to &SW1.

The operand of a SETB statement can also be a *logical expression* that is evaluated by the assembler as true or false. If the expression it true, the SET symbol is assigned the value 1. If the expression is false, zero is assigned. Logical expressions are composed of two arithmetic expressions or two character expressions connected by one of the *logical operators* illustrated in figure 11-13.

The expressions that are compared by the logical operators can be self-defining terms, arithmetic expressions composed of arithmetic

True logical expressions

Statement			Variable values
&X3	SETB	(8 GT 3)	
&LIMIT	SETB	(&INDEX LE &HIGH)	&INDEX=19 &HIGH=20
&SWITCH	SETB	(&PARM1+5 NE &PARM2*3)	&PARM1=4 &PARM2=6
&DONE	SETB	(4 EQ L'&KEY2)	Length of &KEY2 is 4

False logical expressions

Statement			Variable values
&B1	SETB	(&NAME EQ 'FIRST')	&NAME='BRK'
&B2	SETB	(T'&P1 NE 'C')	Type code of &P1='C'
&SYMB	SETB	(&KEY4 EQ &END)	&KEY4='NXT' &END='END'

Figure 11-14   Some SETB statements with logical expressions as operands

operators and variable names, or symbol attributes. In the first group of examples in figure 11-14, the logical expressions are all true, so the value assigned in each case is 1. In the second group of SETB statements in figure 11-14, each logical expression is false so the value assigned to the binary SET symbol is zero.

The SETC statement   Character SET symbols are assigned values with a SETC statement. The operand can be a self-defining character string, another variable symbol, or any combination or concatenation of the two. The operand can also be an attribute of a variable symbol. Except for an attribute operand, the operand must be enclosed in single quotes as in the examples in figure 11-15.

Some SET statement examples   Figure 11-16 gives several examples of each type of SET statement and shows the resulting value assigned to the symbol. Note that, in the third SETC statement, two periods in a character string are required for one period to show in the resulting value because a period is the concatenation character. Similarly, two consecutive apostrophes are required for one apostrophe to show in the resulting value.

Statement			Remark
&STRING	SETC	'KEY'	The operand is a self-defining string.
&NAME	SETC	'&KEY1'	The operand is a variable symbol.
&NAME	SETC	'MR &KEY1'	The operand is a string plus a variable symbol.
&TYPE	SETC	T'&PARM1	The operand is the type attribute.

Figure 11-15   Different types of operands allowed in the SETC statement

Conditional assembly statements

Normally, the assembler processes the instructions in a source program in sequence. When you use conditional assembly statements, though, you can control the sequence in which the source statements are processed. For instance, you can cause the assembler to skip some of the instructions and jump ahead in the source statement sequence. And, you can cause the assembler to branch backward in the sequence so some of the source code can be processed again, just as if it had been coded in the source program more than once.

The primary conditional assembly statements are the AGO and AIF statements. They are similar to an unconditional branch instruction and a conditional branch instruction, but they direct the assembly of the source program rather than the execution of the object program. Related to the use of the AGO and AIF statements are the MNOTE, MEXIT, and ANOP statements.

The AGO statement   To illustrate the AGO statement, let's consider the portion of the macro definition in figure 11-17. Here, the AGO statement causes the assembler to skip ahead to the last MVC instruction. As a result, the two LA instructions, the first MVC instruction, and any other instructions before .END aren't generated in the resulting source code.

Here, the label .END is called a *sequence symbol*. Sequence symbols are labels that can be referred to in conditional assembly statements in order to direct the assembly sequence, but they aren't generated with the rest of the statement that they label. A period is the first character of a sequence symbol.

The AIF statement   The operand of the AIF statement must be a logical expression followed by a sequence symbol. A logical expression is formed just as it is in a SETB statement. If the expression is true, the assembler

Statement examples			Symbol values	Assigned value
&A72	SETA	72		72
&NBR	SETA	&INDEX+10	&INDEX=3	13
&LIMIT	SETA	&BASE*5-&ORG	&BASE=100,&ORG=37	463
&LGTH	SETA	L'&P1-1	Length of &P1=7	6
&SW1	SETB	0		0
&YES	SETB	(&PARM2 EQ 'YES')	&PARM2='NO'	0
&TOOLONG	SETB	(L'&FLD LE 256)	Length of &FLD=180	1
&STRING	SETC	'AB C'		'AB C'
&NAME	SETC	'&KEY1'	&KEY1=JONES	'JONES'
&NAME	SETC	'MR .&KEY1'	&KEY1=JONES	'MR JONES'
&PRT1	SETC	'MR.. &KEY1'	&KEY1=BOLTZ	'MR. BOLTZ'
&TNAME	SETC	T'&NAME	Type attribute of &NAME=C	'C'

Figure 11-16   Some additional SET statement examples

```
          .
          .
          .
     AGO  .END
     LA   &R1,256(&R1)
     LA   &R2,256(&R2)
     MVC  0(256,&R2),0(&R1)
          .
          .
.END MVC  0(&LGTH,&R2),0(&R1)
          .
          .
```

Figure 11-17   Part of a macro definition that shows the use of the AGO instruction

branches to the sequence symbol that follows the logical expression. If the expression is false, the assembler continues processing the statements sequentially.

In the example that follows, a variable symbol, &LGTH, is compared to a value of 256:

```
AIF   (&LGTH LE 256).SHORT
```

If &LGTH is less than or equal to 256, the expression is true and the assembler branches to the statement starting with the sequence symbol .SHORT. If the expression is false, the assembler processes the statement after the AIF statement.

When you code a logical expression, you can use the operators OR, AND, and NOT in various combinations to form complex logical expressions. For example, the logical expression

```
(&A GT 14 AND &B LT 12)
```

is true only if both logical terms are true. In contrast,

```
(&A GT 14 OR &B LT 12)
```

is true if either one or both of the logical terms are true.

Sometimes, it's necessary to use multiple sets of parentheses to group the various logical expressions so they will be evaluated properly:

```
((&A GT 2 AND &A LT 13) OR
(&A GT &B AND NOT &A GT 15))
```

In this example, if either of the internal expressions is true, the overall expression is true. Since the internal expressions are made up of two expressions in AND relationships, both expressions in the AND relationships must be true to make an internal expression true. Although the AND, OR, and NOT operators can be used in logical expressions for both SETB and AIF statements, they are used most often in AIF statements.

The MNOTE statement   Macro definitions often include some checking or editing of the macro instruction in the source program. When they do, conditional assembly statements are used to check that all the necessary operands are present, that certain operands are numeric, and so on. If any improper conditions are found, the MNOTE statement can be used to cause an error message to be printed on both the source listing and the diagnostic listing.

To illustrate, look at the GET macro in figure 11-18. Here, the second AIF statement tests the type attribute of the filename operand (&FILEN) to see if it is equal to 'O.' If the operand isn't omitted, the expansion continues with the sequence symbol .ONE. If the operand is omitted, the MNOTE statement causes the message NO FILENAME SPECIFIED to be printed on the assembly listing.

The first operand of the MNOTE statement is the *severity code*. If a severity code is present, the message will be printed in the diagnostic listing at the end of the assembly listing as well as in the source listing immediately following the macro. If the severity-code operand is omitted, the statement is written like this:

```
MNOTE 'NO FILENAME SPECIFIED'
```

Then, the MNOTE message is only printed in the source listing. Although the severity code in the MNOTE statement causes the MNOTE message to be printed in the diagnostic listing, the severity code has no function in terms of DOS/VSE.

The MEXIT statement   The MEXIT statement causes the assembler to stop the macro expansion and go back to the source program. It is generally used when an uncorrectable error is detected, such as an invalid operand. An MEXIT can have a sequence symbol, but no operands. In the GET macro definition in figure 11-18, you can see that two MEXIT statements have been used.

The ANOP statement   The ANOP statement is a no-operation statement. It is used to provide a statement on which to place a sequence symbol when the sequence symbol can't be coded directly on the model statement. In figure 11-18, all of the sequence symbols, from .ONE to .THIRT, are coded on ANOP statements.

Some related ideas

When to use internal comments   An *internal comment* has .* in columns 1 and 2 and any characters in the remaining columns. Unlike a regular comment, though, an internal comment isn't printed on the source listing when the macro is expanded. However, it prints when the macro definition itself is listed.

Internal comments can be used in any macro definition. However, you shouldn't use them unnecessarily. In general, we recommend that you use them only to identify or to clarify a segment of code.

How to use character selection   Statement number 27000025 in the GET macro definition in figure 11-18 illustrates the selection of characters from a character string:

```
AIF    ('&FILEN'(1,1) NE '(').TWO
```

Here, the first part of the logical expression

```
'&FILEN'(1,1)
```

means: select a character string beginning in position 1 of &FILEN and continue for a length of 1. In this case, the first character of the filename operand is compared to a left parenthesis. Although the presentation of the GET macro in chapter 5 didn't mention it, the filename operand of GET can be the number of a register enclosed in parentheses. If used, the register is expected to contain the address of the DTF. This AIF statement is thus checking to see if the register notation is used.

The same type of character selection is made in statement number 24000025 of the SAVE macro definition in figure 11-19. This AIF instruction checks to see that parentheses surround the registers specified as the operand of the macro, which is a sublist operand. It uses a SET symbol, &KAREGS, to specify the character position to check for the right parenthesis. A value is assigned to &KAREGS by the preceding statement, which is a SETA statement that assigns the count attribute of the SAVE operand to &KAREGS.

```
 1              MACRO                                                   00000000
 2 &LABEL GET &FILEN,&PARAM,&RPL=
 3 ✿ IOCS - GET - 5745-SC-IOX - REL 29.0                              12000029
 4              AIF    (T'&RPL NE '0').NINE                            12050028
 5              AIF    (T'&FILEN NE '0').ONE                           15000025
 6              MNOTE  0,'NO FILENAME SPECIFIED.SET TO ''✿'''          18000025
 7 &LABEL       L      1,=A(✿)             ✿✿✿✿✿ERROR-PATCH DTF TABLE ADDRESS  21000025
 8              AGO    .THREE                                          24000025
 9 .ONE         ANOP                                                   
10              AIF    ('&FILEN'(1,1) NE '(').TWO                      27000025
11              AIF    ('&FILEN(1)' EQ '1').FOUR                       30000025
12 &LABEL       LR     1,&FILEN(1)                GET DTF TABLE ADDRESS  33000025
13              AGO    .THREE                                          36000025
14 .TWO         ANOP                                                   
15 &LABEL       L      1,=A(&FILEN)               GET DTF TABLE ADDRESS  42000025
16 .THREE       ANOP                                                   
17              AIF    (T'&PARAM EQ '0').EIGHT                         45000025
18              AIF    ('&PARAM'(1,1) EQ '(').SIX                      48000025
19              L      0,=A(&PARAM)               GET WORK AREA ADDRESS  51000025
20              AGO    .EIGHT                                          54000025
21 .SIX         ANOP                                                   
22              AIF    ('&PARAM(1)' NE '1').SEVEN                      57000025
23              MNOTE  0,'INVALID REGISTER SPECIFICATION FOR WORKAREA'  60000025
24              LR     0,0                ✿✿✿✿✿ERROR-PATCH REGISTER NUMBER  63000025
25              AGO    .EIGHT                                          66000025
26 .SEVEN       ANOP                                                   
27              AIF    ('&PARAM(1)' EQ '0').EIGHT                      69000025
28              LR     0,&PARAM(1)                GET WORK AREA ADDRESS  72000025
29 .EIGHT       ANOP                                                   
30              L      15,16(1)                   GET LOGIC MODULE ADDRESS  75000025
31              BAL    14,8(15)                   BRANCH TO GET ROUTINE  78000025
32              MEXIT                                                  81000025
33 .FOUR        ANOP                                                   
34 &LABEL       DC     OH'0'                                          87000025
35              AGO    .THREE                                          90000025
36 .NINE        ANOP                                                   
37              AIF    (N'&SYSLIST EQ 0).TEN                           90100028
38              MNOTE  0,'POSITIONAL PARAMETERS NOT ALLOWED IN AM/0 GET'  C90150029
39                                                        @DA01534     90160029
40              MEXIT                                                  90200028
41 .TEN         ANOP                                                   
42              AIF    ('&RPL'(1,1) NE '(').ELEVEN                     90300028
43              AIF    ('&RPL(1)' NE '1').TWELF                        90350028
44 &LABEL       DC     OH'0'                               @DM03696    90400028
45              AGO    .THIRT                                          90450028
46 .TWELF       ANOP                                                   
47 &LABEL       LR     1,&RPL(1)           GET RPL ADDRESS    @DM03696  90550028
48              AGO    .THIRT                                          90600028
49 .ELEVEN      ANOP                                                   
50 &LABEL       L      1,=A(&RPL)          GET RPL ADDRESS    @DM03696  90700028
51 .THIRT       ANOP                                                   
52              LA     0,4                 INSERT GET CODE   @DM03696   90800028
              L      15,24(0,1)           GET ADDRESS OF ACB   @DM03696  90850028
              L      15,8(0,15)           GET ADDRESS OF AM/0 MODULE  @DM03696  90900028
              BALR   14,15                CALL AM/0         @DM03696    90950028
              MEND                                                     93000025
```

Figure 11-18   The GET macro definition

```
1             MACRO                                                      00000000
2 &NAME SAVE &REGS
3   LCLA &R1,&R2,&KAREGS
4 * SUPERVISOR - SAVE - 5745-SC-SUP - REL. 28.0                         12000028
5            AIF    (T'&REGS(1) EQ 'N').E                               14000025
6         MNOTE 1,'FIRST REGISTER NOT A SELF-DEFINING VALUE. 14 ASSUMED.'  16000025
7            AGO    .F                                                  18000025
8 .E         ANOP
9 &KAREGS    SETA   K'&REGS                                             22000025
10           AIF    ('&REGS'(1,1) EQ '(' AND '&REGS'(&KAREGS,1) EQ ')').C  24000025
11        MNOTE 0,'OPERAND NOT ENCLOSED IN PARENTHESES - IN ERROR IF    *26000025
12                 MORE THAN ONE OPERAND'                              28000025
13 &R1       SETA   &REGS                                               30000025
14           AGO    .D                                                 32000025
15 .C        ANOP
16 &R1       SETA   &REGS(1)                                            36000025
17 .D        ANOP
18           AIF    (&R1 NE 13 AND &R1 LE 15).A                         38000025
19        MNOTE 3,'1ST REG MUST NOT BE 13 OR GREATER THAN 15. 14 ASSUMED.'  40000025
20 .F        ANOP
21 &R1       SETA   14                                                  44000025
22 .A        ANOP
23           AIF    (N'&REGS EQ 1).ST                                   46000025
24           AIF    (T'&REGS(2) EQ 'N').H                               48000025
25        MNOTE 1,'2ND REGISTER NOT A SELF-DEFINING VALUE.12 ASSUMED.'  3-8 50000025
26           AGO    .G                                                  52000025
27 .H        ANOP
28 &R2       SETA   &REGS(2)                                            56000025
29           AIF    (&R1 GE 14 AND (&R2 GE &R1 AND &R2 LE 15 OR &R2 LE 12) 0X58000025
30                R &R1 LE &R2 AND &R2 LE 12).B
31        MNOTE 3,'IMPROPER RANGE OF REGISTERS. 2ND REG = 12 ASSUMED.'  62000025
32 .G        ANOP
33 &R2       SETA   12                                                  66000025
34 .B        ANOP
35 &NAME     STM    &R1,&R2,12+4*(&R1+2-(&R1+2)/16*16)(13)              70000025
36           MEXIT                                                      72000025
37 .ST       ANOP
38 &NAME     ST     &R1,12+4*(&R1+2-(&R1+2)/16*16)(13)                  76000025
39           MEND                                                       78000025
```

Figure 11-19   The SAVE macro definition

When to check for operand omissions   When you code a macro definition that checks the validity of the operands in the macro instruction, most of the routine is likely to be involved with the checking. Nevertheless, most macro definitions should at least check for operand omissions that will lead to program errors. If an omitted operand just means that a default value will be used, your macro definition doesn't have to check to make sure that the operand is present. But operand omissions often mean that the macro cannot be generated properly. As a result, omission checking is done in the IBM-supplied standard macros. And you should code routines for omission checking in your macros if they are of any consequence.

Three macro definitions for text manipulation

The GET and SAVE macros   Figures 11-18 and 11-19 present the source listings for the IBM GET and SAVE macros. As you have already seen, they illustrate extensive use of conditional assembly statements. By studying them, you can get a better appreciation for what writing a complex macro definition involves. If you relate the definitions to the code generated by the macros in your assembly listings, you should be able to figure you how your code was expanded. But it's not easy.

A move-long macro   To give you a chance to study a text-manipulation macro that isn't quite so complex, figure 11-20 presents a move-long macro. You don't need a macro like this on a System/370 because the MVCL statement does the same function. But I wrote a macro like this many years ago for the System/360 to get around the 256-byte limitation of the MVC instruction.

The move-long macro allows a move of any number of bytes to be coded in a single macro instruction. The first two operands name the receiving and sending fields; the third operand specifies the number of bytes to be moved. During macro expansion, the macro will generate one or more MVC instructions that move the data in 256-byte chunks plus one last MVC instruction that moves 256 bytes or fewer.

To show how this macro definition is expanded, assume that

```
MOVERCD   MOVEL OUTA,RCD,600
```

has been coded in a program. This means the following assignments are made at the start of the macro expansion: &LABEL=MOVERCD, &RFLD=OUTA, &SFLD=RCD, and &LGTH=600. Then, the symbols &DISP, &ALGTH, and &FIRST are declared so the first two are given initial values of zero and &FIRST is given an initial value of null. At this point the assembler reaches these SET statements:

```
&ALGTH    SETA    &LGTH
&FIRST    SETC    '&LABEL'
```

The first statement assigns the value 600 to &ALGTH; the second assigns the string MOVERCD to &FIRST.

Next, the assembler encounters this AIF statement:

```
.LOOP      AIF     (&ALGTH LE 256).LAST
```

Since &ALGTH has a value of 600, the statement is false, no branch takes place, and this statement is reached by the assembler:

```
&FIRST    MVC     &RFLD+&DISP.(256),&SFLD+&DISP
```

When the current variable values are substituted in this statement, the following source instruction is expanded into the source program:

```
MOVERCD   MVC     OUTA+0(256),RCD+0
```

Macro definition

```
           MACRO
&LABEL     MOVEL   &RFLD,&SFLD,&LGTH
           LCLA    &DISP,&ALGTH
           LCLC    &FIRST
&ALGTH     SETA    &LGTH
&FIRST     SETC    '&LABEL'
.LOOP      AIF     (&ALGTH LE 256).LAST
&FIRST     MVC     &RFLD+&DISP.(256),&SFLD+&DISP
&DISP      SETA    &DISP+256
&ALGTH     SETA    &ALGTH-256
&FIRST     SETC    ''
           AGO     .LOOP
.LAST      ANOP
&FIRST     MVC     &RFLD+&DISP.(&ALGTH),&SFLD+&DISP
           MEND
```

Macro instruction

```
MOVERCD   MOVEL  OUTA,RCD,600
```

Macro expansion

```
MOVERCD   MVC    OUTA+0(256),RCD+0
          MVC    OUTA+256(256),RCD+256
          MVC    OUTA+512(88),RCD+512
```

Figure 11-20   A move-long macro definition for the System/360

Then, the assembler reaches these statements:

```
&DISP      SETA    &DISP+256
&ALGTH     SETA    &ALGTH-256
&FIRST     SETC    ''
           AGO     .LOOP
```

As a result, the value of &DISP is increased by 256, the value of &ALGTH is decreased by 256, and the value of &FIRST is set to a null string. The AGO statement then branches the assembler back to the first statement in the loop.

The second time through the loop, the value of &ALGTH is 344 so the AIF still doesn't branch. Then, the following source instruction is generated:

```
MVC    OUTA+256(256),RCD+256
```

Note here that no label is given to the instruction since &FIRST has a null value at this time.

The third time through the loop, &ALGTH has a value of 88 so the branch to .LAST takes place. Since the operation code of this statement is ANOP, the assembler goes on to the MVC model statement so this final source instruction is generated:

```
MVC     OUTA+512(88),RCD+512
```

When the assembler reaches the MEND statement, it returns to the source instructions following the MOVEL macro.

Discussion

Although this topic is intended to familiarize you with advanced macro writing techniques, it is only a start. Before you can write macros such as the GET or SAVE, you'll probably have to put many hours of study into macro writing. If you want to learn some of the additional macro writing facilities, you can find them in *OS/VS—DOS/VSE—VM/370 Assembler Language*(GC33-4010). At this time, however, you should be able to write simple text-manipulation macros like the move-long macro without too much difficulty.

Terminology

text insertion
text insertion with modification
text manipulation
SET symbol
conditional assembly statement
local SET symbol
global SET symbol
symbol declaration
length attribute
type attribute
number attribute
sublist
subscript
count attribute
arithmetic expression
self-defining term
arithmetic operator
logical expression
logical operator
sequence symbol
severity code
internal comment

Objective

Given specifications for a text-manipulation macro, code its macro definition. Your definition will require the use of SET symbols and conditional assembly statements.

Chapter 12

Floating-point arithmetic

Floating-point is the most powerful form of System/370 arithmetic for several reasons. First, it's faster than fixed-point binary or decimal arithmetic. Second, the floating-point data format can store a wider range of values than the other formats. Third, the floating-point format can store fractional values and, when the floating-point instructions are executed, they automatically align the decimal positions.

In business data processing, however, there is little need for this power. In fact, due to the problem of converting data to and from floating-point format, floating-point instructions are rarely used for business arithmetic. So, as you study this chapter, we think you should have one major objective: to develop a better understanding of high-level languages that use floating-point instructions in the resulting object code.

Data formats   Floating-point data is stored in a fullword (*short form*) or a doubleword (*long form*) as illustrated in figure 12-1. The difference between short and long form is the number of digits that can be carried in the fraction. This is referred to as the *precision* of a number. In short form, which is often called *single precision*, the equivalent of about 7 decimal digits can be stored in the fraction; in long form, which is often called *double precision*, the equivalent of about 16 decimal digits can be stored.

In either form, the leftmost bit represents the sign of the field: "off" represents plus, and "on" represents minus. The next seven bits represent the *exponent* of the number; the remaining bits (bits 8-31 in the short form, 8-63 in the long form) represent the *fraction*. This is something like the exponential notation that you may have used in chemistry or physics classes in which a value like 1,563,487 can be written as $0.1563487E+7$ meaning 0.1563487×10^7 (10^7 means 10 to the seventh power). The expo-

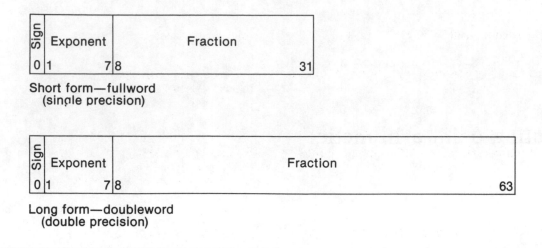

Short form—fullword
(single precision)

Long form—doubleword
(double precision)

Figure 12-1   Floating-point data formats

nent (in this case, +7) is sometimes called the *characteristic*; the fraction (in this case, 0.1563487) is sometimes called the *mantissa*.

The format of a floating-point exponent   The exponent in the floating-point format is expressed as a power of 16 (instead of 10). This exponent value is stored as a binary number in bits 1-7. To allow both plus and minus exponents, the exponent is stored in *excess-64 format*. This means that the value stored as the exponent is 64 more than the actual exponent. If, for example, the value stored is 65, it really means 65 minus 64, or 1. Thus, the fraction is multiplied by 16 to the first power. If the exponent value is less than 64, it indicates a negative exponent; for instance, a value of 62 means 62 minus 64, or an exponent of -2. (Negative exponents allow storage of very small fractional values as in 0.18×10^{-12} which equals .00000000000018.) Because the seven exponent bits can represent a number from 0 through 127, the exponent can range from -64 to +63. Thus, the range of a floating-point number in either form is approximately from 10^{-78} to 10^{+75}.

The format of a floating-point fraction   The fraction portion of a floating-point number assumes a decimal point before bit number 8. Thus, the place values of bits 8 through 31 in the short form, or bits 8 through 63 in the long form, are 2^{-1}, 2^{-2}, 2^{-3}, 2^{-4}, and so on. The fractional values of these place values are 1/2, 1/4, 1/8, 1/16, and so on. Figure 12-2 illustrates some short-form floating-point numbers in binary along with their decimal equivalents. Unlike fixed-point format, negative fractions are not in complement form.

How to normalize a floating-point number   A floating-point value is *normalized* if the fraction bits have been shifted left as much as possible so that the exponent is at the minimum possible value. In contrast, the last

Sign	Exponent	Fraction			Determining value
0	1000000	10100000	00000000	00000000	Exponent $= (64 - 64) = 0; 16^0 = 2^0$ Fraction $= (2^{-1} + 2^{-3})$ Value $= 2^0(2^{-1} + 2^{-3}) = (2^{-1} + 2^{-3}) = (.500 + .125) = 0.625$
1	1000001	01100000	00000000	00000000	Exponent $= (65 - 64) = 1; 16^1 = 2^4$ Fraction $= (2^{-2} + 2^{-3})$ Value $= -2^4(2^{-2} + 2^{-3}) = -(2^2 + 2^1) = -(4 + 2) = -6$
0	0111110	01000000	00000000	00000000	Exponent $= (62 - 64) = -2; 16^{-2} = 2^{-8}$ Fraction $= (2^{-2})$ Value $= 2^{-8}(2^{-2}) = (2^{-10}) = \dfrac{1}{1024} = .009765625$
0	1000100	00001001	00000000	00100000	Exponent $= (68 - 64) = 4; 16^4 = 2^{16}$ Fraction $= (2^{-5} + 2^{-8} + 2^{-18})$ Value $= 2^{+16}(2^{-5} + 2^{-8} + 2^{-18}) = (2^{11} + 2^8 + 2^{-2})$ $= (2048 + 256 + 0.25) = 2304.25$

Figure 12-2   Some floating-point numbers and their equivalents

example in figure 12-2 is *unnormalized*. In this case, the fraction can be shifted left four bits and the exponent reduced by one without changing the value stored. Since normalization allows a maximum number of fraction bits to be carried, thereby offering the highest level of precision, floating-point fields are usually normalized. Although there are eight instructions for manipulating unnormalized fields and there are cases when these instructions have value, they are rarely used. As a result, they aren't covered in this book.

How to define a floating-point field   To define a floating-point field, you use the type codes E and D. Type code E indicates short form and type code D indicates long form as illustrated in figure 12-3. As you can see, you can write the nominal value in an E or D type definition in regular decimal form or in exponential notation. If you use exponential notation, the exponent in decimal must be preceded by E and a plus or minus sign. The E type reserves a fullword of storage; the D type reserves a doubleword.

Figure 12-4 illustrates some additional constant definitions with the hex constant shown as it will appear both on an assembly listing and in a storage dump. Notice that hex 40 in the exponent portion of a field is

```
SINGLE      DS      E
DOUBLE      DS      D
FPVAL1      DC      E'3.141596'
FPVAL2      DC      D'1.86E+5'
FPVAL3      DC      E'-1.0E-6'
```

Figure 12-3   Some floating-point field definitions

equivalent to a zero exponent (64 minus 64). Note also that a value like 0.1 can't be expressed exactly in floating-point. In the single precision format, for example, the hex representation is 4019999A where 40 is the exponent and 19999A is the fraction. This is an approximate value of .09999999.

Instructions

As in fixed-point binary arithmetic, all arithmetic operations for floating-point are performed in registers. For this purpose, a System/370 provides four *floating-point registers*. These are doubleword registers that are used only for floating-point operations. The registers are numbered 0, 2, 4, and 6, and they accommodate both short- and long-form data. For short-form instructions, only the first of the two words in each register are used; for the long-form instructions, both words are used.

There are 44 floating-point instructions on the System/370. They cover operations for loading, storing, addition, subtraction, multiplication, division, and comparison. The 32 instructions that are summarized in figure 12-5 are presented in this topic.

Store   There are two forms of the floating-point store instruction as indicated in figure 12-5. In these instructions, as in all floating-point instructions, the character E in the operation code means short form and the character D means long form. The operands of all the floating-point instructions also have identical requirements: the first operand must always be one of the floating-point register numbers; the second operand must be either a fullword (short form), a doubleword (long form), or another floating-point register.

Load   In addition to the basic forms of the load instruction, several special forms are available. These special instructions load a value while forcing the sign of the value to be positive, negative, or the opposite of its original value. Because negative floating-point numbers aren't stored in complement form, the load complement instructions change the sign of a field by reversing only the sign bit.

Add and subtract   The add and subtract instructions follow a similar pattern. When these instructions are executed, the value in the second operand is added to or subtracted from the first operand with the result replacing the first operand. Any alignment of decimal points is performed automatically, and the result is normalized before it is placed in the first operand register.

Hex code on assembly listing	Source code		Object code in storage dump
+00.000000	DC	E'0'	00000000
+41.100000	DC	E'1'	41100000
+43.FFF000	DC	E'4095'	43FFF000
+44.100000	DC	E'4096'	44100000
-41.100000	DC	E'-1'	C1100000
-43.FFF000	DC	E'-4095'	C3FFF000
-44.100000	DC	E'-4096'	C4100000
+40.800000	DC	E'0.5'	40800000
+41.180000	DC	E'1.5'	41180000
+40.19999A	DC	E'0.1'	4019999A
+3F.28F5C3	DC	E'0.01'	3F28F5C3
+3E.418937	DC	E'0.001'	3E418937
+48.4C2CBC	DC	E'12.78E+8'	484C2CBC
+51.56BC76	DC	E'1E+20'	5156BC76
-6A.BF9572	DC	E'-2.8E+50'	EABF9572
+00.00000000000000	DC	D'0'	0000000000000000
+41.10000000000000	DC	D'1'	4110000000000000
+40.80000000000000	DC	D'0.5'	4080000000000000
+40.1999999999999A	DC	D'0.1'	401999999999999A
+17.3BD0F495A9703E	DC	D'0.1E-49'	173BD0F495A9703E
+40.1F9ADD3739635F	DC	D'12345.6789E-5'	401F9ADD3739635F

Figure 12-4   Some representations of floating-point numbers as they would appear in an assembly listing and a storage dump

Multiply   The floating-point multiply instruction can have either a storage field or another floating-point register as the second operand. When the instruction is executed, the first operand is multiplied by the second with the product replacing the first operand. Like signs result in a positive result, unlike signs in a negative result. An *exponent overflow* exception occurs if the resulting exponent value is greater than 127 and *exponent underflow* occurs if it's less than 0.

Divide   The floating-point divide instruction is similar. When executed, the quotient replaces the dividend in the first operand register and no remainder is saved. Exponent overflow and underflow can occur as in a multiply instruction, and an attempt to divide by zero leads to a floating-point divide exception.

Compare   The floating-point compare instructions provide an arithmetic comparison of floating-point values. After a compare instruction, you normally use a conditional branch instruction to test the condition code and branch accordingly.

Operation code	Instruction name	Example	
STE	Store short	STE	2,FPSAVE
STD	Store long	STD	4,FPDBLE
LE	Load short	LE	4,FWORD
LD	Load long	LD	6,DWORD
LER	Load short RR	LER	0,4
LDR	Load long RR	LDR	2,0
LPER	Load positive short	LPER	2,NEGF
LPDR	Load positive long	LPDR	4,NEGD
LNER	Load negative short	LNER	2,POSF
LNDR	Load negative long	LNDR	4,POSD
LCER	Load complement short	LCER	6,COMPF
LCDR	Load complement long	LCDR	6,COMPD
AE	Add short	AE	0,FACT1
AD	Add long	AD	4,DFACT
AER	Add short RR	AER	0,6
ADR	Add long RR	ADR	4,6
SE	Subtract short	SE	2,SUBWORD
SD	Subtract long	SD	6,DBLESUB
SER	Subtract short RR	SER	4,2
SDR	Subtract long RR	SDR	6,0
ME	Multiply short	ME	0,FACT
MD	Multiply long	MD	4,FACT
MER	Multiply short RR	MER	2,4
MDR	Multiply long RR	MDR	2,6
DE	Divide short	DE	2,DIV
DD	Divide long	DD	4,DDIVS
DER	Divide short RR	DER	2,0
DDR	Divide long RR	DDR	2,6
CE	Compare short	CE	2,VAL1
CD	Compare long	CD	6,VAL2
CER	Compare short RR	CER	0,2
CDR	Compare long RR	CDR	2,4

Figure 12-5   The floating-point instructions

Imprecision in floating-point arithmetic

One thing you should understand about floating-point arithmetic is that it doesn't always give exact results. For example, you have already seen how some decimal values (like 0.1) can't be expressed exactly in hexadecimal floating-point format. Another problem is that hex digits on the right of a fraction may be lost during an arithmetic operation.

To illustrate, suppose the add-long instruction adds two values, one with a hex exponent of 40, another with a hex exponent of 43. Prior to addition, the fraction with the smaller exponent is shifted right three hex digits to align the fractions. This means the rightmost 12 bits of the smaller number are moved out of the register, which can mean lost hex digits. After addition, the result is normalized (if necessary), so the result is shifted left.

To reduce the number of lost digits in floating-point arithmetic operations, the electronic circuitry that actually does the shifting has four extra bit positions to the right of the fraction that is shifted. These four bit positions are called a *guard digit*. Then, if a fraction is shifted right three hex digits, only two of the digits are lost when the result is normalized. Nevertheless, the result of a floating-point operation is likely to be less precise than that of a fixed-point binary or decimal operation.

This imprecision is an important notion to grasp because it can affect the coding of branching operations. To illustrate, suppose a program compares a floating-point constant of 0.1 with a field in which a decreasing value eventually should reach 0.1. When they are equal, the program should branch. Since the constant 0.1 can't be represented exactly and since the manipulated value may lose digits as it approaches 0.1, the two fields may never be exactly equal. Because of this, a branch code of BNL or BNH should be used so the program will branch when the manipulated value equals or passes the constant value. If BE is used, the program may never branch.

Data conversion

The main reason floating-point arithmetic isn't used in business programming is that data conversion is a problem. Since there is no instruction that converts other data formats to floating-point format, you must code a conversion routine. Figure 12-6, for example, illustrates a simple routine that converts an EBCDIC input field to floating point. It is relatively simple because the input format is rigid: the leftmost column of the ten-column field contains the sign, followed by a four-column integer, followed by a decimal point, followed by a four-column decimal fraction. Imagine how much more complex a FORTRAN conversion routine must be since the decimal point can be anywhere in a field and E notation is optional.

In figure 12-6, the integer and fraction portions are converted to floating point separately and then added together. First, the digits are converted to binary in register 7. Then, a valid floating-point exponent value followed by binary zeros is placed into register 6 using the load instruction. In this case, an exponent of hex 4E (the equivalent of +14) is placed in the register. Since there are 14 hex digits in the fraction portion of a double precision field, this means the decimal point is assumed to be to the right of all the hex digits in the fraction. In other words, the value stored in registers 6 and 7 is a valid, unnormalized whole number.

At this point, the value in register 6 and 7 is loaded into floating-point register 0 and a value of zero is added to it. After the addition takes place, the result is automatically normalized so the original integer value is shifted left as many hex digits as appropriate and the exponent is reduced accordingly. That means floating-point register 0 contains the proper normalized floating-point number for the integer portion of the input field.

The conversion of the fraction takes place in the same manner as the integer conversion until after the decimal fraction is loaded as an integer into floating-point register 2. Then, the value is divided by 10,000 so it takes on its true fractional value.

Next, the routine adds the fractional value of the input field in floating-point register 2 to the integer value in floating-point register 0. After the addition takes place, the floating point value is stored in the field named FPVAL.

To make sure the sign of the field is correct, the routine then tests the first byte of the input field for a minus sign. If a minus sign is present, a one bit is ORed into the first bit position of FPVAL using the OI instruction (described in detail in chapter 10). This makes FPVAL negative.

Discussion

As I mentioned earlier, floating-point instructions are rarely used for business arithmetic. Instead, the floating-point facilities are used for solving scientific problems—ones in which very large or very small values may be involved or ones in which decimal alignment may be extremely difficult to keep track of when using fixed-point arithmetic.

The vast majority of scientific programming, however, isn't done in assembler language. Instead, a mathematical language such as FORTRAN is used. As a result, it is unlikely that you will ever actually use floating-point instructions in an assembler language program.

Terminology

short form	mantissa
long form	excess-64 format
precision	normalized
single precision	unnormalized
double precision	floating-point register
exponent	exponent overflow
fraction	exponent underflow
characteristic	guard digit

Objective

Give two reasons why a numeric result that is derived by floating-point instructions may not be exactly equal to a result that is derived by fixed-point instructions.

```
                .
                .
CONV     PACK   DWORD,RINT
         CVB    7,DWORK
         L      6,EXPONENT
         STM    6,7,DWORK
         LD     0,DWORK
         AD     0,FPZERO
         PACK   DWORK,RFRAC
         CVB    7,DWORK
         L      6,EXPONENT
         STM    6,7,DWORK
         LD     2,DWORK
         DD     2,FRACADJ
         ADR    0,2
         STD    0,FPVAL
         CLI    RSIGN,C'-'
         BNE    CONT
         OI     FPVAL,X'80'
CONT            .
                .
                .
DWORK    DS     D
FPVAL    DS     D
FPZERO   DC     D'0'
FRACADJ  DC     D'1.0E+4'
EXPONENT DC     X'4E000000'
                .
                .
                .
RECVAL   DS     0CL10     (SXXXX.XXXX)
RSIGN    DS     C
RINT     DS     CL4
RPOINT   DS     C
RFRAC    DS     CL4
```

Figure 12-6   A floating-point conversion routine

Section 4

Assembler language for DASD access methods

This section shows you how to use the DASD access methods in assembler language. That includes the native access methods (SAM, ISAM, and DAM) as well as the VSAM access methods. You can study this section any time after you complete section 2.

This section is designed so you have to read chapter 13 on SAM files before you read the other chapters in the section. However, once you read chapter 13, you can read any one of the other chapters in this section. For instance, you may find that you only need information on SAM and VSAM files, so you will only read chapter 13 and chapter 16 in this section.

If you use assembler language today, you will most likely use SAM and VSAM files at one time or another. However, you may never need to use ISAM and DAM files. On the other hand, if you are asked to modify an old program that uses ISAM or DAM, the material in chapters 14 and 15 will come in handy.

Chapter 13

The Sequential Access Method (SAM)

In section 2 of this book, you were introduced to the coding for sequential input files. Since they are relatively simple in concept, I hope you haven't had any problem understanding how they are used.

In this chapter, I'm going to give you more information about using sequential files. In topic 1, you'll learn about variable-length records and blocks. In topic 2, you'll learn assembler language for sequential input, output, and update files in both fixed-length and variable-length format. Finally, in topic 3, you'll learn more about the VSE JCL you use for sequential files. You can read this chapter any time after you complete section 2.

TOPIC 1   SAM concepts

The *Sequential Access Method (SAM)* is used to store records on a DASD and to retrieve them from a DASD in sequential order. When a SAM file is created on a DASD, the records are written on the device one after the other starting with the first record position in the area for the file and continuing until all of the records have been written in the area or there's no more room for the next record. When a sequential file is read, the records are read starting with the record in the first record position and continuing until an end-of-file record is read. An *end-of-file record* on a CKD device is simply a count area that indicates a data area with a length of zero.

Because SAM files are relatively simple conceptually, there's no point in dwelling on them. In this topic, then, I'll simply review blocked records, introduce you to variable-length records, and give you some ideas about how to determine block sizes.

Blocked records

In chapter 1, I introduced you to *blocked records*. This simply means that more than one record in a file is stored in a *block* of records on a DASD. For example, in a file with a *blocking factor* of ten, ten records are stored in each block. Blocking records makes efficient use of disk space because less space is used up in the gaps between records or blocks. It can also speed up I/O operations because only one I/O execution is required to read or write an entire block of records.

To read blocked records, a program must deblock the records. To illustrate, suppose a program reads a block of ten records. This means that one I/O instruction reads a block of ten records into storage. Then, the program must process one of the ten records at a time, just as if the records were presented to it in unblocked format. The routine that does this is called a *deblocking routine*. Similarly, a program that writes a block of records requires a *blocking routine* to assemble the records in a block before they are written to a DASD.

You have already learned how to deblock sequential input records in two ways. First, in chapter 5, you learned how to use a work area for deblocking. In this case, the next record in the file is moved from the I/O area into your work area each time a GET instruction is executed. Then, in chapter 7, you learned how to use an I/O register for deblocking. In this case, the records in the block stay in the I/O area. However, the address in the I/O register is adjusted each time a GET instruction is executed so it always points to the start of the next record to be processed. In both of these cases, if the records are blocked ten to a block, the GET instruction only reads a block into the input area once for every ten times the instruction is executed. As you will see in the next topic, you can provide for blocking records in much the same way that you provide for deblocking records.

Variable-length records

When the records in a file vary in length, they are referred to as *variable-length records*. Sometimes, for example, a file will consist of more than one type of record. Then, if these record types have different lengths, the file consists of variable-length records. For instance, a set of records representing one transaction may consist of a header record that is 250-bytes long, detail records that are 50-bytes long, and a trailer record that is 150-bytes long. In this case, the maximum record length in the file is 250 bytes.

Another type of variable-length record consists of a *root segment* plus a variable number of other segments. For example, inventory records that give warehouse locations may be in variable-length format. In this case, the root segment of each record contains the basic inventory data like item number, item description, total quantity on hand, and so on. Then, a variable number of additional segments follow the root segment. These segments (one for each warehouse location in which some of the item is stored) specify the warehouse location (typically, warehouse number and bin number), the quantity stored there, and maybe even the date it was stored. As a result, an item stored in only one location has only one of these location segments attached to the root segment; an item stored in 10 locations has 10 location segments.

Like fixed-length records, variable-length records are stored one after another in consecutive order. If the records are blocked, each block contains as many records as will fit in the maximum block size. So the system knows how long the blocks and the records are, each block and each record is preceded by a four-byte length field as illustrated in figure 13-1. For each record, the number of bytes contained in the record, including the four-byte record-length field, is recorded as a binary value in the first two bytes of the record-length field. The second two bytes are reserved for use by DOS and usually contain EBCDIC blanks. For each block, the number of bytes contained in the block, including the four-byte block-length field, is recorded in the block-length field. This field is in the same format as the record-length field.

When one of your programs creates a variable-length record, it must calculate the record length and store it in the record-length field before the record can be written. Since the length is stored in binary format, the length is usually accumulated in a register and stored using the store-halfword instruction. The block length, however, is calculated automatically and stored in the block-length field.

Determining block size

When you write a program that reads a sequential file, you normally are given the block size as part of the program specifications. For fixed-length records, the block size is a multiple of the record size. For variable-length records, the block size must provide for at least one record of maximum length.

However, when you write a program that creates a sequential file, you may not be given the block size. If you know that your operations group is going to determine the block size for your program after you test

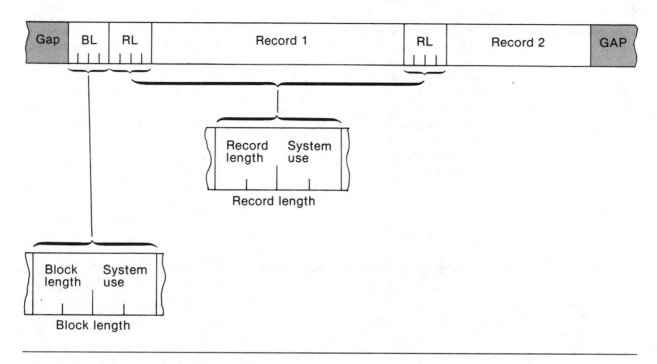

Figure 13-1   The format of blocked variable-length records

it, this presents no problem. In this case, you simply assume that the records will be blocked and select a block size that is consistent with your test data. You understand that your program will be changed later on so it uses a block size that maximizes program and storage efficiency.

On the other hand, if you are asked to select an efficient block size, you should know that block sizes of around 4000 bytes tend to maximize program and storage efficiency. This means that blocks of this size minimize the number of I/O operations required to read or write a file while they maximize the amount of data that can be stored on a track of a DASD. Although larger block sizes can improve these two factors even more, they continue to increase the size of your program which can decrease its efficiency. As a result, it becomes a case of diminishing returns.

As a rule of thumb, then, you should select a block size that is close to 4000 bytes long. In addition, if the file will always be stored on the same type of DASD, you should select a block size that is consistent with the device type. To do this, you use the tables in the manual for the device.

Terminology
Sequential Access Method
SAM
end-of-file record
blocked records
block
blocking factor
deblocking routine
blocking routine
variable-length record
root segment

Objective

1. Explain how blocking records can reduce the time required to read or write a file.

2. Describe the format for blocked, variable-length records.

TOPIC 2 Assembler language for SAM files

In chapter 5, you were introduced to sequential disk file processing in the reorder-listing program. However, that chapter only showed you how to process input files with blocked or unblocked fixed-length records. In this topic, I'll show you how to use sequential update and output files as well as input files in both fixed- and variable-length formats. First, I will present the operands of the DTFSD that I didn't present in chapter 5. Then I will present two programs that illustrate sequential file processing.

DTFSD operands

There are 23 different keyword operands that can be used in a DTFSD macro. However, only eleven of these are used frequently. This subset is summarized in figure 13-2. Since you were introduced to part of this subset in chapter 5, I will only present the new information at this time.

BLKSIZE   When you use a sequential disk file for input, you specify the physical length of a block of data in the BLKSIZE operand. However, when you create a new file (an output file), the I/O area must also provide for an eight-byte count area at the start of the block. As a result, the BLKSIZE operand and the I/O area definition must reflect these additional bytes.

Fortunately, the programmer isn't responsible for moving any data into this eight-byte count area. This is done automatically in an assembler language program.

RECFORM   The RECFORM operand specifies how the records in a file are formatted on the disk. Disk records can be blocked fixed-length (FIX-BLK), unblocked fixed-length (FIXUNB), blocked variable-length (VARBLK), or unblocked variable-length (VARUNB). If the RECFORM operand is omitted, FIXUNB is assumed.

RECSIZE   The RECSIZE operand specifies the physical length of a single record and is only required if the file contains fixed-length blocked records. This makes sense because if the records are unblocked, the BLKSIZE operand specifies the record size. And, if the records are variable length, each record can have a different size.

TYPEFLE   The TYPEFLE operand specifies whether a file is to be used for input or output. Since the default value is INPUT, the TYPEFLE operand only needs to be coded for output files.

UPDATE   The UPDATE operand is only specified if the records in a file are to be updated in place. This means that a record is read, its data is updated in a work area or an I/O area in storage, and the record is written back onto the DASD in its original location. When the UPDATE operand is specified, the TYPEFLE operand must specify INPUT.

Two illustrative programs

Because sequential files are relatively simple in concept, you shouldn't have much trouble coding the assembler language for processing them. As a result, I'll only present two short programs in this topic to illustrate the use of the assembler language macros for SAM files.

An update program that uses fixed-length records   Figure 13-3 gives a program overview for a simple update program. Briefly, a shipment file is used to update an order master file representing unfilled customer orders. Both files are in sequence by product number within order number. After an order record has been updated, it is written in its original location on the order file and a report record is written on a report file. This report file is used later as input to a disk-to-printer program. But if a shipment record doesn't have a matching order record, the unmatched transaction is printed on the error listing. This program, of course, is unrealistic because it has been simplified for illustrative purposes.

Figure 13-4 presents a traditional flowchart for this program and figure 13-5 presents its assembler language code. As you might guess, the decision block on the flowchart is the critical point in the program. Here, the control number (order number plus product number) in the shipment record (the transaction) is compared with the control number in the order record (the master). A *control number*, or *control field*, is a field or combination of fields within a record or set of records that determines the processing of a program. As you study the logic in the flowchart, remember that both transaction and master file are in sequence by product number within order number. Otherwise, this control-number comparison wouldn't work correctly.

If the control numbers are equal (T=M), the order record is updated and written back onto the file and a report record is written on the report file. If the control number in the transaction record is greater than the one in the master record (T>M), another master record is read and the loop repeats. If the control number in the transaction is less than the one in the master (T<M), it indicates an *unmatched transaction*. In this case, an error line is printed, another transaction is read, and processing continues.

The only other point of interest in the flowchart is the end-of-file processing for the master file. If this end-of-file condition is reached before the end of the shipment file, it indicates one or more unmatched shipment records. Then, the program prints an error line on the error listing, reads another shipment record, and repeats the loop. When the shipment end-of-file is reached within this loop, the program ends.

Priority	Keyword	Programmer code	Remarks
Required	BLKSIZE	Length of I/O area	Block length; for output files, it must include 8 bytes for the count area.
Optional	RECFORM	FIXUNB FIXBLK VARUNB VARBLK	FIXBLK for fixed-length blocked records; VARBLK for variable-length blocked records; FIXUNB is the default.
Optional	RECSIZE	Record length	Use only if RECFORM is FIXBLK.
Optional	TYPEFLE	INPUT OUTPUT	INPUT is the default so this operand is usually omitted for input files.
Optional	UPDATE	YES	Used only when records are to be updated in place; TYPEFLE must be INPUT.
Required	IOAREA1	Name of first I/O area	Length must equal block length.
Optional	IOAREA2	Name of second I/O area	Must be same length as first I/O area.
Optional	WORKA	YES	When used, records will be read into or written from the area named in the related GET or PUT statement. Don't use if IOREG is specified.
Optional	IOREG	Register number (nn)	When used, the register will give the address of the next record to be processed. Don't use if WORKA = YES is specified. IOREG is illustrated in topic 3 of chapter 7.
Required for input files	EOFADDR	Label of first instruction of EOF routine	Required for input files.
Optional	DEVADDR	Logical unit name in form SYSxxx	Programmer logical units are commonly used; only required when no EXTENT statement is used in the JCL for the file.

Figure 13-2   DTFSD operand summary

Program: ORDUPD Update order file	Page: 1
Designer: Anne Prince	Date: 11-06-85

Input/output specifications

File	Description	Use
SHIPTR	Shipment transaction file	Input
ORDERS	Order master file	Update
RPTTR	Report transaction file	Output
ERRLIST	Printer file: Error transaction listing	Output

Process specifications

The order master file contains records of items that have been ordered but not shipped with one record for each item on order. The shipment transaction file is used to update this file in place with one record for each item that has just been shipped. Both files are in sequence by product code within order number, and there can only be one shipment transaction for a matching order record. To update a master record, the program moves the product code, quantity shipped, and shipment date from the shipment record into the corresponding fields of the master record.

If a transaction is processed correctly, a copy of the updated order record should be written in the report transaction file for use by a report-preparation program later on. If the program can't find a matching master record for a transaction, a line should be printed on the error listing. This listing is simplified for illustrative purposes, so the format of a record line is simply the 24 bytes of the transaction record followed by the message, UNMATCHED SHIPMENT TRANSACTION. Also, the program doesn't have to provide for page overflow or headings on this error listing.

Shipment record format

Bytes	Field name
1-2	Transaction code
3-6	Order number
7-12	Product code
13-16	Quantity shipped
17-24	Shipment date (MM/DD/YY)

Order record format

Bytes	Field name
1-4	Customer number
5-24	Customer name
25-28	Order number
29-34	Product code ordered
35-38	Quantity ordered
39-46	Date ordered (MM/DD/YY)
47-52	Product code shipped
53-56	Quantity shipped
57-64	Date shipped (MM/DD/YY)
65-80	Not used

All data is in character (C) format.

Figure 13-3   A program overview for a sequential update program

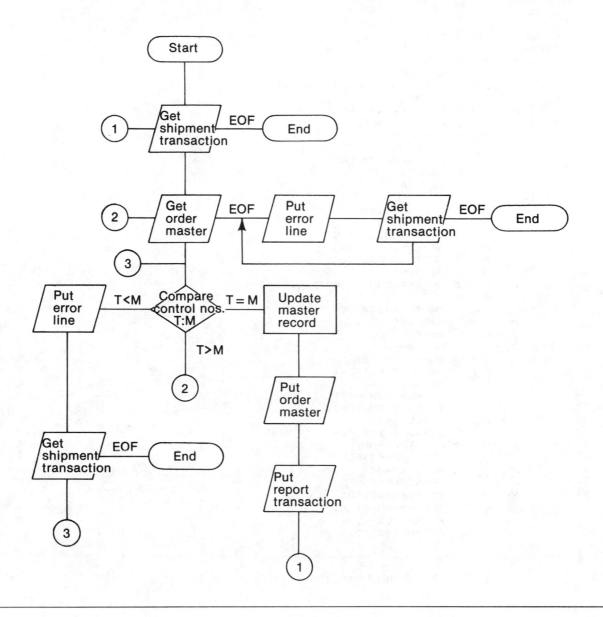

Figure 13-4   A flowchart for the sequential update program

```
ORDUPD      START   0
BEGIN       BALR    3,0
            USING   *,3
            USING   SHIPMASK,4
            OPEN    SHIPTR,ORDERS,RPTTR,ERRLIST
READSHIP    GET     SHIPTR
READORD     GET     ORDERS,ORDWORK
TEST        CLC     ORDCTL,SHCTL
            BL      READORD
            BE      MATCH
            MVC     ERRTR,SHIPMASK
            PUT     ERRLIST
            GET     SHIPTR
            B       TEST
MATCH       MVC     ORPRODSH,SHPROD
            MVC     ORQTYSH,SHQTY
            MVC     ORDATESH,SHDATE
            PUT     ORDERS,ORDWORK
            PUT     RPTTR,ORDWORK
            B       READSHIP
EOFSHIP     CLOSE   SHIPTR,ORDERS,RPTTR,ERRLIST
            EOJ
EOFORD      MVC     ERRTR,SHIPMASK
            PUT     ERRLIST
            GET     SHIPTR
            B       EOFORD
SHIPTR      DTFSD   BLKSIZE=240,                                    X
                    RECFORM=FIXBLK,                                 X
                    RECSIZE=24,                                     X
                    IOAREA1=SHIPIN1,                                X
                    IOAREA2=SHIPIN2,                                X
                    IOREG=(4),                                      X
                    EOFADDR=EOFSHIP
ORDERS      DTFSD   BLKSIZE=400,                                    X
                    RECFORM=FIXBLK,                                 X
                    RECSIZE=80,                                     X
                    UPDATE=YES,                                     X
                    IOAREA1=ORDIO1,                                 X
                    IOAREA2=ORDIO2,                                 X
                    WORKA=YES,                                      X
                    EOFADDR=EOFORD
```

Figure 13-5   A sequential update program (part 1 of 2)

If you look at the DTFSD for the shipment file in figure 13-5, you can see that it uses two I/O areas along with an I/O register, register 4. Then, a USING statement relates register 4 to the DSECT named SHIPMASK. As a result, the names in the DSECT refer to the fields within each record in the shipment file. Since I presented the use of an I/O register in chapter 7, you shouldn't have any trouble understanding how this works in this program.

In the DTFSD for the order master file, UPDATE=YES is specified along with WORKA=YES. This means that the master record in the work area will be written in the location from which the master record was originally read. As a result, you shouldn't issue a PUT instruction for an

```
RPTTR      DTFSD BLKSIZE=408,                                                    X
                 RECFORM=FIXBLK,                                                 X
                 RECSIZE=80,                                                     X
                 TYPEFLE=OUTPUT,                                                 X
                 IOAREA1=RPTIO1,                                                 X
                 IOAREA2=RPTIO2,                                                 X
                 WORKA=YES
ERRLIST    DTFPR BLKSIZE=132,                                                    X
                 IOAREA1=ERRLINE,                                                X
                 DEVADDR=SYSLST
SHIPIN1    DS    CL240
SHIPIN2    DS    CL240
ORDIO1     DS    CL400
ORDIO2     DS    CL400
RPTIO1     DS    CL408
RPTIO2     DS    CL408
ERRLINE    DS    0CL132
           DC    20C' '
ERRTR      DS    CL24
           DC    CL88'          UNMATCHED SHIPMENT TRANSACTION'
SHIPMASK   DSECT
SHTRCODE   DS    CL2
SHCTL      DS    0CL10
SHORDNBR   DS    CL4
SHPROD     DS    CL6
SHQTY      DS    CL4
SHDATE     DS    CL8
ORDUPD     CSECT
ORDWORK    DS    0CL80
           DS    CL24
ORDCTL     DS    0CL10
ORDNBR     DS    CL4
ORPRODOR   DS    CL6
ORQTYOR    DS    CL4
ORDATEOR   DS    CL8
ORPRODSH   DS    CL6
ORQTYSH    DS    CL4
ORDATESH   DS    CL8
           DS    CL16
           END   BEGIN
```

Figure 13-5   A sequential update program (part 2 of 2)

update file without first issuing a GET instruction.

In the DTFSD for the report file, the BLKSIZE is 408 and the RECSIZE is 80. Since this is an output file, the I/O area must provide for the 8-byte count area. In other words, the records are blocked with a blocking factor of five, so the I/O area is 400 bytes plus 8 bytes, or 408 bytes.

Notice that the DEVADDR operand isn't specified in the DTFs for any of the disk files. When this operand is omitted, EXTENT statements in the JCL for running the program provide the logical unit addresses for the disk files. You will learn how to code EXTENT statements in the next topic.

A disk-to-printer program that uses variable-length records   Figure 13-6 presents the program overview for a variable-length, disk-to-printer program. This program prepares a listing of students and courses as indicated in the print chart in figure 13-7. As you can see in figure 13-6, the student master file consists of a root segment plus course segments with one course segment for each course a student is taking. In this school, a student may take up to ten courses in a semester, so the maximum number of course segments in a record is ten. Again, this program is unrealistic because it has been simplified for illustrative purposes.

The logic of the program is simple. For each course segment of each student record, a line is printed on the student course listing. For the first course for each student, the information in the root segment is printed along with the course information. Otherwise, only the course information is printed in a line.

Figure 13-8 is the assembler language listing for this program. Although there is little in this program that is new to you, other than the characteristics of the file, there are a few things I would like to point out.

First, notice that the DTFSD for the student master file specifies blocked, variable-length records with a block size of 704 bytes. Since the minimum block length is ten course segments (310 bytes) plus one root segment (33 bytes) plus the block and record length fields (8 bytes), this block size is satisfactory for testing the program. Later on, the block size can be increased by the operations department to improve execution and storage efficiency. When the program is executed, the actual sizes of the blocks will vary depending on the number of courses taken by each student. But since the deblocking routine is handled automatically by assembler language, you don't have to worry about the actual size of each block.

Second, take a look at the procedure I used to determine if there are additional course segments to be processed for each student record read. First, register 5 is loaded with the actual record length. Next, the length of the root segment is subtracted from register 5. As a result, the length remaining in register 5 is the length of the course segments. Then, after each course segment is processed, the length of a single course segment is subtracted from register 5 and the resulting length is compared to zero. If the length is equal to zero, it means that all course segments have been processed and the next student record is read. Otherwise, the next course segment is processed.

Third, look at the definition of the work area for the variable-length record. As I explained in the last topic, the first two bytes of a variable-length record contain the record length. Since the length is stored in binary format, it is defined as a halfword in the first field before the root segment. Then, the next two bytes are reserved for use by the operating system.

Finally, note that I coded a DSECT for the course segments. After each new student record is read, the base register for the DSECT is loaded with the address of the course segment area in the student record. Then, after each course segment is processed, if another segment is present, the register is increased by 31 bytes so it addresses the next segment.

Program: DSKTOPRT Prepare course listing	Page: 1
Designer: Anne Prince	**Date:** 11-06-85

Input/output specifications

File	Description	Use
STUDENT	Student master file (variable length records)	Input
CRSELST	Printer file: Student course listing	Output

Process specifications

This program prepares a student course listing from a student master file. This file consists of variable-length records. The root segment gives information about the student. Each course segment gives information about one course that the student is taking with a maximum of ten course segments per student.

The format of the listing, which is shown on the next page, is simplified for illustrative purposes. To further simplify, the program doesn't have to provide for page overflow or headings on this listing. To prepare the listing, the program prints one line for each course segment in a record. For the first course segment line, the program also prints the information in the root segment.

Student master record format

Segment	Bytes	Field name	Format
Root	1-6	Student ID number	CL6
	7-31	Student name	CL25
	32-33	Total credit hours	PL2
Course	1-4	Course code	CL4
	5-29	Course title	CL25
	30-31	Course credit hours	PL2

Figure 13-6   A program overview for a variable-length, disk-to-printer program

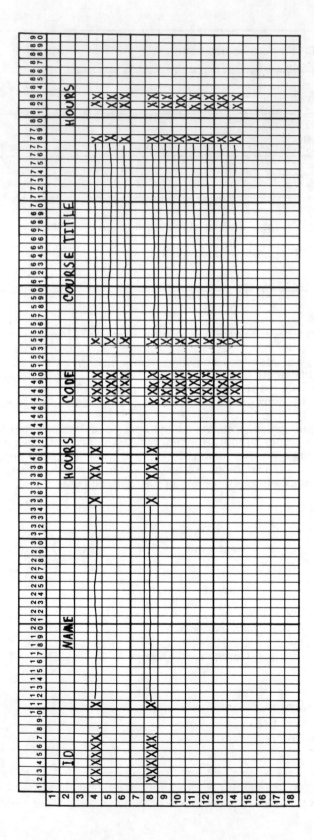

Figure 13-7   A print chart for the variable-length, disk-to-printer program

```
DSKTOPRT START 0
BEGIN     BALR  3,0
          USING *,3
          USING SCOURSE,4          ASSIGN R4 AS BASE FOR DSECT
          OPEN  STUDENT,CRSELST
READSTUD  GET   STUDENT,STUDREC
          MVC   LSID,SID
          MVC   LSNAME,SNAME
          MVC   LSHOURS,HRSEDIT
          ED    LSHOURS,SHOURS
          LA    4,SSEGAREA          LOAD FIRST SEGMENT ADDRESS
          LH    5,SLGTH             LOAD R5 WITH RECORD LENGTH
          S     5,=F'37'            SUBTRACT ROOT SEGMENT LENGTH
NXTCRSE   MVC   LCNBR,SCNBR
          MVC   LCNAME,SCNAME
          MVC   LCHRS,HRSEDIT
          ED    LCHRS,SCHRS
          PUT   CRSELST,LLINE
          MVI   LLINE,X'40'
          MVC   LLINE+1(131),LLINE
          S     5,=F'31'            SUBTRACT SEGMENT LENGTH
          C     5,=F'0'
          BNH   READSTUD
          LA    4,31(4)             ADJUST ADDRESS IN R4 TO NEXT SEGMENT
          B     NXTCRSE
EOFDISK   CLOSE STUDENT,CRSELST
          EOJ
STUDENT   DTFSD BLKSIZE=704,                                              X
                RECFORM=VARBLK,                                           X
                IOAREA1=STUDIN1,                                          X
                IOAREA2=STUDIN2,                                          X
                WORKA=YES,                                                X
                EOFADDR=EOFDISK
```

Figure 13-8   A variable-length disk-to-printer program (part 1 of 2)

Discussion
: If you understand the programs presented in this topic, you shouldn't have any problem with sequential files. In contrast, it's considerably more difficult to use ISAM, DAM, and VSAM files. You'll learn about these files in the next three chapters.

Terminology
: control number
control field
unmatched transaction

Objective
: Given program specifications that require the use of one or more SAM files, code an assembler language program that satisfies the specifications.

```
CRSELST   DTFPR BLKSIZE=132,                                                X
                IOAREA1=PRTOUT1,                                            X
                IOAREA2=PRTOUT2,                                            X
                WORKA=YES,                                                  X
                DEVADDR=SYSLST
STUDIN1   DS    CL704
STUDIN2   DS    CL704
PRTOUT1   DS    CL132
PRTOUT2   DS    CL132
HRSEDIT   DC    X'4020214B21'
STUDREC   DS    0CL347
SLGTH     DS    H                       DEFINE RECORD LENGTH IN BINARY
          DS    CL2
SID       DS    CL6
SNAME     DS    CL25
SHOURS    DS    PL2
SSEGAREA  DS    CL310
SCOURSE   DSECT
SCNBR     DS    CL4
SCNAME    DS    CL25
SCHRS     DS    PL2
DSKTOPRT  CSECT
LLINE     DS    0CL132
          DS    C' '
LSID      DS    CL6
          DC    3C' '
LSNAME    DS    CL25
          DC    C' '
LSHOURS   DS    CL5
          DC    3C' '
LCNBR     DS    CL4
          DC    3C' '
LCNAME    DS    CL25
LCHRS     DS    CL5
          DC    51C' '
          END   BEGIN
```

Figure 13-8   A variable-length disk-to-printer program (part 2 of 2)

TOPIC 3   VSE JCL for SAM files

In chapter 3, I introduced you to the JCL required to compile and test disk-to-printer programs that use sequential files. Now, in this topic, I am going to expand upon that presentation. First, I will review the use of the ASSGN and DLBL statements. Then, I will present the EXTENT statement, which I didn't present in chapter 3.

As I explain these statements, I will refer to the JCL procedure in figure 13-9. This is the JCL I used for testing the update program in figure 13-5.

The ASSGN statement

The ASSGN statement is used to assign the files defined in your program to physical I/O devices. It is used to temporarily override any standard assignments. For example, these are the ASSGN statements in figure 13-9:

```
// ASSGN    SYS008,290
// ASSGN    SYS009,290
// ASSGN    SYS010,290
```

The first operands name the logical units and the second operands specify the physical addresses of the devices to which the logical units are to be assigned. In this case, all of the logical units are assigned to the DASD device at address 290. These assignments are in effect from the time the ASSGN statement is read until the end of the job or until another ASSGN statement changes an assignment. When the job ends, the logical unit reverts to its standard assignment.

Generally, if a file your program uses is on a device that has a standard assignment to a logical unit, you will relate your file to the logical unit for that device. Then, you won't need to code an ASSGN statement for that file when you test your program. You will note in figure 13-9, for example, that ASSGN statements are only coded for the disk files. The DTF instruction for the printer file uses the DEVADDR operand to relate the file to a logical unit that has a standard assignment to a printer.

When the DTF for a sequential file doesn't include the DEVADDR operand, the file must be related to a logical unit by the EXTENT statement in the JCL. In fact, none of the DTFs for the disk files in the program in figure 13-5 use the DEVADDR operand, so all three files must have EXTENT statements. In a moment, I'll explain how an EXTENT statement relates a file to a logical unit.

The DLBL statement

All disk files in the standard file organizations have standard disk labels. This means that a DLBL statement must be included in the JCL for programs that use disk files so these labels can be checked for input files and created for output files. The DLBL statement names the file and describes its characteristics. The basic format of the DLBL statement is this:

```
// DLBL   filename,'file-id',date,code
```

Although the DLBL statement has other operands, you won't need to use them for processing sequential files.

The filename operand   The filename operand is the only required operand of the DLBL statement. It must be one to seven alphameric characters long, and it must begin with a letter. Note, though, that the value you code doesn't refer to the file's label. Instead, it refers to the symbolic name given in the DTF for the file. In the first DLBL statement in figure 13-9, for example, the filename SHIPTR refers to the name of the DTF for the shipment transaction file in the program in figure 13-5.

The file-id operand   The name in the file's physical label is what you code for file-id. You can omit the file-id, but if you do, the value you coded for the filename is substituted for it. So, you usually need to code the file-id for an input file. It can be up to 44 alphameric characters long, and it must be enclosed within apostrophes.

The date operand   When a new file is created, one of the functions of the label checking routine is to check the DASD area the new file will use to insure that it's not already occupied. If it is occupied, the expiration date of the existing file is checked to be sure that the date has passed. If it has passed, the new file is written over the existing file.

When you create a new file, you can code the date operand to specify when the file should expire. If you omit the date operand, the file is automatically assigned a seven-day retention period. So, if you need to retain the file for more than seven days, you have to code the date operand. To access an existing file, you don't need to code the date operand because it is ignored anyway. In figure 13-9, the date operand is omitted for all of the files, so the output file is assigned a retention period of seven days.

You can code the date operand in two ways: as a retention period or as an expiration date. When you code the retention period, you code the number of days the new file is to be retained (between 0 and 9999). Alternatively, you can code an expiration date in the format yy/ddd, where yy is the year and ddd is the day. If, for example, you create a file on July 2, 1986, that you want to be retained for 15 days, you can code either 15 as the retention period or 86/181 as the expiration date. Both cause the file to expire on July 17, 1986.

The code operand   The code operand indicates what type of file the DLBL statement is for. You can omit the code operand for a SAM file because the default value indicates a SAM file. In figure 13-9, the code operand is omitted for all files so sequential files are assumed. If you want to code this operand for a sequential file, the code is SD.

```
// JOB       ORDUPD
// OPTION    LINK
// EXEC      ASSEMBLY
   .
   .     SOURCE PROGRAM
   .
// LIBDEF    CL,TO=USRCL4
// EXEC      LNKEDT
// ASSGN     SYS008,290
// ASSGN     SYS009,290
// ASSGN     SYS010,290
// DLBL      SHIPTR,'ORDUPD.SHIPMENT.TRANSACTIONS'
// EXTENT    SYS008,,,,1200,10
// DLBL      ORDERS,'ORDUPD.ORDER.MASTERS'
// EXTENT    SYS009,,,,700,40
// DLBL      RPTTR,'ORDUPD.REPORT.TRANSACTIONS'
// EXTENT    SYS010,,,,1360,10
// EXEC
/&
```

Figure 13-9   The VSE JCL for the sequential update program in figure 13-5

The EXTENT statement

The EXTENT statement can be considered an extension to the DLBL information for a file and must always be placed directly after the related DLBL statement. In figure 13-9, each DLBL statement has one EXTENT statement related to it. But you can code as many EXTENT statements as are needed for a file. If you remember from chapter 1, an *extent* is an area assigned to a file. In a *multi-extent file*, more than one area is assigned to the file.

For a one-extent SAM file that is used for input, you don't have to use EXTENT statements. That's why I didn't present the EXTENT statement in chapter 3. However, for SAM output files or for multi-extent files, EXTENT statements are required.

The EXTENT statement specifies the location of the related disk file. The basic format of the EXTENT statement is this:

```
// EXTENT logical-unit,volser,,sequence,location,size
```

The two commas in succession in the format above indicate that one operand is missing. However, you don't need the missing operand for sequential files. In the EXTENT statements in figure 13-9, the four commas in succession mean that the volser and sequence operands are missing too. As you will see, you can usually omit these three operands in your EXTENT statements.

The logical-unit operand   This is a six-character operand that specifies the logical unit for the file. As a result, when you use an EXTENT statement, you don't code the DEVADDR operand in the DTF for the file. In figure 13-9, you can see that the first EXTENT statement relates the SHIPTR file to logical unit SYS008. In figure 13-5, you can see that the DTF named SHIPTR doesn't have a DEVADDR operand.

As I've mentioned, the logical unit is related to a physical device either by a standard assignment or an ASSGN statement. In figure 13-9, the first EXTENT statement refers back to the first ASSGN statement, which relates SYS008 to the device at address 290. In other words, SHIPTR in the DTF is related to logical unit SYS008 by the EXTENT statement, which is related to the device at address 290 by the ASSGN statement.

If you omit the logical-unit operand, the one from the preceding EXTENT statement is used. And if you omit the logical unit operand on the first EXTENT statement in a job, the symbolic name specified in the application program is used as the default. To avoid possible confusion, then, we recommend that you code the logical-unit operand.

The volser operand   This operand specifies the six-character volume serial number for the volume that contains the extent. If you code it, VSE checks to make sure the correct pack is mounted on the physical unit. If you don't code it, VSE doesn't check the volume label.

The sequence operand   Although you code only one DLBL statement to identify a DASD file, you may need to code more than one EXTENT statement for a sequential file. For instance, a file may be located in cylinders 11-13, 25-30, and 46-51 of a disk pack. Or, it may be so large that it takes up two full disk packs. In these cases, you code one EXTENT statement for each extent used by the file, and you must code the sequence operand in each statement.

The sequence operand is a one- to three-digit value between 0 and 255 that specifies the sequence number of the extent within a multi-extent file. Since the first extent of a file is numbered zero and the default is zero, you normally omit this operand for a file with only one extent.

The location and size operands   The location and size operands in the EXTENT statement specify where a file can be found on a DASD. The location operand specifies where a file extent begins. For a CKD DASD, you give the relative track number of the first track the file uses. For an FBA DASD, you give the number of the first block the file uses.

To specify how large a file is, you use the size operand of the EXTENT statement. For a CKD device, you code the number of tracks the file uses. For an FBA device, you code the total number of blocks the file uses.

For instance, the first EXTENT statement in figure 13-9 is for a CKD device:

```
// EXTENT  SYS008,,,,1200,10
```

It indicates that the file begins at relative track number 1200 and that it occupies 10 tracks. Where relative track 1200 is depends upon the device being used. If, for example, the device is a 3350 with 30 tracks per cylinder, relative track 1200 is the first track of cylinder 40 (since all numbering starts with zero rather than one, cylinder 40 is actually the 41st cylinder). Then, since the entire file occupies just 10 tracks, it takes up just one-third of cylinder 40.

Discussion

To code the JCL for a SAM file used in one of your programs, you need to know the physical address of the device the file is located on as well as the file-id for the file. In addition, for an output or a multi-extent file, you need to know the location and size for each extent used by the file. If you created the file in the first place, you will already have all of this information. Otherwise, you can get it by listing the VTOC for the volume the file is on. If you want more information about the JCL for sequential files, we recommend our *DOS/VSE JCL* by Steve Eckols.

Terminology

extent
multi-extent file

Objective

Given the file specifications for a program that processes one or more SAM files, code the JCL for running the program.

Chapter 14

The Indexed
Sequential Access Method (ISAM)

Although sequential file organization has its advantages, it also has limitations. For example, although a blocked sequential file makes maximum use of the storage capacity of a DASD, it has many of the limitations of a tape file. To update a sequential file, all of the records in the file must be read rather than just those affected by transactions, and the entire file has to be rewritten in order to add a record to the file. Using indexed sequential organization, the records in a file are stored so that they can be read sequentially or randomly, and records can be added to a file without having to rewrite the entire file.

Under VSE, you can use either ISAM or VSAM for creating and processing indexed sequential files. Although ISAM was widely used during the 1970s, it has been superseded by VSAM. As a result, ISAM is rarely used today in new programs, but most shops still use many old programs that process ISAM files. That's why you may never need to use ISAM for new program development, but you may use ISAM when you modify old programs.

In case you do need to use ISAM someday, this chapter shows you how to use it. Topic 1 presents the ISAM concepts you need to be familiar with. Topic 2 presents assembler language for ISAM files. Topic 3 presents the JCL you need to know for processing ISAM files.

TOPIC 1   ISAM concepts

Before you can write assembler language programs that process ISAM files, you need to understand how they are organized. As a result, this topic introduces you to the ISAM concepts you need to know.

ISAM file organization

The *Indexed Sequential Access Method (ISAM)* is designed to allow both sequential and random processing of DASD files. As a result, the structure of an ISAM file is more complicated than that of a SAM file. It contains not only a sequential grouping of data records, but also index elements and, usually, overflow areas.

The prime data area   The *prime data area* of an ISAM file is just what its name implies: it contains the bulk of the file's data records. Within the prime data area, records are ordered sequentially based on their key values.

The *key* field in each record in an ISAM file contains a value that uniquely identifies it. For instance, customer number or code is usually the key field in a customer file, and the customer numbers are assigned so each customer has its own number. Similarly, inventory number or code is usually the key field in an inventory file.

Indexes   To retrieve records at random, ISAM requires an index structure. Every ISAM file uses two kinds of indexes to locate specific records: a cylinder index and track indexes. In addition, large ISAM files may use a third index type: a master index. After I describe cylinder and track indexes, I'll describe the master index.

The *cylinder index* contains one entry for each cylinder in the prime data area. Each entry contains two elements: (1) the highest key value of the records stored in the cylinder and (2) the address of a lower level index for that cylinder, the track index. The *track index*, located at the beginning of each cylinder in the prime data area, contains one entry for each track within that cylinder. Like the entries in the cylinder index, each entry in the track index contains two elements: (1) the highest key value of the records stored on the track and (2) the track number itself.

Figure 14-1 shows how ISAM locates a record using the cylinder and track indexes. Here, the record with the key value 428 is to be retrieved. Searching the cylinder index, ISAM determines that the record is on cylinder 11. Then, searching the track index, ISAM determines that the record is on track 7 of that cylinder. Finally, by searching track 7, ISAM finds the record with key value 428.

If an ISAM file is large, the cylinder index may require several tracks. When that's the case, the time required to locate an entry in it can be too time-consuming to be acceptable. If so, the file may be created with an optional master index. The *master index* points directly to each track of the cylinder index. As a result, the time required to search the cylinder index is reduced.

Overflow areas   An ISAM file can include *overflow areas* that are used when records are added to a file. As a result, the entire file doesn't have to be rewritten to add new records in their proper positions within the key sequence, as is the case with a SAM file. When records are added to an overflow area, the index structure is updated so records can still be retrieved in key sequence.

There are two kinds of overflow areas you should be familiar with: cylinder overflow areas and the independent overflow area. When you use *cylinder overflow areas*, one or more tracks in each cylinder in the prime data area are reserved for inserted records. When you use an *independent overflow area*, one or more cylinders, usually located at the end of a file area, are reserved for additions to the file.

When records are added to an overflow area, the index structure is adjusted to point to them. As more and more records are added to the file, it becomes necessary at some point to *reorganize* it. When a file is reorganized, the records in the independent overflow area are moved into the prime data area and the index structure is rebuilt. If ISAM files that have many insertions aren't periodically reorganized, serious performance degradation can result.

ISAM file handling logic

When an ISAM file is created, the records are written in key sequence in the prime data area. As the records are written, the indexes are created to allow the records in the file to be accessed directly. When all of the records have been stored in the file, an end-of-file record is written just as if the file had sequential organization.

After the file has been loaded, track 1 of each cylinder contains the track index records. Any area left on track 1 and all of the remaining tracks, excluding those reserved for cylinder overflow, contain the records of the file in sequence. The tracks that make up the cylinder overflow area contain no data at all, and the independent overflow area contains no data either.

Before new records are added to a file, the file handling logic is fairly simple. For sequential retrieval, the records in the prime data area are read one after the other. For random retrieval, after the proper cylinder is located, the track index is checked to locate the track the record is on. Then, the prime data area on that track is searched to find the record with the appropriate key.

After new records have been added to the file, this logic becomes more complicated. Index entries for the overflow areas have to be used and existing records have to be moved to the overflow areas to make room for new records. From a programmer's point of view, though, you don't need to know how records are added to the overflow areas or how they

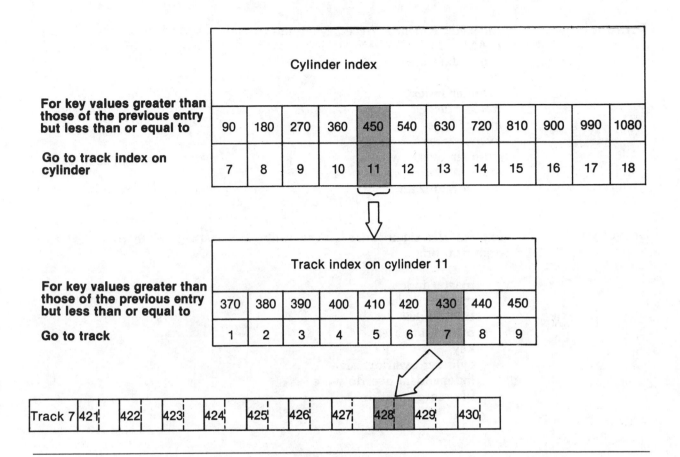

Figure 14-1 How ISAM searches cylinder and track indexes to locate a record

are retrieved from them since ISAM handles this logic for you. You should realize, though, that ISAM processing becomes more and more inefficient as the number of records in the overflow areas increases. That's why these files need to be reorganized frequently.

Discussion   Although ISAM file organization offered the benefits of both sequential and random processing, it was relatively inefficient. That's why it has been superseded by VSAM. In comparision, VSAM for indexed sequential files is more efficient no matter what type of file processing is being done: creating a file, adding records to a file, retrieving records sequentially, or retrieving records randomly.

Terminology

Indexed Sequential Access Method
ISAM
prime data area
key
cylinder index
track index
master index
overflow area
cylinder overflow area
independent overflow area
file reorganization

Objective

Explain the significance of the following as they relate to ISAM file organization:

master index
cylinder index
track index
prime data area
key
cylinder overflow area
independent overflow area
file reorganization

TOPIC 2   Assembler language for ISAM files

Because the organization of ISAM files is complex, the assembler language for processing them is complex too. For instance, you need to know 23 DTF operands for ISAM files. In addition, you need to use several new macros. In this topic, I will first present the macros that you need for ISAM file processing. Then, I will introduce you to ISAM error status bytes. Last, I will present three illustrative ISAM programs and describe two other file-handling functions.

DTFIS operands

To define an ISAM file, you use the DTFIS macro. Figure 14-2 summarizes the most widely used operands of this macro. Some of these operands, such as RECFORM and RECSIZE, you are already familiar with. The rest of them are new to you.

DSKXTNT   The DSKXTNT operand indicates the number of extents for a file. There are always at least two extents for an ISAM file: one for the prime data area and one for the cylinder index. In addition, there will be one extent for a master index if one is used, another for an independent overflow area if one is used, plus any extra extents for the prime data area.

IOROUT   The IOROUT operand indicates the function to be performed on the file. The options include loading a file, adding records to a file, retrieving records from a file, or adding records to and retrieving records from a file. If you will be updating records in place, you need to specify the retrieve option. In case it's not obvious, *loading* an ISAM file means creating the file.

KEYLEN   The KEYLEN operand specifies the number of bytes in the key for a file. It is required for all ISAM files whether they are being retrieved sequentially or randomly.

NRECDS   You will remember from the DTFSD macro that the BLKSIZE and RECSIZE operands were required for fixed-length, blocked records. In contrast, the NRECDS operand is required when blocked records are used in an ISAM file. In this operand, you give the blocking factor for the file.

DEVICE   The device operand simply specifies the type of device on which the file is located. The default is 2311 so you need to code this operand unless you're still using a 2311 or simulating one on some other device.

HINDEX   It is possible to have the cylinder index and master index on a device other than the device for the prime area. For instance, the master

Priority	Keyword	Programmer code	Remarks
Required	DSKXTNT	Number of extents	
Required	IOROUT	LOAD ADD RETRVE ADDRTR	Specify type of processing: loading file, adding records, retrieving (also updating in place), or add/retrieve.
Required	RECFORM	FIXUNB FIXBLK	FIXUNB for unblocked records; FIXBLK for blocked records.
Required	RECSIZE	Record length	
Required	KEYLEN	Key length	Length of key area for file.
Optional	NRECDS	Number of records per block	Required for RECFORM = FIXBLK. The default is one.
Optional	DEVICE	Device number	Specify the type of DASD that holds the prime data area.
Optional	HINDEX	Device number	Specify the type of DASD that holds the highest level index. Usually, the same as DEVICE.
Optional	MSTIND	YES	Indicates that a master index is used for this file.
Optional	INDAREA	Name of user area reserved to hold cylinder index in storage	The cylinder index can be held in storage to process records faster. INDAREA names the storage area; INDSIZE specifies the number of bytes.
Optional	INDSIZE	Number of bytes reserved to store cylinder index in INDAREA field	Must be included if INDAREA is coded. Most effective size is large enough to hold entire index: (Number of prime cylinders plus 4) times (key length + 6).
Optional	CYLOFL	Number of tracks per cylinder for overflow records	Depends on addition activity.
Optional	KEYLOC	Starting position of key field in blocked records	For blocked records, the key is embedded in the data of each record. Required if RECFORM = FIXBLK.

Figure 14-2   DTFIS operand summary (part 1 of 2)

Priority	Keyword	Programmer code	Remarks
Optional	KEYARG	Name of user key field	In random retrieval, the user supplies the key of the record to be read or written in this field. Also used to specify the starting key for skip sequential processing.
Optional	TYPEFLE	RANDOM SEQNTL RANSEQ	Coded only when IOROUT = RETRVE or ADDRTR. It indicates random, sequential, or combination retrieval.
Optional	IOAREAL	Name of I/O area for load function	Must be coded if IOROUT = LOAD, ADD, or ADDRTR. See figure 14-3 to determine the size of the area.
Optional	IOAREAR	Name of I/O area for random processing	Must be coded if IOROUT = RETRVE or ADDRTR and TYPEFLE = RANDOM or RANSEQ. See figure 14-3 to determine the size of the area.
Optional	IOAREAS	Name of I/O area for sequential processing	Must be coded if IOROUT = RETRVE or ADDRTR and TYPEFLE = SEQNTL or RANSEQ. See figure 14-3 to determine the size of the area.
Optional	IOAREA2	Name of second I/O area for load or sequential retrieve	Two I/O areas can be used for loading or sequential processing. This length must be the same as for IOAREAL or IOAREAS.
Optional	WORKL	Name of work area for load or add	For unblocked records, the work area must hold the key and the record. For blocked records, the work area only holds the records.
Optional	WORKR	Name of work area for random processing	The work area length must be one record length.
Optional	WORKS	YES	Indicates that GET or PUT will specify the work area. The work area length must be the same as for WORKL.
Optional	IOREG	Register number (nn)	For loading or sequential processing, records can be processed in the I/O area. Then, the I/O register points to the record being processed.

Figure 14-2   DTFIS operand summary (part 2 of 2)

and cylinder index can be on a 2314, while the prime data area is on a 3330. If this is the case, the HINDEX operand specifies the device for the highest index used. In practice, though, the indexes and the prime area are usually on the same device.

MSTIND The MSTIND operand simply specifies that a master index is used for the file. If it is specified, an additional extent must be included in the DSKXTNT operand.

INDAREA and INDSIZE It is possible to have the cylinder index read into storage at the start of a program. Then, the searches through the index are done at CPU speeds rather than at the slower DASD speeds. This can improve processing speeds dramatically by cutting down on access-mechanism movement and rotational delay.

   If this feature is used, the INDAREA operand gives the name of the index area in storage and the INDSIZE operand gives the number of bytes in the area. Although the formula in the summary will calculate the number of bytes required for the entire cylinder index, you can specify less than this maximum number. If you do, only a portion of the cylinder index will be read into storage at one time with a resulting decrease in efficiency.

CYLOFL The CYLOFL operand specifies the number of tracks on each cylinder that are reserved for cylinder overflow. If a file is being loaded or records are being added to a file, this operand must be specified. If zero is specified, cylinder overflow areas aren't used. Then, overflow records will be put in the independent overflow area if there is one.

KEYLOC When ISAM records are blocked, only the highest control field number in the block is stored in the key area for the block. That means *embedded keys* (keys within the actual records) must be used for finding individual records. In this case, the KEYLOC operand gives the starting byte of the key field within each record. If, for example, the control field is found in bytes 11-15 of a record, you code this operand as KEYLOC=11. By combining this operand with the KEYLEN operand, the assembler can tell where a key field is located within a record.

KEYARG The KEYARG field specifies the name of the field that will contain the key of the record to be processed. This operand must be included for random reading and writing operations. It must also be specified if sequential retrieval is to be performed beginning with a record key other than the first key in the file.

IOAREAL, IOAREAR, and IOAREAS The IOAREAL, IOAREAR, or IOAREAS operand specifies the name of the I/O area for loading, random processing, and sequential processing, respectively. For an ISAM file, the I/O area length depends on whether the program loads a file, processes a file sequentially, processes it randomly, or adds records to it. The length varies because different items are read into storage or are required for output depending on the function being performed. Sometimes only the data area is involved; sometimes count, key, or sequence-link fields are involved.

A *sequence-link field* is an extra field in a record in an overflow area that is used to link records in the overflow area sequentially. This field is ten bytes long. Although you don't have to know how this field provides the linkage between overflow records, you do have to know its length to calculate the length of some required I/O areas.

The I/O area length requirement is summarized in figure 14-3. For example, the I/O area for adding unblocked records to a file must be the eight bytes for the count area plus the key length plus ten bytes for the sequence-link field plus the record length. When adding blocked records to a file, the I/O area length is usually count plus key plus data; however, if the data area is very small, the minimum I/O area length is count plus key plus sequence-link field plus one record length.

IOAREA2   To improve processing efficiency, you can specify a second I/O area by using the IOAREA2 operand. Note in the summary in figure 14-2, though, that you can only specify a second area for loading or sequential processing operations. When you use a second I/O area, its length must be the same as the one used for the IOAREAL or IOAREAS area.

WORKL, WORKR, and WORKS   When processing ISAM files, different elements may be read into an input area or be required by an output area. It depends on the function being performed, whether the records are blocked or unblocked, and whether the data involves a prime track or an overflow area. If, for example, an unblocked record is read randomly from an overflow area, the ten-byte sequence-link field will precede the data. If the record is read from a prime track, it will be followed by ten unused bytes in the I/O area. For this reason, a work area, rather than an I/O register, is generally used with ISAM files. To define a work area, use the righthand column in figure 14-3 to determine what the contents of the work area will be.

For a load or add function, the WORKL operand is used to specify the name of the work area. For a random processing function, the WORKR operand is used. In contrast, for a file being retrieved sequentially, you code the WORKS operand as WORKS=YES to specify that a work area is being used. In this case, you code the name of the work area in the GET and PUT macros used for reading and writing the file on a sequential basis.

Other macros for ISAM file handling

When processing ISAM files, there are several other macros you need to use. These are summarized in figure 14-4. Since the formats and functions of these macros are simple, I will only cover them briefly here. Then, you will see how they are used in the illustrative programs.

Function	Record format	I/O area keyword	I/O area length	Work area keyword	Work area contents
Load	Unblocked	IOAREAL IOAREA2	C + K + RL	WORKL	Key + record
Load	Blocked	IOAREAL IOAREA2	C + K + D	WORKL	Record
Add	Unblocked	IOAREAL	C + L + SL + RL	WORKL	Key + record
Add	Blocked	IOAREAL	C + K + D or C + K + SL + RL, the larger	WORKL	Record
Retrieve sequentially	Unblocked	IOAREAS IOAREA2	K + SL + RL	WORKS	Key + record
Retrieve sequentially	Blocked	IOAREAS IOAREA2	D or SL + RL, the larger	WORKS	Record
Retrieve randomly	Unblocked	IOAREAR	SL + RL	WORKR	Record
Retrieve randomly	Blocked	IOAREAR	D or SL + RL, the larger	WORKR	Record

Codes: C = Count area = 8 bytes
       K = Key area
     RL = Record length
      D = Data area
     SL = Sequence-link field = 10 bytes

Figure 14-3   I/O and work area summary for ISAM files

The GET and PUT macros   If you review the third group of macros in figure 14-4, you can see that the GET and PUT macros are used for sequential processing of an ISAM file. These macros are used just as they are for SAM files. If a work area is used, you code the name of the work area as the second operand in either of these macros. If the records are processed in an I/O area by using an I/O register, you omit the second operand. In most cases, though, you will use a work area for ISAM file processing.

The READ and WRITE macros   The READ and WRITE macros for loading or random processing are similar to the GET and PUT macros for sequential processing. The READ macro reads a record from the input file into the associated I/O area. The first operand of the macro is the filename and the second operand is always the word KEY.

Loading

```
SETFL filename
WRITE filename,NEWKEY
ENDFL filename
```

Additions

```
WRITE filename,NEWKEY
WAITF filename
```

Sequential retrieval and updating

```
SETL   filename,BOF
SETL   filename,KEY
SETL   filename,GKEY
GET    filename
GET    filename,workarea
PUT    filename
PUT    filename,workarea
ESETL  filename
```

Random retrieval and updating

```
READ   filename,KEY
WAITF filename
WRITE filename,KEY
WAITF filename
```

Random additions and retrieval

```
READ   filename,KEY
WAITF filename
WRITE filename,KEY
WAITF filename
WRITE filename,NEWKEY
WAITF filename
```

Figure 14-4   ISAM I/O macro summary

The WRITE macro writes a record from the I/O area to the output file. The first operand is the filename and the second operand is either KEY or NEWKEY. If a record that is being written already exists, KEY is used. This means that the record is being written back on the file in its original location. If a new record is being written to a file, NEWKEY is used.

When you code the READ and WRITE macros, you don't code the name of the work area as one of the operands. That's because the name of the related work area is specified in the DTFIS for the file. So, when a record is read or written using the READ or WRITE macros, the data is automatically moved to or from the work area specified in the DTF.

The SETFL and ENDFL macros   The SETFL (set file load mode) macro prepares, or formats, portions of the disk for the indexes that will be stored on it. This macro must be coded whenever a file is being loaded or extended. It is usually coded as part of the housekeeping routine. Its only operand is the filename.

The ENDFL (end file load mode) macro also requires only the filename as its operand. When executed, this macro causes the last block of data to be written on the disk (even if it isn't completely filled) followed by an end-of-file record. The ENDFL macro also performs some final operations on the index records. It can only be executed after the SETFL macro and must always precede the CLOSE macro.

The SETL and ESETL macros   Before a program can begin sequential processing, the SETL (set limits) macro must be issued. This macro can initialize sequential processing in four ways. The first operand gives the filename, while the second operand of the macro specifies which of the four ways you want to use as follows:

```
SETL    filename,BOF
SETL    filename,KEY
SETL    filename,GKEY
SETL    filename,idname
```

The most common starting point is at the first record of the file. This is specified by coding BOF (beginning of file) as the second operand.

If you want to start processing at a specific key in a file, you must code the KEYARG operand too. Then, before SETL is executed with KEY as the second operand, the starting key must be placed in the KEYARG field.

You can also specify a *generic key*. For example, if a file contains account master records keyed by account number, you can specify that processing is to start with the first account in the 1000 series without knowing if the first key is 1002, 1009, or whatever. The KEYARG field is then set to 1000 at the start of the program, and the SETL macro is coded with GKEY as the second operand.

The last form of the SETL macro specifies the starting point by giving the name of the field that contains the disk address of the first record to be processed. However, this form of SETL is almost never used, so you don't have to worry about it.

To end sequential processing, the ESETL (end set limit) macro is used. If the records being processed are blocked, this macro causes the last block to be written on the file if a PUT has been issued. This macro, which has the filename as its only operand, is used in combination with the SETL macro. It should precede a CLOSE for the file.

In some programs, SETL and ESETL are coded several times in order to start and end processing at several different points in a file. First one section of the file is processed, then another section, and so on. This type of processing is called *skip-sequential processing*. Using the account master record as an example, the program could process the records from keys 1000-1500, followed by the records from keys 500-750, followed by the records from keys 2800-2850.

The WAITF macro   The WAITF macro must be coded following any ISAM READ or WRITE, except when loading or extending a file. When you *extend* an ISAM file, you add records to the file that have keys greater than the highest key in the file, and these records are stored in the prime data area.

The WAITF macro is coded with the filename as its only operand. It causes the program to wait until the I/O operation is completed before continuing the program. This macro is necessary because VSE doesn't wait to make sure an I/O operation is completed before it returns control to a program. If, for example, you issue a READ macro and follow it with instructions that are to process the data just read, the execution of the processing instructions may begin before the data from the record has been read into storage. However, if you code the WAITF macro after the READ macro, you can be sure that the data has been read into storage before your program starts to process it.

The ISAM error status byte

When a program performs ISAM I/O operations, several errors can occur. When you're loading an ISAM file, for example, the file may require more space than the JCL for the job provides for it. Similarly, when adding records to a file, there may not be enough room for a record in the cylinder overflow or independent overflow area. When errors like this occur, an error byte for the file is updated by VSE to show that the error occurred.

The name of the error byte for an ISAM file is the name of the DTFIS for the file followed by the letter C. For example, INVMSTRC is the name of the error byte for an ISAM file that has a DTF named INVMSTR. The meanings of the bits within this error byte are summarized in figures 14-5 and 14-6. Figure 14-5 applies to errors that can occur during load operations only. Figure 14-6 applies to errors that can occur during addition, retrieval, or combined addition and retrieval operations. In the illustrative programs that follow, you'll see how the ISAM error bytes can be used.

Three illustrative programs

If you understand the ISAM concepts, you shouldn't have much trouble coding assembler language programs that process ISAM files. Once you know the ISAM function your program needs to perform, you can use figures 14-2 through 14-6 to get the coding information you need. To illustrate, figures 14-7 through 14-9 present three programs that show you how to perform basic ISAM functions.

Although all three programs specify 2311s as the devices used for the ISAM files and indexes, you should realize that this device is just about obsolete. On our system, though, we have software that simulates 2311s on FBA devices, and we used this software for testing the illustrative programs. Since you will almost surely use other devices for your ISAM files, you will use other device numbers in your DTFs.

Bit	Cause	Explanation
0	DASD error	Any uncorrectable DASD error has occurred (except wrong length record).
1	Wrong length record	A wrong length record has been detected during an I/O operation.
2	Prime data area full	The next to the last track of the prime data area has been filled during the load or extension of the data file. The program should issue the ENDFL macro and a load extend should be done on the file with new extents given.
3	Cylinder index area full	The cylinder index area is not large enough to contain all the entries needed to index each cylinder specified for the prime data area. This condition can occur during the execution of the SETFL macro. The user must extend the upper limit of the cylinder index by using a new EXTENT statement in the JCL for the job.
4	Master index full	The master index area is not large enough to contain all the entries needed to index each track of the cylinder index. This condition can occur during the execution of the SETFL macro. The user must extend the upper limit of the master index by using a new EXTENT statement in the JCL for the job.
5	Duplicate record	The record being loaded is a duplicate of the previous record.
6	Sequence check	The record being loaded is not in the sequential order required for loading.
7	Prime data area overflow	There is not enough space in the prime data area to write an EOF record. This condition can occur during the execution of the ENDFL macro.

Figure 14-5   The ISAM error-status byte for IOROUT=LOAD

A file creation program   Loading an ISAM file is much like creating a sequential file. Usually, a sequential input file provides the data that goes into each ISAM record. Since the ISAM records must be loaded in key sequence, the input file records must also be in key sequence.

Figure 14-7 presents a program that loads an ISAM file of inventory records from a sequential disk file. The new records are to be 70 bytes long. The basic processing loop of the program reads a record from the sequential file, moves and packs its data into the ISAM record, and writes an output record.

You normally have to make several decisions about an ISAM file before you can code a load program for it. You must decide what blocking factor to use, whether a master index is necessary, how much overflow area should be reserved, and what types of overflow areas should be used. In the program in figure 14-7, I assumed that the file would be a maximum

Bit	Cause	Explanation
0	DASD error	Any uncorrectable DASD error has occurred (except wrong length record).
1	Wrong length record	A wrong length record has been detected during an I/O operation.
2	End of file	The EOF condition has been encountered during the execution of a sequential retrieval function.
3	No record found	The record to be retrieved has not been found in the data file. This applies to a random READ or a sequential SETL macro.
4	Illegal ID specified	The ID specified in the SETL macro is outside the prime data area extents.
5	Duplicate record	The record to be added to the file has a duplicate record key in the file.
6	Overflow area full	An overflow area in a cylinder is full and no independent overflow area has been specified or the independent overflow area is full, so the addition cannot be made.
7	Overflow record	The record just read in a retrieval function is in an overflow area.

Figure 14-6   The ISAM error-status byte for IOROUT=ADD, RETRVE, or ADDRTR

of 4500 records with nine records per block. I also assumed that a single track per cylinder would be enough overflow area for the file. Because this file is small, a master index isn't needed. As a result, the file can be described in two disk extents: one for the cylinder index and the other for the prime data area.

In figure 14-7, the DTFIS for the inventory master file reflects these decisions. Since the file will reside on a 2311, both DEVICE and HINDEX specify 2311. Then, DSKXTNT specifies 2 extents for the file, CYLOFL specifies 1 track per cylinder, and the MSTIND operand is omitted. KEYLEN is 6 bytes, and because this is a blocked file, KEYLOC must be included. Since the key, item number, begins in the second byte of the record, KEYLOC=2. TYPEFLE and KEYARG are omitted since they apply only to retrieval programs.

IOAREAL names the output area (MSTRIO) that I have reserved, and the length of MSTRIO is 644 bytes: 8 bytes for count, 6 for key, and 630 for the block of nine records. You can get the information for this calculation from the summary in figure 14-3. WORKL names the work area for the master file (MSTRRCD) in which each new record will be constructed. Since the records will be blocked, MSTRRCD reserves enough space for the record, but no extra space for the key (see figure 14-3).

Before the main processing loop, the program uses the SETFL macro. Then, the main loop begins with the GET macro for the input file. After a record is read, the new master record is constructed in the work area. To write the record on the ISAM file, the WRITE macro is used with NEWKEY as the second operand.

When control is returned to the program following the WRITE macro, the status of the WRITE operation is indicated in the error status byte named INVMSTRC. Then, the program checks this byte to find out if the WRITE operation was successful. If none of the error bits are on, the new record is assumed to have been written successfully and the program continues by reading the next input record. If any of the bits in INVMSTRC are on, however, the program issues the DUMP macro, which causes a storage printout and program termination. If all the records are successfully loaded, the program issues the ENDFL macro.

In a production program, you would check the error status byte in more detail. For instance, you might check for duplicate records or sequence errors, print those records on an error list, and then try to continue to load the file. Or you might check for the prime area being full, and if it is, print an error message, issue the ENDFL macro, and end the program. Remember, then, that the program in figure 14-7 is only designed to illustrate the use of the ISAM macros; it is certainly not realistic in other ways.

If you check the work area for the master record in figure 14-7, you can see that the first byte is named MDELCODE, which stands for deletion code. It is set to hex zeros by the MVI instruction near the start of the main processing loop. Later on in this topic, I'll explain how deletion codes are used for ISAM files.

A random update program   Figure 14-8 is a program that updates an ISAM file on a random basis. The input file is a sequential shipment transaction file; the updated file is the ISAM inventory master file that was created by the program in figure 14-7. The basic logic of this program is to read a shipment transaction, read the master record with the same key on a random basis, and rewrite the updated master record in its original location on the DASD.

Because the cylinder index is going to be processed in storage, INDAREA=INDEX is specified in the DTFIS. Then, INDSIZE=168 is given for the size of this index area (10 cylinders plus 4 equals 14; key length of 6 plus 6 equals 12; 14 times 12 equals 168 bytes for the cylinder index). In the data definitions, the area named INDEX is defined as a 168-byte field to correspond to these DTF operands.

Because the records are blocked, the I/O area is 630 bytes; that is, the length of the data area. Similarly, the work area is the length of one record. Because random processing is used, the DTF keywords for the I/O area and the work area are IOAREAR and WORKR.

The processing of the program should be easy for you to follow. After an input record has been read, the item number in the transaction record is moved to the KEYARG field named ITEMKEY. The READ macro then tries to read the master record randomly by key. Following the READ macro is the WAITF macro.

```
INVLOAD   START  0
BEGIN     BALR   3,0
          USING  *,3
          OPEN   INPUT,INVMSTR
          SETFL  INVMSTR                    PREPARE DISK FOR LOADING
READREC   GET    INPUT,INPTWRKA
          MVI    MDELCODE,X'00'
          MVC    MSTRRCD+1(32),INPTWRKA
          PACK   MORDQTY,IORDQTY
          PACK   MORDPT,IORDPT
          PACK   MSAFSTK,ISAFSTK
          PACK   MONHAND,IONHAND
          PACK   MONORD,IONORD
          PACK   MALLOC,IALLOC
          WRITE  INVMSTR,NEWKEY             WRITE ISAM OUTPUT RECORD
          CLI    INVMSTRC,X'00'            COMPARE STATUS-BYTE TO HEX ZEROS
          BE     READREC
          DUMP
EOFDSK    ENDFL  INVMSTR                    FINISH LOAD ROUTINE
          CLOSE  INPUT,INVMSTR
          EOJ
INPUT     DTFSD  BLKSIZE=248,                                              X
                 RECFORM=FIXBLK,                                           X
                 RECSIZE=62,                                               X
                 IOAREA1=INPTDSKA,                                         X
                 WORKA=YES,                                                X
                 EOFADDR=EOFDSK
INVMSTR   DTFIS  DSKXTNT=2,                                                X
                 IOROUT=LOAD,                                              X
                 RECFORM=FIXBLK,                                           X
                 RECSIZE=70,                                               X
                 KEYLEN=6,                                                 X
                 NRECDS=9,                                                 X
                 DEVICE=2311,                                              X
                 HINDEX=2311,                                              X
                 CYLOFL=1,                                                 X
                 KEYLOC=2,                                                 X
                 IOAREAL=MSTRIO,                                           X
                 WORKL=MSTRRCD
INPTDSKA  DS     CL248
MSTRIO    DS     CL644
INPTWRKA  DS     0CL62
IITEM     DS     CL6
IDESC     DS     CL20
IUM       DS     CL4
IORDPOL   DS     CL2
IORDQTY   DS     CL5
IORDPT    DS     CL5
ISAFSTK   DS     CL5
IONHAND   DS     CL5
IONORD    DS     CL5
IALLOC    DS     CL5
MSTRRCD   DS     0CL70
MDELCODE  DS     CL1
MITEM     DS     CL6
MDESC     DS     CL20
MUM       DS     CL4
MORDPOL   DS     CL2
MORDQTY   DS     PL4
MORDPT    DS     PL4
MSAFSTK   DS     PL4
MONHAND   DS     PL4
MONORD    DS     PL4
MALLOC    DS     PL4
          DC     13X'00'
          END    BEGIN
```

Figure 14-7   An ISAM file-creation program

```
RDMUPD    START  0
BEGIN     BALR   3,0
          USING  *,3
          OPEN   SHIPTR,ERRMSG,INVMSTR
READSHP   GET    SHIPTR,SHPWRKA
          MVC    ITEMKEY,SHPITEM
          READ   INVMSTR,KEY
          WAITF  INVMSTR
          TM     INVMSTRC,X'FE'        TEST BITS 0-6
          BZ     FOUND                 BRANCH IF BITS 0-6 ARE ALL ZERO
          TM     INVMSTRC,X'EE'        TEST BITS 0-2 AND 4-6
          BZ     NOTFOUND              BRANCH IF THEY ARE ALL ZERO
          DUMP
NOTFOUND  MVC    LITEM,SHPITEM
          MVC    LERR(15),=C'NO RECORD FOUND'
          PUT    ERRMSG
          B      READSHP
FOUND     PACK   PACKQTY,SHPQTY
          SP     MONHAND,PACKQTY
          WRITE  INVMSTR,KEY
          WAITF  INVMSTR
          B      READSHP
EOFINPT   CLOSE  SHIPTR,ERRMSG,INVMSTR
          EOJ
SHIPTR    DTFSD  BLKSIZE=240,                                        X
                 RECFORM=FIXBLK,                                     X
                 RECSIZE=24,                                         X
                 IOAREA1=SHIPIO,                                     X
                 WORKA=YES,                                          X
                 EOFADDR=EOFINPT
ERRMSG    DTFPR  BLKSIZE=132,                                        X
                 IOAREA1=ERRLINE,                                    X
                 DEVADDR=SYSLST
```

Figure 14-8   An ISAM random update program (part 1 of 2)

After the WAITF macro, the program tests the status byte to see if
any errors occurred during the execution of the READ macro. If bit 3 is
on, the program should print an error message since this means that the
master record can't be found. If bit 7 is on, the program should ignore it
since this means that the master record came from an overflow area rather
than a prime track, and that has no effect on the program. If any of the
other bits are on, the program uses the DUMP macro to get a storage
printout and end the program.

To test the error bits, the program uses the test-under-mask (TM)
instruction. This instruction, which is described in detail in chapter 10, lets
you test the condition of any bit within a byte. The branch instruction
that follows it can then branch according to the resulting condition code.

To illustrate, consider the first two instructions that test the error
status byte in figure 14-8:

```
          TM       INVMSTRC,X'FE'
          BZ       FOUND
```

```
INVMSTR   DTFIS  DSKXTNT=2,                                              X
                 IOROUT=RETRVE,                                          X
                 RECFORM=FIXBLK,                                         X
                 RECSIZE=70,                                             X
                 KEYLEN=6,                                               X
                 NRECDS=9,                                               X
                 DEVICE=2311,                                            X
                 HINDEX=2311,                                            X
                 INDAREA=INDEX,                                          X
                 INDSIZE=168,                                            X
                 CYLOFL=1,                                               X
                 KEYLOC=2,                                               X
                 KEYARG=ITEMKEY,                                         X
                 TYPEFLE=RANDOM,                                         X
                 IOAREAR=MSTRIO,                                         X
                 WORKR=MSTRRCD
SHIPIO    DS     CL240
MSTRIO    DS     CL630
ERRLINE   DS     0CL132
          DC     5C' '
LITEM     DS     CL6
          DC     52C' '
LERR      DS     CL15
          DC     54C' '
PACKQTY   DS     PL4
INDEX     DS     CL168
ITEMKEY   DS     CL6
SHPWRKA   DS     0CL24
          DS     CL6
SHPITEM   DS     CL6
SHPQTY    DS     CL4
          DS     CL8
MSTRRCD   DS     0CL70
MDELCODE  DS     CL1
MSTITEM   DS     CL6
MDESC     DS     CL20
          DS     CL18
MONHAND   DS     PL4
          DS     CL21
          END    BEGIN
```

Figure 14-8   An ISAM random update program (part 2 of 2)

The TM instruction tests the status bits indicated by the immediate operand, X'FE', to see whether they are 1s or 0s. Since hex FE is binary 1111 1110, the first 7 bits (bits 0-6) of INVMSTRC are tested. Then, if they are all zeros (meaning the record has been read without error), the program will branch to FOUND since the operation code BZ means branch if zeros. If at least one of the bits is on, however, the branch will not take place. Then, the program executes these instructions:

```
          TM     INVMSTRC,X'EE'
          BZ     NOTFOUND
          DUMP
```

Since hex EE is binary 1110 1110, all bits but the "not found" and "overflow record" bits are tested by the TM instruction. If they are all zeros, it means the previous BZ instruction didn't branch because the "not found" bit was on. Then, the program branches to the routine named NOTFOUND. If this second BZ operation doesn't branch, it indicates one of the other errors so the program executes the DUMP macro and the program ends.

If the error status byte indicates no errors, the on hand field in the inventory master record is updated. Then, the WRITE macro, with KEY as the second operand, writes the record on the disk in its original location. Since the record has just been read, the KEYARG field still contains the record key. Again, after the WRITE macro, a WAITF macro must be issued to make sure that the operation has been completed before processing continues. When the end of the transaction file is reached, the EOF routine closes the files and ends the job.

A sequential retrieval program   Figure 14-9 presents a program that illustrates sequential record retrieval. It reads the inventory master file created by the program in figure 14-7 and prepares an inventory report from it. Since the logic of the program is straightforward, you should have no difficulty following it once you learn the new elements it presents.

If you review the program, you can see that many of the DTFIS operands are the same as those used in the random retrieval program. For sequential processing, though, the cylinder index isn't brought into storage because it isn't accessed often. Therefore, the INDAREA and INDSIZE operands are omitted. IOROUT still specifies RETRVE, but TYPEFLE must now be changed to SEQNTL, and KEYARG can be omitted. Also, the keyword IOAREAS replaces the keyword IOAREAR, and WORKS=YES replaces WORKR=MSTRRCD.

The I/O macros used to perform the sequential processing are the GET and PUT. They are coded just as they are for SAM files. In this program, only the GET is used since no update is performed. Since I specified WORKS=YES in the DTFIS, the GET includes a second operand that names the work area.

Notice that the SETL and ESETL macros are used before and after the main processing routine. As explained earlier, these macros must be present to begin and end the sequential processing of an ISAM file. In this program, all of the records in the ISAM file are processed, so the SETL macro uses the BOF operand, and the ESETL macro is issued after all records have been read.

To determine the end-of-file condition for an ISAM file, the program must check the error status byte after each GET to see if bit number 2 has been turned on (see the bit summary in figure 14-6). If it is on, the program must branch to an end-of-file routine. In figure 14-9, these instructions test the status byte after the GET is issued:

```
TM      INVMSTRC,X'FE'
BZ      PROCESS
TM      INVMSTRC,X'20'
BO      EOFMSTR
DUMP
```

The first TM instruction tests whether any of bits 0-6 are on. If all are zero, the branch to PROCESS takes place and the mainline routine continues. If not, the second TM instruction tests bit 2. If it is on indicating end-of-file, the program branches to the EOF routine (BO means branch if ones). Otherwise, some error is indicated, the DUMP macro is issued, and the program ends.

The rest of the program should be clear to you. One point of interest is the editing of the six output fields starting with RORDQTY before a line is printed. Since the edit pattern uses field separators (hex 22s) and since all six packed fields are adjacent in storage, only one edit instruction is needed. This use of field separators is described in detail in chapter 10.

Other file-handling functions

The three programs I've just illustrated should give you examples that you can use for most of the ISAM programming you'll ever do. However, you should be aware that there are two other functions that I haven't illustrated. These are adding records to a file and deleting records from a file. So let me briefly describe programs that perform these functions.

File additions   A program that adds records to an ISAM file is much like a program that loads records. However, there are four differences that you should be aware of.

First, the IOROUT operand of the DTFIS specifies ADD instead of LOAD. Second, SETFL and ENDFL aren't required for an add program. Third, although the NEWKEY form of the WRITE macro is used to add records, the bits in the status byte for the add program have the meanings given in figure 14-6, not those given in figure 14-5. Fourth, for file additions, the WAITF macro must follow the WRITE macro, but it isn't required for file loading.

In addition to these differences, the error-checking routine in a file-addition program is likely to be more complicated than it is in a load program. If a record to be added to a file has a key that is a duplicate of one already on the file, an error message is usually printed and the program goes on to the next input record. If a record can't be added to a file because there is no room for it, a message is usually printed and the program ends.

File deletions   The ISAM access method doesn't directly provide for deleting records from an ISAM file. However, a standard technique has been developed to simulate deletion. When you use this technique, one byte in a record (usually the first byte of the record unless it is part of the key) is reserved for a deletion code. To delete a record, then, a program turns this byte on (hex FF is commonly used to show that the byte is on). This indicates that the record has been deleted.

Note, however, that the deleted records actually remain on the file until it is reorganized. As a result, all of the programs that process the file must ignore the records that have the deletion code turned on. To reorganize the file, a reload program reads the old file, ignoring records

```
INVSTAT   START  0
BEGIN     BALR   3,0
          USING  *,3
          OPEN   INVMSTR,STATUS
          SETL   INVMSTR,BOF              START PROCESSING WITH FIRST RECORD
NXTRCD    GET    INVMSTR,MSTRRCD
          TM     INVMSTRC,X'FE'           TEST BITS 0-6
          BZ     PROCESS                  IF BITS ARE ZERO, CONTINUE
          TM     INVMSTRC,X'20'           TEST BIT 2
          BO     EOFMSTR                  IF BIT 2 IS ON, GO TO EOF ROUTINE
          DUMP                            DUMP STORAGE AND END
PROCESS   MVI    RLINE,X'40'
          MVC    RLINE+1(132),RLINE
          MVC    RITEM,MITEM
          MVC    RDESC,MDESC
          MVC    RUM,MUM
          MVC    RORDPOL,MORDPOL
          MVC    RORDQTY(61),PATTERN
          ED     RORDQTY(61),MORDQTY EDIT SIX FIELDS
          ZAP    AVAILWK,MONHAND
          AP     AVAILWK,MONORD
          SP     AVAILWK,MALLOC
          MVC    RAVAIL,PATTERN
          ED     RAVAIL,AVAILWK
          CP     LCOUNT,=P'50'
          BL     PRTDET
          PUT    STATUS,RHEAD
          ZAP    LCOUNT,=P'0'
          MVI    RCTL,C'0'
PRTDET    PUT    STATUS,RLINE
          AP     LCOUNT,=P'1'
          B      NXTRCD
EOFMSTR   ESETL  INVMSTR                  END SEQUENTIAL PROCESSING
          CLOSE  INVMSTR,STATUS
          EOJ
INVMSTR   DTFIS  DSKXTNT=2,                                                    X
                 IOROUT=RETRVE,                                               X
                 RECFORM=FIXBLK,                                              X
                 RECSIZE=70,                                                  X
                 KEYLEN=6,                                                    X
                 NRECDS=9,                                                    X
                 DEVICE=2311,                                                 X
                 HINDEX=2311,                                                 X
                 CYLOFL=1,                                                    X
                 KEYLOC=2,                                                    X
                 TYPEFLE=SEQNTL,                                              X
                 IOAREAS=MSTRIO,                                             X
                 WORKS=YES
```

Figure 14-9   An ISAM sequential retrieval program (part 1 of 2)

```
STATUS    DTFPR BLKSIZE=133,                                                    X
                IOAREA1=PRTOUT,                                                 X
                WORKA=YES,                                                      X
                DEVADDR=SYSLST,                                                 X
                CTLCHR=ASA
MSTRIO    DS    CL630
PRTOUT    DS    CL133
AVAILWK   DS    PL4
LCOUNT    DC    P'50'
PATTERN   DS    0CL61
          DC    X'40'
          DC    6X'202020202020201222222'
RHEAD     DS    0CL133
          DC    CL105'1                  ITEM      DESCRIPTION              U/M  X
                    OP       ORDQTY     ORDPNT   SAFSTK    ONHAND    ONORDR'
          DC    CL28'     ALLOC     AVAIL        '
RLINE     DS    0CL133
RCTL      DS    CL1
          DS    CL12
RITEM     DS    CL6
          DS    CL2
RDESC     DS    CL20
          DS    CL4
RUM       DS    CL4
          DS    CL2
RCRDPOL   DS    CL2
          DS    CL4
RCRDQTY   DS    CL8
          DS    CL2
RCRDPT    DS    CL8
          DS    CL2
RSAFSTK   DS    CL8
          DS    CL2
RONHAND   DS    CL8
          DS    CL2
RONORD    DS    CL8
          DS    CL2
RALLOC    DS    CL8
          DS    CL2
RAVAIL    DS    CL8
          DS    CL8
MSTRRCD   DS    0CL70
MDELCODE  DS    CL1
MITEM     DS    CL6
MDESC     DS    CL20
MUM       DS    CL4
MCRDPOL   DS    CL2
MORDQTY   DS    PL4
MCRDPT    DS    PL4
MSAFSTX   DS    PL4
MONHAND   DS    PL4
MONORD    DS    PL4
MALLOC    DS    PL4
          DS    CL13
          END   BEGIN
```

Figure 14-9   An ISAM sequential retrieval program (part 2 of 2)

that have been deleted, and loads a new file. Thus, deleted records are dropped from the file.

In the load program in figure 14-7, the ISAM file was created with a deletion code as the first byte in each record. However, the programs in figures 14-8 and 14-9 don't check to see whether a record has been deleted. To handle deletions properly, then, these programs would have to be revised so they treat records marked for deletion as though they aren't on the file.

Discussion

As you should realize by now, the trick to processing ISAM files in assembler language is coding the DTFIS and the other I/O macros properly. To make sure you use the correct macros for each ISAM function, be sure to use the summary in figure 14-4. Notice that the WAITF macro is required after all READ and WRITE macros except when loading a file. It is not required when using GET or PUT.

Terminology

loading a file
embedded key
sequence-link field
generic key
skip-sequential processing
extending a file

Objective

Given program specifications that require the use of ISAM files, code an assembler language program that satisfies the specifications. The specifications may require any of the following functions: loading a file, adding records to a file, deleting records from a file, sequentially or randomly updating a file, and sequentially or randomly retrieving records from a file. They may also require that cylinder overflow, independent overflow, or a cylinder index in storage be used.

TOPIC 3   VSE JCL for ISAM files

In topic 3 of the last chapter, I presented the basic JCL for processing sequential disk files. However, to process ISAM files, you need to know some additional operands of the DLBL and EXTENT statements. This topic will present those operands and show you how they are used in some ISAM job streams.

The DLBL statement

The format of the DLBL statement for ISAM files is this:

```
// DLBL filename,'file-id',date,code
```

Since I presented these operands in the last chapter, I won't describe them now. But you do need to know how to use the code operand for ISAM files.

The code operand   The code operand specifies the access method to be used for the file. To create an ISAM file, the code is ISC. To perform any other processing of an ISAM file, the code is ISE. Since the default is SD, you must code this operand for any ISAM file.

The EXTENT statement

When ISAM files are created, at least two EXTENT statements are required: one for the cylinder index area and one for the prime data area. If a master index or an independent overflow area is to be used, an additional EXTENT statement must be included for each of them.
　　The format of an EXTENT statement for an ISAM file is this:

```
// EXTENT logical-unit,volser,type,sequence,location,size
```

In the last chapter, you learned how to code the logical unit, volser, sequence, location, and size operands, so I'm not going to describe them again. Instead, I'm going to focus on the type operand and its relationship to the sequence operand.

The type and sequence operands   On each EXTENT statement for an ISAM file, you code the type operand. The acceptable codes are shown in figure 14-10. As the sequence values in this figure indicate, you must code the EXTENT statements for an ISAM file in this sequence: first, the EXTENT statement for the master index (if there is one); second, the EXTENT statement for the cylinder index; next, the EXTENT statements for the prime data area (there may be more than one); and last, the EXTENT statement for the independent overflow area (if there is one). As you can see, the first EXTENT statement for an ISAM file isn't necessarily sequence number 0; if an ISAM file doesn't have a master index, the first extent is 1.

ISAM file area	Type value	Sequence value
Master index	4	0
Cylinder index	4	1
Prime data area(s)	1	2,...,n
Independent overflow area	2	n + 1

Figure 14-10   Values for the type and sequence operands in the EXTENT statements for an ISAM file

Two illustrative job streams

Figures 14-11 and 14-12 show two job streams that include DLBL and EXTENT statements for ISAM files. Figure 14-11 shows the JCL that I used to test the file creation program in figure 14-7. If you check the DLBL statement for the ISAM master file, you can see that I gave it a retention period of 10 days and that its code is ISC. If you check the EXTENT statements for the file, you can see that it doesn't have a master index or an independent overflow area. Its cylinder index starts at relative track 740 and is 10 tracks long. Its prime data area starts at relative track 750 and is 20 tracks long. Note that I didn't have to code the logical unit or volume serial number operands in the second EXTENT statement for the file. If they're omitted, VSE assumes that they're the same as in the preceding EXTENT statement.

Figure 14-12 shows the JCL I used to test the random update program in figure 14-8. This time, the code in the DLBL statement for the ISAM master file is ISE and no retention period is specified since the file already exists. Otherwise, the DLBL and EXTENT statements for the ISAM master file are the same as they are in the file creation job stream.

When you test a program, you normally have only two extents for each ISAM file: one for the cylinder index and one for the prime data area. Then, when the program goes into production, the operations group decides how large the file is going to be, whether or not it needs a master index or an independent overflow area, and so on. If these decisions affect the DTFIS for a file, the program is changed and reassembled for final testing.

Discussion

The most difficult part of writing the JCL statements for ISAM files is determining where the index, data, and overflow areas should be located and how large they should be. Once you have this information, though, it is relatively simple to write the DLBL and EXTENT statements for an ISAM file. If you want more information about VSE JCL for ISAM files, we recommend our *DOS/VSE JCL* by Steve Eckols.

Objective

Given the file specifications for a program that processes one or more ISAM files, code the JCL for running the program.

```
// JOB     CREATION
// OPTION LINK
// EXEC    ASSEMBLY
    .
    .  SOURCE PROGRAM
    .
/*
// LIBDEF CL,TO=USRCL4
// EXEC   LNKEDT
// ASSGN  SYS008,290
// ASSGN  SYS009,290
// DLBL   INPUT,'SEQUENTIAL.DISK.RECORDS'
// EXTENT SYS008,CKD001
// DLBL   INVMSTR,'ISAM.INVENTORY.MASTER.FILE',10,ISC
// EXTENT SYS009,CKD001,4,1,740,10
// EXTENT ,,1,2,750,20
// EXEC
/&
```

Figure 14-11   The VSE JCL for testing the ISAM file creation program in figure 14-7

```
// JOB     UPDATE
// OPTION LINK
// EXEC    ASSEMBLY
    .
    .  SOURCE PROGRAM
    .
/*
// LIBDEF CL,TO=USRCL4
// EXEC   LNKEDT
// ASSGN  SYS008,290
// ASSGN  SYS009,290
// DLBL   SHIPTR,'SHIPMENT.RECORDS'
// EXTENT SYS008,CKD001
// DLBL   INVMSTR,'ISAM.INVENTORY.MASTER.FILE',,ISE
// EXTENT SYS009,CKD001,4,1,740,10
// EXTENT ,,1,2,750,20
// EXEC
/&
```

Figure 14-12   The VSE JCL for testing the ISAM update program in figure 14-8

Chapter   15

The Direct Access Method (DAM)

Because of the complexities of direct file processing, the Direct Access Method (DAM) is used infrequently. As a result, you may never be called upon to code routines for DAM files in assembler language. On the other hand, some programmers prefer DAM files for some purposes because they have more control over them than they have over the files of other access methods. As a result, if you know what you're doing, you can write file-handling routines for DAM files that are extremely efficient.

In case you ever use them, this chapter presents what you need to know in order to use DAM files. Topic 1 presents the DAM concepts. Topic 2 presents assembler language for DAM files. Topic 3 presents the JCL you need to know for processing DAM files.

TOPIC 1   DAM concepts

The main concern when creating DAM files is determining where to store each record. The main concern when accessing the records in DAM files is finding each record. To understand these concerns, you first need to know how you can address the records in a file when using DAM. Then, you need to become familiar with the techniques you can use to store and locate records. In this topic, I'll first present the DAM disk address formats. Then, I'll introduce you to file-handling techniques for DAM files.

DAM disk address formats

To access records in a DAM file, you must supply the proper disk address each time a record is read or written. In other words, as far as DAM is concerned, the records in a direct file have no sequence or organization. Only the disk addresses matter.

Figure 15-1 summarizes the three types of disk addresses you can use with DAM. As you will see, the second and third formats have a distinct advantage over the first, so you probably won't use the first format in new programs. However, you might come in contact with the first format when you work with old programs.

Physical disk address format   The first format is cylinder number, head number, and record number. These values are supplied as hex (binary) values in an eight-byte format. For most devices, bytes 0-2 aren't used so they are set to hex zeros. In particular, bytes 1-2 apply to a data cell device that is all but obsolete. Bytes 3-4 must specify the cylinder number. If, for example, a device has 200 cylinders, the cylinder number can range from zero through 199. Bytes 5-6 must contain the head number, which is the same as the track number within the cylinder. If, for example, a device has 20 disk surfaces, the head numbers can range from 0 through 19. Finally, byte 8 is for record number. If the records are to be referred to by keys, the record number must be set to zero. But if the records are referred to by record number, it must be a value from 1 to the number of records stored on the track.

Relative track address format in zoned decimal   The second disk address format is relative track number plus record number, both as zoned-decimal values. A *relative track number* is the number of the track that a record is supposed to be on relative to the first track in the area for the file. Since the first track in a file is always relative track number zero, the relative track number can range from zero to the total number of tracks allocated to the file minus one.

The first eight bytes of this addressing format specify the relative track number in zoned decimal form. If, for example, you wanted to read a record located on track zero of cylinder 62 within a file that began on track zero of cylinder 60 on a 3330, the value in the relative track number

field should be 38 since there are 19 usable tracks in each cylinder of a
3330. For a record on track 15 of cylinder 63, the relative track number
should be 72.

The last two bytes of this format must contain the record number as a
zoned decimal value. Again, if the records are to be referred to by key, the
record number should be zero. Otherwise, the record number can range
from one to the number of records per track.

When you use this address format, you don't have to be concerned
with the actual location of a file as you do when you use the physical
address format. A reference to relative track 38, for instance, will search
the proper track whether the file begins on cylinder 60 or cylinder 128.
That means that a file can be moved from one area of a disk to another
without modifying the program. As a result, you'll probably use this
address format or the one that follows whenever you use DAM files.

Relative track address format in hex   The third address format shown
in figure 15-1 is also relative track number plus record number. In this format, however, the values are in hex (binary) rather than zoned decimal.
Bytes 0-2 must contain the relative track number, and byte 3 must hold the
record number.

An introduction to file-handling techniques for DAM files

Before you can create a direct file, you usually develop a routine that will
determine the placement of each record in the file. A routine like this can
be called a *randomizing routine* because it assigns disk locations to the
records of a file on a random basis. A randomizing routine for a DAM file
converts the value of a field within a record (usually, the key field) to a
disk address in one of the three forms that is acceptable to DAM.

Because the purpose of this book is to teach you assembler language,
not how to develop randomizing routines, I'm not going to try to present
different techniques that can be used in randomizing routines. If you ever
use DAM, you'll probably be able to develop your own routines without
any special training. Otherwise, you can do some research on your own to
learn more about randomizing routines. At this time, then, I will present
only one example of a randomizing routine so you have the general idea of
what one entails.

Figure 15-2 presents a simple example of a randomizing routine for
loading and accessing the records in a DAM file. In this case, 3000 inventory master records are supposed to be stored in a disk area consisting of
200 tracks with a maximum of 20 records per track. These records are supposed to be in count-key-data format so they can be accessed by relative
track number plus key. As you would guess, the key area for each record
will contain the part number of the inventory item. Since the part numbers
are seven digits long in character format, the key areas are seven bytes
long.

Format 1:
An 8-byte physical disk address in hex (MBBCCHHR)

Bytes	Format	Contents	Remarks
0	M	Module number	Usually X'00' for disk.
1-2	BB	Bin number	Always X'0000' for disk.
3-4	CC	Cylinder number	Range is from zero to number of cylinders per device minus 1.
5-6	HH	Head (or track) number	Range is from zero to the number of tracks per cylinder minus 1.
7	R	Record number	Zero if records are accessed by key. Otherwise, the number of the record on the track ranging from 1 to the number of records on the track.

Format 2:
A 10-byte relative track address in zoned decimal (TTTTTTTTRR)

Bytes	Format	Contents	Remarks
0-7	TTTTTTTT	Relative track number	Range is from zero to the number of tracks allocated to the file.
8-9	RR	Record number	Zero if records are accessed by key. Otherwise, the number of the record on the track ranging from 1 to the number of records on the track.

Format 3:
A 4-byte relative track address in hex (TTTR)

Bytes	Format	Contents	Remarks
0-2	TTT	Relative track number	Range is from zero to the number of tracks allocated to the file.
3	R	Record number	Zero if records are accessed by key. Otherwise, the number of the record on the track ranging from 1 to the number of records on the track.

Figure 15-1   Disk address formats for the DAM access method

Since 3000 records can be stored in only 150 tracks with 20 records per track, you can see that 1000 of the record positions won't be used for this file. These positions can be used for records that are added to the file later on. Also, as you will see in a moment, they make it easier for the file loading routine to find available record positions for the records of the file. In general, then, you allocate more space to a direct file than is actually needed for the number of records in the file.

The problem of the randomizing routine is to convert a record's part number, which may range from 0000000 through 9999999 to a relative track number between 0 and 199. This data will be used to move the access mechanism to the selected cylinder and to turn the selected head on. Then, the appropriate record can be located by searching for a key equal to the record's part number.

One common method used for calculating relative track number is called the *division/remainder method*. In figure 15-2, this method is used to calculate the relative track number for a record by dividing the part number by the number of tracks allocated to the file. Since 200 tracks are allocated to the file, each part number is divided by 200. Then, the remainder is a number between zero and 199, so it can be used as the relative track number for the record.

The problem with this method is that the calculation may generate the same track number for more than 20 records, but each track can hold a maximum of 20 records. This means that *track overflow* will occur for the 21st record that is assigned to each track and all subsequent records that are assigned to that track. As a result, the routines for loading and accessing the records in the file must provide for track overflow.

If you check the routines for loading and accessing records in figure 15-2, you can see that they provide for track overflow in a straightforward manner. If a track is full when a loading routine tries to write a record on it, the routine writes the record on the next available record location in the tracks that follow it. If the routine can't find an open location after looking for one in ten successive tracks, it prints an error message, skips the record, and continues the loading process with the next record in the input file.

The accessing routine in figure 15-2 is consistent with the loading routine. If an accessing routine can't find a record on a track, it searches for the record in the tracks that follow. After ten tracks have been searched, the accessing routine assumes the record can't be found. Since 1000 extra record positions are assigned to the file, the loading routine should be able to find open positions for each record without too much searching. Similarly, the accessing routine shouldn't have to do too much searching to find a record either.

Although this example is quite simple, I hope you get the general idea of what the file-handling routines for a DAM file must provide for. Sometimes, if the keys of the file are planned with direct file processing in mind, the routine can be quite simple with no provision for track overflow because it won't ever be necessary. Sometimes, it can be extremely difficult to develop a routine that provides for track overflow and that still runs with satisfactory efficiency.

Characteristics of the file

A file of 3000 inventory master records is to be stored in a DAM file of 200 tracks with a maximum of 20 records per track. The records will be stored in count-key-data format, and they will be accessed by relative track number plus key.

Problem of the randomizing routine

To convert the seven-digit key (part number) of each master record to a relative track number.

The division/remainder method for calculating relative track number

Divide the key in each master record by 200. Then, the remainder is a number between 0 and 199 that can be used as the relative track number for the record.

The routine for loading the records in the file

1. Convert the part number to relative track number using the division/ remainder method.

2. Write the record in the next available record position on the relative track. If the track is full, write the record in the next available record position on any of the nine tracks that follow. If relative track 199 is reached, continue the search for an open position with relative track zero. If an open position can't be found in the relative track or the nine tracks that follow, print an error message and skip the record.

The routine for accessing the records in the file

1. Convert the part number of the desired record to relative track number using the division/remainder method.

2. Search the relative track for a key equal to the key of the desired record. If an equal key can't be found, search the next track in sequence and continue the search until a total of ten tracks have been searched. If the relative track number reaches 199 during the search, continue with relative track zero. If a record can't be found in the relative track or the nine tracks that follow, stop searching and assume the record can't be found.

3. When an equal key is found, read the record that follows the key area.

Figure 15-2   One method of loading and accessing the records in a direct file using DAM

When records in a DAM file are blocked, additional programming is required because DAM doesn't provide for blocked records. As a result, you must provide your own blocking and deblocking routines. To load a blocked file, the records have to be randomized to a block of records rather than to a relative track. Then, overflow records for each block can be stored in the next available block or in separate overflow areas. To access the records, the randomizing routine must search the selected block and the related overflow areas until the desired record is found. Because of these complications, DAM files are usually unblocked.

Discussion

As you will see in the next topic, the assembler language macros for DAM files are relatively difficult to use. In addition, the routines for loading and accessing DAM files are likely to be relatively difficult to design and code. Because of these difficulties, DAM files are used infrequently.

Terminology

relative track number
randomizing routine
division/remainder method
track overflow

Objective

Describe the two disk address formats that DAM offers for accessing a record by relative track number plus key or record number.

TOPIC 2   Assembler language for DAM files

Because direct files can be processed in many different ways, I will make no attempt to illustrate the most common processing patterns for DAM files. Instead, I will start by presenting the DTF operands and I/O macros for DAM files. Then, I will present two simple programs that illustrate the use of DAM files. When you complete this chapter, you should be able to apply the DAM macros to a wide range of programming problems.

DTFDA operands

The DTF macro for DAM files is the DTFDA. The most widely used operands for the DTFDA macro are summarized in figure 15-3. Although this summary is largely self-explanatory, here is some additional information about some of the operands.

IOAREA1   The label of the I/O area is coded in this operand. To determine the number of bytes required in the I/O area for the file, use the table in figure 15-4. The contents of the I/O area are determined by the disk format (count-data or count-key-data) and by the I/O macro used. If more than one macro is used for one direct file, the I/O area must provide for the largest possible I/O area content. The program must then process the varying contents of the I/O area by using appropriate dummy sections or work areas.

RECFORM   Although you can provide blocking and deblocking routines of your own, DAM regards all records as unblocked. The records can be fixed-length, variable-length, or undefined. In most cases, you will use FIXUNB for unblocked, fixed-length records.

If VARUNB is specified, the programmer is responsible for calculating the record and block lengths and for placing them in the appropriate format in the first eight bytes of the I/O area. The format for record and block length is the same as it is for variable-length SAM files, as described in chapter 13. However, the variable-length format for DAM files is rarely used.

When UNDEF is specified, the records can be fixed- or variable-length, blocked or unblocked. When UNDEF is coded, the RECSIZE operand must also be included.

RECSIZE   If RECFORM=UNDEF, the RECSIZE operand must be included and must specify a register number. When an undefined record is read, the I/O module puts the length of the record into this register as a binary value. Similarly, before an undefined record can be written, the length of the record must be put into this register.

KEYLEN   The KEYLEN operand must specify the length of the keys if the file is in count-key-data format. It should be omitted if the file is in count-data format.

Priority	Keyword	Programmer code	Remarks
Required	BLKSIZE	Length of I/O area	See IOAREA1 for length.
Required	IOAREA1	Name of I/O area	Length of I/O area must include 8 bytes for the count area if AFTER = YES is coded; it must include bytes for the key area if KEYLEN is coded.
Optional	RECFORM	FIXUNB VARUNB UNDEF	If UNDEF is coded, RECSIZE must be coded.
Optional	RECSIZE	Register number (nn)	Required if RECFORM = UNDEF. Register must contain the record length in binary before a WRITE is issued. The length of a record will be put into this register after a READ.
Optional	KEYLEN	Length of key	Used only if file is in count-key-data format.
Required	TYPEFLE	INPUT OUTPUT	The default is INPUT.
Optional	DSKXTNT	Maximum number of extents for a file	Indicates that relative track addresses are used.
Optional	DEVADDR	Logical unit	Required only when no EXTENT statement is provided.
Required	SEEKADR	Name of disk-address field	The length of this address field depends on the address format: 8 bytes for physical address, 10 bytes for relative track address in decimal, 4 bytes for relative track address in hex.
Optional	KEYARG	Name of key field	Used only if KEYLEN is coded. Length of the KEYARG field should be equal to the key length. The key must be placed in this field before a READ or WRITE by key.
Optional	RELTYPE	HEX DEC	Specifies that the format of a relative track address is hex (4 bytes) or decimal (10 bytes).

Figure 15-3   DTFDA operand summary (part 1 of 2)

Priority	Keyword	Programmer code	Remarks
Required	ERRBYTE	Name of error-code field	The user must define this two-byte field for error indications. See figure 15-5 for a description of the error codes.
Optional	IDLOC	Name of disk-address field	The length of IDLOC must be the same as the length of the SEEKADR field. An address will be placed in this field after a READ or WRITE in the same format as SEEKADR. See figure 15-6 to determine which address is placed in this field.
Optional	XTNTXIT	Label of first instruction in an extent processing routine	Lets the user code a routine that captures extent information. The label is branched to during the execution of the OPEN macro. See figure 15-7 for more details.
Optional	READID	YES	READ by ID will be used.
Optional	READKEY	YES	READ by KEY will be used.
Optional	WRITEID	YES	WRITE by ID will be used.
Optional	WRITEKY	YES	WRITE by KEY will be used.
Optional	AFTER	YES	WRITE AFTER or RZERO will be used.
Optional	SRCHM	YES	Requests a search of multiple tracks to the end of a cylinder during a READ or WRITE by KEY.

Figure 15-3   DTFDA operand summary (part 2 of 2)

Macro instruction	I/O area contents with KEYLEN	I/O area contents without KEYLEN
`READ    filename,KEY`	Data	Illegal
`READ    filename,ID`	Key and data	Data
`WRITE   filename,KEY`	Data	Illegal
`WRITE   filename,ID`	Key and data	Data
`WRITE   filename,RZERO`	Not used	Not used
`WRITE   filename,AFTER`	Count, key, and data	Count and data

Figure 15-4   I/O area contents based on macro type

DSKXTNT   The DSKXTNT operand must be included when relative track addresses are used. It should be omitted when cylinder and head addresses are used. This operand specifies the number of extents used for a file, which is usually one.

SEEKADR   The SEEKADR operand specifies the label of the disk address field. This field must be of proper length for the type of reference that you selected: eight bytes for cylinder and head addresses, ten bytes for relative track in zoned decimal, and four bytes for relative track in hex.

RELTYPE   If relative track addresses are used, this entry is coded either DEC to indicate that the 10-byte decimal format is used, or HEX to indicate that the four-byte hex format is used.

KEYARG   The KEYARG operand should be coded for files in count-key-data format that are processed using the KEY form of READ or WRITE. It names a field in which the program must place the key of the desired record before issuing an I/O macro. If a count-key-data file is read by ID (record number), the key of the record that is read will be placed in this field by the I/O module.

SRCHM   The SRCHM operand stands for *search multiple tracks*. If the file is in count-key-data format, this operand will cause a READ or WRITE by KEY to search beyond the track indicated in the disk address. If the specified key is not found on the indicated track, the search will continue on subsequent tracks until the record is found or the end of the cylinder is reached.

ERRBYTE   THe ERRBYTE operand gives the name of a two-byte field in your program that will be used to indicate processing errors. Figure 15-5 lists all of the error conditions that can be posted. When I explain the illustrative programs in this topic, it will help you understand which type of error is applicable to which type of READ or WRITE macro.

IDLOC   If the IDLOC operand is coded, the ID (disk address) of a record will be placed in the specified field after each READ or WRITE operation. The returned ID will be in the same format as that used by the SEEKADR field.

Figure 15-6 shows what the contents of the IDLOC field will be after each I/O operation. The contents will be the address of the next record in the file, except when the KEY form of the READ or WRITE is used with the SRCHM option. In this case, the address of the record just read or written is placed in the IDLOC field. If a record isn't found, an error indication will be posted in the ERRBYTE field; then, the contents of the IDLOC field are unpredictable.

Byte	Bit	Meaning
0	0	Not used
	1	Wrong length record
	2	Nondata transfer (hardware I/O error)
	3	Not used
	4	No room found (WRITE AFTER only)
	5	Not used
	6	Not used
	7	Reference outside file extents
1	0	Data check in count area
	1	Track overrun
	2	End of cylinder (SRCHM)
	3	Data check in reading key or data
	4	No record found
	5	End-of-file record read
	6	End-of-volume reached (multi-volume files)
	7	Not used

Figure 15-5   ERRBYTE bit meanings

Macro instruction	ID supplied with SRCHM	ID supplied without SRCHM
READ filename,KEY	Same record	Next record
READ filename,ID	Next record	Next record
WRITE filename,KEY	Same record	Next record
WRITE filename,ID	Next record	Next record

Figure 15-6   ID supplied in IDLOC after a READ or WRITE macro has been issued

XTNTXIT   This operand gives the address of an instruction that control is passed to during the execution of the OPEN macro for the file. When control is passed to this instruction, register 1 will contain the address of a 14-byte field that contains the extents of the file in the form shown in figure 15-7. This extent information can then be saved for use in randomizing routines. In general, this extent information is only needed when cylinder and head addressing is used.

Bytes	Contents
0	Extent type code as specified in the EXTENT statement
1	Extent sequence number
2-5	Lower limit of the extent in binary (CCHH)
6-9	Upper limit of the extent in binary (CCHH)
10-11	Symbolic unit number in binary
12-13	Not used

Note: At entry to user's XTNTXIT routine, register 1 contains the address of the 14-byte area described above.

Figure 15-7 Format of the extent area for an XTNTXIT routine

Other macros required for DAM file processing

To process DAM files, only four other macros are required. They are the READ, WRITE, WAITF, and LBRET macros. These macros are summarized in figure 15-8.

The READ and WRITE macros DAM files are processed using READ and WRITE macros. When you read or write a record, you can refer to it by its record number on a track or by its key. If you want to refer to it by record number (or ID), you code:

```
    READ  filename,ID
 or WRITE filename,ID
```

In this case, the program must supply the proper ID in the SEEKADR field.

If you want to refer to a record by key, the file must be in count-key-data format. Then, you code:

```
    READ  filename,KEY
 or WRITE filename,KEY
```

In this case, the SEEKADR field must contain the proper track address, but the record number must be set to zero. Also, the KEYARG field must contain the key of the record to be read or written.

Two other formats of the WRITE macro are also used in processing DAM files. Before creating a direct file, you may need to clear the disk area of previous data. In this case, a special form of the WRITE macro is used:

```
WRITE filename,RZERO
```

Macro format	Meaning
`READ   filename,KEY`	Read the record with the key specified in the KEYARG field on the track specified in the SEEKADR field.
`READ   filename,ID`	Read the record at the address specified in the SEEKADR field.
`WRITE filename,KEY`	Write a record in the location that has the key specified in the KEYARG field on the track specified in the SEEKADR field.
`WRITE filename,ID`	Write a record at the address specified in the SEEKADR field.
`WRITE filename,RZERO`	Reset record zero on the track specified in the SEEKADR field to indicate that no records are stored on the track.
`WRITE filename,AFTER`	Write a record on the track specified in the SEEKADR field in the next available record location.
`WRITE filename,AFTER,EOF`	Write an end-of-file record on the track specified in the SEEKADR field in the next available record location.
`WAITF filename`	Wait until the I/O operation specified by the preceding I/O macro has finished its execution.
`LBRET`	Return to the OPEN routine. This macro is used in a DSKXTNT routine.

Figure 15-8   I/O macro summary for DAM files

With RZERO as the second operand, the WRITE macro causes the track specified in the SEEKADR field to be prepared for new data. This includes resetting the fields in record zero of the track to indicate that no records are stored on the track. Record zero is never used for storing data; it is used by the VSE access methods.

If you don't use this method of clearing a disk area before creating a file, it must be done by using one of the VSE utility programs called the *clear disk utility*. As you will learn later, there are differences in these two methods of clearing a disk area that will affect the logic of a file creation program.

The other special form of the WRITE macro allows you to write a record in the next available space on a track without knowing which record number it will be. This macro is coded:

```
WRITE filename,AFTER
```

When it has a third operand of EOF, this macro has this form:

```
WRITE filename,AFTER,EOF
```

Then, it causes an end-of-file record to be written in the next available record position. The end-of-file record is only used if the file is processed sequentially by some other program.

The WAITF macro   This macro must follow each READ or WRITE macro that you use. Its format is:

```
WAITF filename
```

This macro is necessary because VSE doesn't wait for an I/O operation to finish before returning control to a program. As a result, you must code the WAITF macro to stop the execution of your program until the preceding I/O operation has been completed.

The LBRET macro   If you use the XTNTXIT operand in the DTFDA, control passes to your routine from the routine for the OPEN macro. Then, to end your XTNTXIT routine and return to the OPEN routine, you use the LBRET (label processing return) macro. It is coded with no operands.

Two illustrative programs

Normally, when a direct file is created, some type of randomizing routine is used to determine the address of each record in the file. However, the illustrative programs in figures 15-9 and 15-10 don't use randomizing routines. Instead, a DAM file is created by writing the records in sequence on the tracks of the file. Then, to access the records, the update program simply searches for the desired records in sequence, one track after another.

For most jobs, of course, this method of loading and accessing records would be so inefficient that it wouldn't be practical. However, if a file is small, this loading and accessing method might be practical. So, as you study these programs, assume that the file will require a maximum of only four tracks. This will make the programs somewhat more realistic. In any event, keep in mind that the purpose of these programs is to show you the assembler language code for DAM files, not the routines that determine disk addresses.

A file creation program   The program in figure 15-9 creates a DAM file of inventory master records from a sequential disk file with records that have a similar format. The key for each output record is the item number (six bytes) and the rest of the record is 50 bytes. If you assume that the entire file will fit on just four tracks of one cylinder, all of the tracks in the file can be searched by using just one READ macro with the SRCHM option on.

In the DTFDA in figure 15-9, the KEYLEN operand must be included to indicate count-key-data format; it is coded with a key length of six bytes. Since the program uses the AFTER form of WRITE in this program, the I/O area must include eight bytes for the count field, six for the key, and 50 for the data, as indicated by the table in figure 15-4. Because of this, the BLKSIZE entry must be 64.

The name of the ERRBYTE field is DAERRS. The name of the SEEKADR field is TRKADDR. Since this program has no need for a returned disk address, IDLOC is omitted. The KEYARG operand is also omitted because the program only uses the RZERO and AFTER forms of WRITE. Since the program uses the hex form of relative track addressing, HEX is used in the RELTYPE operand and the XTNTXIT operand is omitted (the program doesn't need to know the file extents). Since the DSKXTNT operand must be included for relative track addressing, it is coded 1. Of the other possible operands, only AFTER = YES is coded. This is done so the program can use the RZERO and AFTER forms of the WRITE macro.

Notice that the definition of the I/O area, DAOUT, corresponds to the BLKSIZE operand. Space has been reserved for the count, key, and data portions of the record. Similarly, the disk address field, TRKADDR, is coordinated with the RELTYPE operand. This field is four bytes long as required for relative track addresses in binary format. In this program, I reserved those four bytes as a fullword.

Now look at the program logic. After the file has been opened, a small loop is initialized and executed thus clearing the four tracks of the file so the new records can be written:

```
         LA    4,4
         LA    5,0
CLEARTRK ST    5,TRKADDR
         WRITE DAFILE,RZERO
         WAITF DAFILE
         LA    5,256(5)
         BCT   4,CLEARTRK
```

First, register 4 is loaded with a binary value of four so it can be used as a counter for the loop. Then, register 5 is set to zero and stored in the track address field to set the relative track to zero. When the RZERO form of the WRITE is executed the first time, it clears the first track. The WAITF macro then makes sure that the WRITE has finished its operation before processing continues.

When the WRITE RZERO macro has been completed for the first track, the LA instruction is used to increase the contents of register 5 to the next relative track address. Remember that the hex format of the relative track address is TTTR. Thus, the value 256 in the LA instruction changes the contents of register 5 from X'00000000' to X'00000100'. In other words, the relative track number is changed from zero to one. Then, the branch-on-count (BCT) instruction causes the program to repeat the loop three more times thus clearing the second, third, and fourth tracks in the file. After the fourth track has been cleared, register 5 is reset to zero and the program continues.

The second part of the program reads the sequential inventory records. In this main routine, register 5 is used for manipulating the

```
LOADDA    START  O
BEGIN     BALR   3,0
          USING  ≠,3
          OPEN   INPUT,DAFILE
          LA     4,4
          LA     5,0
CLEARTRK  ST     5,TRKADDR
          WRITE  DAFILE,RZERO          CLEAR TRACK FOR NEW RECORDS
          WAITF  DAFILE
          LA     5,256(5)
          BCT    4,CLEARTRK
          LA     5,0
          ST     5,TRKADDR
NXTREC    GET    INPUT,INPTWRKA
          MVC    DITEM,IITEM
          MVC    DDESC,IDESC
          MVC    DUM,IUM
          MVC    DORDPOL,IORDPOL
          PACK   DORDQTY,IORDQTY
          PACK   DORDPT,IORDPT
          PACK   DSAFSTK,ISAFSTK
          PACK   DONHAND,IONHAND
          PACK   DONORD,IONORD
          PACK   DALLOC,IALLOC
WRITE     WRITE  DAFILE,AFTER          WRITE REC AFTER LAST REC ON TRACK
          WAITF  DAFILE
          CLC    DAERRS,=X'0000'       COMPARE ERROR BYTES TO HEX ZEROS
          BE     NXTREC                BRANCH IF ALL BITS ARE ZERO
          CLC    DAERRS,=X'0800'       TEST TO SEE IF BIT 4 IS ON
          BE     NXTTRK                BRANCH IF BIT 4 IS ON
          DUMP
NXTTRK    LA     5,256(5)              INCREASE REL TRACK NO BY 1
          ST     5,TRKADDR             STORE REL TRACK NO IN TRKADDR
          CLC    TRKADDR,=X'00000400'  COMPARE REL TRACK NO WITH 4
          BNL    AREAFULL              BRANCH IF REL TRACK NO NOT LESS 4
          B      WRITE
AREAFULL  DUMP
EOFDSK    WRITE  DAFILE,AFTER,EOF      WRITE EOF RECORD
          CLOSE  INPUT,DAFILE
          EOJ
```

Figure 15-9   A file creation program for a DAM file (part 1 of 2)

relative track address. After a sequential record has been read and the record in the direct file assembled, the AFTER form of the WRITE is issued with the relative track address set to zero. This causes the first record to be written on the first track of the file. While the WRITE is being executed, the WAITF halts processing. When the program continues, it checks to see if the error bytes are all zero. If they are, the program branches to NXTREC so the next record can be written on the file by repeating the loop.

If the error bytes aren't zero, the program tests to see whether bit 4 is on and all other bits are off using this compare logical instruction:

```
CLC    DAERRS,=X'0800'
BE     NXTTRK
```

```
INPUT      DTFSD  BLKSIZE=248,                                         X
                  RECFORM=FIXBLK,                                      X
                  RECSIZE=62,                                          X
                  IOAREA1=INPTDSKA,                                    X
                  WORKA=YES,                                           X
                  EOFADDR=EOFDSK
DAFILE     DTFDA  BLKSIZE=64,                                          X
                  IOAREA1=DAOUT,                                       X
                  KEYLEN=6,                                            X
                  TYPEFLE=OUTPUT,                                      X
                  DSKXTNT=1,                                           X
                  SEEKADR=TRKADDR,                                     X
                  RELTYPE=HEX,                                         X
                  ERRBYTE=DAERRS,                                      X
                  AFTER=YES
INPTDSKA   DS     CL248
DAOUT      DS     OCL64
DCOUNT     DS     CL8
DITEM      DS     CL6
DDESC      DS     CL20
DUM        DS     CL4
DORDPOL    DS     CL2
DORDQTY    DS     PL4
DORDPT     DS     PL4
DSAFSTK    DS     PL4
DONHAND    DS     PL4
DONORD     DS     PL4
DALLOC     DS     PL4
INPTWRKA   DS     OCL62
IITEM      DS     CL6
IDESC      DS     CL20
IUM        DS     CL4
IORDPOL    DS     CL2
IORDQTY    DS     CL5
IORDPT     DS     CL5
ISAFSTK    DS     CL5
IONHAND    DS     CL5
IONORD     DS     CL5
IALLOC     DS     CL5
TRKADDR    DS     F
DAERRS     DS     CL2
           END    BEGIN
```

Figure 15-9   A file creation program for a DAM file (part 2 of 2)

If bit 4 is the only one that is on, it means that there is no room on the track for the current record. Then, the program branches to NXTTRK where the relative track number is increased by one so the record can be written on the next track. It's possible, though, that there are more records in the file than can be stored on the four tracks allocated to the file. As a result, these instructions test the relative track number in TRKADDR after it has been increased by one to make sure it's less than 4:

```
CLC    TRKADDR,=X'00000400'
BNL    AREAFULL
B      WRITE
```

If it isn't less than four, the program branches to AREAFULL and a DUMP macro terminates the program. If it is less than four, the program branches to WRITE and the record is written on the new track.

If any bit in DAERRS is on other than bit 4, it indicates that an unexpected I/O error has occurred. In this case, the program reaches the DUMP macro. This instruction prints a storage dump and causes program termination.

If all input records are read and written on the file without problems, the program issues an AFTER EOF form of the WRITE macro. This causes an end-of-file record to be written. Then, the program ends.

Although this program uses WRITE RZERO to clear the disk for file creation, a disk can also be cleared by using the clear disk utility that I mentioned earlier. When this utility is used, however, the tracks are not only cleared, they are formatted. If, for example, the clear disk utility were used for this file, the tracks would be formatted with count areas, key areas, and data areas. Furthermore, each count area would contain a disk address including cylinder number, head number, and record number. Then, the WRITE AFTER macro couldn't be used to store the actual data on the disk. Instead, the program would have to supply the record number for each record to be written on the disk and use the WRITE ID form of the macro. It is important to understand this difference in methods of clearing disk areas for DAM files because it has a significant effect on the file creation logic.

A random update program   Figure 15-10 presents a program that updates the DAM file created by the program in figure 15-9. In this program, a SAM file of shipment transactions is used to update the inventory master records.

Before getting into the main part of the program, let me discuss the DTFDA that describes the inventory master file. This time the file will be processed by using only the KEY form of the READ macro. As a result, the I/O area and the BLKSIZE operand need to account for only the data portion of the record as indicated by the table in figure 15-4. Since I omitted the TYPEFLE operand, the default value, INPUT, is assumed. The required SEEKADR operand names the disk address field, TRACK, and, since I have no need for the returned disk address, I have omitted the IDLOC operand. The KEYARG operand gives the name of the field in which I will place the key of the record to be read (ITEMKEY) before reading the records by key. I again elected to use the binary format of relative track addressing so the RELTYPE operand specifies HEX. Of the operands that indicate the type of I/O macros to be issued, I coded READKEY=YES and SRCHM=YES to indicate that the records will be searched for by key and that a single READ macro will search an entire cylinder. I coded WRITEKY=YES since the records will be rewritten on the file using keys after they are updated.

Notice in the data definitions following the DTFDA that the attributes of the fields correspond to the DTF entries. The length of the KEYARG field, ITEMKEY, is six bytes; the ERRBYTE field, ERRS, is two bytes; and the disk address field, TRACK, is four bytes. For this program, I defined the relative track address field as hex zeros so it will address relative track zero. I will leave this field set to zero throughout the program, so each READ will search for a key beginning on the first track of the file. Then, since SRCHM=YES is specified, the succeeding tracks will also be searched by the READ macro until the key is found or the end of the cylinder has been reached. To prevent unnecessary searching, I will use appropriate JCL statements to allocate this file to the last four tracks of a cylinder.

Now look at the instructions to see how the program works. First, a transaction record is read and the item number is moved into the key field of the inventory master record (ITEMKEY). Then, the KEY form of the READ is issued and a WAITF macro follows. This causes a search of the four-track file starting with the first track of the file. When the I/O operation finishes, the program checks the ERRBYTE field to find out the results.

If the key is found and the record is successfully read, the ERRBYTE field will have all bits off. In this case, the program branches to FOUND. Then, the program updates the master record and writes it back on the file using the KEY form of the WRITE macro followed by a WAITF macro. This causes the master record to be rewritten on the file in its original location.

If all four tracks of the file are searched but the record isn't found, two bits will be on in the ERRBYTE field: (1) the bit that indicates that no record has been found and (2) the bit that indicates that the end of the cylinder has been reached. To test these bits, the test-under-mask (TM) instruction is used. If you're not familiar with this instruction, chapter 10 describes it in detail. However, the descriptions that follow should help you understand its operation.

The first TM instruction tests the bits in the first ERRBYTE byte as follows:

```
CHKERRS1 TM      ERRS,X'FF'
         BM      DISASTER
```

Since the mask is hex FF, which is binary 11111111, it means all the bits will be tested. If any of these bits are on, it indicates that an unexpected I/O error has occurred. (BM means branch if mixed). Then, the program branches to DISASTER and a PDUMP macro is issued.

If none of the bits in the first error byte are on, the program tests the second error byte using these instructions:

```
CHKERRS2 TM      ERRS+1,X'D7'
         BM      DISASTER
```

Since hex D7 is binary 1101 0111, this TM instruction tests all the bits of the second error byte except bit 2 for the no-record-found condition and bit 4 for the end-of-cylinder condition. If any of the tested bits are on, the

```
UPDTDA     START  0
BEGIN      BALR   3,0
           USING  *,3
           OPEN   SHIPTR,REPORT,INVMSTR
READSHIP   GET    SHIPTR,SHPWRKA
           MVC    ITEMKEY,SHPITEM
           READ   INVMSTR,KEY              READ DAM RECORD BY KEY
           WAITF  INVMSTR
           CLC    ERRS,=X'0000'            COMPARE ERROR BYTES WITH HEX ZEROS
           BE     FOUND
CHKERRS1   TM     ERRS,X'FF'              TEST ALL BITS IN FIRST ERROR BYTE
           BM     DISASTER                BRANCH IF ANY BITS ARE ON
CHKERRS2   TM     ERRS+1,X'D7'            TEST BITS IN SECOND ERROR BYTE
           BM     DISASTER                BRANCH IF ANY TESTED BITS ARE ON
NORECFND   MVC    ERRITEM,ITEMKEY
           PUT    REPORT
           B      READSHIP
FOUND      PACK   QTYSHIP,SHPQTY
           SP     MONHAND,QTYSHIP
           WRITE  INVMSTR,KEY             WRITE DAM RECORD BY KEY
           WAITF  INVMSTR
           B      READSHIP
DISASTER   PDUMP  INVMSTR,OPENSW
EOFINPT    CLOSE  SHIPTR,REPORT,INVMSTR
           EOJ
SHIPTR     DTFSD  BLKSIZE=240,                                          X
                  RECFORM=FIXBLK,                                       X
                  RECSIZE=24,                                           X
                  IOAREA1=SHPREC,                                       X
                  WORKA=YES,                                            X
                  EOFADDR=EOFINPT
INVMSTR    DTFDA  BLKSIZE=50,                                           X
                  IOAREA1=MSTRIO,                                       X
                  KEYLEN=6,                                             X
                  TYPEFLE=INPUT,                                        X
                  DSKXTNT=1,                                            X
                  SEEKADR=TRACK,                                        X
                  KEYARG=ITEMKEY,                                       X
                  RELTYPE=HEX,                                          X
                  ERRBYTE=ERRS,                                         X
                  READKEY=YES,                                          X
                  WRITEKY=YES,                                          X
                  SRCHM=YES
```

Figure 15-10   A random update program for a DAM file (part 1 of 2)

program branches to DISASTER. Otherwise, it indicates that the only bits that are on are bits 2 and 4. As a result, the program continues with the next intructions, which cause a line to be printed on the error listing.

If an I/O error has occurred, the PDUMP macro at DISASTER causes a partial storage dump. It prints the contents of storage between the DTFDA macro and the field named OPENSW. This information will help me figure out why the error took place. Following the PDUMP macro, the files are closed, and the program ends.

```
REPORT     DTFPR  BLKSIZE=132,                                              X
                  IOAREA1=ERRMSG,                                           X
                  DEVADDR=SYSLST
SHPREC     DS     CL240
MSTRIO     DS     OCL50
MDESC      DS     CL20
MUM        DS     CL4
MORDPOL    DS     CL2
MORDQTY    DS     PL4
MORDPT     DS     PL4
MSAFSTK    DS     PL4
MONHAND    DS     PL4
MONORD     DS     PL4
MALLOC     DS     PL4
SHPWRKA    DS     OCL24
           DS     CL6
SHPITEM    DS     CL6
SHPQTY     DS     CL4
           DS     CL8
ERRMSG     DS     OCL132
           DC     5C' '
           DC     CL15'NO RECORD FOUND'
           DC     5C' '
ERRITEM    DS     CL6
           DC     101C' '
OPENSW     DC     X'00'
ERRS       DS     CL2
TRACK      DC     X'00000000'
ITEMKEY    DS     CL6
QTYSHIP    DS     PL4
           END    BEGIN
```

Figure 15-10   A random update program for a DAM file (part 2 of 2)

Discussion

As you should now start to appreciate, DAM files are more difficult to use than SAM and ISAM files. The DTF is more complex, the I/O macros are a little more complicated, and you must provide all of the file handling logic yourself. Because of these difficulties, DAM files aren't popular. In some cases, though, a DAM file can offer a good solution to a particular programming need.

Terminology

search multiple tracks
clear disk utility

Objective

Given program specifications that require the use of DAM files, code a program that satisfies the specifications.

TOPIC 3   VSE JCL for DAM files

The JCL required for DAM files is almost identical to that for SAM files. For that reason, I won't cover the required JCL statements in detail here. Instead, I will simply present an example of the JCL required for processing a DAM file.

A job stream for creating a DAM file

Figure 15-11 is the job stream I used for assembling and testing the file creation program in figure 15-9. The DLBL and EXTENT statement for the DAM file can be used whether the file is an input, output, or update file.

The only new thing here is the type code on the DLBL statement, which must be DA for a DAM file. The rest of the code you should already be familiar with. The file is to reside on the volume CKD001 starting at relative track number 776 and occupying 4 tracks. I selected these location and size values so the file will reside on the last four tracks of a cylinder. As I explained when I described the file creation program, this will make the update program run more efficiently.

Direct files can reside in more than one extent on the same volume or on multiple volumes. When this is the case, multiple EXTENT statements must be coded. Otherwise, the coding for DAM files is quite routine.

Discussion

There are other operands that can be coded on both the DLBL and EXTENT statements for a DAM file, but they are beyond the scope of this book. If you want more information about the JCL for DAM files, we recommend our *DOS/VSE JCL* by Steve Eckols.

Objective

Given the file specifications for a program that processes a DAM file, write the JCL for running the program.

```
// JOB     CREATION
// OPTION  LINK
// EXEC    ASSEMBLY
    .
    .   SOURCE PROGRAM
    .
/*
// LIBDEF  CL,TO=USRCL4
// EXEC    LNKEDT
// ASSGN   SYS008,290
// ASSGN   SYS009,290
// DLBL    INPUT,'SEQUENTIAL.DISK.RECORDS'
// EXTENT  SYS008,CKD001
// DLBL    INVMSTR,'DAM.INVENTORY.MASTER.FILE',10,DA
// EXTENT  SYS009,CKD001,,,776,4
// EXEC
/&
```

Figure 15-11   The VSE JCL for testing the DAM file creation program in figure 15-9

Chapter 16

The Virtual Storage
Access Method (VSAM)

VSAM (*Virtual Storage Access Method*) is the predominant DASD access method on VSE systems. But VSAM does more than just replace SAM, ISAM, and DAM with its entry-sequenced, key-sequenced, and relative-record data sets. It also provides efficiency improvements and better space management facilities than the native VSE access methods. In addition, it includes a multifunction utility program called *Access Method Services* (*AMS*) that lets you perform a variety of file-related functions.

Because VSAM is such a comprehensive access method, I couldn't begin to present everything there is to know about it in one chapter. Instead, I will present only the minimum that you need to know to write simple assembler programs that process VSAM files. Topic 1 introduces you to VSAM concepts and terminology. Topic 2 presents the assembler language for VSAM files. Topic 3 presents the JCL for VSAM files.

TOPIC 1   VSAM concepts

This topic introduces you to the terms and concepts you need to understand for processing VSAM files. First, it describes VSAM catalogs and areas. Then, it shows you how the three kinds of VSAM files are organized. By the way, the facilities this topic describes are for VSE/VSAM release 3.0, so if you're using a different release, some details may differ. Nevertheless, the basic concepts are the same.

VSAM CATALOGS

DASD files that use VSE's native access methods are identified with labels stored in the VTOC of the volume on which they reside. In contrast, individual VSAM files don't have VTOC labels. They're identified by information stored in VSAM *catalogs*.

VSAM uses two kinds of catalogs: a *master catalog* and *user catalogs*. There's only one master catalog on a system. It stores label information for all user catalogs. In addition, it may store information for some VSAM data files. More often, though, information for a VSAM file is stored in a user catalog. The file is then said to be "cataloged" in and "owned" by the user catalog.

Figure 16-1 shows the relationships among the master catalog, user catalogs, and files. The shaded areas in the figure represent areas under the control of VSAM. Notice that there's no more than one catalog on each volume; that's a VSAM rule.

A catalog can own items on more than just the volume where it resides. For instance, user catalog 3 owns VSAM files on volumes 3, 4, and 5. Notice also that a catalog can own VSAM files that are on volumes that have other catalogs. For instance, user catalog 3 owns VSAM files on volume 3, but volume 3 contains user catalog 2. It's even possible for non-VSAM files to be cataloged in a VSAM catalog.

VSAM AREAS

Data spaces   The areas labelled "VSAM files" in figure 16-1 represent VSAM *data spaces*. As far as VSE is concerned, those areas are just that: VSAM space. The VSAM files that reside within a VSAM space (there may be many) aren't recorded in the VTOC. What's in the VSAM spaces is transparent to standard VSE facilities.

In the simplest case, an entire DASD volume can be defined as one VSAM space. But it's possible for only a part of a volume to be defined as a VSAM space. In figure 16-1, all of volume 4 is defined as VSAM space, but only part of volume 5 is. It's also possible for several VSAM data spaces to be defined on the same volume, as with volumes 1, 2, and 3 in the figure.

Clusters   In VSAM terms, a file, or *data set*, is a *cluster*. A cluster consists of a *data component* plus an optional *index component*. Before any records can be written to a VSAM file, you have to use AMS to define its cluster. This is in contrast to files managed by the native VSE access methods. With them, all you have to do is open the file and it's ready for use. However, once a cluster is defined, VSAM determines where the file is located. You don't have to worry about finding a free extent for it as you do with SAM, ISAM, and DAM files.

Control intervals and control areas   The unit of data that VSAM transfers between DASD and virtual storage is the *control interval*. A control interval may contain one or more fixed or variable length records, but the control interval itself is always fixed length. VSAM determines the optimum control interval size for a file based on the characteristics of the file and the DASDs that store it.

The VSAM control interval concept is much like blocking used with non-VSAM files. However, a control interval contains control information that isn't in a block. In addition, part of a control interval may be left empty so additions to the file can be made easily. That's not true, of course, for blocks in files that are managed by the native VSE access methods.

A group of adjacent control intervals forms a *control area* within a data space. When you define a cluster, VSAM preformats control areas so they can be processed more efficiently. Just as sections within control intervals may be left empty to make additions easier, entire control intervals within control areas may be left empty.

Figure 16-2 illustrates the structure of a VSAM file's data component. Several control areas make up the data component of a cluster. Within each control area are several control intervals, each containing data records and control information. Of course, figure 16-2 is simplified. A typical VSAM file's data component consists of many control areas, each with perhaps hundreds of control intervals.

VSAM FILE ORGANIZATIONS

The three VSAM file organizations parallel the native VSE access methods. An *entry-sequenced data set* (*ESDS*) is a VSAM file with sequential organization; a *key-sequenced data set* (*KSDS*) is a VSAM file with indexed sequential organization; and a *relative-record data set* (*RRDS*) is a VSAM file with direct organization. But don't confuse these VSAM organizations with the VSE native access methods. For example, even though a VSAM ESDS has sequential organization, SAM can't process it.

Entry-sequenced data sets   An ESDS simply consists of a data component. All additions to it are made at the end of the file. Within an ESDS, records are identified by *relative byte addresses*, or *RBAs*. The RBA is an indication of how far, in

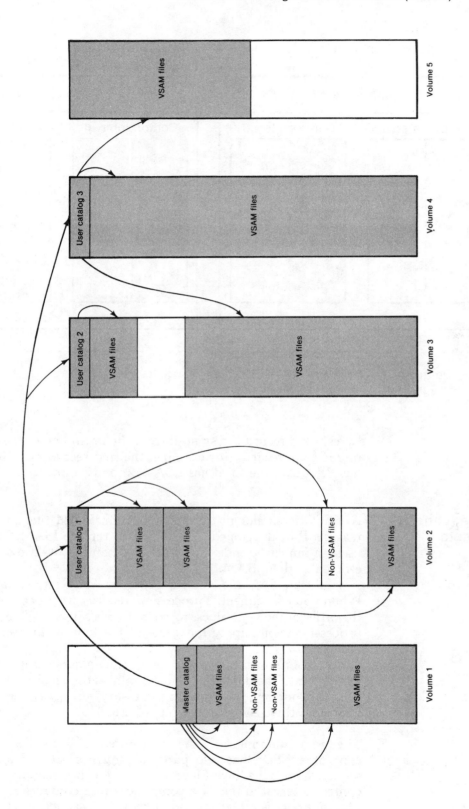

Figure 16-1   Possible VSAM catalog and file relationships

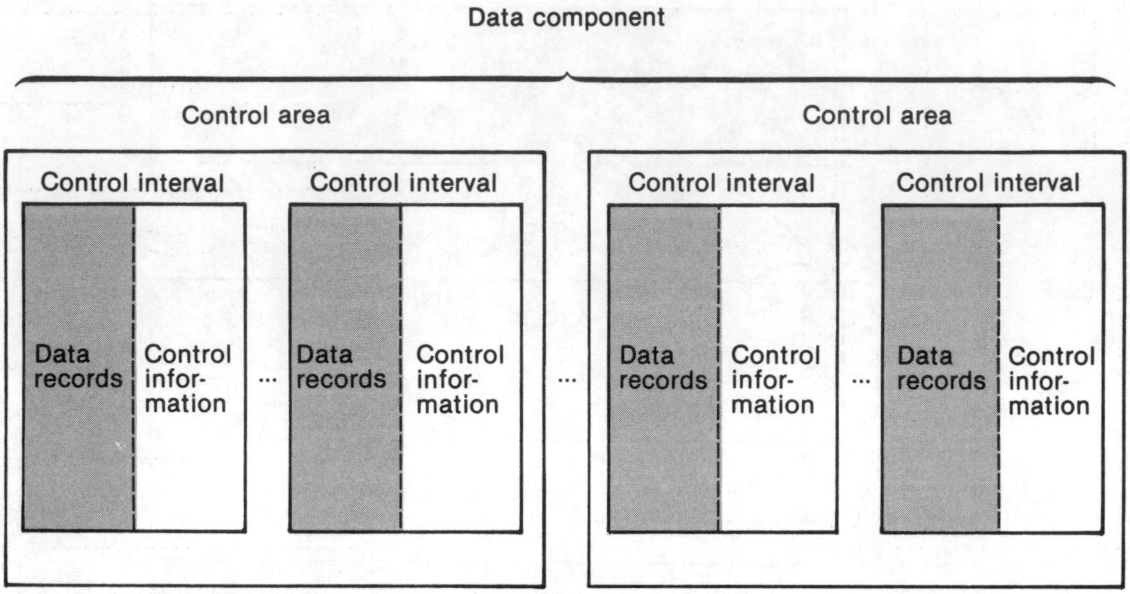

Data component

Figure 16-2   Structure of a VSAM file's data component

bytes, each record is displaced from the beginning of the file. In an ESDS of 256-byte records, for example, the first record has RBA 0, the second has RBA 256, the third has RBA 512, and so on.

Key-sequenced data sets

A KSDS is similar in many ways to an ISAM file. In fact, one of the reasons IBM developed VSAM was to replace ISAM. However, VSAM uses an improved index structure and handles overflow processing more efficiently than ISAM.

Like an ISAM file, you can process a KSDS sequentially or randomly. When you use sequential processing, records are processed one at a time in the order of the key values stored in the file's index. When you use random processing, you supply the value of the key in the record you want to access.

A KSDS consists of two components: a data component and an index component. The data component contains the records and the index component contains the indexes necessary to access them. Figure 16-3 illustrates these two components of a KSDS.

The index component   As you can see in figure 16-3, the index component of a KSDS has two parts: a *sequence set* and an *index set*. The sequence set is the lowest level of the index. It is searched to determine the control interval in the data component that contains a particular record. The index set is a higher level index to the sequence set.

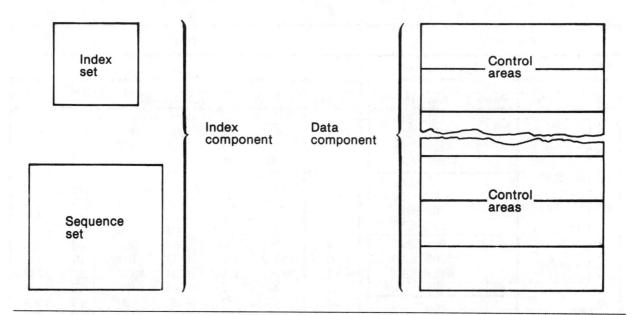

Figure 16-3   Elements of a KSDS

To understand how this works, consider the KSDS in figure 16-4. Here, the key value is a four-digit item number in a file of inventory records. The index set contains four entries, each with a pointer to a record in the sequence set as well as the highest key value referenced in that sequence set record. Each record in the sequence set in turn contains pointers to control intervals in the data component and the highest key value in each of them. In the data component, records are stored sequentially by key value.

To find a record, VSAM searches the index set sequentially for a key value greater than or equal to that of the desired record. When it's found, VSAM searches the indicated record in the sequence set sequentially to find the control interval that contains the record. Then, VSAM reads that control interval and searches it sequentially until it finds the data record.

For example, to retrieve the record with the key value 1239, VSAM first searches the index set in the index component to determine the record in the sequence set to access (record 3). Then, the entries in the sequence set record are searched to find the control interval in the data component that contains the record (control interval 11). Finally, VSAM reads control interval 11 and retrieves record 1239.

Free space in a KSDS   When a KSDS is defined, free space is reserved to accommodate new records. This space can be reserved in two ways: (1) space within each control interval may be left empty, and (2) entire control intervals may be left empty. When you define a KSDS with AMS, you can specify both types of free space.

Index component					Data component						
Index set (level 1)		Sequence set									
Key	Pointer	Record	Key	Pointer	Control interval	Keys in control interval					
397	S1	1	187	C1	1	012	041	049	094	101	187
			284	C2	2	188	210	218	247	250	284
940	S2		322	C3	3	287	291	294	301	307	322
			397	C4	4	341	348	354	363	370	397
1391	S3	2	513	C5	5	410	415	420	434	470	513
			641	C6	6	585	592	601	615	621	641
1833	S4		787	C7	7	660	680	685	710	740	787
			940	C8	8	812	819	901	914	927	940
		3	991	C9	9	951	957	967	984	985	991
			1205	C10	10	1032	1105	1117	1121	1187	1205
			1297	C11	11	1207	1208	1231	1239	1250	1297
			1391	C12	12	1330	1337	1341	1355	1366	1391
		4	1522	C13	13	1410	1415	1423	1480	1481	1522
			1639	C14	14	1523	1530	1537	1539	1599	1639
			1740	C15	15	1641	1645	1691	1701	1703	1740
			1833	C16	16	1748	1780	1788	1790	1805	1833

Figure 16-4   Accessing a record in a KSDS

Figure 16-5 shows a control area that consists of four control intervals. Three of the four each contain three records and enough free space for two more so 40 percent of the free space is available in each of these control intervals. The numbers in each record area indicate key values (notice that they're in sequence). The fourth control interval contains no records. So 25 percent of the control intervals in the control area are free.

When a record is added to a KSDS, it's inserted in its correct sequential location in the data component and the records that follow it in the control interval are moved down one position. That's what figure 16-6 shows. It indicates what the control area in figure 16-5 would look like after record 6494 is added to the file.

This is like what happens when a record is added to a track in an ISAM file that has free space in its cylinder overflow area. VSAM differs, however, because it moves records within the control interval in a virtual storage buffer. It doesn't actually rewrite the records on a DASD until the space in the buffer is needed by another control interval. As a result, insertions in a KSDS are processed more efficiently than insertions in an ISAM file.

If an insertion is to be made into a control interval that's already full, the records that would otherwise follow it are written to a free control

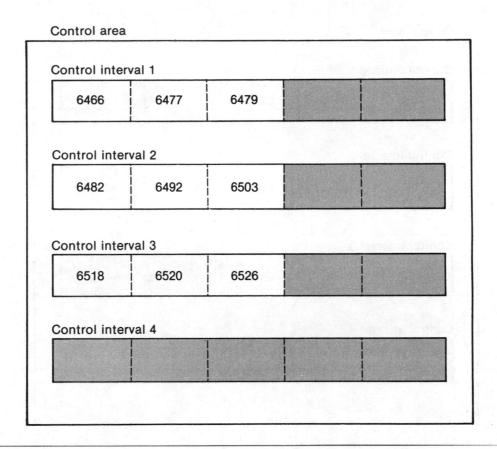

Figure 16-5   Free space distribution in the data component of a KSDS

interval (that would be the fourth control interval in figure 16-5 or 16-6). This is called a *control interval split*. Then, the free space in both the original control interval and the one used for overflow is available for insertions. Compare this to the relatively clumsy way ISAM handles insertions.

When a record is deleted from a VSAM KSDS, it's actually removed from its control interval and the space it occupied is available for a new record. Under ISAM, deletions are logical rather than physical; logically deleted records still remain in an ISAM file, using valuable storage space. Because deletions don't waste space in the VSAM file and because insertions are handled more sensibly, a KSDS doesn't have to be reorganized as often as an equivalent ISAM file.

Relative-record data sets

You can implement a VSAM file with direct organization as a relative-record data set (RRDS). Frankly, as with DAM files, there are relatively few applications in which an RRDS is a substantially better choice than a

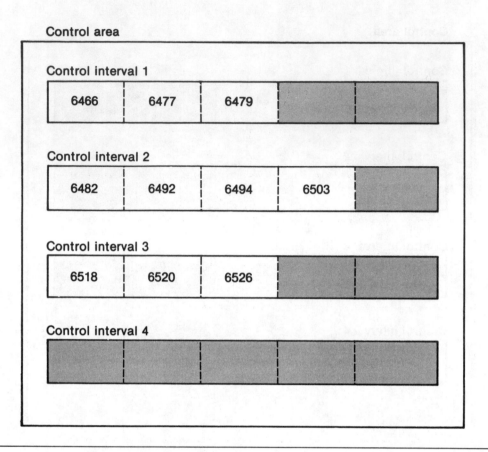

Control area

Control interval 1

| 6466 | 6477 | 6479 | | |

Control interval 2

| 6482 | 6492 | 6494 | 6503 | |

Control interval 3

| 6518 | 6520 | 6526 | | |

Control interval 4

| | | | | |

Figure 16-6   Free space distribution in the data component of a KSDS after adding a record to it

KSDS. Even so, I want to give you a brief description of an RRDS.

Figure 16-7 shows a VSAM RRDS. The file consists of *record slots* that contain either data or free space. Each record slot is numbered, and it's those numbers, called *relative record numbers*, or *RRNs*, that identify records. If, for example, a file consists of one thousand slots, the slots are identified by relative record numbers from 1 through 1000.

When an RRDS is processed sequentially, the record slots are accessed in sequential order. If a slot doesn't contain any data, it's skipped over. When a program processes an RRDS randomly, it accesses slots, not records, so it's possible for a program to access a slot that doesn't have a record in it. For example, in figure 16-7, that would happen if you accessed slot 6, 9, 15, 16, 18, or 20.

Additions to an RRDS can be handled in two ways. First, records can be added to the end of the file. Alternatively, records can be inserted in empty slots wherever they exist in the file. To do so, however, the application program has to be able to identify the slots that are empty.

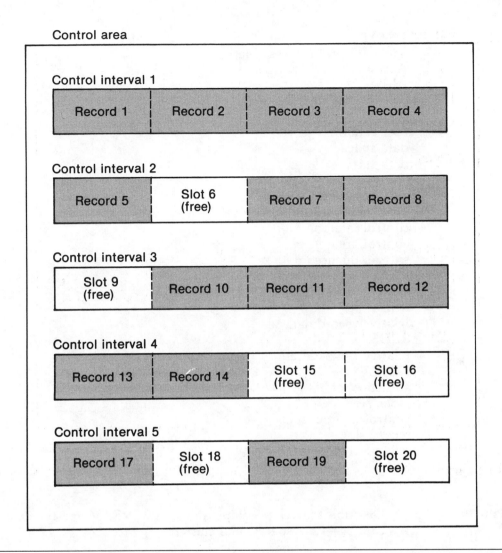

Figure 16-7   Record organization in an RRDS

When records in an RRDS are processed randomly, they are accessed by RRNs. As a result, an RRDS doesn't need an index component and doesn't have one. That explains why an RRDS can often be processed more efficiently than a KSDS. As a result, if an application lends itself to an RRN addressing scheme, an RRDS can be a practical alternative to a KSDS.

DISCUSSION   If this is your first introduction to VSAM, it may seem complex to you. Although VSAM is complicated, however, it's a significant improvement over the native VSE access methods. In particular, as you will see in the next topic, VSAM offers dramatic improvements in efficiency.

Terminology   VSAM
                         Virtual Storage Access Method
                         Access Method Services
                         AMS
                         catalog
                         master catalog
                         user catalog
                         data space
                         data set
                         cluster
                         data component
                         index component
                         control interval
                         control area
                         entry-sequenced data set
                         ESDS
                         key-sequenced data set
                         KSDS
                         relative-record data set
                         RRDS
                         relative byte address
                         RBA
                         sequence set
                         index set
                         control interval split
                         record slot
                         relative record number
                         RRN

Objectives   1.   Describe the relationships among the VSAM master catalog, user
                        catalogs, data spaces, and clusters.

                   2.   Name and describe the three VSAM file organizations.

TOPIC 2   Assembler language for VSAM files

As you might guess, the assembler language for processing VSAM files is complex. In particular, you need to learn several new macros for VSAM file handling, some with extensive lists of operands. In this topic, though, I won't try to present all the VSAM macros and all the operands. Instead, I will present a subset that you will find useful for application programming. Then, if you need to code VSAM functions that aren't presented in this topic, you will have the background you need to research the VSAM manuals on your own.

In this topic, I will first present the macros that you need to define and access VSAM files. Then, I will present some other macros that you may find useful when processing VSAM files. Last, I will present three illustrative programs that use VSAM files.

MACROS FOR DEFINING VSAM FILES AND THEIR ACCESSES

To access a file using one of the native access methods, you must define the characteristics of the file by coding a DTF macro. However, this macro isn't used for VSAM files. Instead, you code three different macros: the ACB, EXLST, and RPL macros. These macros define a file, provide for error-handling routines, and define access requests to the file.

The ACB macro

The *ACB (access method control block)* macro provides some basic information about a VSAM file. So you must code one ACB macro for each VSAM file that your program uses. Figure 16-8 summarizes the most commonly used operands of the ACB macro. I will cover each of them in detail.

The AM operand   The AM (access method) operand specifies whether you're defining a VSAM or VTAM control block. Unless your shop uses VTAM as well as VSAM, there is no particular reason for coding this operand. This operand is used only for documentation.

The BUFND, BUFNI, and BUFSP operands   The BUFND, BUFNI, and BUFSP operands specify the number and size of the I/O buffers needed for data and index control intervals. Although these operands are important for program efficiency, their use is beyond the scope of this book. As a result, the illustrative programs use the default values for these operands.

The DDNAME operand   The DDNAME operand is used to specify the name of the file. It must be the same as the name specified in the DLBL statement for the file. If this operand is omitted, the label of the ACB macro must be the same as the filename used in the DLBL statement.

Priority	Keyword	Programmer code	Remarks
Optional	AM	VSAM	Used for documentation only.
Optional	BUFND	Number of I/O buffers used for data control intervals	If you specify less than the minimum, VSAM overrides your specification. The default is 2.
Optional	BUFNI	Number of I/O buffers used for index control intervals	If you specify less than the minimum, VSAM overrides your specification. The default is 1.
Optional	BUFSP	Size of an area for data and index I/O buffers	Must be at least as large as the buffer space size recorded in the catalog entry for the file. The default is the size recorded in the catalog.
Optional	DDNAME	Filename to be used in the DLBL statement for the file	If you omit this operand, the DLBL filename must be the same as the name of the ACB macro.
Optional	EXLST	Address of the EXLST macro	The EXLST macro generates a list of addresses for user routines. As a result, the address of the EXLST macro is the address of an address list. This operand is usually coded with the label of the EXLST macro.
Optional	MACRF	Types of processing that the file will do	See figure 16-9 for the format of this operand.

Figure 16-8   The operands of the ACB macro

The EXLST operand   The EXLST operand specifies the address of the EXLST macro. This address is usually supplied in the form of a label, so this operand usually gives the label of the EXLST macro. Since the EXLST macro generates a list of addresses for exit routines, this operand actually gives the address of a list of addresses.

The MACRF operand   The MACRF operand specifies the type of processing to be performed on the file. Figure 16-9 gives the format of the MACRF operand along with its most commonly-used options. Notice that the options are in groups and that the underlined word in each group is the default value. The brackets before and after each word in each group indicate that the enclosed word is optional. The use of brackets to mean optional is used throughout this topic.

     The first group of options specifies the type or types of accesses to be used for a file: address, control interval, or key. Accessing by address is used for ESDS files in which the records are accessed by relative byte addresses. Accessing by key is used for either KSDS or RRDS files in which the records are accessed by keys or relative record numbers.

Operand format

```
MACRF=([ADR][,CNV][,KEY]

       [,DIR][,SEQ][,SKP]

       [,IN][,OUT])
```

Code	Meaning
ADR	Access by relative byte address
CNV	Access by control interval
KEY	Access by key
DIR	Direct processing
SEQ	Sequential processing
SKP	Skip sequential processing
IN	Used for input only
OUT	Used for output or both input and output

Figure 16-9   The format of the MACRF operand of the ACB macro

Although you'll probably never use *control interval access*, let me describe it briefly. When you use control interval access, data is retrieved and stored by control intervals rather than by single records. A control interval is identified by specifying its relative byte address. When you use this access method, the programmer is responsible for determining the relative byte addresses for the control intervals.

The second group of options of the MACRF operand specifies the type of processing to be performed: direct, sequential, or skip sequential. *Skip sequential processing* means processing a portion of a file in sequence, then skipping to another portion of the file and processing it, and so on. Normally, an ESDS is processed using sequential processing, while a KSDS or RRDS can be processed using any of the three processing methods.

The third group of options specifies whether a file is to be used as input only or output. If OUT is specified, the file can be used for output only or for both input and output.

Although I won't illustrate it in this book, it is acceptable to code more than one of the options from each group. If, for example, you will be processing records both directly and sequentially, you code your MACRF operand like this:

```
MACRF=(KEY,DIR,SEQ,IN)
```

Then, before you issue a GET macro, you must specify which processing method you want to use. You will see how this works when I discuss the RPL macro. Note in the coding for the macro above that the operands are enclosed within parentheses with no intervening blanks.

The EXLST macro

The *EXLST (exit list)* macro is optional. It produces a list of addresses for routines that VSAM may branch to. Then, when the related VSAM condition occurs, VSAM exits its routine and passes control to the programmer's routine for handling that condition.

Figure 16-10 lists the possible operands of the EXLST macro. Again, the AM operand is used only for documentation. The rest of the operands give the addresses of routines that are to be executed when specific VSAM conditions occur. Normally, an address is given as the label of the first instruction of the programmer's routine.

The operand that you will probably use most frequently is EODAD. This means that VSAM should exit to the addressed routine when an end-of-data-set (end-of-file) condition occurs. You'll see this operand used in one of the illustrative programs.

The other operands are used for specialized processing functions that are beyond the scope of this book. The EXCPAD operand can be used to provide an exit for a routine that provides for overlapped VSAM I/O operations and processing. The JRNAD operand can be used to provide an exit for a routine that records VSAM transactions. And the LERAD and SYNAD operands can be used to provide exits for routines that handle logical errors (LERAD) and physical errors (SYNAD).

After the address (or label) of each exit routine, you can code two options. The first indicates whether the exit is active or inactive. Since A is underlined, the default is active, so the VSAM exit will take place if this option isn't specified. In contrast, if an option is specified as inactive (N), the exit won't take place even though the operand is coded. Then, to change this option to active, the program must issue the MODCB macro, which will be presented in a moment.

The second option indicates that the programmer's routine is a phase stored in a core image library. Then, the address given in this operand must be the address of a field that contains the name of the phase in the core image library.

The RPL macro

The *RPL (request parameter list)* macro generates the information needed to access a record in a file. Then, when you use a GET, PUT, ERASE, or POINT macro, you usually code the label of the RPL macro as the only operand. Figure 16-11 presents a list of the most commonly used operands of the RPL macro.

The ACB operand   The ACB operand specifies the address of the ACB macro generated for the file. The address is usually coded as the label of the ACB macro.

The AREA operand   The AREA operand specifies the address of the work area to be used for the file being defined. What this work area contains depends on whether the OPTCD parameter specifies locate mode or move mode. In *locate mode*, each record is processed in a VSAM buffer area (not a work area), so VSAM puts the address of the record in this work area. In *move mode*, each record is processed in this work area.

Macro format

```
EXLST   [AM=VSAM]
        [,EODAD=(address[, {A}  ][,L])]
                          {N}

        [,EXCPAD=(address[, {A}  ][,L])]
                           {N}

        [,JRNAD=(address[, {A}  ][,L])]
                          {N}

        [,LERAD=(address[, {A}  ][,L])]
                          {N}

        [,SYNAD=(address[, {A}  ][,L])]
                          {N}
```

Code	Meaning
EODAD	End of data set
EXCPAD	Execute channel program
JRNAD	Journal
LERAD	Logical error
SYNAD	Physical error
A	Active
N	Inactive
L	The exit routine is a phase that is stored in the core image library.

Figure 16-10   The format of the EXLST macro

The AREALEN operand   The AREALEN operand specifies the length of the work area identified by the AREA operand. If the records are being processed in move mode, the work area must be large enough to hold the largest record that will be processed. If the records are being processed in locate mode, the work area must be at least four bytes long to hold the address of the record in the VSAM buffer.

The RECLEN operand   The RECLEN operand specifies the length of the records in the file. You only need to specify this operand for a PUT request. If the records are variable-length, you need to use the MODCB macro to modify this value each time a record with a different length is to be written on the file. For a GET request, VSAM puts the length of each record read into this field.

The ARG operand   The ARG operand specifies the address of the field containing the search argument for the record to be retrieved from or written on a file. It is normally coded with the label of the field that contains

Priority	Keyword	Programmer code	Remarks
Required	ACB	Address of the ACB macro	Usually, the label of the ACB macro.
Optional	AM	VSAM	Used for documentation only.
Required	AREA	Address of the work area for the file	For move mode, VSAM uses this area as a work area for records that are read or written. For locate mode, VSAM puts the address of the record being processed into this work area.
Required	AREALEN	Length of the work area	For move mode, the work area must be large enough to store the largest record retrieved or written. For locate mode, it must be at least 4 bytes long so it can hold the address of the record in the VSAM buffer.
Optional	RECLEN	Length of data record	For a PUT request, the program must store the length of the output record in this field. For a GET request, VSAM puts the length of the record in this field.
Optional	ARG	Address of the field that contains the search argument	Used with the GET, POINT, and PUT macros.
Optional	OPTCD	Types of access	See figure 16-12 for the format of this operand.

Figure 16-11   The operands of the RPL macro

the search argument. When direct processing is used, the search argument is the key value for a KSDS, the relative record number for an RRDS, or the RBA for an ESDS. (Generic keys can also be used, but I'm not going to cover them in this book.)

The OPTCD operand   The OPTCD operand specifies how the records in a file are to be accessed. Its format and options are given in figure 16-12. As you can see, the options are in groups, with one default value in each group. The stacking of the items in the groups means that you can only code one option from each group. These options must be consistent with one another, and they must also be consistent with the options coded in the MACRF operand of the ACB macro.

The first two groups of options correspond to the options of the MACRF operand in the ACB macro. The third group specifies whether a file is to be processed in a forward or backward direction. The fourth group specifies whether processing is to start with the last record in the file

Operand format

Code	Meaning
ADR	Access by relative byte address
CNV	Access by control interval
KEY	Access by key
DIR	Direct processing
SEQ	Sequential processing
SKP	Skip sequential processing
FWD	Forward sequential processing
BWD	Backward sequential processing
ARD	Start sequential processing (forward or backward) with the record identified by the ARG field.
LRD	For backward processing, start with the last record in the file.
NSP	No updating (for direct processing only; VSAM is positioned at the next record for subsequent processing)
NUP	No updating (VSAM is not positioned for subsequent processing)
UPD	Record updating
LOC	Locate mode (records will be processed in the VSAM buffer area)
MVE	Move mode (records will be processed in a work area)

Figure 16-12   The format of the OPTCD operand of the RPL macro

or with the record identified by the data in the ARG field. The fifth group specifies whether each record is to be updated and, if not, which record should be read next. The last group specifies whether the records will be processed in locate mode or move mode.

When I presented the MACRF operand of the ACB macro, I pointed out that you could specify more than one type of accessing and processing for a single VSAM file. In the OPTCD operand of the RPL macro, though, you can only specify one option in each group. Then, when you want to change to another set of the options that were specified in the MACRF operand, you must use the MODCB macro to change the RPL options. (Although you can code more than one RPL for a file, you only do this if you are processing a file by two different sets of options simultaneously, which is beyond the scope of this book.)

MACROS FOR REQUESTING ACCESS TO VSAM FILES

In order to access VSAM files, you use the OPEN, CLOSE, GET and PUT macros. In addition, you can use the ERASE macro to delete a record and the POINT macro to position VSAM for a record access.

The OPEN and CLOSE macros

The formats of the OPEN and CLOSE macros for VSAM files are the same as for non-VSAM files. The operands are the addresses of the ACBs for the files to be processed. These addresses are normally coded as the labels given to the ACB macros, but they can also be coded as register numbers in parentheses. Then, the registers must contain the appropriate addresses when the macros are executed.

If both VSAM and non-VSAM files are coded as operands in the same OPEN or CLOSE macros, the VSAM files should always be coded together. I will explain this in a moment when I discuss the use of the LTR instruction.

The GET and PUT macros

The GET and PUT macros have the format illustrated in figure 16-13. As you can see, the only operand required is the address of the associated RPL. This address is usually the label given to the RPL macro, but it can also be the number of the register that contains the address of the related RPL macro.

The ERASE macro

The ERASE macro deletes a record from a file. It has the same format as the GET and PUT macros, as illustrated in figure 16-13. Again, the only operand is the address of the related RPL macro. Before issuing the ERASE macro, the record to be deleted must be retrieved for update.

This macro illustrates one advantage that VSAM has over ISAM. If you've read chapter 14, you should remember that ISAM doesn't provide for record deletion. The only way to physically delete records from a file is to ignore records that are marked for deletion during the reorganization of the file. In contrast, the ERASE macro causes a record to be physically deleted from a file so the space can be used for another record.

The POINT macro

You use the POINT macro to position VSAM at a specific record within a file. The position is determined by the value given in the ARG field that is defined by the RPL macro. The POINT macro is generally used to set a starting point for sequential or skip sequential processing. Its format is the same as the format of the GET and PUT macros, as illustrated in figure 16-13.

```
{GET  }          RPL=  {label of RPL macro}
{PUT  }                {(register)          }
{ERASE}
{POINT}
```

Macro	Request
GET	Retrieve a record
PUT	Store a record
ERASE	Delete a record
POINT	Position for access

Figure 16-13   The format of the GET, PUT, ERASE, and POINT macros

MACROS FOR CONTROL BLOCK MANIPULATION

When you use assembler language, you can examine, test, and modify the information that is stored in the control block for a VSAM file. You do this by using the SHOWCB, TESTCB, and MODCB macros. In addition, you can generate the control block for a file without using the ACB, EXLST, and RPL macros. You do this by using the GENCB macro. All of these macros are called *control block manipulation macros.*

Although you don't have to use these macros much in simple application programs, they are extremely useful when you want to perform systems programming functions. As a result, you should be familiar with them. Then, you can do more research on them later on when you see the need for them in your assembler language programs.

The SHOWCB macro

Figure 16-14 presents the operands of the SHOWCB macro. This macro lets you examine the fields generated by an ACB, EXLST, or RPL macro. It does this by putting the contents of the specified fields into the work area specified.

To use this macro effectively, you must know the keywords for the fields that you want to capture. To start, a keyword in the SHOWCB macro can be most any keyword of the ACB, EXLST, RPL, or GENCB macros. If, for example, you want to examine the address of the EXLST macro, you code the SHOWCB macro like this:

```
SHOWCB ACB=INVMSTR,AREA=SHOWADDR,
       FIELDS=EXLST,LENGTH=4
```

Then, the address of the EXLST is put into the first four bytes of the field named SHOWADDR. If two or more keywords are coded, you must separate them with commas and enclose them in parentheses.

Priority	Keyword	Programmer code	Remarks
Required	ACB EXLST RPL	Address of ACB, EXLST, or RPL macro	Usually coded with the label of the selected macro.
Optional	AM	VSAM	Used for documentation only.
Required	AREA	Area in which VSAM will put the contents of the specified fields	The contents of the fields are placed in the area in the order in which they are specified.
Required	FIELDS	List of fields to be examined in this format: (keyword[,keyword...])	A field in the list can be most any keyword of the ACB, EXLST, RPL, or GENCB macros; the length of any ACB, EXLST, or RPL macro using the keyword ACBLEN, EXLLEN, or RPLLEN; or any attribute of an open file or index.
Required	LENGTH	Length of the area specified as the AREA operand	Each field of an ACB, EXLST, or RPL macro is a fullword except for DDNAME, which is two fullwords.
Optional	OBJECT	DATA or INDEX	Specifies whether the attributes of a file's data or its index are to be examined.

Figure 16-14   The operands of the SHOWCB macro

You can also use the SHOWCB macro to examine the length of any ACB, EXLST, or RPL macro. To do this, the keywords are ACBLEN, EXLLEN, and RPLLEN.

Finally, you can use this macro to examine any attribute of an open file. To do this, you use the keywords in figure 16-15. Although this isn't a complete list, it includes most of the commonly used attributes for an open file. If, for example, you want to know the percent of free control intervals in the control areas of a frequently used file, you can code the SHOWCB macro like this:

```
SHOWCB ACB=INVMSTR,AREA=FREECI,FIELDS=FS,LENGTH=4
```

This statement puts the percentage of free control intervals in the file labeled INVMSTR into the four-byte work area named FREECI. If this macro is executed each time a file is opened, you can keep track of the free space available in the file. When an attribute can apply to either the data or index component of a file, you use the DATA or INDEX operand to specify which attribute the SHOWCB macro should capture.

Keyword	Meaning
AVSPAC	Number of bytes of available space
BUFNO	Number of buffers being used
CINV	Size of a control interval
FS	Percent of free control intervals
KEYLEN	Length of the key field
LRECL	Maximum record length
NCIS	Number of control-interval splits
NDELR	Number of records deleted from the file
NEXT	Number of extents allocated to the file
NINSR	Number of records inserted into the file
NLOGR	Number of records in the file
NRETR	Number of records retrieved from the file
NUPDR	Number of data records updated in the file
RKP	Position of the record key relative to the beginning of the file

Figure 16-15   Some common attributes of an open file that can be examined by the SHOWCB macro

The TESTCB macro

Figure 16-16 gives the operands of the TESTCB macro. It is similar to the SHOWCB macro except that it tests rather than captures the one specified field. It can test one of the fields of an ACB, EXLST, or RPL macro or one of the attributes of an open file such as those listed in figure 16-15. It compares the values of the specified field with the value specified in the macro.

In addition to the attributes given in figure 16-15, the TESTCB macro can test if a file is open as in this instruction:

```
TESTCB ACB=INVMSTR,OFLAGS=OPEN
```

Here, the keyword is OFLAGS and the value is OPEN. Then, your program can branch depending on the results of the test using the mnemonic operation codes for branching such as BE and BNE.

You can also use the TESTCB macro to test the results of an I/O operation. You do this by coding the keyword FDBK (feedback) and the error code you want to compare it with. Figure 16-17 gives some of the common error codes you are likely to test for when using the FDBK keyword. If, for example, you want to test whether a record couldn't be added to a KSDS because it had a duplicate key, you could code the TESTCB macro this way:

```
TESTCB RPL=INVMSTR,FDBK=8
BE     DUPKEY
```

Here, the program branches to DUPKEY when a record can't be written because it has a duplicate key.

Priority	Keyword	Programmer code	Remarks
Required	$\left\{ \begin{array}{l} \text{ACB} \\ \text{EXLST} \\ \text{RPL} \end{array} \right\}$	Address of ACB, EXLST, or RPL macro	Usually coded with the label of the selected macro.
Optional	AM	VSAM	Used for documentation only.
Optional	ERET	Address of error routine	If the condition specified can't be tested, VSAM branches to the address specified in this operand. The routine at this address can inspect the return code in register 15 to determine the problem.
Required	keyword	Field to be tested	The field specified can be any keyword of the ACB, EXLST, RPL, or GENCB macros; the length of any ACB, EXLST, or RPL macro using the keyword ACBLEN, EXLLEN, or RPLLEN; or any attribute of an open file or index.
Optional	OBJECT	DATA or INDEX	Specifies whether the attributes of a file's data or its index are to be examined.

Figure 16-16   The operands of the TESTCB macro

The MODCB macro

The MODCB macro is used to modify the control blocks generated by the ACB, EXLST, RPL, and GENCB macros. Its standard format is given in figure 16-18.

Although you probably won't use it often, let me give you two examples of situations in which you might need to use it. First, if you need to access a file using two different types of processing in the same program (not simultaneously), you have to change the access request specified in the RPL for that file. The only way to do that is to code a MODCB macro. Second, if you're processing a file of variable-length records, you need to change the record length field of the RPL each time the record length changes.

To illustrate, consider this MODCB macro:

```
MODCB RPL=INVRPL,OPTCD=(DIR)
```

This changes the processing option in the OPTCD operand of the RPL macro from sequential to direct. Then, if the program needs to change back to sequential processing, it must issue this macro:

```
MODCB RPL=INVRPL,OPTCD=(SEQ)
```

As you can see, then, the MODCB macro lets you change the starting values of the ACB, EXLST, or RPL macros whenever you need to.

Code	Explanation
8	Duplicate key
12	Record out of sequence
16	No record found
68	Access requested doesn't match access specified
92	A PUT for update or an ERASE is issued without a preceding GET for update
104	Invalid or conflicting RPL options or parameters

Figure 16-17   Some common VSAM error codes for the FDBK keyword of the TESTCB macro

Priority	Keyword	Programmer code	Remarks
Required	{ ACB EXLST RPL }	Address of ACB, EXLST, or RPL macro	Type of control block to be modified.
Optional	AM	VSAM	Used for documentation only.
Required	Operand keyword	New value for operand	The operand keywords are those used in the ACB, EXLST, and RPL macros.

Figure 16-18   The operands of the MODCB macro

The GENCB macro

The GENCB macro is used to generate VSAM control blocks at program execution time instead of at assembly time. As a result, this macro can take the place of a set of ACB, EXLST, and RPL macros for a file. Its operands are shown in figure 16-19.

The benefit of using GENCB is that your programs don't have to be reassembled each time the specifications for a control block change (due to a new release of VSAM, for example). Instead, the GENCB macro generates the control blocks in the current format each time the program is executed. The drawback, of course, is that it takes additional processing time and storage to generate these macros each time a program is executed.

Priority	Keyword	Programmer code	Remarks
Required	BLK	ACB, EXLST, or RPL	Type of control block to be generated.
Optional	AM	VSAM	Used for documentation only.
Optional	COPIES	Number of control blocks to be generated	If multiple control blocks are generated, they are identical and MODCB must be used to modify them. The default is 1.
Optional	keyword	Characteristics of the control block in this form: keyword = value	The keywords and values that can be coded are the same as those used in the ACB, EXLST, and RPL macros. If a keyword is omitted, VSAM provides default values.
Optional	WAREA	The address of the area in which VSAM is to put the control block	If this operand isn't coded, VSAM will obtain an area in which to put the control block.
Optional	LENGTH	Length of the area specified as the WAREA operand	The length required for a control block can be determined by coding a SHOWCB macro. This area is required if the WAREA operand is coded.

Figure 16-19   The operands of the GENCB macro

THREE ILLUSTRATIVE PROGRAMS

To show how the VSAM macros are used within programs, I'm now going to present three simple programs that use VSAM files. If you read the chapter on ISAM, you'll see that these programs are like the ones that were used to illustrate ISAM coding. In the first program, a KSDS master file is created from a SAM file. In the second program, the KSDS master file is updated based on the transactions in an ESDS transaction file. In the third program, a report is prepared by reading the KSDS master file sequentially.

A file creation program

Figure 16-20 presents a program that loads a KSDS file of inventory records from a SAM disk file. The new records are to be 70 bytes long. The basic processing loop of the program reads a record from the sequential file, moves and packs its data into the KSDS record, and writes an output record.

To start, look at the ACB and RPL macros for the inventory master file. If these macros look brief, remember that the cluster (file) must be

```
INVLOAD   START  0
BEGIN     BALR   3,0
          USING  *,3
          OPEN   INPUT,INVMSTR
          LTR    15,15                TEST FOR VSAM I/O ERROR
          BNZ    DUMP
READREC   GET    INPUT,INPTWRKA
          MVC    MSTRRCD(32),INPTWRKA MOVE 32 BYTES TO OUTPUT AREA
          PACK   MORDQTY,IORDQTY      PACK INPUT FIELDS
          PACK   MORDPT,IORDPT
          PACK   MSAFSTK,ISAFSTK
          PACK   MONHAND,IONHAND
          PACK   MONORD,IONORD
          PACK   MALLOC,IALLOC
          PUT    RPL=RPL1             WRITE OUTPUT RECORD
          LTR    15,15                TEST FOR VSAM I/O ERROR
          BZ     READREC
DUMP      DUMP
EOFDSK    CLOSE  INPUT,INVMSTR
          LTR    15,15                TEST FOR VSAM I/O ERROR
          BNZ    DUMP
          EOJ
INPUT     DTFSD  BLKSIZE=248,                                            X
                 RECFORM=FIXBLK,                                         X
                 RECSIZE=62,                                             X
                 IOAREA1=INPTDSKA,                                       X
                 EOFADDR=EOFDSK,                                         X
                 WORKA=YES
INVMSTR   ACB    MACRF=OUT
RPL1      RPL    ACB=INVMSTR,                                            X
                 AREA=MSTRRCD,                                           X
                 AREALEN=70,                                             X
                 RECLEN=70
INPTDSKA DS      CL248
INPTWRKA DS      0CL62
IITEM     DS     CL6
IDESC     DS     CL20
IUM       DS     CL4
IORDPOL   DS     CL2
IORDQTY   DS     CL5
IORDPT    DS     CL5
ISAFSTK   DS     CL5
IONHAND   DS     CL5
IONORD    DS     CL5
IALLOC    DS     CL5
MSTRRCD   DS     0CL70
MITEM     DS     CL6
MDESC     DS     CL20
MUM       DS     CL4
MORDPOL   DS     CL2
MORDQTY   DS     PL4
MORDPT    DS     PL4
MSAFSTK   DS     PL4
MONHAND   DS     PL4
MONORD    DS     PL4
MALLOC    DS     PL4
          DC     14X'00'
          END    BEGIN
```

Figure 16-20   A VSAM KSDS file creation program

defined by the AMS program. As a result, VSE already knows that the file is going to be key sequenced, that its keys are in the first six bytes of each record, and so on. Then, the ACB macro only has to specify that the file will be an output file. And the RPL macro only has to give the name and size of the work area for the file and the size of each output record. Because the defaults in both the ACB and RPL macros are for sequential processing by key, they don't have to be specified in these macros.

If you look at the instruction after each VSAM access request macro in the program, you'll see that it's an LTR instruction. You can find this instruction after the OPEN, PUT, and CLOSE macro for the KSDS file. As you will learn in a moment, each LTR instruction tests the contents of register 15. Why? Because VSAM places a return code in register 15 after each I/O request to tell what the result of the request was. Furthermore, VSAM doesn't automatically cancel a program when an I/O error occurs. Instead, the program must check the contents of register 15 and provide appropriate error-handling routines.

When the LTR instruction is executed, it moves the contents of the register specified as operand 2 into the register specified as operand 1 and sets the condition code according to the value of operand 2 (plus, minus, or zero). In figure 16-20, though, both operand 1 and operand 2 specify the same register:

```
LTR     15,15
```

As a result, the effect is to set the condition code based on the value in register 15. Then, the condition code can be tested using a branch instruction. If it doesn't indicate a zero value, an error has occurred. If an error is indicated in the program in figure 16-20, the program issues the DUMP macro and terminates.

When you use the LTR instruction to test the return code following an OPEN or CLOSE macro, you must be careful about the sequence in which you code the operands of the OPEN or CLOSE macro if they are for both VSAM and non-VSAM files. If all the VSAM files are listed consecutively, the return code generated will apply to all of the VSAM files. However, if the VSAM and non-VSAM files are interspersed, the return code will only apply to the VSAM files that follow the last non-VSAM file listed. For this reason, when you code your OPEN and CLOSE macros, we recommend that you list all non-VSAM files first, followed by all VSAM files.

You should also notice in the program in figure 16-20 that no I/O areas have been coded for the inventory master file. Unlike the native access methods, VSAM automatically provides I/O buffers for storing the index and data records. Since move mode is the RPL default value, each record is moved into the I/O buffer from the work area named MSTRRCD before it is written. This work area is defined in the RPL for the file.

A random
update program

Figure 16-21 is a program that updates a KSDS file on a random basis. The input file is an ESDS shipment transaction file. The updated file is the KSDS inventory master file that was created by the program in figure 16-20. The basic logic of this program is to read a shipment transaction, to read the master record with the same key on a random basis, and to rewrite the updated master record in its original location on the file. This program also prints a report listing any records that aren't found in the master file.

To define the ESDS transaction file, both the ACB and RPL macros specify access by address (ADR). This is required because access by key is the default. In addition, the EXLST macro is used for this file. It specifies an exit routine for an end-of-data-set condition. That means that VSAM will automatically branch to the address specified (EOFINPT) when the end-of-file condition is detected.

To define the KSDS master file, the ACB macro specifies direct processing (DIR) of an output (OUT) file. Similarly, the OPTCD operand of the RPL macro specifies direct processing (DIR) and record updating (UPD). In addition, the ARG operand is coded in the RPL macro to specify the field (ITEMKEY) that will contain the key of the master record to be processed.

If you read through the program, you can see that the logic is straightforward. Again, the LTR instruction is used after each VSAM access request macro to see whether an I/O error has occurred. If an error has occurred during any I/O operation other than the GET for the KSDS master file, the program branches to DUMP and the program terminates. However, if an error is detected after the GET macro for the KSDS master file, the program branches to ERROR so the program can test for the not-found condition by using the TESTCB macro.

The test for the not-found condition is coded this way:

```
ERROR      TESTCB RPL=RPL2,FDBK=16
           BNE    DUMP
```

The feedback field specified in the TESTCB macro (FDBK) contains more information about a VSAM I/O area. Figure 16-17 lists some of the most common codes you may need to test for, and you can find a complete list of these codes in IBM's *VSE/VSAM Messages and Codes (SC24-5146)*. In the instruction above, the TESTCB macro tests to see if FDBK is equal to 16, which is the error code that indicates a not-found condition. If the error is a not-found condition, the program continues by printing a line on the error listing. Otherwise, the program branches to DUMP where the DUMP macro is issued.

```
UPDTINV   START  0
BEGIN     BALR   3,0
          USING  *,3
          OPEN   ERRMSG,SHIPTR,INVMSTR
          LTR    15,15                        TEST FOR VSAM I/O ERROR
          BNZ    DUMP
READSHP   GET    RPL=RPL1                     READ VSAM RECORD FOR FILE 1
          LTR    15,15                        TEST FOR VSAM I/O ERROR
          BNZ    DUMP
          MVC    ITEMKEY,SHPITEM
          GET    RPL=RPL2                     READ VSAM RECORD FOR FILE 2
          LTR    15,15                        TEST FOR VSAM I/O ERROR
          BNZ    ERROR
          PACK   QTYONHND,SHPQTY
          SP     MONHAND,QTYONHND
          PUT    RPL=RPL2                     UPDATE VSAM RECORD IN FILE 2
          LTR    15,15                        TEST FOR VSAM I/O ERROR
          BNZ    DUMP
          B      READSHP
ERROR     TESTCB RPL=RPL2,FDBK=16             TEST FOR NO RECORD FOUND
          BNE    DUMP
          MVC    LITEM,SHPITEM
          PUT    ERRMSG
          B      READSHP
DUMP      DUMP
EOFINPT   CLOSE  ERRMSG,SHIPTR,INVMSTR
          LTR    15,15                        TEST FOR VSAM I/O ERROR
          BNZ    DUMP
          EOJ
SHIPTR    ACB    EXLST=EXIT,                                          X
                 MACRF=ADR
EXIT      EXLST  EODAD=EOFINPT
RPL1      RPL    ACB=SHIPTR,                                          X
                 AREA=SHPWRKA,                                        X
                 AREALEN=24,                                          X
                 OPTCD=ADR
INVMSTR   ACB    MACRF=(DIR,OUT)
RPL2      RPL    ACB=INVMSTR,                                         X
                 AREA=MSTRRCD,                                        X
                 AREALEN=70,                                          X
                 RECLEN=70,                                           X
                 ARG=ITEMKEY,                                         X
                 OPTCD=(DIR,UPD)
ERRMSG    DTFPR  BLKSIZE=132,                                         X
                 IOAREA1=ERRLINE,                                     X
                 DEVADDR=SYSLST
ERRLINE   DS     0CL132
          DC     5C' '
LITEM     DS     CL6
          DC     52C' '
LERR      DC     CL15'NO RECORD FOUND'
          DC     54C' '
ITEMKEY   DS     CL6
QTYONHND  DS     PL4
SHPWRKA   DS     0CL24
          DS     CL6
SHPITEM   DS     CL6
SHPQTY    DS     CL4
          DS     CL8
MSTRRCD   DS     0CL70
MSTITEM   DS     CL6
MDESC     DS     CL20
          DS     CL18
MONHAND   DS     PL4
          DS     CL22
          END    BEGIN
```

Figure 16-21   A VSAM KSDS random update program

A sequential retrieval program

Figure 16-22 presents a program that illustrates sequential retrieval of a KSDS file. It reads the inventory master file created by the program in figure 16-20 and prepares an inventory report from it. Since the logic of the program is straightforward, you should have little difficulty understanding it.

If you review the macros that define the master file, you can see that the RPL specifies locate mode for the file. As a result, the AREALEN is only four, because it will only contain the address of the record that is being processed. The record will reside in the VSAM buffer area. Note also that the EXLST macro specifies an exit routine for the end-of-file condition on the master file. This will cause an automatic branch to EOFMSTR when there are no more records in the master file.

Again, LTR instructions are used to test register 15 after each VSAM access request macro. If an error is detected, the program branches to DUMP and terminates.

To provide for locate mode processing, the program uses a DSECT in combination with register 4. Then, after each GET macro for the master file, VSAM moves the address of the record into MSTRADR, and the program loads the contents of MSTRADR into register 4. As a result, the instructions of the program will address the fields of MSTRRCD properly.

DISCUSSION

You may have noticed that I didn't present a programming example using a relative-record file. However, the coding of the macros for an RRDS is similar to the coding for a KSDS since the relative-record numbers are treated as keys. With this in mind, you should be able to develop assembler language programs that use simple ESDS, KSDS, and RRDS files at this time.

On the other hand, you should realize that this topic is at best an introduction to VSAM processing in assembler language. As such, it doesn't begin to present all of the VSAM functions that you code when you use assembler language. For example, files can be set up with more than one key. Also, it's okay for the secondary keys to have duplicates. And on and on. If you want to do some research on your own, be sure to get the IBM manual called *Using VSE/VSAM Commands and Macros (SC24-5144).*

Terminology

ACB	RPL
access method control block	request parameter list
control-interval access	locate mode
skip sequential processing	move mode
EXLST	control block manipulation macro
exit list	

Objective

Given specifications for an application program that processes simple VSAM files (ESDS, KSDS, or RRDS), develop a program that satisfies the specifications.

```
INVSTAT   START 0
BEGIN     BALR  3,0
          USING *,3
          USING MSTRAREA,4
          OPEN  REPORT,INVMSTR          OPEN FILES
          LTR   15,15                   TEST FOR VSAM I/O ERROR
          BNZ   DUMP
PROCESS   GET   RPL=RPL1                READ VSAM RECORD
          LTR   15,15                   TEST FOR VSAM I/O ERROR
          BNZ   DUMP
          L     4,MSTRADR
          MVI   RLINE,X'40'
          MVC   RLINE+1(132),RLINE
          MVC   RITEM,MITEM
          MVC   RDESC,MDESC
          MVC   RUM,MUM
          MVC   RORDPOL,MORDPOL
          MVC   RORDQTY(61),PATTERN
          ED    RORDQTY(61),MORDQTY     EDIT SIX FIELDS
          ZAP   AVAILWK,MONHAND
          AP    AVAILWK,MONORD
          SP    AVAILWK,MALLOC
          MVC   RAVAIL,PATTERN
          ED    RAVAIL,AVAILWK
          CP    LCOUNT,=P'50'
          BL    PRTDET
          PUT   REPORT,RHEAD
          ZAP   LCOUNT,=P'0'
          MVI   RCTL,C'0'
PRTDET    PUT   REPORT,RLINE
          AP    LCOUNT,=P'1'
          B     PROCESS
DUMP      DUMP
EOFMSTR   CLOSE REPORT,INVMSTR          CLOSE FILES
          LTR   15,15                   TEST FOR VSAM I/O ERROR
          BNZ   DUMP
          EOJ
INVMSTR   ACB   EXLST=EXITS
EXITS     EXLST EODAD=EOFMSTR
RPL1      RPL   ACB=INVMSTR,                                    X
                AREA=MSTRADR,                                   X
                AREALEN=4,                                      X
                OPTCD=(LOC)
REPORT    DTFPR BLKSIZE=133,                                    X
                IOAREA1=PRTOUT,                                 X
                WORKA=YES,                                      X
                DEVADDR=SYSLST,                                 X
                CTLCHR=ASA
PRTOUT    DS    CL133
AVAILWK   DS    PL4
LCOUNT    DC    P'50'
PATTERN   DS    0CL61
          DC    X'40'
          DC    6X'202020202020201222222'
MSTRADR   DS    F
```

Figure 16-22   A VSAM KSDS disk-to-printer program (part 1 of 2)

```
MSTRAREA  DSECT
MSTRRCD   DS      0CL70
MITEM     DS      CL6
MDESC     DS      CL20
MUM       DS      CL4
MORDPOL   DS      CL2
MORDQTY   DS      PL4
MORDPT    DS      PL4
MSAFSTX   DS      PL4
MONHAND   DS      PL4
MONORD    DS      PL4
MALLOC    DS      PL4
          DS      CL14
INVSTAT   CSECT
RHEAD     DS      0CL133
          DC      CL105'1                   ITEM        DESCRIPTION                         U/M   X
                  OP        ORDQTY        ORDPNT        SAFSTK        ONHAND        ONORDR'
          DC      CL28'       ALLOC        AVAIL                '
RLINE     DS      0CL133
RCTL      DS      CL1
          DS      CL12
RITEM     DS      CL6
          DS      CL2
RDESC     DS      CL20
          DS      CL4
RUM       DS      CL4
          DS      CL2
RORDPOL   DS      CL2
          DS      CL4
RORDQTY   DS      CL8
          DS      CL2
RORDPT    DS      CL8
          DS      CL2
RSAFSTK   DS      CL8
          DS      CL2
RONHAND   DS      CL8
          DS      CL2
RONORD    DS      CL8
          DS      CL2
RALLOC    DS      CL8
          DS      CL2
RAVAIL    DS      CL8
          DS      CL8
          END     BEGIN
```

Figure 16-22   A VSAM KSDS disk-to-printer program (part 2 of 2)

TOPIC 3   VSE JCL for VSAM files

Before you can store data in a VSAM file, you must define it using a VSAM utility program called AMS (or IDCAMS). Once you do this, the information that defines and locates the file is in the file's VSAM catalog. As a result, you don't need to code EXTENT and ASSGN statements for VSAM files since this data is already stored in catalogs. However, you do need to be familiar with some new operands for the DLBL and EXEC statements in order to run a VSAM job. You also need to know how to identify the VSAM catalogs that are required by a job stream.

In this topic, I'll start by presenting some catalog considerations. Then, I'll present the DLBL and EXEC statements as they are used for VSAM jobs. As you read this topic, please refer to figure 16-23. It presents the VSE JCL that I used for testing the update program in figure 16-21.

VSAM catalog considerations

Because VSAM catalogs are used to locate VSAM files, you have to include DLBL statements for the catalogs that own the files your jobs use. That's why all jobs that access VSAM files require a DLBL statement for the VSAM master catalog. The name of the master catalog is IJSYSCT. As a result, its DLBL statement should look something like this:

```
// DLBL   IJSYSCT,'VSAM.MASTER.CATALOG',,VSAM
```

Because this DLBL statement is required by any job that accesses VSAM files, it should be stored as a system standard label. If it is, you don't have to include it in your job streams. Then, you only have to identify the user catalogs that your jobs require. In figure 16-23, there is no DLBL statement for the VSAM master catalog because it is stored as a system standard label on our system.

The DLBL statement

A simplified version for the format of the DLBL statement for VSAM files is this:

```
// DLBL filename,'file-id',,VSAM,[CAT=catalog-name]
```

Although there are several other operands that can be coded for VSAM files, they are beyond the scope of this book.

The first four operands are the same as in the other DLBL statements you've seen. The filename operand specifies the name the application program uses to refer to the VSAM file. In an assembler language program, this is the label of the ACB macro or the name specified in the DDNAME operand of the ACB macro. The file-id operand is the name given to the file when it was defined. The third DLBL operand, which is normally date, doesn't have an effect for a VSAM file since the expiration date of a

```
// JOB      UPDTVSAM
// OPTION   LINK
// EXEC     ASSEMBLY
   .
   .  SOURCE PROGRAM
   .
/*
// LIBDEF   CL,TO=USRCL4
// EXEC     LNKEDT
// DLBL     IJSYSUC,'MMA.USER.CATALOG',,VSAM,CAT=IJSYSCT
// DLBL     SHIPTR,'VSAM.ESDS.SHIPMENT.TRANSACTIONS',,VSAM
// DLBL     INVMSTR,'VSAM.KSDS.INVENTORY.MASTERS',,VSAM
// EXEC     ,SIZE=AUTO
/&
```

Figure 16-23   The VSE JCL for testing the VSAM KSDS update program in figure 16-21

VSAM file is specified when it is defined. The code operand is VSAM whether the file is a KSDS, an ESDS, or an RRDS.

The fifth operand, CAT, is optional as indicated by the brackets. It is a keyword operand that you use to specify which catalog owns the file. The value you code for CAT is the filename of the catalog from a preceding DLBL statement. You don't always have to code the CAT operand, however. If all of the VSAM files in a job are owned by the same user catalog, you can define one job catalog instead of coding the CAT operand on each of the DLBL statements for the VSAM files used in the job.

A *job catalog* is a VSAM user catalog that is defined for one job. To specify a job catalog, you code a DLBL statement with the filename IJSYSUC, as in this example:

```
// DLBL   IJSYSUC,'MMA.USER.CATALOG',,VSAM,CAT=IJSYSCT
```

If you code a DLBL statement like this one, the system assumes that all the VSAM files used in the job are owned by the user catalog rather than the master catalog. Since most applications are designed so related files are owned by the same catalog, this works well. Notice that I coded CAT=IJSYSCT to indicate that the master catalog owns the job catalog. If you refer to the job stream in figure 16-23, you can see that the CAT operands are omitted from the DLBL statements for the two files used in the job because both of them are owned by the job catalog.

To access a VSAM file that isn't owned by the job catalog, you code the CAT operand on its DLBL statement. For that to work, however, you need to code a DLBL statement for the second user catalog with a filename other than IJSYSUC. This is illustrated in figure 16-24. Here, the DLBL statement for the second user catalog has the filename INVCAT. Then, the CAT operand in the DLBL statement for the second file specifies INVCAT as the catalog that owns it. Note that the CAT operand isn't coded on the DLBL statement for the first file, SHIPTR, because it is owned by the job catalog.

```
// DLBL IJSYSUC,'MMA.USER.CATALOG',,VSAM,CAT=IJSYSCT
// DLBL SHIPTR,'VSAM.ESDS.SHIPMENT.TRANSACTIONS',,VSAM
// DLBL INVCAT,'INVENTORY.USER.CATALOG',,VSAM,IJSYSCT
// DLBL INVMSTR,'INVENTORY.MASTER.RECORDS',,VSAM,INVCAT
```

Figure 16-24   A job stream that defines VSAM files that are cataloged in two different user catalogs

The EXEC statement

When you code an EXEC statement to invoke a program that uses VSAM files, you need to include a SIZE operand as in this EXEC statement format:

```
// EXEC program-name,SIZE=AUTO
```

The SIZE operand specifies the additional area required for the VSAM I/O buffers and control blocks. Although the size operand can be coded in several different ways, we recommend that you code it as AUTO. That way the additional space will be allocated automatically.

In the job stream in figure 16-23, you can see that the EXEC statement for testing the update program is coded as:

```
// EXEC   ,SIZE=AUTO
```

As in other assemble-and-test jobs, the program name is omitted.

Discussion

At this point, I think you can see that it's relatively easy to code the JCL for VSAM files. In particular, you don't have to worry about coding the exact location and size for a VSAM file. Instead, VSAM keeps track of that information for you in its catalogs.

I want you to realize, though, that this topic is just a brief introduction to the JCL required for using VSAM files. It doesn't show you how to define a VSAM space or cluster using IDCAMS, and it doesn't present all the DLBL operands that can be used with VSAM files. If you want more information about VSE JCL for VSAM files, we recommend our *DOS/VSE JCL* by Steve Eckols.

Terminology

job catalog

Objective

Given the file specifications for a program that uses one or more VSAM files, code the JCL for running the program.

Section 5

Program development techniques

This section contains three chapters. Chapter 17 shows you how to assemble a source program and correct any diagnostic errors it contains. You can read this chapter any time after you complete chapter 5. But we recommend that you read it just before you assemble your first program or right after you get your first diagnostics.

Chapter 18 shows you how to test and debug a program. Again, you can read this chapter any time after you complete chapter 5. But we recommend that you read it just before you test your first program or right after you get your first test run output.

Chapter 19 is an optional chapter, but one that we believe will help you become a more effective programmer. You can think of it as an idea chapter that you can read any time after you complete chapter 8. We recommend, though, that you read it sooner rather than later, because it's likely to give you ideas that will help you do your case study problems more efficiently.

Chapter 17

How to assemble a source program and correct its diagnostics

After you code a source program and enter it into the system, you must assemble it using a procedure like the one presented in chapter 3. Then, if the assembly produces any diagnostic messages, you must correct them and reassemble the program until it assembles without diagnostics. At that time, you can test and debug the program as described in the next chapter.

This chapter starts by presenting the assembly output you are likely to get when you assemble a source program. Then, it shows you how to go about correcting diagnostics. You can read this chapter any time after you complete chapter 5 of this book. But the best time is probably just before you assemble your first program or right after you assemble it.

ASSEMBLY OUTPUT

When a program is assembled, several different types of output are printed. These are illustrated in figures 17-1 through 17-5. This assembly output is for the refined reorder-program presented in topic 2 of chapter 5. However, we've put a few coding errors into the program so the assembly produces some diagnostics.

Each type of assembly output starts on a new page and continues for as many pages as needed. In sequence, the normal assembly output consists of (1) the external symbol dictionary, (2) the assembly listing, (3) the relocation dictionary, (4) the cross-reference listing, and (5) the diagnostic and statistic listing.

The external symbol dictionary

Figure 17-1 presents the *external symbol dictionary* for the reorder-listing program. This dictionary gives information that is needed by the linkage editor. After you read chapter 8, you'll know what a CSECT and an EXTRN are so this dictionary will have more meaning for you. In brief,

SYMBOL	TYPE	ID	ADDR	LENGTH	LD-ID
REORDLST	SD (CSECT)	001	000000	0005CC	
IJDFAZIW	ER (EXTRN)	002			

Figure 17-1   The external symbol dictionary for the reorder-listing program

though, the dictionary in figure 17-1 says that the control section (CSECT) named REORDLST (that is, the reorder-listing program) uses an external symbol (EXTRN) named IJDFAZIW (that is, the name of an I/O module). As a result, the linkage editor must establish the linkage between these two modules.

Because the linkage editor produces similar information, you won't need to use external symbol dictionaries in this course. As a result, we won't show them in the assembly output for any of the other programs in this book. And we won't mention them any more in this book.

The assembly listing

Sometimes, all of the assembly output is referred to as the assembly listing. More precisely, though, the *assembly listing* for the reorder-listing program is just the listing shown in figure 17-2. From left to right, there are six columns of information on the assembly listing. Since it contains considerable information, I will go over each column in detail.

The source statement column   The rightmost column of the assembly listing, headed SOURCE STATEMENT, is a listing of the source program. In addition, though, instructions generated from macro instructions are shown. These are preceded by a plus sign. For example, the GET macro has generated 5 statements, the first of which is a comment. Similarly, the DTFPR macro has generated 20 lines of source code.

After the END statement in the source listing are data definitions representing the literals used by the program. For example, the last three statements represent the literals used for packed values 50, 1, and 0. The other literal definitions are those generated by macros. For the most part, they are address constants as presented in chapter 7.

The statement number column   To the left of the source statements is a column headed STMT, short for statement number. This column gives a number to each of the source statements of the program. The statement numbers are then used in the cross-reference and diagnostic listings to refer to the source statements.

The location counter column   The leftmost column of information is headed LOC, which stands for *location counter*. The location counter is a field that is used during assembly to keep track of the starting location of each machine instruction or data field of the program. For the first machine instruction, BALR, the location is the value given in the START instruction (in this case, zero). For each subsequent instruction or data definition, the location is determined by adding the length of the instruction or field to the previous location counter value. Since BALR is a two-byte instruction, the second machine instruction has a location of 000002.

Notice that the location values are given in hex. If you scan the LOC column, you can see that the increments from instruction to instruction are two, four or six bytes. These, of course, are the lengths of the System/370 instructions. If a source line doesn't generate any object code, the location counter value is not increased.

For data definitions, the location counter is increased by the total number of bytes reserved (that is, the duplication factor times the length modifier). To illustrate, look at statements 118 and 119. Because the duplication factor is zero in statement 118, both INVWRKA and INVITNBR have the same location counter value, hex 632. As a result, both labels address the same byte of storage. However, INVWRKA will have a length attribute of 50 and INVITNBR will have a length attribute of 5.

The object code column   The second column from the left is headed OBJECT CODE. This column shows the actual machine language assembled for a statement just as it will be stored in the computer. It is in hex notation with two hex digits representing one byte of storage. If a statement causes no object code to be generated, this column is blank.

For instructions, there are two, four, or six bytes represented in the object code column. The format of this data corresponds to the instruction formats presented in chapter 4. The BALR statement, for instance, is translated into two bytes of object code, hex 0530. The first byte is the operation code, hex 05; the second byte holds two register numbers, 3 and 0. Similarly, the MVC instruction in statement 29 is translated into hex D21337FD3635. By referring to the MVC instruction format, you can determine that D2 is the operation code, hex 13 is the length, address 1 consists of a base address in register 3 plus a displacement of hex 7FD, and so on.

For DC statements, the object code column usually shows only the first eight bytes of the field. If you want all of the defined data to print, you can use a PRINT assembler command as described in chapter 6. Remember that DS statements do not cause object code to be created even if they are given nominal values.

You might notice that ***ERROR*** is printed in the object code column when the assembler cannot create object code due to a diagnostic error. As you will see, the diagnostics refer to these statements so the errors can be corrected.

The operand address columns   The ADDR1 and ADDR2 columns give the location counter values for operands 1 and 2 of each instruction. If an operand is a register or if no operand is present, the corresponding column is left blank. As you will see in the next chapter, the location values are helpful when you are debugging.

```
                                              DOS/VSE ASSEMBLER 10.23  86-01-06                    PAGE    2

LOC      OBJECT CODE      ADDR1  ADDR2  STMT   SOURCE STATEMENT

000000                                    1    REORDLST START 0                                             00000100
000000   0530                    00002    2    BEGIN    BALR  3,0            LOAD BASE REGISTER             00000200
                                           3             USING *,3                                          00000300
                                           4             OPEN  INVMAST,PRTOUT                               00000400
000002   0700                             5+*   IOCS - OPEN - 5745-SC-IOX - REL 28.0                        12000028
000004                                    6+           CNOP  0,4                                            20000025
                                          7+           DC    0F'0'                                          22000025
000004   4110 3596      00598             8+           LA    1,=C'$$BOPEN '                                 46000025
000008   4500 3012      00014             9+IJJ00001   BAL   0,*+4+4*(3-1)                                  54000025
00000C   00000000                        10+           DC    A(INVMAST)                                     64000025
                  *** ERROR ***
000010   00000110                        11+           DC    A(PRTOUT)                                      64000025
000014   0A02                            12+           SVC   2                                              74000025
                                         13    READINV  GET   INVMAST,INVWRKA  READ RECORD INTO WORK AREA   00000500
000016                                   14+*   IOCS - GET - 5745-SC-IOX - REL 29.0                         12000029
000016   5810 35A6      005A8            15+READINV    L     1,=A(INVMAST)    GET DTF TABLE ADDRESS         42000025
00001A   5800 35AA      005AC            16+           L     0,=A(INVWRKA)    GET WORK AREA ADDRESS         51000025
00001E   58F1 0010      00010            17+           L     15,16(1)         GET LOGIC MODULE ADDRESS      75000025
000022   45EF 0008      0008             18+           BAL   14,8(15)         BRANCH TO GET ROUTINE         78000025
000026   FA20 3530 35C8 00592 005CA      19           AP    COUNT,=P'1'       ADD ONE TO COUNT             00000600
00002C   F224 3584 32D4 00586 002D6      20           PACK  WRKAVAIL,INVONHND                              00000700
000032   F224 3587 32D9 00589 002DB      21           PACK  WRKONORD,INVONORD                              00000800
                                         22           ADD   WRKAVAIL,WRKONORD ADD ON HAND AND ON ORDER     00000900
                  *** ERROR ***
000038   F224 358A 32CF 0058C 002D1      23           PACK  WRKORDPT,INVORDPT                              00001000
00003E   F922 3584 358A 00586 0058C      24           CP    WRKAVAIL,WRKORDPT COMPARE AVAILABLE, REORDER POINT  00001100
000044   47B0 3014      00016            25           BNL   READINV                                        00001200
000048   F224 358D 32AC 0058F 002AE      26           PACK  PACKAREA,INVITNBR                              00001300
                                         27           MVL   PRTITNBR,PATTERN1                              00001400
                  *** ERROR ***
00004E   DE05 346E 358D 00470 0058F      28           ED    PRTITNBR,PACKAREA EDIT ITEM NUMBER FIELD       00001500
000054   D213 3479 32B1 0047B 002B3      29           MVC   PRTITDES,INVITDES MOVE ITEM DESCRIPTION        00001600
00005A   F224 358D 32CA 0058F 002CC      30           PACK  PACKAREA,INVPRICE                              00001700
000060   D206 3491 357D 00493 0057F      31           MVC   PRTPRICE,PATTERN2                              00001800
000066   DE06 3491 358D 00493 0058F      32           ED    PRTPRICE,PACKAREA EDIT UNIT PRICE              00001900
00006C   D205 349C 3577 0049E 00579      33           MVC   PRTAVAIL,PATTERN1                              00002000
000072   DE05 349C 3584 0049E 00586      34           ED    PRTAVAIL,WRKAVAIL EDIT AVAILABLE               00002100
000078   D205 34A6 358A 004A8 0058C      35           MVC   PRTORDPT,PATTERN1                              00002200
00007E   DE05 34A6 358A 004A8 0058C      36           ED    PRTORDPT,WRKORDPT EDIT ORDER POINT             00002300
000084   F911 3593 35C6 00595 005C8      37           CP    LINECNT,=P'50'    COMPARE LINE COUNT TO 50     00002400
00008A   4740 30C6      000C8            38           BL    PRTDET            BRANCH ON LOW TO PRTDET       00002500
                                         39           PUT   PRTOUT,HDGLINE1   PRINT FIRST HEADING LINE      00002600
                                         40+*   IOCS AND DEVICE INDEPENDENT I/O - PUT - 5745-SC-IOX - REL. 29.0   05000029
00008E   5810 35AE      005B0            41+           L     1,=A(PRTOUT)      GET DTF TABLE ADDRESS        15000025
000092   5800 35B2      005B4            42+           L     0,=A(HDGLINE1)    GET WORK AREA ADDRESS        46000025
000096   58F1 0010      00010            43+           L     15,16(1)          GET LOGIC MODULE ADDRESS  3-5  54000025
00009A   45EF 000C      0000C            44+           BAL   14,12(15)         BRANCH TO PUT ROUTINE     3-5  55000025
                                         45           PUT   PRTOUT,HDGLINE2   PRINT SECOND HEADING LINE     00002700
                                         46+*   IOCS AND DEVICE INDEPENDENT I/O - PUT - 5745-SC-IOX - REL. 29.0   05000029
00009E   5810 35AE      005B0            47+           L     1,=A(PRTOUT)      GET DTF TABLE ADDRESS        15000025
0000A2   5800 35B6      005B8            48+           L     0,=A(HDGLINE2)    GET WORK AREA ADDRESS        46000025
```

Figure 17-2   The assembly listing for the reorder-listing program (part 1 of 4)

```
                                                    PAGE    3

                            DOS/VSE ASSEMBLER 10.23  86-01-06

LOC    OBJECT CODE  ADDR1 ADDR2  STMT  SOURCE STATEMENT

0000A6 58F1 0010    00010         49+      L     15,16(1)          GET LOGIC MODULE ADDRESS       3-5 54000025
0000AA 45EF 000C          0000C   50+      BAL   14,12(15)         BRANCH TO PUT ROUTINE          3-5 55000025
                                  51       PUT   PRTOUT,HDGLINE3   PRINT THIRD HEADING LINE           00002800
                                  52+*  IOCS AND DEVICE INDEPENDENT I/O - PUT - 5745-SC-IOX - REL. 29.0  05000029
0000AE 5810 35AE    005B0         53+      L     1,=A(PRTOUT)      GET DTF TABLE ADDRESS              15000025
0000B2 5800 35BA    005BC         54+      L     0,=A(HDGLINE3)    GET WORK AREA ADDRESS              46000025
0000B6 58F1 0010    00010         55+      L     15,16(1)          GET LOGIC MODULE ADDRESS       3-5 54000025
0000BA 45EF 000C          0000C   56+      BAL   14,12(15)         BRANCH TO PUT ROUTINE          3-5 55000025
0000BE F810 3593 35C9 00595 0046F 57       ZAP   LINECNT,=P'0'     RESET LINE COUNT TO ZERO           00002900
0000C4 92F0 346D    0046F         58       MVI   PRTDCTL,C'0'      MOVE ZERO TO DETAIL CONTROL BYTE   00003100
                                  59 PRTDET PUT   PRTOUT,PRTDETL   PRINT DETAIL LINE
                                  60+*  IOCS AND DEVICE INDEPENDENT I/O - PUT - 5745-SC-IOX - REL. 29.0  05000029
0000C8 5810 35AE    005B0         61+PRTDET L     1,=A(PRTOUT)     GET DTF TABLE ADDRESS              15000025
0000CC 5800 35BE    005C0         62+      L     0,=A(PRTDETL)     GET WORK AREA ADDRESS              46000025
0000D0 58F1 0010    00010         63+      L     15,16(1)          GET LOGIC MODULE ADDRESS       3-5 54000025
0000D4 45EF 000C          0000C   64+      BAL   14,12(15)         BRANCH TO PUT ROUTINE          3-5 55000025
0000D8 FA10 3593 35C8 00595 0046F 65       AP    LINECNT,=P'1'     ADD ONE TO LINE COUNT              00003200
0000DE 9240 346D    0046F         66       MVI   PRTDCTL,C' '      MOVE BLANK TO DETAIL CONTROL BYTE  00003400
0000E2 47F0 3014    00016         67       B     READINV           BRANCH TO READINV                  00003400
0000E6 DE06 34F3 3590 004F5 00592 68 INVEOF ED   CNTPATRN,COUNT    EDIT COUNT                         00003500
                                  69       PUT   PRTOUT,CNTLINE    PRINT COUNT LINE                   00003600
                                  70+*  IOCS AND DEVICE INDEPENDENT I/O - PUT - 5745-SC-IOX - REL. 29.0  05000029
0000EC 5810 35AE    005B0         71+      L     1,=A(PRTOUT)      GET DTF TABLE ADDRESS              15000025
0000F0 5800 35C2    005C4         72+      L     0,=A(CNTLINE)     GET WORK AREA ADDRESS              46000025
0000F4 58F1 0010    00010         73+      L     15,16(1)          GET LOGIC MODULE ADDRESS       3-5 54000025
0000F8 45EF 000C          0000C   74+      BAL   14,12(15)         BRANCH TO PUT ROUTINE          3-5 55000025
                                  75       CLOSE INVMAST,PRTOUT
                                  76+*  IOCS AND DEVICE INDEPENDANT I/O - CLOSE - 5745-SC-IOX - REL. 28.0  08100028
0000FC                            77+      CNOP  0,4                                                 20000025
0000FC                            78+      DC    0F'0'                                               22000025
0000FC 4110 359E    005A0         79+      LA    1,=C'$$BCLOSE'                                      46000025
000100 4500 310A    0010C   80+IJJC0008    BAL   0,*+4+4*(3-1)                                       54000025
000104 00000000                   81+      DC    A(INVMAST)                                          64000025
       *** ERROR ***
000108 00000110                   82+      DC    A(PRTOUT)                                           64000025
00010C 0A02                       83+      SVC   2                                                   74000025
                                  84       EOJ
                                  85+*  SUPVR COMMN MACROS - EOJ - 5745-SC-SUP - REL. 28.0            40000028
00010E 0A0E                       86+      SVC   14                                                  50000025
                                  87 *  THE INVENTORY FILE DEFINITION FOLLOWS                         00003900
                                  88 INVMAST DTFSE BLKSIZE=50,                                      X00004000
       *** ERROR ***
                                                  IOAREA1=INVIO1,                                   X00004100
                                                  IOAREA2=INVIO2,                                   X00004200
                                                  EOFADDR=INVEOF,                                   X00004300
                                                  DEVADDR=SYS008,                                   X
                                                  WORKA=YES                                          00004400
                                  89 *  THE PRINTER FILE DEFINITION FOLLOWS                           00004500
                                  90 PRTOUT DTFPR DEVADDR=SYSLST,                                   X00004600
                                                  IOAREA1=PRTIO1,                                   X00004700
                                                  IOAREA2=PRTIO2,                                   X00004800
```

Figure 17-2   The assembly listing for the reorder-listing program (part 2 of 4)

```
                                              DOS/VSE ASSEMBLER 10-23 86-01-06                    PAGE    4

LOC     OBJECT CODE       ADDR1 ADDR2  STMT   SOURCE STATEMENT

                                              5745-SC-IOX - REL.1.3    @DY28915   02870000
000110                                  91+* IOCS AND DEV INDEPENDENT I/O DTFPR               X00004900
                                        92+        WORKA=YES,                                 X00005000
                                                   BLKSIZE=133,                               X00005100
                                                   CTLCHR=ASA                                  60000025
000110  00008000J000                    93+PRTOUT   DC  0D'0'                                   70000028
000116  00                              94+        DC  X'000080000000'   RES. COUNT, COM. BYTES BTS   JJ 61510028
000117  03                              95+        DC  AL1(0)            LOGICAL UNIT CLASS            70200028
000118  00000138                        96+        DC  AL1(3)            LOGICAL UNIT              JJ 71000028
00011C  00000000                        97+        DC  A(*+32)           CCW ADDR.                 JJ 71200028
000120  00                              98+        DC  4X'00'            CCB-ST BYTE,CSW CCW ADDRESS 4-0 71750027
000121  000000                          99+        DC  AL1(0)            SWITCH 3   ADDR OF LOGIC MODUL3-8  JJ 76800025
000124  08                             100+        DC  VL3(IJDFAZIW)     DTF TYPE (PRINTER)        JJ 77580028
000125  36                             101+        DC  X'08'             SWITCHES                     77600025
000126  09                             102+        DC  AL1(54)           NORMAL COMM. CODE         4-0 78000027
000127  09                             103+        DC  AL1(9)            CONTROL COMM. CODE        4-0 78400027
000128  000001A5                       104+        DC  AL1(9)            ADDRESS OF DATA IN IOAREA1    78800025
00012C  00000000                       105+        DC  A(PRTIO1+1)       BUCKET                    3-5 84000025
000130  0700  00000                    106+        DC  4X'00'            PUT LENGTH IN REG12 (ONLY UNDEF.  84800025
000132  4700  0000                     107+        NOPR 0                LOAD USER POINTER REG        86400025
000136  0000                           108+        NOP 0                 NOT USED                  3-5 89600025
000138  0900022A20000084               109+        DC  2X'00'                                     4-0 90400027
                               00140           CCW 9,PRTIO2+1,X'20',133-1                            92000025
                                       110+IJJZ0010 EQU *
                                       111+* THE DATA DEFINITIONS FOR THE TWO INVENTORY FILE I/O AREAS FOLLOW  00005300
000140                                 112 INVIO1   DS  CL50                                    00005400
000172                                 113 INVIO2   DS  CL50                                    00005500
                                       114 * THE DATA DEFINITIONS FOR THE TWO PRINTER OUTPUT AREAS FOLLOW  00005600
0001A4                                 115 PRTIO1   DS  CL133                                   00005700
000229                                 116 PRTIO2   DS  CL133                                   00005800
                                       117 * THE DATA DEFINITIONS FOR THE INVENTORY FILE WORK AREA FOLLOW  00005900
0002AE                                 118 INVWRKA  DS  0CL50                                   00006000
0002AE                                 119 INVITNBR DS  CL5                                     00006100
0002B3                                 120 INVITDES DS  CL20                                    00006200
0002C7                                 121          DS  CL5                                     00006300
0002CC                                 122 INVPRICE DS  CL5                                     00006400
0002D1                                 123 INVORDPT DS  CL5                                     00006500
0002D6                                 124 INVONHND DS  CL5                                     00006600
0002DB                                 125 INVONORD DS  CL5                                     00006800
                                       126 * THE DATA DEFINITIONS FOR THE PRINTER HEADING LINES FOLLOW  00006900
0002E0                                 127 HDGLINE1 DS  0CL133                                  00007000
0002E0  F1                             128          DC  C'1'                                    00007100
0002E1  4040404040404040               129          DC  24C' '                                 00007200
0002F9  D9C5D6D9C4C5D940               130          DC  C'REORDER LISTING'                      00007300
000308  4040404040404040               131          DC  93C' '                                 00007400
000365                                 132 HDGLINE2 DS  0CL133                                  00007500
000365  F0                             133          DC  C'0'                                    X00007600
000366  40C9E3C5D4404040               134          DC  C' ITEM    ITEM   UNIT                  00007700
                                                        REORDER'
0003A5  4040404040404040               135          DC  69C' '                                 00007700
0003EA                                 136 HDGLINE3 DS  0CL133                                  00007900
0003EA  40                             137          DC  C' '                                    00008000
```

Figure 17-2   The assembly listing for the reorder-listing program (part 3 of 4)

```
LOC    OBJECT CODE          ADDR1 ADDR2  STMT  SOURCE STATEMENT

0003EB 404D5D64B404040            138          DC    C'    NO.   DESCRIPTION    PRICE    AVAILABLE         X00008100
                                                     POINT'                                                 00008200
000429 40404040404040404040       139          DC    70C' '                                                00008300
                                  140   *  THE DATA DEFINITIONS FOR THE PRINTER DETAIL LINE FOLLOW         00008400
0046F                             141   PRTDETL  DS   0CL133                                               00008500
0046F                             142   PRTDCTL  DS   CL1                                                  00008600
00470                             143   PRTITNBR DS   CL6                                                  00008700
00476  4040404040                 144            DC   5C' '                                                00008800
0047B                             145   PRTITDES DS   CL20                                                 00008900
0048F  40404040                   146            DC   4C' '                                                00009000
00493                             147   PRTPRICE DS   CL7                                                  00009100
0049A  40404040                   148            DC   4C' '                                                00009200
0049E                             149   PRTAVAIL DS   CL6                                                  00009300
004A4  40404040                   150            DC   4C' '                                                00009400
004A8                             151   PRTORDPT DS   CL6                                                  00009500
004AE  404040404040404040         152            DC   70C' '                                               00009600
                                  153   *  THE DATA DEFINITIONS FOR THE FINAL TOTAL LINE FOLLOW           00009700
0004F4                            154   CNTLINE  DS   0CL133                                               00009800
0004F4 60                         155            DC   C'-'                                                 00009900
0004F5 402020 6B202020            156   CNTPATRN DC   X'402020 6B202020'                                   00010000
0004FC 40D9C5C3D6D9C4E2           157            DC   C' RECORDS IN THE INPUT FILE'                        00010100
00516  404040404040404040         158            DC   99C' '                                               00010200
                                  159   *  THE DATA DEFINITIONS THAT FOLLOW DEFINE OTHER WORK AREAS NEEDED 00010300
                                  160   *  BY THE PROGRAM                                                  00010400
000579 4020202020 2020            161   PATTERN1 DC   X'40202020202020'                                    00010500
00057F 40202021 4B2020            162   PATTERN2 DC   X'40202021 4B2020'                                   00010600
000586                            163   WRKAVAIL DS   PL3                                                  00010700
000589                            164   WRKONORD DS   PL3                                                  00010800
00058C                            165   WRKORDPT DS   PL3                                                  00010900
00058F                            166   PACKAREA DS   PL3                                                  00011000
000592 00000C                     167   COUNT    DC   PL3'0'                                               00011100
000595 050C                       168   LINECNT  DC   P'50'                                                00011200
                     00000        169            END  BEGIN                                                00011300
000598 5B5BC2D6D7C5D540           170                  =C'$$BOPEN '
0005A0 5B5BC2C3D3D6E2C5           171                  =C'$$BCLOSE'
0005A8 00000000                   172                  =A(INVMAST)
       *** ERROR ***
0005AC 000002AE                   173                  =A(INVWRKA)
0005B0 00000110                   174                  =A(PRTOUT)
0005B4 000002E0                   175                  =A(HDGLINE1)
0005B8 00000365                   176                  =A(HDGLINE2)
0005BC 000003EA                   177                  =A(HDGLINE3)
0005C0 0000046F                   178                  =A(PRTDETL)
0005C4 000004F4                   179                  =A(CNTLINE)
0005C8 050C                       180                  =P'50'
0005CA 1C                         181                  =P'1'
0005CB 0C                         182                  =P'0'
```

Figure 17-2   The assembly listing for the reorder-listing program (part 4 of 4)

ESDID FOR ADDR CON	ESDID FOR REF SYMBOL	TYPE	LENGTH	ADDRESS	
001	+001	A	4	000010	86-01-06
001	+001	A	4	000108	
001	+001	A	4	000118	
001	+002	V	3	000121	
001	+001	A	4	000128	
001	+001	CCW	3	000139	
001	+001	A	4	0005AC	
001	+001	A	4	0005B0	
001	+001	A	4	0005B4	
001	+001	A	4	0005B8	
001	+001	A	4	0005BC	
001	+001	A	4	0005C0	
001	+001	A	4	0005C4	

Figure 17-3   The relocation dictionary for the reorder-listing program

The relocation dictionary

Figure 17-3 is the relocation dictionary for the reorder-listing program. However, you won't need to use these dictionaries in this course. As a result, these dictionaries won't be shown in the assembly output for any other programs in this book.

The cross-reference listing

Figure 17-4 is the *cross-reference listing* for the reorder-listing program. In the SYMBOL column of this listing, you can see the labels of all instructions or fields used in the program. For instance, BEGIN is the name of the first machine instruction in the program, and INVORDPT is the name of one of the fields in the input work area. Near the end of the listing, you can see that literals are included in the cross-reference listing. The literals for values of 0, 1, and 50 were coded in the source program. But the literals generated by macro instructions are also listed. Because this is a *sorted* cross-reference listing (the option is SXREF), the symbol names are listed in alphabetical order.

Four of the columns to the right of each symbol name give information that is useful when you are correcting diagnostics or debugging. First, the LEN column gives the length attribute of each label. For instance, BEGIN, which is the label of the BALR instruction, has a length attribute of 2; INVITDES has a length attribute of 20. Second, the VALUE column gives the location counter value assigned to the label. Third, the DEFN column gives the number of the statement that defines the label. And fourth, the REFERENCES column gives the numbers of all statements that use the label as an operand. If necessary, more than one line is used for these reference numbers.

The diagnostics and statistics listing

Figure 17-5 shows the *diagnostics and statistics listing* for the reorder-listing program. In practice, this name is shortened to *diagnostic listing*. For each diagnostic message on the listing, you can see the statement number of the instruction in error (STMNT) followed by an error message number (ERROR NO.) followed by an error message (MESSAGE).

An error number, like IPK097, refers to an expanded explanation of the error message that can be found in IBM's *Guide to the DOS/VSE Assembler* (GC33-4024). In general, though, the messages on the diagnostic listing tell you all you need to know so you should rarely need this manual.

In addition to the diagnostics, this listing also gives some program information that includes a list of the macros used, the options used for the assembly, and the number of bytes the assembler was run in. Of these, the option list will probably be the most interesting to you. As you can see in figure 17-5, this assembly of the reorder-listing program was done with the SXREF and RLD options on. So, if you don't want the cross-reference listing or relocation dictionary, you can turn these options off as described in topic 2 of chapter 3. For most assemblies, though, you will want a cross-reference listing.

HOW TO CORRECT DIAGNOSTICS

When it comes to correcting diagnostics, you should realize from the start that the assembler's ability to find errors is limited. It can find coding errors like invalid operation codes, invalid formats for operands, undefined labels, and missing commas, but it cannot detect errors in the logic of a program. As a result, it's possible to write a series of statements that assemble without error but that make no sense at all as far as the function of a program is concerned.

You should also know that the assembler does not require strict alignment of statement parts even though the programs in this book are all coded with the operation codes starting in column 10 and the operands starting in column 16. Although the label must start in column 1, the operation code can start anywhere as long as one or more blanks separate it from the label. Similarly, the operands can start anywhere as long as one or more blanks separate them from the operation code. If a statement doesn't have a label, the operation code can start anywhere after column 1. Of course, the sequence from left to right in the statement is critical; it must be label followed by operation code followed by operands.

Although the assembler can produce many different diagnostic messages, the majority of errors are covered by just a few messages. To illustrate, the diagnostic listings in figures 17-5 and 17-6 present some of the common messages. Both of these listings are for the same reorder-listing program, but with different coding errors. As you will see, it's relatively easy to figure out how to correct the coding errors, even though the messages aren't always clear.

CROSS-REFERENCE

PAGE 7

86-01-06

SYMBOL	LEN	ID	VALUE	DEFN	REFERENCES				
BEGIN	00002	001	000000	00002	0169	0179			
CNTLINE	00133	001	0004F4	00154	0179				
CNTPATRN	00007	001	0004F5	00156	0068				
COUNT	00003	001	000592	00167	0019	0175			
HDGLINE1	00133	001	0002E0	00127	0175				
HDGLINE2	00133	001	000365	00132	0176				
HDGLINE3	00133	001	0003EA	00136	0177				
INVITDES	00020	001	0002B3	00120	0029				
INVITNBR	00005	001	0002AE	00119	0026				
INVMAST	#####		UNDEFINED	#####	0010	0081	0172		
INVONHND	00005	001	0002D6	00124	0020				
INVONORD	00005	001	0002DB	00125	0021				
INVORDPT	00005	001	0002D1	00123	0023				
INVPRICE	00005	001	0002CC	00122	0030				
INVWRKA	00050	001	0002AE	00118	0173				
LINECNT	00002	001	000595	00168	0037	0057	0065		
PACKAREA	00003	001	00058F	00166	0026	0028	0030	0032	
PATTERN1	00006	001	000579	00161	0033	0035			
PATTERN2	00007	001	00057F	00162	0031				
PRTAVAIL	00006	001	00049E	00149	0033	0034			
PRTDCTL	00001	001	00046F	00142	0058	0066			
PRTDET	00004	001	0000C8	00061	0038				
PRTDETL	00133	001	00046F	00141	0178				
PRTIO1	00133	001	0001A4	00115	0104				
PRTIO2	00133	001	000229	00116	0109				
PRTITDES	00020	001	00047B	00145	0029				
PRTITNBR	00006	001	000470	00143	0028				
PRTORDPT	00006	001	0004A8	00151	0035	0036			
PRTOUT	00006	001	000110	00093	0011	0082	0174		
PRTPRICE	00007	001	000493	00147	0031	0032			
READINV	00004	001	000016	00015	0025	0067			
WRKAVAIL	00003	001	000586	00163	0020	0024	0034		
WRKONORD	00003	001	000589	00164	0021	0024			
WRKORDPT	00003	001	00058C	00165	0023	0024	0036		
=A(CNTLINE)	00004	001	0005C4	00179	0072				
=A(HDGLINE1)	00004	001	000584	00175	0042				
=A(HDGLINE2)	00004	001	000588	00176	0048				
=A(HDGLINE3)	00004	001	0005BC	00177	0054				
=A(INVMAST)	00004	001	0005A8	00172	0015				
=A(INVWRKA)	00004	001	0005AC	00173	0016				
=A(PRTOUT)	00004	001	0005B0	00174	0041	0047	0053	0061	0071
=A(PRTDETL)	00004	001	0005C0	00178	0062				
=C'$$BOPEN '									

Figure 17-4   The cross-reference listing for the reorder-listing program (part 1 of 2)

The first diagnostic listing

In figure 17-5, there are six diagnostic messages. All of these relate to invalid operation codes. The second diagnostic message, for example, is UNDEFINED OP CODE 'ADD', OR MACRO NOT FOUND. It refers to statement 22. Since ADD is an invalid operation code, the assembler was unable to create the object code for this statement so it printed the diagnostic message. In this case, of course, the operation code should be AP.

The message says "or macro not found," because it's possible that the programmer meant to use a macro with the name ADD. However, the assembler couldn't find an ADD macro in any source statement library in the search chain either. So the statement is still in error. Chapters 6 and 11 in this book present more information about macros that should make this portion of the message more meaningful to you.

The third diagnostic has a similar message. This time the message was caused by the invalid operation code MVL instead of the intended MVC. An error like this is often just a typographical error made during the entry of the source program.

The fifth diagnostic is for an undefined operation code in statement 88. In this case, the source program has DTFSE for the operation code when DTFSD is correct. Because of this error, the label of the DTFSD, INVMAST, is not considered to be defined. This is shown in the cross-reference listing.

The error in the operation code for the DTFSD also accounts for the other three diagnostic messages in figure 17-5. All of these refer to an undefined symbol, INVMAST, which is the label of the DTFSD. These diagnostics refer to the instructions in statements 10, 81, and 171, which are generated by the OPEN, CLOSE, and GET macros. The instructions in these lines all define an address constant, A(INVMAST), for the DTF statement. You will learn more about address constants in chapters 6 and 8.

When a diagnostic is caused by an undefined operation code, it's usually easy to correct the coding error. At first, it might be confusing when the diagnostic refers to an instruction generated by a macro. However, if you study the macro rather than the generated instructions, you should be able to find a coding error in it.

PAGE   8   86-01-06

CROSS-REFERENCE

```
SYMBOL    LEN  ID VALUE  DEFN   REFERENCES
          00008 001 000598 00170  0008
=C'$$BCLOSE'
          00008 001 0005A0 00171  0079
=P'0'     00001 001 0005CB 00182  0057
=P'1'     00001 001 0005CA 00181  0019  0065
=P'50'    00002 001 0005C8 00180  0037
```

Figure 17-4 The cross-reference listing for the reorder-listing program (part 2 of 2)

PAGE   9   86-01-06

DIAGNOSTICS AND STATISTICS

```
STMNT  ERROR NO.  MESSAGE
 10    IPK156  SYMBOL 'INVMAST' UNDEFINED
 22    IPK097  UNDEFINED OP CODE 'ADD', OR MACRO NOT FOUND
 27    IPK097  UNDEFINED OP CODE 'MVL', OR MACRO NOT FOUND
 81    IPK156  SYMBOL 'INVMAST' UNDEFINED
 88    IPK097  UNDEFINED OP CODE 'DTFSE', OR MACRO NOT FOUND
172    IPK156  SYMBOL 'INVMAST' UNDEFINED
```

THE FOLLOWING MACRO NAMES HAVE BEEN FOUND IN MACRO INSTRUCTIONS
OPEN   GET   ADD   MVL   PUT   CLOSE   EOJ   DTFSE   DTFPR

OPTIONS FOR THIS ASSEMBLY - ALIGN, LIST, SXREF, LINK, RLD, NODECK, NOEDECK

THE ASSEMBLER WAS RUN IN 7833480 BYTES
END OF ASSEMBLY

Figure 17-5 The diagnostics and statistics listing for the reorder-listing program

The second diagnostic listing

Figure 17-6 illustrates the assembly output for another version of the reorder-listing program. This output includes the assembly listing, the sorted cross-reference listing, and the diagnostic listing. This diagnostic listing illustrates some common coding errors that weren't shown in the first listing.

The diagnostic for statement 33 indicates INVALID DELIMITER. A delimiter is a character, normally a comma or parenthesis, that is used to separate operands. In the case of statement 33, a comma is present, but it is followed by a blank instead of the next operand. The statement can be corrected by deleting the blank.

The diagnostic for statement 226 indicates CONSTANT FIELD MISSING OR PRECEDED BY INVALID FIELD. Actually, however, it's the operation code that's wrong. It should be DS instead of DC. Because the operand was coded without a nominal value, the assembler assumed the operand was incorrect. This in turn accounts for the diagnostics that refer to statements 23, 24, and 36: WRKORDPT is undefined. As a result, these statements don't have to be corrected.

The reverse of this mistake (coding DS for DC) is also common. When you do this, though, the error won't be caught by the assembler because it is acceptable to have a nominal value in a DS operand. This is a more serious error than coding DC for DS because the program is assembled but the intended value isn't put into the field. As a result, an error will normally result when the program is executed.

The diagnostic message for statement 91 illustrates a special type of error. An MNOTE message is generated when an error is present in a macro statement. It usually means that one of the operands for the macro is missing, has an invalid value, or is in conflict with another operand. If you look at the statement referred to by the diagnostic, you will often find additional diagnostic information. In this case, statement 91 says that no work area or I/O register is specified and that register 2 has been assigned as the I/O register. Since two I/O areas are used, either a work area or an I/O register must be present.

If you look at the DTFSD that precedes statement 91, you can see that WORKA=YES has been specified. Why, then, did this diagnostic message get printed? If you look more closely, you can see that the operand on the line before the WORKA operand doesn't end in a comma. As a result, the assembler assumes that it is the last operand in the DTF. And that means that the line with the WORKA operand is treated as a comment.

With this as background, you should be able to figure out the other errors indicated by the diagnostic listing in figure 17-6. They are all relatively simple coding errors in DS or DC instructions, machine instructions, or macro instructions.

PAGE 2

DOS/VSE ASSEMBLER 15.03   86-01-06

LOC	OBJECT CODE	ADDR1	ADDR2	STMT	SOURCE STATEMENT			
000000				1	REORDLST	START	0		00000100
000000	0530			2	BEGIN	BALR	3,0	LOAD BASE REGISTER	00000200
			00002	3		USING	*,3		00000300
				4		OPEN	INVMAST,PRTOUT		00000400
000002	0700			5+*	IOCS - OPEN - 5745-SC-IOX - REL 28.0				12000028
000004				6+		CNOP	0,4		20000025
				7+		DC	0F'0'		22000025
000004	4110 39CE		009D0	8+		LA	1,=C'$$BOPEN '		46000025
000008	4500 3012		00014	9+IJJ00001	BAL	0,*+4+4*(3-1)		54000025
000000	00000128			10+		DC	A(INVMAST)		64000025
000010	000001C8			11+		DC	A(PRTOUT)		64000025
000014	0A02			12+		SVC	2		74000025
000016				13	READINV	GET	INVMAST,INVWORKA	READ RECORD INTO WORK AREA	00000500
000016				14+*	IOCS - GET - 5745-SC-IOX - REL 29.0				12000029
000016	5810 39DE		009E0	15+READINV	L	1,=A(INVMAST)		42000025
00001A	5800 39E2		009E4	16+		L	0,=A(INVWORKA)	GET DTF TABLE ADDRESS	51000025
00001E	58F1 001D		00010	17+		L	14,8(1)	GET WORK AREA ADDRESS	75000025
000022	45EF 0008		00008	18+		BAL	14,8(15)	GET LOGIC MODULE ADDRESS	78000025
								BRANCH TO GET ROUTINE	
000026	FA20 39C4 3A00	009C6 00A02		19		AP	COUNT,=P'1'	ADD ONE TO COUNT	00000600
00002C	F224 39B3 370B	009BD 0070D		20		PACK	WRKAVAIL,INVONHND		00000700
000032	F224 39BE 3710	009C0 00712		21		PACK	WRKONORD,INVONORD		00000800
000038	FA22 39B3 39BE	009BD 009C0		22		AP	WRKAVAIL,WRKONORD	ADD ON HAND AND ON ORDER	00000900
00003E	0000 0000 0000			23		PACK	WRKORDPT,INVORDPT		00001000
	*** ERROR ***								
000044	0000 0000			24		CP	WRKAVAIL,WRKORDPT	COMPARE AVAILABLE, REORDER POINT	00001100
	*** ERROR ***								
00004A	0000 0000			25		BNL	READIV		00001200
	*** ERROR ***								
00004E	F224 39C1 36E8	009C3 006EA		26		PACK	PACKAREA,INVITNBR		00001300
000054	D205 38A5 39AE	008A7 009B0		27		MVC	PRTITNBR,PATTERN1	EDIT ITEM NUMBER	00001400
00005A	DE05 38A5 39C1	008A7 009C3		28		ED	PRTITNBR,PACKAREA		00001500
000060	D213 38B0 36ED	008B2 006EF		29		MVC	PRTIDES,INVITDES	MOVE ITEM DESCRIPTION	00001600
000066	F224 39C1 3701	009C3 00703		30		PACK	PACKAREA,INVPRICE		00001700
00006C	D206 38C8 39B4	008CA 009B6		31		MVC	PRTPRICE,PATTERN2	EDIT UNIT PRICE	00001800
000072	DE06 38C8 39C1	008CA 009C3		32		ED	PRTPRICE,PACKAREA		00001900
000078	0000 0000 0000			33		MVC	PRTAVAIL,PATTERN1		00002000
	*** ERROR ***								
00007E	DE05 38C3 39BB	008D5 009BD		34		ED	PRTAVAIL,WRKAVAIL	EDIT AVAILABLE	00002100
000084	D205 38DD 39AE	008DF 009B0		35		MVC	PRTORDPT,PATTERN1		00002200
00008A	0000 0000 0000			36		ED	PRTORDPT,WRKORDPT	EDIT ORDER POINT	00002300
	*** ERROR ***								
000090	0000 0000 0000			37		CP	LINECNT,=P'50'	COMPARE LINE COUNT TO 50	00002400
	*** ERROR ***								
000096	4740 30D2		000D4	38		BL	PRTDET	BRANCH ON LOW TO PRTDET	00002500
				39		PUT	PRTOUT,HDGLINE1	PRINT FIRST HEADING LINE	00002600
				40+*	IOCS AND DEVICE INDEPENDENT I/O - PUT - 5745-SC-IOX - REL. 29.0				05000029
00009A	5810 39E6		009E8	41+		L	1,=A(PRTOUT)	GET DTF TABLE ADDRESS	15000025
00009E	5800 39EA		009EC	42+		L	0,=A(HDGLINE1)	GET WORK AREA ADDRESS	46000025
0000A2	58F1 0010		00010	43+		L	15,16(1)	GET LOGIC MODULE ADDRESS	54000025
0000A6	45EF 000C		0000C	44+		BAL	14,12(15)	BRANCH TO PUT ROUTINE	55000025
				45		PUT	PRTOUT,HDGLINE2	PRINT SECOND HEADING LINE	00002700

Figure 17-6 Assembly output for another version of the reorder-listing program (part 1 of 9)

```
LOC    OBJECT CODE    ADDR1 ADDR2   STMT  SOURCE STATEMENT

0000AA 5810 39E6      009E8          46+* IOCS AND DEVICE INDEPENDENT I/O - PUT - 5745-SC-IOX - REL. 29.0   05000029
0000AE 5800 39EE      009F0          47+        L     1,=A(PRTOUT)          GET DTF TABLE ADDRESS           15000025
0000B2 58F1 0010      00010          48+        L     0,=A(HDGLINE2)        GET WORK AREA ADDRESS           46000025
0000B6 45EF 000C      0000C          49+        L     15,16(1)              GET LOGIC MODULE ADDRESS    3-5 54000025
                                     50+        BAL   14,12(15)             BRANCH TO PUT ROUTINE       3-5 55000025
                                     51         PUT   PRTOUT,HDGLINE3       PRINT THIRD HEADING LINE        05000029
0000BA 5810 39E6      009E8          52+* IOCS AND DEVICE INDEPENDENT I/O - PUT - 5745-SC-IOX - REL. 29.0   05000029
0000BE 5800 39F2      009F4          53+        L     1,=A(PRTOUT)          GET DTF TABLE ADDRESS           15000025
0000C2 58F1 0010      00010          54+        L     0,=A(HDGLINE3)        GET WORK AREA ADDRESS           46000025
0000C6 45EF 000C      0000C          55+        L     15,16(1)              GET LOGIC MODULE ADDRESS    3-5 54000025
                                     56+        BAL   14,12(15)             BRANCH TO PUT ROUTINE       3-5 55000025
0000CA 0000 0000 0000                57         ZAP   LINECNT,P'0'          RESET LINE COUNT TO ZERO        00002900
              *** ERROR ***
0000D0 92F0 38A4      008A6          58 PRTDET  MVI   PRTDCTL,C'0'          MOVE ZERO TO ASA CONTROL BYTE   00003000
                                     59         PUT   PRTOUT,PRTDETL        PRINT DETAIL LINE               00003100
0000D4 5810 39E6      009E8          60+* IOCS AND DEVICE INDEPENDENT I/O - PUT - 5745-SC-IOX - REL. 29.0   05000029
0000D8 5800 39F6      009F8          61+PRTDET  L     1,=A(PRTOUT)          GET DTF TABLE ADDRESS           15000025
0000DC 58F1 0010      00010          62+        L     0,=A(PRTDETL)         GET WORK AREA ADDRESS           46000025
0000E0 45EF 000C      0000C          63+        L     15,16(1)              GET LOGIC MODULE ADDRESS    3-5 54000025
                                     64+        BAL   14,12(15)             BRANCH TO PUT ROUTINE       3-5 55000025
0000E4 0000 0000 0000                65         AP    LINECNT,=P'1'         ADD ONE TO LINE COUNT           00003200
              *** ERROR ***
0000EA 9240 38A4      008A6          66         MVI   PRTDCTL,C' '          MOVE BLANK TO ASA CONTROL BYTE  00003300
0000EE 47F0 3014      00016          67 INVEOF  B     READINV                                               00003400
0000F2 DE06 392A 39C4 0092C          68         ED    CNTPATRN,COUNT        EDIT COUNT                      00003500
                                     69         PUT   PRTOUT,CNTLINE        PRINT COUNT LINE                00003600
0000F8 5810 39E6      009E8          70+* IOCS AND DEVICE INDEPENDENT I/O - PUT - 5745-SC-IOX - REL. 29.0   05000029
0000FC 5800 39FA      009FC          71+        L     1,=A(PRTOUT)          GET DTF TABLE ADDRESS           15000025
000100 58F1 0010      00010          72+        L     0,=A(CNTLINE)         GET WORK AREA ADDRESS           46000025
000104 45EF 000C      0000C          73+        L     15,16(1)              GET LOGIC MODULE ADDRESS    3-5 54000025
                                     74+        BAL   14,12(15)             BRANCH TO PUT ROUTINE       3-5 55000025
                                     75         CLOSE INVMAST,PRTOUT                                        00003700
                                     76+* IOCS AND DEVICE INDEPENDANT I/O - CLOSE - 5745-SC-IOX - REL. 28.0 08100028
000108                               77+        CNOP  0,4                                                   20000025
000108                               78+        DC    0F'0'                                                 22000025
000108 4110 39D6      009D8          79+        LA    1,=C'$$BCLOSE'                                        46000025
00010C 4500 3116      00118          80+IJJC0008 BAL  0,*+4+4*(3-1)                                         54000025
000110 00000128                      81+        DC    A(INVMAST)                                            64000025
000114 000001C8                      82+        DC    A(PRTOUT)                                             64000025
000118 0A02                          83+        SVC   2                                                     74000025
                                     84         EOJ                                                         00003800
                                     85+* SUPVR COMMN MACROS - EOJ - 5745-SC-SUP - REL. 28.0                40000028
00011A 0A0E                          86+        SVC   14                                                    50000025
                                     87 * THE INVENTORY FILE DEFINITION                                    000003900
                                     88 INVMAST DTFSD BLKSIZE=500,                                         X00004000
                                                     RECFORM=FIXBLK,                                       X00004100
                                                     RECSIZE=50,                                           X00004200
                                                     IOAREA1=INVIO1,                                       X00004300
                                                     IOAREA2=INVIO2,                                       X00004400
                                                     WORKA=YES,                                            X00004500
                                                     EOFADDR=INVEOF,                                       X00004600
```

Figure 17-6   Assembly output for another version of the reorder-listing program (part 2 of 9)

```
LOC     OBJECT CODE        ADDR1 ADDR2  STMT   SOURCE STATEMENT                    DOS/VSE ASSEMBLER 15.03   86-01-06        PAGE    4

                                        89* SEQUENTIAL DISK IOCS - DTFSD - 5745-SC-DSK (G98)   @D37ZDHK  01450000
                                               DEVADDR=SYS008                                                      00004700
                                        90*,NO EOFADDR SPEC.SET TO *
                                        91*,NO WORKAREA OR IOREG SPEC..IOREG SET TO REG 2
0011C   00000000                        92+          DC    0D'0'                                          @D35DE98  38140035
00120   00000000                        93+          DC    F'0'             RESERVED FOR IBM USE          @D35DE98  38147035
00124   000001B0                        94+          DC    A(IJGZ0010)      VERSION 3 DTF AREA POINTER    @D35DE98  38154035
00128                                   95+          DC    0D'0'                                                    39000025
00128   0000800400040000                96+INVMAST   DC    X'0000800040000'  CCB                                    39300025
0012E   FF                              97+          DC    AL1(255)         LOGICAL UNIT CLASS                       39400025
0012F   FF                              98+          DC    AL1(255)         LOGICAL UNIT NUMBER                      39500025
00130   0000019C                        99+          DC    A(IJGC0010)      CCB-CCW ADDRESS                          39600025
00134   0000000C                       100+          DC    4X'00'           CCB-ST BYTE,CSW CCW ADDRESS  3-3         39700025
00138   00                             101+          DC    AL1(0)                                                   39800002
00139   000000                         102+          DC    X'000000'        LOGIC MODULE ADDRESS         @D35DE98    39800002
0013C   20                             103+          DC    X'20'            DTF TYPE                     @D36KE97    39820002
0013D   4A                             104+          DC    AL1(74)          OPEN/CLOSE INDICATORS                    54800025
00145   00                             105+INVMASTS  DC    CL7'INVMAST'     FILENAME                                 55200025
00146   0000000C0000                   106+          DC    X'00'            INDICATE 2311                @DL2W720    55958034
0014C   0000                           107+          DC    6X'00'           BCCHHR ADDR OF F1 LABEL IN VTOC          56100025
0014E   08                             108+          DC    2X'00'           VOL SEQ NUMBER                           56200025
0014F   00                             109+          DC    X'08'            OPEN COMMUNICATIONS BYTE                 56300025
00150   00                             110+          DC    X'00'            XTENT SEQ NO OF CURRENT EXTENT           56400025
00151   000151                         111+          DC    X'00'            XTENT SEQ NO LAST XTENT OPENED           56500025
00154   20                             112+          DC    AL3(*)           USER'S LABEL ADDRESS                     56700025
00155   0003EC                         113+          DC    X'20'            DATAFILE VERSION 3 BIT       @D35DE98    57068035
00158   8000000C                       114+          DC    AL3(INVIO2)      ADDRESS OF 2ND. IOAREA       @DL30SMD    57100030
0015C   0000                           115+          DC    X'8000000C'      CCHH ADDR OF USER LABEL TRACK            57400025
0015E   00000000                       116+          DC    2X'00'           LOWER HEAD LIMIT                         57500025
00162   0000                           117+          DC    4X'00'           XTENT UPPER LIMIT                        57600025
00164   0000FF00                       118+INVMASTS  DC    2X'00'           SEEK ADDRESS-BB                          57700025
00168   00                             119+          DC    X'0000FF00'      SEARCH ADDRESS-CCHH                      57800025
00169   000169                         120+          DC    X'00'            RECORD NUMBER                            57900025
0016C   00000000                       121+          DC    AL3(*)           EOF ADDRESS                              58100025
00170   06                             122+          DC    4X'00'           CCHH CONTROL FIELD           3-2         58500025
00171   04                             123+          DC    AL1(6)           R   CONTROL FIELD                        58700025
00172   01F3                           124+          DC    B'00000100'                                               59000025
00174   FFFFFFFF                       125+          DC    H'499'           SIZE OF BLOCK-1                          59200025
00179   000000                         126+          DC    5X'FF'           CCHHR BUCKET                 3-7         60100025
0017C   5821 0058         00058        127+          DC    3X'00'                                                   60500025
00180   00001FE                        128+          L     2,88(1)          LOAD USER'S IOREG            4-0         60800027
00184   00000032                       129+          DC    A(INVIO1)        DEBLOCKER-INITIAL POINTER                61700025
00188   000003EB                       130+          DC    F'50'            DEBLOCKER-RECORD SIZE        4-0         62700027
0018C   0A                             131+          DC    A(INVIO1+500-1)  DEBLOCKER LIMIT                          63600025
0018D   000000                         132+          DC    AL1(10)          LOGICAL INDICATORS                       63700025
00190   0700016240000006               133+          DC    AL3(0)           USER'S ERROR ROUTINE         4-0         63800025
00198   3100016440000005               134+IJGC0010  CCW   X'31',*-46,64,6  SEEK                                     63900025
001A0   0800019800000000               135+          CCW   8,*-52,64,5      SEARCH ID EQUAL                          64000025
001A8   06000IF8000001F4               136+          CCW   8,*-8,0,0        TIC                          4-0         64400027
                                       137+          CCW   6,INVIO1,0,500   READ DATA
```

Figure 17-6   Assembly output for another version of the reorder-listing program (part 3 of 9)

PAGE   5

DOS/VSE ASSEMBLER 15.03   86-01-06

LOC	OBJECT CODE	ADDR1	ADDR2	STMT	SOURCE STATEMENT			
		001B0		138+IJGZ0010	EQU	*		@D35DE98 74835035
0001B0	8C			139+	DC	AL1(140)	VERSION 3 FLAGS	@D35DE98 74840035
0001B1	000000			140+	DC	AL3(0)	VERSION 3 FLAGS	@D35DE98 74850035
0001B4	00000000			141+	DC	AL4(0)	CISIZE IF PRESENT	@D35DE98 74860035
0001B8	00000000			142+	DC	AL4(0)	PHYSICAL BLOCK SIZE	@D356EE3 74870035
0001BC	0000			143+	DC	AL2(0)	NUMBER OF PHYSICAL	@D356EE3 74920035
				144+*			BLOCKS/CI	@D356EE3 74970035
0001BE	00			145+	DC	AL1(0)	NUMBER OF PHYSICAL	@D356EE3 75020035
				146+*			BLOCKS/TRACK	@D356EE3 75070035
0001BF	00			147+	DC	AL1(0)	UPPER LIMIT RECD NUMBER	@D356EE3 75120035
0001C0	00000000			148+	DC	A(0)	DATA SECURITY PLIST PTR	@D350EE3 75170035
		001C4		149+IJJZ0010	EQU	*		@D35DE98 75270035
				150	* THE PRINTER FILE DEFINITION			
				151	PRTOUT DTFPR BLKSIZE=133,			X00004800
						IOAREA2=PRTIO2,		X00004900
						WORKA=YES,		X00005100
						DEVADDR=SYSLST,		X00005200
						CTLCHR=ASA		X00005300
				152+* IOCS AND DEV INDEPENDENT I/O DTFPR 5745-SC-IOX - REL.1.3			@DY28915 02870000
				153+0,NO IOAREA1 SPECIFIED. SET TO *			
0001C4	00000000			154+	DC	0D'0'		60000025
0001C8	0000800000000000			155+PRTOUT	DC	X'000080000000000'	RES. COUNT, COM. BYTES BTS JJ	61510028
0001CE	00			156+	DC	AL1(0)	LOGICAL UNIT CLASS	70000025
0001CF	03			157+	DC	AL1(3)	LOGICAL UNIT	70200028
0001D0	000001F0			158+	DC	A(*+32)	CCW ADDR.	71000028
0001D4	00000000			159+	DC	4X'00'	CCB-ST BYTE,CSW CCW ADDRESS JJ	71200028
0001D8	00			160+	DC	AL1(0)	SWITCH 3 4-0	71750027
0001D9	000000			161+	DC	VL3(IJDFAZIW)	ADDR OF LOGIC MODUL3-8 JJ	76800025
0001DD	08			162+	DC	X'08'	DTF TYPE (PRINTER) JJ	77580028
0001DD	36			163+	DC	AL1(54)	SWITCHES	77600025
0001DE	09			164+	DC	AL1(9)	NORMAL COMM. CODE 4-0	78000027
0001DF	09			165+	DC	AL1(9)	CONTROL COMM. CODE 4-0	78400027
0001E0	000001E1			166+	DC	A(*+1)	ADDRESS OF DATA IN IOAREA1	78800025
0001E4	00000000			167+	DC	4X'00'	BUCKET 3-5	84000025
0001E8	0700			168+	NOPR	0	PUT LENGTH IN REG12 (ONLY UNDEF.	84800025
0001EA	4700 0000	00000		169+	NOP	0	LOAD USER POINTER REG	86400025
0001EE	0000			170+	DC	2X'00'	NOT USED 3-5	90400027
0001F0	0900006620000084			171+	CCW	9,PRTIO2+1,X'20',133-1	4-0	92000025
		001F8		172+IJJZ0011	EQU	*		00005500
				173	* THE DATA DEFINITIONS FOR THE TWO INVENTORY FILE I/O AREAS			00005600
0001F8				174	INVIO1	DS	CL500	00005700
0003EC				175	INVIO2	DS	CL500	00005800
				176	* THE DATA DEFINITIONS FOR THE TWO PRINTER OUTPUT AREAS			00005900
0005E0				177	PRTIO1	DS	CL133	00006000
000665				178	PRTIO2	DS	CL133	00006100
				179	* THE DATA DEFINITIONS FOR THE INVENTORY FILE WORK AREA			00006200
0006EA				180	INVWRKA	DS	0CL50	00006300
0006EA				181	INVITNBR	DS	CL5	00006400
0006EF				182	INVITDES	DS	CL20	00006500
				183		DS	C5	

*** ERROR ***

Figure 17-6   Assembly output for another version of the reorder-listing program (part 4 of 9)

```
LOC      OBJECT CODE        ADDR1 ADDR2   STMT  SOURCE STATEMENT

000703                                    184   INVPRICE  DS   CL5                              00006600
000708                                    185   INVRORDPT DS   CL5                              00006700
00070D                                    186   INVONHND  DS   CL5                              00006800
000712                                    187   INVONORD  DS   CL5                              00006900
                                          188   *    THE DATA DEFINITIONS FOR THE PRINTER      00007000
                                                      HEADING LINES
000717                                    189   HDGLINE1  DS   0CL133                           00007100
000717  F1                                190             DC   C'1'                             00007200
000718  4040404040404040                  191             DC   24C' '                           00007300
000730  D9C5D6D9C4C5D940                  192             DC   C'REORDER LISTING'               00007400
00073F  4040404040404040                  193             DC   93C' '                           00007500
00079C                                    194   HDGLINE2  DS   0CL133                           00007600
00079C  F0                                195             DC   C'0'                             00007700
00079D  40C9E3C5D4404040                  196             DC   C' ITEM          ITEM      UNIT  X00007800
                                                               REORDER'                          00007900
0007DC  4040404040404040                  197             DC   69C' '                           00008000
000821                                    198   HDGLINE3  DS   0CL133                           00008100
000821  40                                199             DC   C' '                             00008200
000822  4040D5D54B404040                  200             DC   C' NO.     DESCRIPTION    PRICE  AVAILABLEX00008300
                                                               POINT'                            00008400
000860  4040404040404040                  201             DC   70C' '                           00008500
                                          202   *    THE DATA DEFINITIONS FOR THE PRINTER      00008600
                                                      DETAIL LINE
0008A6                                    203   PRTDETL   DS   0CL133                           00008700
0008A6                                    204   PRTDCTL   DS   CL1                              00008800
0008A7                                    205   PRTITNBR  DS   CL6                              00008900
0008AD  40404040                          206             DC   5C' '                            00009000
0008B2                                    207   PRTITDES  DS   CL20                             00009100
0008C6  40404040                          208             DC   4C' '                            00009200
0008CA                                    209   PRTPRICE  DS   CL7                              00009300
0008D1  40404040                          210             DC   4C' '                            00009400
0008D5                                    211   PRTAVAIL  DS   CL6                              00009500
0008DB  40404040                          212             DC   4C' '                            00009600
0008DF                                    213   PRTORDPT  DS   CL6                              00009700
0008E5  4040404040404040                  214             DC   70C' '                           00009800
                                          215   *    THE DATA DEFINITIONS FOR THE COUNT LINE   00009900
00092B                                    216   CNTLINE   DS   0CL133                           00010000
00092B  60                                217             DC   C'-_'                            00010100
00092C  4020206B202020                    218   CNTPATRN  DC   X'402020 6B202020'               00010200
000933  40D9C5C3D6D9C4E2                  219             DC   C' RECORDS IN THE INPUT FILE'    00010300
00094D  4040404040404040                  220             DC   99C' '                           00010400
                                          221   *    THE DATA DEFINITIONS FOR THE WORK FIELDS  00010500
0009B0  4020202020202020                  222   PATTERN1  DC   X'402020202020'                  00010600
0009B6  402020214B2020                    223   PATTERN2  DC   X'402020 214B2020'               00010700
0009BD                                    224   WRKAVAIL  DS   PL3                              00010800
0009C0                                    225   WRKONORD  DS   PL3                              00010900
        *** ERROR ***                     226   WRKORDPT  DC   PL3                              00011000
0009C3                                    227   PACKAREA  DS   PL3                              00011100
0009C6  00000C                            228   COUNT     DC   PL3'0'                           00011200
        *** ERROR ***                     229   LINECNT   DC   '50'                             00011300

                            00000         230             END  BEGIN                            00011400
```

Figure 17-6   Assembly output for another version of the reorder-listing program (part 5 of 9)

```
LOC    OBJECT CODE      ADDR1 ADDR2  STMT  SOURCE STATEMENT

0009D0 5B5BC2D6D7C5D540                231          =C'$$BOPEN '
0009D8 5B5BC2C3D3D6E2C5                232          =C'$$BCLOSE'
0009E0 00000128                        233          =A(INVMAST)
0009E4 00000000                        234          =A(INVWORKA)
       *** ERROR ***
0009E8 000001C8                        235          =A(PRTOUT)
0009EC 00000717                        236          =A(HDGLINE1)
0009F0 0000079C                        237          =A(HDGLINE2)
0009F4 00000821                        238          =A(HDGLINE3)
0009F8 000008A6                        239          =A(PRTDETL)
0009FC 0000092B                        240          =A(CNTLINE)
000A00 050C                            241          =P'50'
000A02 1C                              242          =P'1'
```

Figure 17-6   Assembly output for another version of the reorder-listing program (part 6 of 9)

CROSS-REFERENCE

SYMBOL	LEN	ID	VALUE	DEFN	REFERENCES			
BEGIN	00002	001	000000	00002	0230			
CNTLINE	00133	001	000928	00216	0240			
CNTPATRN	00007	001	00092C	00218	0068			
COUNT	00003	001	0009C6	00228	0019	0068		
HDGLINE1	00133	001	000717	00189	0236			
HDGLINE2	00133	001	00079C	00194	0237			
HDGLINE3	00133	001	000821	00198	0238			
IJGC0010	00008	001	000190	00134	0099			
IJGZ0010	00001	001	0001B0	00138	0094			
INVIO1	00500	001	0001F8	00174	0129	0131	0137	
INVIO2	00500	001	0003EC	00175	0114			
INVITDES	00020	001	0006EF	00182	0029			
INVITNBR	00005	001	0006EA	00181	0026			
INVMAST	00006	001	000128	00096	0010	0081	0233	
INVONHND	00005	001	00070D	00186	0020			
INVONORD	00005	001	000712	00187	0021			
INVORDPT	00005	001	000708	00185	0023			
INVPRICE	00005	001	000703	00184	0030			
INVWORKA	*****		UNDEFINED	*****	0234			
LINECNT	*****		UNDEFINED	*****	0037	0057	0065	
PACKAREA	00003	001	0009C3	00227	0026	0028	0030	0032
PATTERN1	00006	001	0009B0	00222	0027	0035		
PATTERN2	00007	001	0009B6	00223	0031			
PRTAVAIL	00006	001	0008D5	00211	0033	0034		
PRTDCTL	00001	001	0008A6	00204	0058	0066		
PRTDET	00004	001	0000D4	00061	0038			
PRTDETL	00133	001	0008A6	00203	0239			
PRTIO2	00133	001	000665	00178	0171			
PRTITDES	00020	001	0008B2	00207	0029			
PRTITNBR	00006	001	0008A7	00205	0027	0028		
PRTORDPT	00006	001	0008DF	00213	0035	0036		
PRTOUT	00006	001	0001C8	00155	0011	0082	0235	
PRTPRICE	00007	001	0008CA	00209	0031	0032		
READINV	00004	001	000016	00015	0025	0067		
READIV	*****		UNDEFINED	*****	0025			
WRKAVAIL	00003	001	0009BD	00224	0020	0022	0024	0034
WRKONORD	00003	001	0009C0	00225	0021	0022		
WRKORDPT	*****		UNDEFINED	*****	0023	0024	0036	
=A(CNTLINE)	00004	001	0009FC	00240	0072			
=A(HDGLINE1)	00004	001	0009EC	00236	0042			
=A(HDGLINE2)	00004	001	0009F0	00237	0048			
=A(HDGLINE3)	00004	001	0009F4	00238	0054			
=A(INVMAST)	00004	001	0009E0	00233	0015			
=A(INVWORKA)	00004	001	0009E4	00234	0016			
=A(PRTOUT)								

Figure 17-6   Assembly output for another version of the reorder-listing program (part 7 of 9)

CROSS-REFERENCE

SYMBOL	LEN	ID	VALUE	DEFN	REFERENCES			
=A(PRTDETL)								
	00004	001	0009E8	00235	0041	0047	0053	0061 0071
=C'$$BOPEN '								
	00004	001	0009F8	00239	0062			
=C'$$BCLOSE'								
	00008	001	0009D0	00231	0008			
=P'1'								
	00008	001	0009D8	00232	0079	0065		
	00001	001	000A02	00242	0019			
=P'50'								
	00002	001	000A00	00241	0037			

Figure 17-6   Assembly output for another version of the reorder-listing program (part 8 of 9)

DIAGNOSTICS AND STATISTICS

STMNT	ERROR NO.	MESSAGE
23	IPK156	SYMBOL 'WRKORDPT' UNDEFINED
24	IPK156	SYMBOL 'WRKORDPT' UNDEFINED
25	IPK156	SYMBOL 'READIV' UNDEFINED
33	IPK122	INVALID DELIMITER, ','
36	IPK156	SYMBOL 'WRKORDPT' UNDEFINED
37	IPK156	SYMBOL 'LINECNT' UNDEFINED
57	IPK156	SYMBOL 'LINECNT' UNDEFINED
57	IPK116	INVALID SELF-DEFINING TERM, 'P'0''
65	IPK156	SYMBOL 'LINECNT' UNDEFINED
90	IPK216	MNOTE GENERATED
91	IPK216	MNOTE GENERATED
153	IPK216	MNOTE GENERATED
183	IPK112	INVALID CHARACTER IN CONSTANT, '5'
226	IPK128	CONSTANT FIELD MISSING OR PRECEDED BY INVALID FIELD, ' '
229	IPK123	INVALID TYPE SPECIFICATION, ''50''
234	IPK156	SYMBOL 'INVWORKA' UNDEFINED

THE FOLLOWING MACRO NAMES HAVE BEEN FOUND IN MACRO INSTRUCTIONS
OPEN   GET   PUT   CLOSE   EOJ   DTFSD   DTFPR

OPTIONS FOR THIS ASSEMBLY - ALIGN, LIST, SXREF, LINK, RLD, NODECK, NOEDECK

THE ASSEMBLER WAS RUN IN 7833480 BYTES
END OF ASSEMBLY

Figure 17-6   Assembly output for another version of the reorder-listing program (part 9 of 9)

DISCUSSION   When you correct diagnostics, you normally take the diagnostics in sequence and correct operation codes and operands as necessary. But if you come to a message that you can't figure out, you can skip it at first since one of the later diagnostics may indicate its cause. If after going through all diagnostics, there are still a few you can't figure out, you might try reassembling the program with all other errors corrected. On some occasions, this will solve your problem because the problem diagnostics were caused by errors you have already corrected.

Terminology   external symbol dictionary
assembly listing
location counter
cross-reference listing
diagnostics and statistics listing
diagnostic listing

Objective   Given the assembly output for a program including diagnostics, correct the source code so it will assemble without errors.

Chapter 18

How to test and debug
an assembler language program

When you *test* a program, you try to find all the errors the program contains. When you *debug* a program, you try to correct the errors that you found when you tested it. In topic 1 of this chapter, you'll learn a general procedure for testing a program. Then, in topic 2, you'll learn some specific techniques for debugging a program. You can read this chapter any time after you complete chapter 5. But the best time is probably right before you test your first assembler language program or right after you discover your first bugs.

TOPIC 1   How to test a program

In general, programs are tested in three phases: unit test, systems test, and acceptance test. The *unit test* is the programmer's test of his or her own program. In this phase of testing, you should do your best to make sure that all the modules in your program function properly. Since you know your program better than anyone else, you are the person most qualified to test it.

The *system test* is designed to test the interfaces between the programs within a system. For instance, if you're writing an update program, the system test will determine whether or not the edit programs create transaction files that are acceptable to your program. But if the test data used for the edit programs is incomplete, the output from the edit programs will be an inadequate test of your update program. So you can't rely on the system test to test all aspects of your program.

The *acceptance test* is designed to determine whether the programs in a system perform the way that the user intended them to. Although the data for this test should be developed by a creative person with plenty of testing experience, this isn't always the case. So you can't count on this phase of testing to test all aspects of your program either. To a large extent, then, the burden of proof is on the programmer in the unit test.

Although this book isn't designed to teach you precise procedures for unit testing a production program, I would like to give you a few ideas that will help you test your programs more effectively. Most important, we recommend that you take the time to plan your test runs. All too often, it seems, programmers test their programs without any planning. As a result, their programs are *not* tested by all the possible combinations of data, and they are put into production with dozens of bugs.

It's relatively easy, though, to create a test plan for a program. Once you have one, you are more likely to create test data that adequately tests your program. Then, you will have a solid basis for believing that your program is free of bugs after you test it on the data you have created. In general, if your test plan is good, you are likely to do an adequate job of testing. If it isn't, you most likely won't do an adequate job of testing.

How to create a test plan

Before you start your *test plan*, you should review your program and list all the conditions that you must test for. To do this, you should review your program specifications, your design document, and even your assembler language code, writing down any conditions that come to mind as you review these items. Then, if you create test data that tests for all of these conditions, you increase the likelihood that your program will be adequately tested.

Figure 18-1 is a *condition list* that I developed for the refined reorder-listing program of chapter 5. Although making a list like this can be a laborious job if the program is large, you really have no other choice. If your job as programmer is to prove that your program works for all possible conditions, you must know what those conditions are. As you will see, however, your test data usually won't have to be extensive just because your list of conditions is long.

After you have made your list of conditions, you are ready to create the test plan. Specifically, you want to decide in what sequence the conditions should be tested. The intent here is to discover the major problems first. So, you should start by testing the main functions and conditions of the program. Then, once you are satisfied that they are working properly, you can go on to test the less critical conditions.

Figure 18-2 shows a test plan for the refined reorder-listing program. Although this program is extremely limited, I think it will give you an idea of what a test plan should look like. As you can see, I've decided that I will only need to have two test runs. The first one will test the main function of the program. It will also test the main condition: whether available is equal to, is less than, or is greater than the reorder point. Then, the second test run can test all of the remaining functions and conditions, including page overflow.

You should notice in figure 18-2 that I didn't provide for every condition that is listed in figure 18-1. When I reflected upon them, I decided that I didn't need to test the program using an empty master file since this condition shouldn't occur in the first place and since it shouldn't cause any problems if it does occur no matter how the program handles it. When you create a test plan, you should consider every condition on your condition list even though you may decide that you don't have to test for some of them. If you decide *not* to test a condition, you should have a good reason for your decision.

As you create your test plan, you should also decide where the test data will come from. Will you code the data yourself and create the proper input files using utilities? Will you use a test data generator? Can you copy some "live" data for your test files? Does another program create test data that you can use? Here again, you should make these decisions in a thoughtful, controlled manner.

How to create test data

As a general rule, the *test data* you use in your first test runs for a program should be low in volume, often just a couple of records for each input file. That way, it's relatively easy to figure out what output your program should produce. For instance, the three records listed in figure 18-3 are enough for the first phase of testing shown in the test plan in figure 18-2. Record 1 will cause a greater-than comparison of available and reorder point, record 2 will cause a less-than comparison, and record 3 will cause an equal comparison.

Program: REORDLST	Page: 1
Designer: Anne Prince	Date: 07-31-85

Test conditions

1. Are all records in the inventory master file processed?

2. What happens if the master file is empty?

3. Does the program branch properly depending on the relationship between available stock and reorder point?

4. Are all the fields on the report edited properly?

5. Does page overflow work properly?

6. Do heading lines print properly?

7. Are the correct number of lines printed on each page?

8. Is the spacing between lines on the reorder listing okay?

9. Is the total count correct?

Figure 18-1   A list of test conditions for the reorder-listing program

Program: REORDLST Prepare Reorder Listing		Page: 1
Designer: Anne Prince		Date: 07-31-85
Test phase	**Data**	**Data source**
1. Main branching logic	Three inventory master records; one with available = reorder point, one with available > reorder point, and one with available < reorder point	Self
2. Page overflow	Enough inventory master records to cause page overflow	Test data generator

Figure 18-2   A test plan for the reorder-listing program

	Item number	Description	Unit price	On hand quantity	On order quantity	Reorder point
Record 1	00101	GENERATOR	12345	00070	00050	00100
Record 2	00103	HEATER SOLENOID	98765	00034	00000	00050
Record 3	95432	AAAAAAAAAAAAAAAAAAAA	00005	15000	05000	20000

Figure 18-3   Test data for the first test run for the reorder-listing program

After a program has been tested on small volumes of data, the program can be tested on a volume of data that is large enough to test all the conditions that may occur. In the case of the reorder-listing program, for example, the input file must contain enough records to force page overflow. If a program is large, the test plan may require several low-volume tests and several high-volume tests.

If you don't know what the output of a test run should be, you can't tell if your program worked properly. So, after you create the test data for a test run, you should figure out what the output should be. In some cases, doing this will also help you uncover problems in your specifications and program design.

How to document a test run

After you have created the necessary test data for each test phase, you are ready to perform the test run. Then, after each execution of a test run, you compare the actual output of the test run with the expected output. If the program involves tape or disk input or output, appropriate listings of the input and output files must be made before and after the test run. In a disk-update run, for example, the contents of the disk file must be printed before testing and after testing to see what changes were made in the file. In a disk-to-printer program, though, only the printed output usually needs to be checked because you already know what data the disk file contains. In any event, if the actual output disagrees with the expected output, you must find the cause of the error, change the source code, and test again.

After a test run, you should document it so you can review your test runs if that should become necessary. In some shops, in fact, you may be required to document each of your test runs. In general, your documentation for a test run should consist of the items listed in figure 18-4. Because a typical programmer works on more than one program at a time, this documentation can save a considerable amount of backtracking and confusion.

The documentation for a test run

1.   The assembly listing for the test run marked with changes that should be made for the next test run

2.   A listing of each input file used for the test run

3.   The printed output for the test run

4.   A listing of each file that is created or updated by the test run

---

Figure 18-4   The documentation for a test run

Discussion   Normally, in a programming course, you don't have to develop your own test data. Instead, it is provided for you. That way, everyone in the class should get the same test results if they write the program correctly. This makes it easy for your instructor to check your work. Nevertheless, you should know how to create test data for an assembler language program so you can do production work later on.

The point of this topic, of course, is to get you to test your production programs in an orderly fashion. If you take the time to develop condition lists and test plans before you start to test your programs, we're confident that you'll test your programs more effectively.

Terminology   unit test
system test
acceptance test
test plan
condition list
test data

Objective   Given a program's specifications and its design document, create a test plan and test data for it.

TOPIC 2   How to debug a program

When you test a program, there are two possible outcomes. First, the program can run to completion. This is often referred to as a *normal termination*, a *normal end-of-job*, or a *normal EOJ*. Second, the program can be cancelled. This is referred to as an *abnormal termination*, or an *abend*. In the remainder of this chapter, I'll show you how to debug programs that end normally or abnormally.

HOW TO DEBUG A PROGRAM THAT ENDS IN A NORMAL TERMINATION

If the program runs to a normal EOJ, you start by comparing the actual output with expected output. To illustrate, suppose the reorder-listing program runs to completion using the test data in figure 18-3. Suppose also that figure 18-5 gives the actual output of the test run along with the expected output. If you compare the two, you can see that the program has some bugs. In fact, I've highlighted them. Specifically, the unit price isn't edited correctly in the second detail line; the second detail line shouldn't have printed at all since available equals reorder point; and the count of the number of records in the file hasn't printed.

To correct these bugs, you analyze the code that has produced the output, because something must be wrong with it. Since the unit price in figure 18-5 prints correctly in the first detail line, there's probably some minor problem with its edit pattern such as a misplaced or missing significance starter. Since the second detail line prints when it shouldn't, there must be something wrong with the compare and branch instructions that determine when a line is to be printed. And, since the count doesn't print at all, there must be something wrong with the way it's accumulated or the way it is printed.

Since you can encounter so many different kinds of bugs when you test a program, I can't give you a precise procedure for correcting them. As I see it, this is an analytical part of the programmer's job that can't easily be taught. Although certain types of bugs seem to repeat themselves from one program to the next, some bugs are so abstruse that they baffle the most experienced programmers.

How to use debugging instructions and the PDUMP macro   If a program is long or its calculations are complex, it can be extremely difficult to figure out why the actual output isn't what you expected. Then, you may want to add *debugging instructions* to your program.

A debugging instruction is an instruction that you put into your program temporarily to help you figure out why the program isn't working correctly. For instance, you can add debugging instructions that print messages as a program executes. These messages can show the contents of

Expected printer output for the test run

REORDER LISTING

ITEM NO.	DESCRIPTION	UNIT PRICE	AVAILABLE	REORDER POINT
103	HEATER SOLENOID	123.45	34	50

1 RECORDS IN THE FILE

Actual printer output for the test run

REORDER LISTING

ITEM NO.	DESCRIPTION	UNIT PRICE	AVAILABLE	REORDER POINT
103	HEATER SOLENOID	123.45	34	50
95432	AAAAAAAAAAAAAAAAAAAAA	5	65000	65000

▨ RECORDS IN THE FILE

Figure 18-5 The expected output and the actual output for a test run that ends
in a normal program termination

selected storage fields or indicate what routine is being executed. This data
in turn can help you find the source instructions that have caused the
bugs. After the errors have been corrected, you remove the extra
statements from the source code, reassemble it, and test again.

One of the instructions that you may want to add to your program as
a debugging aid is the PDUMP macro as described in chapter 6. This
macro lets you print the contents of a portion of your program in storage
dump format. After you read the rest of this chapter and topic 2 of chapter
6, you will be able to use this macro in your debugging efforts. I'm sure
you will find it useful.

HOW TO DEBUG A PROGRAM
THAT ENDS IN AN ABNORMAL TERMINATION

An abnormal program termination can also be referred to as a *program
check*. A program check indicates that the program tried to do something
invalid like trying to execute the add decimal (AP) instruction on EBCDIC
data. When a program check occurs, you must (1) find the instruction that
led to the program check, (2) find the cause of the error, and (3) correct it.

To illustrate the analysis of a program check, I will use the reorder-
listing program. In the source code of this program, I have included a

minor error that will cause an abend during a test run that uses the test data in figure 18-3. Although the expected printer output is shown in figure 18-5, the program prints nothing during this test run.

Figure 18-6 shows the output of the test run. The first seven parts of this figure are the assembly listing and the cross-reference listing. Then, part 8 is the *linkage editor map* (or just *link edit map*) that was created by the linkage editor. Part 9 is the *program check message*. And parts 10 through 11 are the *storage dump*. The storage dump, also known as a *storage printout*, lists the contents of storage at the time of the program check.

How to find the instruction that caused a program check

To find the instruction that has caused a program check, you use the program check message, the link edit map, and the assembly listing.

The program check message   The program check message tells you (1) the location of the instruction that was being executed when the program was cancelled and (2) the cause of the cancellation. The program check message in part 9 of figure 18-6 tells you that the instruction that caused the program check is located at hex address 37908 and that the cause is DATA EXCEPTION.

Some of the most common causes of program checks are listed in figure 18-7. These should be adequate for most of the program checks you'll experience as part of this course. Later on, if you need to refer to the complete list, you'll find it in *Principles of Operation* (GA22-7070 for the 4300 processors).

As figure 18-7 explains, *data exception* indicates that an operand has invalid data like EBCDIC data for a packed decimal instruction. In contrast, an *operation exception* indicates that the operation code of an instruction is invalid. This can happen, for example, if a branch instruction specifies a data name instead of an instruction label. An *addressing exception* occurs when an instruction tries to address an area in storage outside of the program area. A *decimal overflow exception* occurs when a decimal arithmetic instruction leads to a result larger than the receiving field can hold. And a *decimal divide exception* occurs when the quotient of a decimal divide instruction is larger than the receiving field can hold. By far the most common of the exceptions, though, is the data exception.

The link edit map   To find the instruction that caused the program check, the programmer refers to the link edit map. The link edit map (part 8 in figure 18-6) tells you where your program has been loaded into storage. The LOCORE and HICORE columns give the lowest address and the highest address in hex used by the program. In figure 18-6, these are addresses 37878 and 38369.

In the LABEL column, the names of all *object modules* that make up the complete program (or *phase*) are given. In this case, the phase consists of a module named REORDLST (the name used in the START statement of the reorder-listing program) plus a module named IJDFAZIW (the name of an I/O module). This I/O module is used by REORDLST to control its printing operations.

The LOADED column gives the starting address of each module and the REL-FR gives the *relocation factor* for each module. The relocation factor relates the actual storage locations of your program to the location counter values given in the assembly listing. The actual address of any instruction or data field in storage is the sum of the relocation factor and the location counter value.

How to calculate the location counter value of the instruction that caused a program check   To find out which instruction caused the program check in figure 18-6, you subtract the relocation factor of REORDLST (37878) from the instruction location given in the program check message (37908). The result is the location counter value of the offending instruction (90).

When you do your subtraction, remember that you're working with hex values. The easiest way to do the subtraction, of course, is to use a hex calculator. But if you don't have one with you, you can subtract in much the same way you do decimal subtraction:

$$
\begin{array}{r}
3\ 7\ 9\ 0\ 8 \\
3\ 7\ 8\ 7\ 8 \\
\hline
9\ 0
\end{array}
$$

Starting from the right in this example, 8 from 8 is obviously 0. But to subtract 7 from 0, you must first carry a 1 over from the hundreds decimal position, so you're actually subtracting hex 7 from hex 10. Then, if you realize that hex 10 is decimal 16, you can figure out that hex 7 from hex 10 is hex 9.

How to locate an instruction in the assembly listing   Once you have the location counter value for an instruction, you can find it in the assembly listing. If you scan down the location counter values to a value of hex 90 in the assembly listing in figure 18-6, you can see that statement 37 caused the program check:

```
CP      LINECNT,=P'50'
```

Then, if the cause of the program check isn't obvious, you can examine the data fields involved by looking them up in the storage dump.

DOS/VSE ASSEMBLER 11.46 85-11-13

LOC	OBJECT CODE	ADDR1	ADDR2	STMT	SOURCE STATEMENT		SEQ
000000				1	REORDLST START 0		00000100
000000	0530			2	BEGIN BALR 3,0		00000200
			00002	3	USING *,3	LOAD BASE REGISTER	00000300
				4	OPEN INVMAST,PRTOUT		00000400
000002	0700			5+*	IOCS - OPEN - 5745-SC-IOX - REL 28.0		12000028
000004				6+	CNOP 0,4		20000025
				7+	DC 0F'0'		22000025
000004	4110 39D6		009D8	8+	LA 1,=C'$$BOPEN '		46000025
000008	4500 3012		00014	9+IJJ00001	BAL 0,*+4+4*(3-1)		54000025
00000C	0000012E			10+	DC A(INVMAST)		64000025
000010	000001CE			11+	DC A(PRTOUT)		64000025
000014	0A02			12+	SVC 2		74000025
000016				13 READINV	GET INVMAST,INVWRKA	READ RECORD INTO WORK AREA	00000500
				14+*	IOCS - GET - 5745-SC-IOX - REL 29.0		12000029
000016	5810 39E6		009E8	15+READINV	L 1,=A(INVMAST)	GET DTF TABLE ADDRESS	42000025
00001A	5800 39EA		009EC	16+	L 0,=A(INVWRKA)	GET WORK AREA ADDRESS	51000025
00001E	58F1 0010		00010	17+	L 15,16(1)	GET LOGIC MODULE ADDRESS	75000025
000022	45EF 0008		00008	18+	BAL 14,8(15)	BRANCH TO GET ROUTINE	78000025
000026	FA20 39CC 3A08	009CE	00A0A	19	AP COUNT,=P'1'	ADD ONE TO COUNT	00000600
00002C	F224 39C0 3710	009C2	00712	20	PACK WRKAVAIL,INVONHND		00000700
000032	F224 39C3 3715	009C5	00717	21	PACK WRKONORD,INVONORD		00000800
000038	FA22 39C0 39C5	009C2	009C5	22	AP WRKAVAIL,WRKONORD	ADD ON HAND AND ON ORDER	00000900
00003E	F224 39C6 370B	009C8	0070D	23	PACK WRKORDPT,INVORDPT		00001000
000044	F922 39C0 39C6	009C2	009C8	24	CP WRKAVAIL,WRKORDPT	COMPARE AVAILABLE, REORDER POINT	00001100
00004A	47B0 3014		00016	25	BNL READINV		00001200
00004E	F224 39C9 36E8	009CB	006EA	26	PACK PACKAREA,INVITNBR		00001300
000054	D205 38AA 39B5	008AC	009B5	27	MVC PRTITNBR,PATTERN1		00001400
00005A	DE05 38AA 39CB	008AC	009CB	28	ED PRTITNBR,PACKAREA	EDIT ITEM NUMBER	00001500
000060	D213 38B5 36EF	008B7	006EF	29	MVC PRTITDES,INVITDES	MOVE ITEM DESCRIPTION	00001600
000066	F224 39C9 3706	009CB	00708	30	PACK PACKAREA,INVPRICE		00001700
00006C	D206 38CD 39B9	008CF	009BB	31	MVC PRTPRICE,PATTERN2		00001800
000072	DE06 38CD 39B5	008CF	009B5	32	ED PRTPRICE,PACKAREA	EDIT UNIT PRICE	00001900
000078	D205 38D8 39B5	008DA	009B5	33	MVC PRTAVAIL,PATTERN1		00002000
00007E	DE05 38D8 39C2	008DA	009C2	34	ED PRTAVAIL,WRKAVAIL	EDIT AVAILABLE	00002100
000084	D205 38E2 39B5	008E4	009B5	35	MVC PRTORDPT,PATTERN1		00002200
00008A	DE05 38E2 39C8	008E4	009C8	36	ED PRTORDPT,WRKORDPT	EDIT ORDER POINT	00002300
000090	F911 39CF 3A08	009D1	00A08	37	CP LINECNT,=P'50'	COMPARE LINE COUNT TO 50	00002400
000096	4740 30D2		000D4	38	BL PRTDET	BRANCH ON LOW TO PRTDET	00002500
				39	PUT PRTOUT,HDGLINE1	PRINT FIRST HEADING LINE	00002600
				40+*	IOCS AND DEVICE INDEPENDENT I/O - PUT - 5745-SC-IOX - REL. 29.0		05000029
00009A	5810 39EE		009F0	41+	L 1,=A(PRTOUT)	GET DTF TABLE ADDRESS	15000025
00009E	5800 39F2		009F4	42+	L 0,=A(HDGLINE1)	GET WORK AREA ADDRESS	46000025
0000A2	58F1 0010		00010	43+	L 15,16(1)	GET LOGIC MODULE ADDRESS 3-5	54000025
0000A6	45EF 000C		0000C	44+	BAL 14,12(15)	BRANCH TO PUT ROUTINE 3-5	55000025
				45+	PUT PRTOUT,HDGLINE2	PRINT SECOND HEADING LINE	00002700
				46+*	IOCS AND DEVICE INDEPENDENT I/O - PUT - 5745-SC-IOX - REL. 29.0		05000029
0000AA	5810 39EE		009F0	47+	L 1,=A(PRTOUT)	GET DTF TABLE ADDRESS	15000025
0000AE	5800 39F6		009F8	48+	L 0,=A(HDGLINE2)	GET WORK AREA ADDRESS	46000025
0000B2	58F1 0010		00010	49+	L 15,16(1)	GET LOGIC MODULE ADDRESS 3-5	54000025
0000B6	45EF 000C		0000C	50+	BAL 14,12(15)	BRANCH TO PUT ROUTINE 3-5	55000025
				51	PUT PRTOUT,HDGLINE3	PRINT THIRD HEADING LINE	00002800

Figure 18-6   Test run output for the reorder-listing program: the assembly listing (part 1 of 11)

```
LOC     OBJECT CODE   ADDR1  ADDR2   STMT  SOURCE STATEMENT

                                      52+* IOCS AND DEVICE INDEPENDENT I/O - PUT - 5745-SC-IOX - REL. 29.0        05000029
0000BA  5810 39EE            009F0    53+        L     1,=A(PRTOUT)      GET DTF TABLE ADDRESS             15000025
0000BE  5800 39FA            009FC    54+        L     0,=A(HDGLINE3)    GET WORK AREA ADDRESS             46000025
0000C2  58F1 0010            00010    55+        L     15,16(1)          GET LOGIC MODULE ADDRESS    3-5   54000025
0000C6  45EF 000C            0000C    56+        BAL   14,12(15)         BRANCH TO PUT ROUTINE       3-5   55000025
0000CA  F810 39CF  3A09 009D1 00A0B   57         ZAP   LINECNT,=P'0'     RESET LINE COUNT TO ZERO          00002900
0000D0  92F0 38A9       008AB         58         MVI   PRTDCTL,C'0'      MOVE ZERO TO ASA CONTROL BYTE     00003100
                                      59  PRTDET PUT   PRTOUT,PRTDETL    PRINT DETAIL LINE                 00003000
                                      60+* IOCS AND DEVICE INDEPENDENT I/O - PUT - 5745-SC-IOX - REL. 29.0        05000029
0000D4  5810 39EE            009F0    61+PRTDET  L     1,=A(PRTOUT)      GET DTF TABLE ADDRESS             15000025
0000D8  5800 39FE            00A00    62+        L     0,=A(PRTDETL)     GET WORK AREA ADDRESS             46000025
0000DC  58F1 0010            00010    63+        L     15,16(1)          GET LOGIC MODULE ADDRESS    3-5   54000025
0000E0  45EF 000C            0000C    64+        BAL   14,12(15)         BRANCH TO PUT ROUTINE       3-5   55000025
0000E4  FA10 39CF  3A08 009D1 00A0A   65         AP    LINECNT,=P'1'     ADD ONE TO LINE COUNT             00003200
0000EA  9240 38A9       008AB         66         MVI   PRTDCTL,C' '      MOVE BLANK TO ASA CONTROL BYTE    00003300
0000EE  47F0 3014            00016    67         B     READINV                                            00003400
0000F2  DE06 392F  39CC 00931 009CE   68  INVEOF ED    CNTPATRN,COUNT    EDIT COUNT                        00003500
                                      69         PUT   PRTOUT,CNTLINE    PRINT COUNT LINE                  00003600
                                      70+* IOCS AND DEVICE INDEPENDENT I/O - PUT - 5745-SC-IOX - REL. 29.0        05000029
0000F8  5810 39EE            009F0    71+        L     1,=A(PRTOUT)      GET DTF TABLE ADDRESS             15000025
0000FC  5800 3A02            00A04    72+        L     0,=A(CNTLINE)     GET WORK AREA ADDRESS             46000025
000100  58F1 0010            00010    73+        L     15,16(1)          GET LOGIC MODULE ADDRESS    3-5   54000025
000104  45EF 000C            0000C    74+        BAL   14,12(15)         BRANCH TO PUT ROUTINE       3-5   55000025
                                      75         CLOSE INVMAST,PRTOUT                                      00003700
                                      76+* IOCS AND DEVICE INDEPENDANT I/O - CLOSE - 5745-SC-IOX - REL. 28.0      08100028
000108                                77+        CNOP  0,4                                                20000025
000108  0F'0'                         78+        DC    0F'0'                                              22000025
000108  4110 39DE            009E0    79+        LA    1,=C'$$BCLOSE'                                     46000025
00010C  4500 3116            00118    80+IJC0008 BAL   0,*+4+4*(3-1)                                      54000025
000110  00000128                      81+        DC    A(INVMAST)                                         64000025
000114  000001C8                      82+        DC    A(PRTOUT)                                          64000025
000118  0A02                          83+        SVC   2                                                  74000025
                                      84         EOJ                                                      00003800
                                      85+* SUPVR COMMN MACROS - EOJ - 5745-SC-SUP - REL. 28.0                    40000028
00011A  0A0E                          86+        SVC   14                                                 50000025
                                      87  * THE INVENTORY FILE DEFINITION                                 00003900
                                      88  INVMAST DTFSD BLKSIZE=500,                                     X00004000
                                                         RECFORM=FIXBLK,                                X00004100
                                                         RECSIZE=50,                                    X00004200
                                                         IOAREA1=INVIO1,                                X00004300
                                                         IOAREA2=INVIO2,                                X00004400
                                                         WORKA=YES,                                     X00004500
                                                         EOFADDR=INVEOF,                                X00004600
                                                         DEVADDR=SYS008                                  00004700
                                      89+* SEQUENTIAL DISK IOCS - DTFSD - 5745-SC-DSK (G98)      @D37ZDHK  01450000
00011C  00000000                      90+        DC    0D'0'                                              00003900
000120  00000000                      91+        DC    F'0'          RESERVED FOR IBM USE       @D35DE98  38140035
000120  00000000                      92+        DC    A(IJGZ0010)   VERSION 3 DTF AREA POINTER @D35DE98  38147035
000124  000001B0                      93+        DC    0D'0'                                    @D35DE98  38154035
000128  000080040000                  94+INVMAST DC    X'0000080040000'  CCB                              39000025
                                                                                                          39100025
```

Figure 18-6   Test run output for the reorder-listing program: the assembly listing (part 2 of 11)

```
                                                                              PAGE   4

LOC      OBJECT CODE    ADDR1 ADDR2  STMT   SOURCE STATEMENT              DOS/VSE ASSEMBLER 11.46  85-11-13

00012E   01                           95+        DC   AL1(1)             LOGICAL UNIT CLASS                    39300025
00012F   08                           96+        DC   AL1(8)             LOGICAL UNIT NUMBER                   39400025
000130   00000190                     97+        DC   A(IJGC0010)        CCB-CCW ADDRESS                       39500025
000134   00000000                     98+        DC   4X'00'             CCB-ST BYTE,CSW CCW ADDRESS           39600025
000138   00                           99+        DC   AL1(0)                                                   39700025
000139   000000                      100+        DC   X'000000'          LOGIC MODULE ADDRESS   @D35DE98  3-3  39800002
00013C   20                          101+        DC   X'20'              DTF TYPE               @D36KE97       39820002
00013D   5A                          102+        DC   AL1(90)            OPEN/CLOSE INDICATORS                 54800025
00013E   C9D5E5D4C1E2E3              103+        DC   CL7'INVMAST'       FILENAME                              55200025
000145   00                          104+        DC   X'00'              INDICATE 2311          @DL2W720       55958034
000146   000000000000                105+        DC   6X'00'             BCCHHR ADDR OF F1 LABEL IN VTOC       56100025
00014C   0000                        106+        DC   2X'00'             VOL SEQ NUMBER                        56200025
00014E   08                          107+        DC   X'08'              OPEN COMMUNICATIONS BYTE              56300025
00014F   00                          108+        DC   X'00'              XTENT SEQ NO OF CURRENT EXTENT        56400025
000150   00                          109+        DC   X'00'              XTENT SEQ NO LAST XTENT OPENED        56500025
000151   000151                      110+        DC   AL3(*)             USER'S LABEL ADDRESS                  56700025
000154   20                          111+        DC   X'20'              DATAFILE VERSION 3 BIT @D35DE98       57068035
000155   0003EC                      112+        DC   AL3(INVIO2)        ADDRESS OF 2ND. IOAREA @DL30SMD       57100030
000158   80000000                    113+        DC   X'80000000'        CCHH ADDR OF USER LABEL TRACK         57400025
00015C   0000                        114+        DC   2X'00'             LOWER HEAD LIMIT                      57500025
00015E   00000000                    115+        DC   4X'00'             XTENT UPPER LIMIT                     57600025
000162   0000                        116+INVMASTS DC  2X'00'             SEEK ADDRESS-BB                       57700025
000164   0000FF00                    117+        DC   X'0000FF00'        SEARCH ADDRESS-CCHH                   57800025
000168   00                          118+        DC   X'00'              RECORD NUMBER                         57900025
000169   0000F2                      119+        DC   AL3(INVEOF)        EOF ADDRESS                           58100025
00016C   00000000                    120+        DC   4X'00'             CCHH CONTROL FIELD                    58500025
000170   06                          121+        DC   AL1(6)             R   CONTROL FIELD                     58700025
000171   04                          122+        DC   B'00000100'                                              59000025
000172   01F3                        123+        DC   H'499'             SIZE OF BLOCK-1            3-2         59200025
000174   FFFFFFFFFF                  124+        DC   5X'FF'             CCHHR BUCKET              3-7         59300025
000179   000000                      125+        DC   3X'00'                                                   60100025
00017C   4700 0000      00000        126+        NOP  0                                                        60300025
000180   000001F8                    127+        DC   A(INVIO1)          DEBLOCKER-INITIAL POINTER 4-0        60800027
000184   00000032                    128+        DC   F'50'              DEBLOCKER-RECORD SIZE                 61700025
000188   000003EB                    129+        DC   A(INVIO1+500-1)    DEBLOCKER LIMIT           4-0        62700027
00018C   0A                          130+        DC   AL1(10)            LOGICAL INDICATORS                    63600027
00018D   000000                      131+        DC   AL3(0)             USER'S ERROR ROUTINE                  63700035
000190   0700016240000006            132+IJGC0010 CCW 7,*-46,64,6        SEEK                                  63800025
000198   3100016440000005            133+        CCW  X'31',*-52,64,5    SEARCH ID EQUAL                       63900025
0001A0   0800019800000000            134+        CCW  8,*-8,0,0          TIC                                   64000025
0001A8   060001F8000001F4            135+        CCW  6,INVIO1,0,500     READ DATA                 4-0        64400027
                        001B0        136+IJGZ0010 EQU *                                                        64835035
0001B0   8C                          137+        DC   AL1(140)           VERSION 3 FLAGS        @D35DE98       74840035
0001B1   000000                      138+        DC   AL3(0)             VERSION 3 FLAGS        @D35DE98       74850035
0001B4   00000000                    139+        DC   AL4(0)             CISIZE IF PRESENT      @D35DE98       74860035
0001B8   00000000                    140+        DC   AL4(0)             PHYSICAL BLOCK SIZE    @D356EE3       74870035
0001BC   0000                        141+        DC   AL2(0)             NUMBER OF PHYSICAL     @D356EE3       74920035
                                                                         BLOCKS/CI
0001BE   00                          143+        DC   AL1(0)             NUMBER OF PHYSICAL     @D356EE3       75020035
                                                                         BLOCKS/TRACK           @D356EE3
0001BF   00                          145+        DC   AL1(0)             UPPER LIMIT RECD NUMBER @D356EE3      75120035
```

Figure 18-6   Test run output for the reorder-listing program: the assembly listing (part 3 of 11)

LOC	OBJECT CODE	ADDR1 ADDR2	STMT	SOURCE STATEMENT		
0001C0	00000000		146+	DC	A(0)	DATA SECURITY PLIST PTR	@D350EE3 75170035
		001C4	147+IJJZ0010	EQU	*		@D35DE98 75270035
			148	* THE PRINTER FILE DEFINITION		00004800
			149 PRTOUT	DTFPR	BLKSIZE=133,	X00004900
					IOAREA1=PRTIO1,	X00005000
					IOAREA2=PRTIO2,	X00005100
					WORKA=YES,	X00005200
					DEVADDR=SYSLST,	X00005300
					CTLCHR=ASA	00005400
0001C4	00000000		150+* IOCS AND DEV INDEPENDENT I/O DTFPR 5745-SC-IOX - REL.1.3			@DY28915 02870000
0001C8			151+	DC	0D'0'	60000025
0001C8	00080000000000		152+PRTOUT	DC	X'0000800000000'	RES. COUNT, COMM. BYTES BTS JJ	61510028
0001CE	00		153+	DC	AL1(0)	LOGICAL UNIT CLASS	70000025
0001CF	03		154+	DC	AL1(3)	LOGICAL UNIT	70200028
0001D0	000001F0		155+	DC	A(*+32)	CCW ADDR.	71000028
0001D4	00000000		156+	DC	4X'00'	CCB-ST BYTE,CSW CCW ADDRESS JJ	71200028
0001D8	00		157+	DC	AL1(0)	SWITCH 3 4-0	71750027
0001D9	000000		158+	DC	VL3(IJDFAZIW)	DTF TYPE (PRINTER) JJ	76800028
0001DC	08		159+	DC	X'08'	SWITCHES	77580028
0001DD	36		160+	DC	AL1(54)		77600025
0001DE	09		161+	DC	AL1(9)	NORMAL COMM. CODE 4-0	78000027
0001DF	09		162+	DC	AL1(9)	CONTROL COMM. CODE 4-0	78400027
0001E0	000005E1		163+	DC	A(PRTIO1+1)	ADDRESS OF DATA IN IOAREA1	78800025
0001E4	00000000		164+	DC	4X'00'	BUCKET 3-5	84000025
0001E8	0700		165+	NOPR	0	PUT LENGTH IN REG12 (ONLY UNDEF.	84800025
0001EA	4700 0000	00000	166+	NOP	0	LOAD USER POINTER REG	86400025
0001EE	0000		167+	DC	2X'00'	NOT USED 3-5	89600025
0001F0	09000066620000084		168+	CCW	9,PRTIO2+1,X'20',133-1	4-0	90400027
		001F8	169+IJJZ0011	EQU	*	92000025
			170	* THE DATA DEFINITIONS FOR THE TWO INVENTORY FILE I/O AREAS		00005500
0001F8			171 INVIO1	DS	CL500	00005600
0003EC			172 INVIO2	DS	CL500	00005700
			173	* THE DATA DEFINITIONS FOR THE TWO PRINTER OUTPUT AREAS		00005800
0005E0			174 PRTIO1	DS	CL133	00005900
000665			175 PRTIO2	DS	CL133	00006000
			176	* THE DATA DEFINITIONS FOR THE INVENTORY FILE WORK AREA		00006100
0006EA			177 INVWRKA	DS	0CL50	00006200
0006EA			178 INVITNBR	DS	CL5	00006300
0006EF			179 INVITDES	DS	CL20	00006400
000703			180	DS	CL5	00006500
000708			181 INVPRICE	DS	CL5	00006600
00070D			182 INVORDPT	DS	CL5	00006700
000712			183 INVONHND	DS	CL5	00006800
000717			184 INVONORD	DS	CL5	00006900
			185	* THE DATA DEFINITIONS FOR THE PRINTER HEADING LINES		00007000
00071C			186 HDGLINE1	DS	0CL133	00007100
00071C	F1		187	DC	C'1'	00007100
00071D	404040404040404040		188	DC	24C' '	00007300
000735	D9C5D6D9C4C5D940		189	DC	C'REORDER LISTING'	00007400
000744	4040404040404040		190	DC	93C' '	00007500

Figure 18-6   Test run output for the reorder-listing program: the assembly listing (part 4 of 11)

```
                                              DOS/VSE ASSEMBLER 11.46  85-11-13                    PAGE   6

LOC     OBJECT CODE      ADDR1 ADDR2  STMT  SOURCE STATEMENT

0007A1                                191   HDGLINE2  DS    0CL133                                00007600
0007A1  F0                            192             DC    C'0'                                  00007700
0007A2  40C9E3C5D44404040             193             DC    C' ITEM                   UNIT        X00007800
                                                              REORDER'                           00007900
0007E1  4040404040404040              194             DC    69C' '                                00008000
000826                                195   HDGLINE3  DS    0CL133                                00008100
000826  40                            196             DC    C' '                                  00008200
000827  4040D5D64B404040              197             DC    C' NO.           PRICE    AVAILABLEX00008300
                                                              POINT'                              00008400
000865  404040404040404040           198             DC    70C' '                                00008500
                                      199   *  THE DATA DEFINITIONS FOR THE PRINTER DETAIL LINE   00008600
0008AB                                200   PRTDETL   DS    0CL133                                00008700
0008AB                                201   PRTDCTL   DS    CL1                                   00008800
0008AC                                202   PRTITNBR  DS    CL6                                   00008900
0008B2  4040404040                    203             DC    5C' '                                 00009000
0008B7                                204   PRTITDES  DS    CL20                                  00009100
0008CB  40404040                      205             DC    4C' '                                 00009200
0008CF                                206   PRTPRICE  DS    CL7                                   00009300
0008D6  40404040                      207             DC    4C' '                                 00009400
0008DA                                208   PRTAVAIL  DS    CL6                                   00009500
0008E0  40404040                      209             DC    4C' '                                 00009600
0008E4                                210   PRTORDPT  DS    CL6                                   00009700
0008EA  404040404040404040           211             DC    70C' '                                00009800
                                      212   *  THE DATA DEFINITIONS FOR THE COUNT LINE            00009900
000930                                213   CNTLINE   DS    0CL133                                00010100
000930  60                            214             DC    C'-'                                  00010200
000931  4020206E202020                215   CNTPATRN  DC    X'4020206B202020'                     00010300
000938  40D9C5C3D6D9C4E2              216             DC    C' RECORDS IN THE INPUT FILE'         00010400
000952  4040404040404040             217             DC    99C' '                                00010500
                                      218   *  THE DATA DEFINITIONS FOR THE WORK FIELDS           00010600
0009B5  40202020202020                219   PATTERN1  DC    X'40202020202020'                     00010700
0009BB  402020214B2020                220   PATTERN2  DC    X'402020214B2020'                     00010800
0009C2                                221   WRKAVAIL  DS    PL3                                   00010900
0009C5                                222   WRKONORD  DS    PL3                                   00011000
0009C8                                223   WRKORDPT  DS    PL3                                   00011100
0009CB                                224   PACKAREA  DS    PL3                                   00011200
0009CE  00000C                        225   COUNT     DC    PL3'0'                                00011300
0009D1                                226   LINECNT   DS    P'50'                                 00011400
                            00000     227             END   BEGIN
0009D8  5B5BC2D5D7C5D540              228             =C'$$BOPEN '
0009E0  5B5BC2C3D3D6E2C5              229             =C'$$BCLOSE'
0009E8  0000012B                      230             =A(INVMAST)
0009EC  000006EA                      231             =A(INVWRKA)
0009F0  000001CB                      232             =A(PRTOUT)
0009F4  0000071C                      233             =A(HDGLINE1)
0009F8  000007A1                      234             =A(HDGLINE2)
0009FC  00000826                      235             =A(HDGLINE3)
000A00  000008AB                      236             =A(PRTDETL)
000A04  00000930                      237             =A(CNTLINE)
000A08  050C                          238             =P'50'
000A0A  1C                            239             =P'1'
000A0B  0C                            240             =P'0'
```

Figure 18-6   Test run output for the reorder-listing program: the assembly listing (part 5 of 11)

CROSS-REFERENCE

SYMBOL	LEN	ID	VALUE	DEFN	REFERENCES			
BEGIN	00002	001	000000	00002	0227			
CNTLINE	00133	001	000930	00213	0237			
CNTPATRN	00007	001	000931	00215	0068			
COUNT	00003	001	0009CE	00225	0019	0068		
HDGLINE1	00133	001	00071C	00186	0233			
HDGLINE2	00133	001	0007A1	00191	0234			
HDGLINE3	00133	001	000826	00195	0235			
IJGC0010	00008	001	000190	00132	0097			
IJGZ0010	00001	001	0001B0	00136	0092			
INVEOF	00006	001	0000F2	00068	0119			
INVIO1	00500	001	0001F8	00171	0127	0129	0135	
INVIO2	00500	001	0003EC	00172	0112			
INVITDES	00020	001	0006EF	00179	0029			
INVITNBR	00005	001	0006EA	00178	0026			
INVMAST	00006	001	000128	00094	0010	0081	0230	
INVONHND	00005	001	000712	00183	0020			
INVONORD	00005	001	000717	00184	0021			
INVORDPT	00005	001	00070D	00182	0023			
INVPRICE	00005	001	000708	00181	0030			
INVWRKA	00050	001	0006EA	00177	0231			
LINECNT	00002	001	0009D1	00226	0037	0057	0065	
PACKAREA	00003	001	0009CB	00224	0026	0028	0030	0032
PATTERN1	00006	001	0009B5	00219	0027	0033	0035	
PATTERN2	00007	001	0009BB	00220	0031			
PRTAVAIL	00006	001	0008DA	00208	0033	0034		
PRTDCTL	00001	001	0008AB	00201	0058	0066		
PRTDET	00004	001	0000D4	00061	0038			
PRTDETL	00133	001	0008AB	00200	0236			
PRTIO1	00133	001	0005E0	00174	0163			
PRTIO2	00133	001	000665	00175	0168			
PRTITDES	00020	001	0008B7	00204	0029			
PRTITNBR	00006	001	0008AC	00202	0027	0028		
PRTORDPT	00006	001	0008E4	00210	0035	0036		
PRTOUT	00006	001	0001C8	00152	0011	0082	0232	
PRTPRICE	00007	001	0008CF	00206	0031	0032		
READINV	00004	001	000016	00015	0025	0067		
WRKAVAIL	00003	001	0009C2	00221	0020	0022	0024	
WRKONORD	00003	001	0009C5	00222	0021	0022		
WRKORDPT	00003	001	0009C8	00223	0023	0024	0036	0034
=A(CNTLINE)	00004	001	000A04	00237	0072			
=A(HDGLINE1)	00004	001	0009F4	00233	0042			
=A(HDGLINE2)	00004	001	0009F8	00234	0048			
=A(HDGLINE3)	00004	001	0009FC	00235	0054			
=A(INVMAST)	00004	001	0009E8	00230	0015			
=A(INVWRKA)	00004	001	0009EC	00231	0016			

Figure 18-6   Test run output for the reorder-listing program: the cross-reference listing (part 6 of 11)

CROSS-REFERENCE

SYMBOL	LEN	ID	VALUE	DEFN	REFERENCES				
=A(PRTOUT)									
	00004	OC1	0009F0	00232	0041	0047	0C53	0061	0071
=A(PRTDETL)									
	00004	OC1	000A00	00236	0062				
=C'$$BOPEN '									
	00008	OC1	0009D8	00228	0008				
=C'$$BCLOSE'									
	00008	OC1	0009E0	00229	0079				
=P'0'	00001	OC1	000A0B	00240	0057				
=P'1'	00001	OC1	000A0A	00239	0019	0065			
=P'50'	00002	OC1	000A08	00238	0037				

Figure 18-6 Test run output for the reorder-listing program: the cross-reference listing (part 7 of 11)

11/13/85	PHASE	XFR-AD	LOCORE	HICORE	DSK-AD	LABEL	LOADED	REL-FR	OFFSET	INPUT
										RELOCATABLE
	PHASE**	037878	037878	038369	00048143	REORDLST	037878	000000		SYSLNK
						IJDFAZIW	038288	000A10		IJDFAZIW

Figure 18-6 Test run output for the reorder-listing program: the link-edit map (part 8 of 11)

0S03I PROGRAM CHECK INTERRUPTION - HEX LOCATION 037908 - CONDITION CODE 2 - DATA EXCEPTION
0S00I JOB REORDLST CANCELED
0S07I PROBLEM PROGRAM PSW   031D2000000003790E

Figure 18-6 Test run output for the reorder-listing program: the program check message (part 9 of 11)

```
REORDLST                    11/13/85   11.47.02    CPUID=000118704331000                              PAGE    1

ENDING TASK REGS

GR  0-F   00037F62  00037A0  007AFFFF  4003787A   007AFFFF  00000000  00000000  00037BE0
          40E41002  D7C8C1E2  00000000  007AFFFF   00037878  007B0800  8003789E  00E5E000

FP REG    00000000  00000000  00000000  00000000   00000000  00000000  00000000  00000000
CR  0-F   81400C60  00000000  FFFFFFFF  00000000   00000000  00000000  00000000  00000000
          00000800  00000000  00000000  00000000   00000000  00000000  8F000000  00000000

BG PARTITION
037800  D7C8C1E2  C55C5C5C  031D2000  0003790E     D7C8C1E2  00000000  007AFFFF  00037878    *PHASE***                PHAS*
037820  00780800  8003789E  00E5E000  00037F62     000379A0  007AFFFF  4003787A  007AFFFF    *            V      PHAS  *
037840  00000000  00000000  000378E0  40E41002     00009A08  05CD136A  00000000  00000000    *            U              *
037860  00000000  00000000  00000000  00000000     00000000  05300700  05300700  411039D6    *                        O*
037880  45003012  000379A0  00037A40  0A025810     39E65800  39EA58F1  0010458F  0008FA20    *        W        1        *
0378A0  39CC3A08  F22439C0  3710F224  39C33715     FA2239C0  39C3F224  39C63708  F92239C0    * 2   2C   W   C2 F  9    *
0378C0  39C647B0  3014F224  39C936E8  D20538AA     39B3DE05  38AA39C9  D21338B5  36EDF224    *F  2 I YK    IK     2    *
0378E0  39C93706  D2063BCD  39B9DE06  38CD39C9     D20538D8  39B3DE05  38D839C0  D20538E2    *I K     S F9     IK Q K S*
037900  39B3DE05  38E239C6  F91139CF  3A064740     30D25810  39EE5800  39F258F1  0010458F    * K  K  61 K      K  2 1  *
037920  00C5810  39EE5800  39F658F1  001045EF     000C5810  39EE5800  39FA58F1  001045EF    *      61        K      1  *
037940  00CF810  39CF3A09  92F038A9  581039EE      580039FE  58F10010  45EF000C  FA1039CF    *8    0  1   0     1     *
037960  3A089240  38A947F0  3014DE06  00037A40     581039EE  58003A02  58F10010  45EF000C    *  0    0             1   *
037980  411039DE  45003116  007379A0  00037A40     0A02A0E  39EE5800  39F258F1  00037A28    *    0           1        *
0379A0  00FA8004  0C400108  007B3200  00037C64     00E5E000  205EC9D5  E5D4C1E2  E3000000    *          V    INVMAST    *
0379C0  00000000  00028020  000379C9  20037C64     0000007E  00090000  007E0005  00000000    *         4               *
0379E0  0203796A  00C80009  068401F3  007E0005     01000000  47000000  00037A70  00000032    *                        *
037A00  00037B69  0A000009  070379DA  40000006     00000005  40000005  03037A10  00000000    *                        *
037A20  06037A70  000001F4  8C000000  00000006     00000000  00000000  00000000  00000000    *                        *
037A40  00008000  0C000003  00037A68  000046E0     00038288  08B60909  00037E59  00000000    *                        *
037A60  07004700  00000000  09037EDE  20000084     F0F0F1F0  F3C8C5C1  E3C5D940  E2D6D3C5    *         0      0103HEATER SOLE*
037A80  D5D6C9C4  40404040  40F0F0F3  F3F0F0F0     F4F4F0F0  F0F0F5F0  F0F0F0F3  F4F0F0F0    *NOID    00330044000500000340000*
037AA0  F0F0F5C8  F1F0F5C8  C5C1E3C5  D940E3C3     C5D9D4D6  E2E3C1E3  40404040  F00F7F8F0    *00010105HEATER THERMOSTAT   00780*
037AC0  F0F1F0F1  F0F0F0F0  F1F0F0F0  F0F0F7F0     F0F0F1F0  F0F0F0F0  F3C9E3C5  D440F340    *0101000010000700010000031TEM 3  *
037AE0  40404040  40404040  40404040  40F0F0F6     F3F0F0F0  F0F0F1F0  F0F0F0F0  F0F0F0F1    *            060001300000100001 *
037B00  F2F0F0F0  F0F0F0F0  F0F0F4C9  E3C5D440     F4404040  40404040  40404040  40404040    *20000000004ITEM 4           0*
037B20  F1F2F5F0  F0F1F8F0  F0F0F0F0  F0F0F5F0     F0F0F0F0  F0F0F0F0  F5C9E3C5  F5C9E3C5    *12500180000050000020000000005ITE*
037B40  D440F540  40404040  40404040  40404040     40F0F2F0  F0F0F0F3  F2F5F0F0  F0F0F0F5    *M 5              0200003250000005*
037B60  F0F0F0F0  F0F04150  F0F04150  3EB895F0     50004780  334495F1  50004780  334495F2    *           0   1   2*
037B80  50004780  334495F3  50004780  334495F4     50004780  334495F5  50004780  334495F6    *       3   4   5   6*
037BA0  50004780  334495F7  50004780  334495F8     50004780  334495F9  50004770  33545A50    *       7   8   9     *
037BC0  89F64640  32F49240  878D47F0  335892FF     87BD95FF  87BD4770  3366D214  8508899E    * 6  4  0     K     *
037BE0  924087BD  45B03464  95FF87BD  4770337C     D2148508  89895880  880A07FB  F276882E    *        K     K  2 *
037C00  500E4F70  882E1A67  5A50882A  07FB5810     89FA4100  C00458F0  101858F0  F00805EF    *      0    0  00  *
037C20  12FF4780  343E0700  451033D2  0037C34      8003C34   C0040000  00037F28  D01C9101    *        K      *
037C40  00000000  00380000  00000010  5010D018     58100014  AF040005  1BFF50F0  D01C9101    *                  *
037C60  10864780  34045810  1020BF17  100A5010     D01C4780  3404BFF7  10194770  342A4110    *          7   0   *
037C80  89DE41F0  00000A41  120F4780  341C41F0     000C47F0  343218F1  BF17D01D  4780342A    * 0   0   1     *
```

Figure 18-6   Test run output for the reorder-listing program: the storage dump (part 10 of 11)

Figure 18-6   Test run output for the reorder-listing program: the storage dump (part 11 of 11)

Code	Exception type	Explanation
01	Operation	The machine has encountered an invalid operation code. This is often caused by a branch to a data name or the failure to branch around file or data definitions.
05	Addressing	An instruction has tried to use an address that is beyond the highest valid storage address. This is often caused by loading an incorrect value into a register that is used for addressing.
07	Data	An instruction has tried to operate on data that is invalid for it. Most often, the instruction is trying to do decimal arithmetic on a field that isn't in packed decimal form.
0A	Decimal overflow	A decimal add, subtract, or multiply instruction develops a result that is too large for the receiving field. This is often caused by bad input data.
0B	Decimal divide	A decimal divide instruction develops a quotient that is too large for the receiving field. This is usually caused by a divisor with a zero value.

Figure 18-7   Some common program checks

How to analyze storage dump data

The contents of the 16 general-purpose registers are printed at the start of a storage dump as illustrated in part 10 of figure 18-6. This is followed by the contents of the 8 floating-point registers, the contents of the 16 control registers, the contents of the communication region, and the contents of some other storage areas used by VSE. Last, the contents of the storage positions in your program partition are printed. In figure 18-6, the user's partition starts with the words BG PARTITION.

In figure 18-6, I have omitted the areas after the registers and before the user's partition because you will rarely, if ever, need to use the data in these areas. And you certainly won't need to use them in this course. However, you will want to analyze the data in the registers and in the fields in your program area.

The contents of the registers   The contents of the general-purpose registers are printed in the line headed GR 0-F on the first page of the storage printout. For example, register 3, which is the base register for this program, contained a value of hex 4003787A at the time of the storage dump in figure 18-6. Since only the rightmost three bytes are involved in base addressing, the base address is hex 03787A. This is the address of the first instruction following the BALR. Because the general-purpose registers

Address	Storage contents
37860-37863	00000000
37864-37867	00000000
37868-3786B	00000000
3786C-3786F	00000000
37870-37873	00000000
37874-37877	00000000
37878-3787B	05300700
3787C-3787F	411039D6

Figure 18-8 The contents of storage positions 37860 through 3787F in the storage dump in figure 18-6

are used in many assembler language operations, you will frequently need to analyze the data in these registers.

If you use floating-point operations as described in chapter 12, you may also need to analyze the data in the floating-point registers. The contents of these registers are printed right after those of the general-purpose registers in the line headed FP REG. There are eight of these registers, but they all contained hex zeros at the time the storage dump in figure 18-6 was created.

The contents of the fields in the user's partition   In the storage portion of the storage dump, 32 bytes of storage are printed in groups of four bytes with the address of the first byte of the line in the left margin. The line next to address 37860, for example, displays the 32 bytes from 37860-3787F with all data in hex. In figure 18-8, I have presented the code from this line of the storage dump in a modified form so it's clear what the addresses are and what the storage contents are. If you compare the object code in the assembly listing with the object code starting at address 37878, you will find them identical.

To the right of the eight columns that give the contents of 32 bytes of storage in hex notation is a column of data that represents the same 32 bytes in character notation. If a blank is printed for a storage position, it means the byte either contains a blank or it doesn't contain an EBCDIC code that can be printed. Otherwise, the character representing the code is printed. If, for example, you look at the last page of the storage dump in figure 18-6, you can see the constant word DESCRIPTION in the character portion of the dump. Then, if you relate this to the address at the far left of that line of print, you can determine that DESCRIPTION is stored in bytes 380AD-380B7. And if you analyze the hex portion of the dump for the same bytes of storage, you can see the hex codes for the letters in this word: C4 for D, C5 for E, and so on.

How to calculate the address of a field or an instruction in the storage dump   To locate a field or an instruction in your program area, you must first calculate its starting address. You do this by adding its location counter value to the relocation factor given in the link edit map. You can find the location counter value for a field in the ADDR1 or ADDR2 columns of the assembly listing or in the cross-reference listing. For instance, the ADDR1 column in statement 37 in figure 18-6 gives 9D1 as the location counter value for LINECNT and so does the cross-reference listing. As a result, the address of the field in storage is hex 38249 (hex 9D1 plus hex 37878).

The easiest way to add two hex addresses is to use a hex calculator. But if you don't have one with you, you can do the addition in much the same way you do decimal addition. Just keep in mind that you're working with hex values. For instance,

$$
\begin{array}{r}
3\ 7\ 8\ 7\ 8 \\
9\ D\ 1 \\
\hline
3\ 8\ 2\ 4\ 9
\end{array}
$$

Starting from the right, 8 plus 1 is 9. Next, 7 plus D (decimal 13) is decimal 20, which is hex 14. As a result 1 is carried over to the hundreds column. Then, 1 (the carried digit) plus 8 plus 9 is decimal 18, which is hex 12. Again, a 1 is carried over to the next column. Finally, 1 (the carried digit) plus 7 is 8.

How to locate a field or an instruction in the storage dump   To find a field or an instruction in the storage dump once you know its address, you scan down the column of addresses on the left side of the storage dump until you come to the nearest address below it. Then, you count over until you locate the start of the field.

In the case of LINECNT in figure 18-6, for example, you scan the column of addresses until you come to address 38240. That is, the nearest address below 38249, the address of LINECNT. Then, you count over to the hex digits representing address 38249. Since the first byte of the line starts at address 38240, you count 38240 for the first byte, 38241 for the second byte, and so on.

When you reach byte 38249, you know that this is the start of the LINECNT field. Then, since the LINECNT field is two bytes long, you examine two bytes of data. If you do this, you'll see that the field contains 4040, which isn't valid packed decimal data. So that's the cause of the data exception.

How to debug
a program check within your program

After you've located the instruction in your program that caused the program check and after you've analyzed the related fields in storage, you must still figure out what's wrong with your source code. In many cases, you may be surprised to discover that the bug won't be in the instruction that caused the program check or in the data definitions of the fields that the instruction operates upon. Instead, the bug will be elsewhere in the program.

In the case of the program in figure 18-6, though, the bug is fairly obvious. Since we know that LINECNT contained invalid packed decimal data at the time of the program check, we must find out why it did. Since LINECNT isn't an input field, you have to assume that the error is in the source code, not in the input data. Then, if you check the definition of LINECNT, you can see the error:

```
LINECNT   DS      P'50'
```

Because this definition uses DS instead of DC, the program assembled cleanly but no starting value was given to the field. As a result, LINECNT took on whatever value was left in its storage positions by the previous program. By changing the DS to DC, the bug should be corrected.

Using debugging instructions and the PDUMP macro   If a bug is difficult to isolate, you may not be able to debug it using just the storage dump at the time of the program check. In this case, you may want to add debugging instructions to your program and rerun the test. As I've mentioned, the PDUMP macro is particularly useful as a debugging instruction. By using PDUMP, you can dump portions of your storage area whenever you want to during the execution of your program. For instance, you can dump the contents of selected storage fields before a series of calculations is made and after the calculations are made. Then, you can compare the before and after values to see what went wrong.

How to debug
a program check at an address within a subprogram

The program check in figure 18-6 was caused by an instruction within the user's program. But that isn't always the case. Sometimes, the address of the offending instruction is in one of the other modules listed on the link edit map.

Link edit map

```
11/13/85 PHASE    XFR-AD  LOCORE  HICORE  DSK-AD    LABEL    LOADED  REL-FR OFFSET INPUT

         PHASE*** 037878  037878  038AB9  00048143                                   RELOCATABLE
                                                    CUSTSLS  037878  037878 000000 SYSLNK
                                                    GETIME   038900  038900 001088 SYSLNK
                                                    IJDFAZIW 0389D8  0389D8 001160 IJDFAZIW
```

Program check message

```
0S03I PROGRAM CHECK INTERRUPTION - HEX LOCATION 038964 - CONDITION CODE 1 - OPERATION EXCEPTION
0S00I JOB CUSTSLS  CANCELED
0S07I PROBLEM PROGRAM  PSW     031D100000038966
```

Figure 18-9   Test run output with a program check in the GETIME subprogram

To illustrate, suppose the program check message in figure 18-6 gave 38290 as the address of the instruction that caused the program check. You can see from the link edit map that this instruction is not in the reorder-listing program. Instead, it's in the I/O module named IJDFAZIW. Fortunately, though, the cause of a program check in an I/O module is almost always an improperly coded I/O macro. As a result, you should be able to correct the problem by analyzing the operands in the related macro.

Now, look at the program check message and link edit map in figure 18-9. In this case, the program check occurred when the system was executing an instruction in a module named GETIME. Suppose, though, that this module is a subprogram that you wrote or that one of the programmer's in your shop wrote. It gets the current time from the system and edits it into a field in the main program that you pass to the subprogram.

If you haven't read chapter 8, you'll learn about subprograms and subprogram linkage when you do. For now, though, you should know that you debug a subprogram the same way that you debug a main program. By subtracting the relocation factor for the module from the program check address, you get the location counter value of the offending instruction in the subprogram. Then, you can find this instruction in the assembly listing of the subprogram, analyze related fields in the storage dump, etc.

What if the subprogram has been in use for years and you have to assume that it works correctly? You must then assume that your program didn't call the subprogram correctly. In most cases, this will mean that your program didn't pass its data to the subprogram in the sequence or format that the subprogram expected it to be in. You can correct this type of bug by making sure that your fields are in the right order and the right format. This should be clear to you after you read chapter 8.

Link edit map

```
01/06/86 PHASE    XFR-AD  LOCORE  HICORE  DSK-AD   LABEL     LOADED   REL-FR OFFSET INPUT
         PHASE***  037878  037878  038283  00048143                                   RELOCATABLE
                                                    REORDLST  037878   037878 000000 SYSLNK
UNRESOLVED EXTERNAL REFERENCES                      EXTRN     IJDFAZIW
UNRESOLVED ADCON   AT OFFSET 00037A51

001 UNRESOLVED ADDRESS CONSTANTS
```

Program check message

```
0S03I PROGRAM CHECK INTERRUPTION - HEX LOCATION 00000C - CONDITION CODE 0 - OPERATION EXCEPTION
0S00I JOB DOC18F10 CANCELED
0S07I PROBLEM PROGRAM  PSW    031D00000000000E
```

Figure 18-10   Test run output that indicates a missing I/O module

How to debug a program check at an address outside your partition

Sometimes, a program check will occur at an address that is outside your program's partition. For instance, figure 18-10 shows another program check message and link edit map for the reorder-listing program. This time, though, the address in the program check message is 00000C. A low storage address like this (000000, 000008, and 000010 are also common) indicates that one of the I/O modules required by the program could not be found. Then, when you check the link edit map, you'll find that at least one I/O module could not be found and resulted in an "unresolved address constant" in the program. In figure 18-10, the missing I/O module is IJDFAZIW.

Sometimes, you can correct a problem like this by correcting the search chain for the relocatable libraries. But sometimes the I/O module won't be in any of the system's relocatable libraries. Although you can't be expected to correct a problem like this at your stage of development, it can be corrected by assembling an I/O module with the proper name. The special macros that allow you to do this are described in *VSE/Advanced Functions Macro Reference* (SC24-5211).

From a practical point of view, you will probably want to get help whenever you realize that a program check occurred outside your program's partition. In most cases, an inexperienced person won't be able to debug this type of program check.

A procedure for debugging
abnormal terminations

Because debugging an abnormal termination takes several steps, figure 18-11 summarizes the debugging procedure. If this seems like a lengthy process to go through to find one trivial error, take heart. Once you have found the cause of a program check a few times, you will be able to locate instructions and fields in the storage dump with considerable speed.

DISCUSSION

Debugging is one of the most challenging jobs you will have as a programmer. In a large, complex program, debugging an error can be like solving a mystery. From the output clues, you trace backwards to figure out what happened until you find the culprit: a coding or an input error.

Unfortunately, debugging can also be a frustrating task. Sometimes, a trivial coding error will cause a bug that takes hours or days to corrrect. That's why it's important that you use an orderly procedure like the one in figure 18-11 when you debug your programs.

Terminology

normal termination
normal end-of-job
normal EOJ
abnormal termination
abend
debugging instruction
program check
linkage editor map
link edit map
program check message
storage dump
storage printout
data exception
operation exception
addressing exception
decimal overflow exception
decimal divide exception
object module
phase
relocation factor

Objective

Given test run output for a program, debug it. The test run output will include the assembly listing, link edit map, program check message, and storage printout.

A debugging procedure for abnormal terminations

1. Find the program-check message and record the instruction address and cause. For example: address 37908 due to data exception.

2. Check the link edit map to see which module the program check address is in. If it is in your program or your subprogram, debug the problem as described in steps 3 through 6. If it is in an I/O module, look for the problem in your I/O macros. If it is in a working subprogram developed by someone else, check your program to make sure that your linkage is coded correctly. If it is outside of your partition, get help.

3. Derive the location counter value of the offending instruction by subtracting the relocation factor of your program from the address of the instruction.

4. Look up the instruction in the assembly listing of your program or subprogram by using the location counter value.

5. At this point, you may want to analyze registers, fields, or instructions in the storage dump depending on the type of exception you're dealing with. To find the starting byte of any field or instruction, add its location counter value to the relocation factor. Your analysis may be simple, as in the case of a data exception, or it may be complicated.

6. If you can't debug the problem by analyzing the data in the storage dump, you may want to add debugging statements to the source program, reassemble it, and do the test run again. For instance, you may want to add PDUMP macros to your source program so you can get the before and after values of the fields or registers used by your program. The PDUMP macro is presented in chapter 6.

7. When you find the bug in the source code, correct it, reassemble the source program or subprogram, and rerun the test.

Figure 18-11   A debugging procedure for abnormal terminations

Chapter 19

An introduction
to structured program development

When I presented the program flowchart in chapter 3, I told you that we believe there are better techniques for designing assembler language programs. Then, in chapter 8, I presented modular flowcharting, which we believe is a significant improvement over traditional program flowcharting. Now, in this chapter, I'm going to introduce you to structured program development.

The term *structured programming* includes a collection of techniques that are designed to help you improve both your productivity and the quality of your programs. The techniques include structured program design, structured module planning via pseudocode, structured coding, and top-down testing. When you finish this chapter, I hope you'll agree that structured design techniques are major improvements over both flowcharting and modular flowcharting. And I hope you'll understand that these design techniques make structured coding and top-down testing possible.

You can read this chapter any time after you complete chapter 8. In fact, we recommend that you read it right after you complete chapter 8. Then, you can use the structured techniques in your work on the case study for this course.

I'll start this chapter by presenting the theory of structured programming. Next, I'll show you the design and coding for the reorder-listing program in structured style. Then, I'll show you how to design a program using a structure chart, how to plan the modules of a program using pseudocode, how to code a program in structured style, and how to test a program from the top down.

THE THEORY OF STRUCTURED PROGRAMMING

The basic theory of structured programming is that any program can be written using three logical structures: sequence, selection, and iteration. These structures, illustrated in figure 19-1, have only one entry point and one exit point.

The first structure, the *sequence structure*, is simply a set of imperative statements executed in sequence, one after another. The entry point is at the start of the sequence; the exit point is after the last function in the sequence. A sequence structure may consist of a single function or of many functions.

The second structure, the *selection structure*, is a choice between two, and only two, functions based on a condition. This structure is often referred to as the IF-THEN-ELSE structure, and most programming languages have code that approximates it. Note that one of the functions may be null. In other words, if the condition is not met, the flow of control may pass directly to the structure's exit point with no intervening statements or structures.

The third structure, the *iteration structure*, is often called the DO-WHILE structure. It provides for doing a function as long as a condition is true. As you can see in variation 1 of the iteration structure, the condition is tested before the function is performed. When the condition is no longer true, the program continues with the next structure.

Related to the DO-WHILE structure are the DO-UNTIL and the COBOL PERFORM-UNTIL structures. As you can see in the DO-UNTIL structure in figure 19-1, the condition is tested after the function is performed and the function is performed until a condition is true. In the PERFORM-UNTIL structure, the function is also performed until the condition is true, but it is tested before the function is performed.

Again, let me stress that all of the structures in figure 19-1 have only one entry point and one exit point. As a result, a program made up of these structures will have only one entry point and one exit point. This means the program will be executed in a controlled manner from the first statement to the last. These characteristics make up a *proper program*.

To create a proper program, any of the three structures can be substituted for a function box in any of the other structures. The result will still be a proper program. Conversely, two or more of the basic structures in sequence can be treated as a single function box. This means that structures of great complexity can be created with the assurance that they will have only one entry point and one exit point.

This theory is an important contribution to the art of programming because it places necessary restrictions on program structure. For instance, branch statements or GOTO statements are unacceptable in structured programming. As a result, uncontrolled branching is impossible. This reduces the likelikood of bugs and makes bugs that do occur easier to find and correct. This also makes a structured program easier to read and understand than an unstructured one.

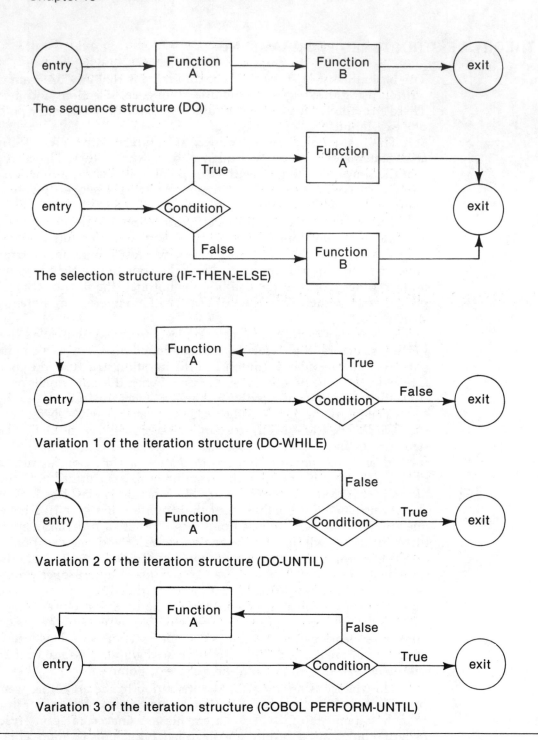

The sequence structure (DO)

The selection structure (IF-THEN-ELSE)

Variation 1 of the iteration structure (DO-WHILE)

Variation 2 of the iteration structure (DO-UNTIL)

Variation 3 of the iteration structure (COBOL PERFORM-UNTIL)

Figure 19-1   The basic structures of structured programming

Unfortunately, assembler language doesn't provide for the selection and iteration structures. And you can't code assembler language programs without using branch instructions in one form or another. So, it's impossible to comply with the principles of structured programming when you develop assembler language programs. That's one reason why assembler language is rarely used today for developing application programs.

On the other hand, you can design an assembler language program using structured design techniques. And you can plan the modules of the program so each one has only one entry and exit point. Then, you can code the modules in a structured style so the progression from one module to another is orderly. And, if you want to, you can test the program using top-down testing. If you do these things, you will get many of the benefits of structured programming, even though your program won't technically comply with the principles of structured programming.

A STRUCTURED VERSION OF THE REORDER-LISTING PROGRAM

Figures 19-2, 19-3, and 19-4 present the documentation for a structured version of the reorder-listing program. This program works like the reorder-listing program presented in topic 2 of chapter 5, except that the current date and time are printed in the first heading line of the reorder listing. Figure 19-2 presents the structure chart for this program. Figure 19-3 presents the pseudocode for the modules of this program. And figure 19-4 presents the assembler language code for this program.

The structure chart

The *structure chart* in figure 19-2 is an index to the subroutines and subprograms used in the assembler language program in figure 19-4. Any box in the structure chart with a number above it becomes a subroutine in the assembler language code. Any box with a stripe in it represents a subprogram called by the program. For instance, box 300 is a subroutine that is named REORD300 in the assembler language code. And the box with the GETIME stripe in it represents a subprogram that is called by module 100 in the reorder-listing program.

When you create a structure chart like the one in figure 19-2, you design from the top down until each box represents a function or subfunction that can be coded in 30 lines or fewer. That way the program consists of modules that are relatively easy to code. In contrast, studies have shown that modules of more than 30 lines become increasingly more difficult to code and understand as their size increases.

One of the benefits of structured design is that it lets you design modules for a program until each module is small enough to be manageable. In addition, a structure chart shows all the modules of a program as well as the relationships between the modules so it becomes an index to the resulting code. In contrast, traditional flowcharting techniques don't help you divide a program into modules. And modular flowcharts don't become an effective index to the resulting code.

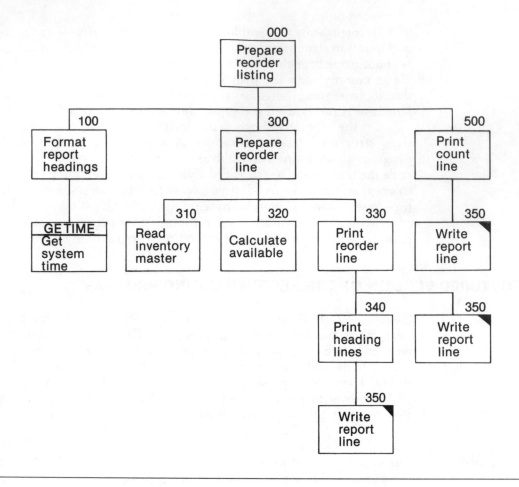

Figure 19-2   A structure chart for a version of the reorder-listing program

The pseudocode

Figure 19-3 presents the *pseudocode* for the modules of the structure chart in figure 19-2. The pseudocode is the plan for the coding of the assembler language modules. In this sense, pseudocode is a replacement for flowcharts. However, you only use the sequence, iteration, and selection structures when you use pseudocode so your modules only have one entry and exit point. In addition, you can create and modify pseudocode much more easily than you can create and modify flowcharts.

The source listing

Figure 19-4 presents the source listing for the program that is planned by the pseudocode in figure 19-3. Here, you can see that one subroutine is coded for each of the subroutine boxes in the structure chart. For instance, the program consists of subroutines named REORD000, REORD100, REORD300, REORD310, and so on. In this program, module 330 is the

```
REORD000:     Prepare reorder listing

DO REORD100.
OPEN files.
DO REORD300
    UNTIL all records processed.
DO REORD500.
CLOSE files.
EOJ.


REORD100:     Format report heading

Get system date.
CALL GETIME.
Format heading.


REORD300:     Prepare reorder line

DO REORD310.
IF NOT end-of-file
    DO REORD320
    IF available not less than reorder-point
        DO REORD330.


REORD310:     Read inventory master

Read inventory master.
IF end-of-file
    set EOFSWTCH to X'FF'
ELSE
    add 1 to record count.


REORD320:     Calculate available

Calculate available.


REORD330:     Print reorder line

IF line count = 54
    DO REORD340.
Format reorder line.
Move reorder line to printer work area.
DO REORD350.
```

Figure 19-3   Pseudocode for the modules of the reorder-listing program that is charted in figure 19-2 (part 1 of 2)

longest module, but it consists of only 22 lines. As a result, the entire program is relatively easy to read and understand.

If you review the code, you can see that comment lines have been used to identify the modules in the program. They are also used to identify groups of data definitions. This helps make the program easy to read. Otherwise, the coding is much like the coding presented in chapter 8.

```
REORD340:     Print heading lines

Move heading line 1 to printer work area.
DO REORD350.
Move heading line 2 to printer work area.
DO REORD350.
Move heading line 3 to printer work area.
DO REORD350.
Reset line count to zero.
Set ASA control character to double spacing.


REORD350:     Write report line

Write line on printer.
Add 1 to line count.


REORD500:     Print count line

Format count line.
Move count line to printer work area.
DO REORD350.
```

Figure 19-3   Pseudocode for the modules of the reorder-listing program that is charted in figure 19-2 (part 2 of 2)

HOW TO DESIGN A PROGRAM USING A STRUCTURE CHART

To develop a structure chart, you start at the top with one box that represents the entire program. At the next level, you draw a box for the one primary function that the top-level box requires. You also add boxes at this level for any functions that must be done before or after the primary function. Then, you expand each of the functions at the second level into subfunctions. You continue in this way until each box on the chart represents a function or subfunction that can be coded with limited difficulty.

To name the functions and subfunctions represented by the boxes of a chart, you use a verb, one or two adjectives, and a noun. Thus, the name of the top-level box in figure 19-2 is "prepare reorder listing." And the name of box 310 is "read inventory master."

I'm now going to present a five-step procedure for developing structure charts. This introductory procedure should help you design the programs required by the case study in appendix B. And it should help you design production programs of limited length and complexity.

```
✽
✽    MODULE 000:    PREPARE REORDER LISTING
✽
REORDLST  START   0
BEGIN     BALR    3,0
          USING   ✽,3
          BAL     11,REORD100
          OPEN    INVMAST,PRTOUT
DU000N1   BAL     11,REORD300
          CLI     EOFSWTCH,X'FF'
          BNE     DU000N1
ENDOJOB   BAL     11,REORD500
          CLOSE   INVMAST,PRTOUT
          EOJ
✽
✽    MODULE 100:    FORMAT REPORT HEADINGS
✽
REORD100  COMRG
          MVC     HDG1DATE,0(1)
          LA      13,SUBSAVE
          CALL    GETIME,(HDG1TIME)
          BR      11
SUBSAVE   DS      18F
✽
✽    MODULE 300:    PREPARE REORDER LINE
✽
REORD300  ST      11,REOSAV11
          BAL     11,REORD310
IF300N1   CLI     EOFSWTCH,X'FF'
          BE      R300EXIT
IF300N1A  BAL     11,REORD320
IF300N2   CP      WRKAVAIL,WRKORDPT
          BNL     R300EXIT
IF300N2A  BAL     11,REORD330
R300EXIT  L       11,REOSAV11
          BR      11
REOSAV11  DS      F
✽
✽    MODULE 310:    READ INVENTORY MASTER
✽
REORD310  GET     INVMAST,INVWRKA
          AP      COUNT,=P'1'
          B       R310EXIT
INVEOF    MVI     EOFSWTCH,X'FF'
R310EXIT  BR      11
✽
✽    MODULE 320:    CALCULATE AVAILABLE
✽
REORD320  PACK    WRKAVAIL,INVONHND
          PACK    WRKONORD,INVONORD
          AP      WRKAVAIL,WRKONORD
          PACK    WRKORDPT,INVORDPT
          BR      11
```

Figure 19-4   The source listing for the structured reorder-listing program that is planned by the pseudocode in figure 19-3 (part 1 of 4)

```
*
*   MODULE 330:    PRINT REORDER LINE
*
REORD330 ST       11,PRTSAV11
         MVI      PRTDETL,X'40'
         MVC      PRTDETL+1(132),PRTDETL
IF330N1  CP       LINECNT,=P'54'
         BL       IF330N1B
IF330N1A BAL      11,REORD340
IF330N1B PACK     PACKAREA,INVITNBR
         MVC      PRTITNBR,PATTERN1
         ED       PRTITNBR,PACKAREA
         MVC      PRTITDES,INVITDES
         PACK     PACKAREA,INVPRICE
         MVC      PRTPRICE,PATTERN2
         ED       PRTPRICE,PACKAREA
         MVC      PRTAVAIL,PATTERN1
         ED       PRTAVAIL,WRKAVAIL
         MVC      PRTORDPT,PATTERN1
         ED       PRTORDPT,WRKORDPT
         MVC      PRTAREA,PRTDETL
         BAL      11,REORD350
         L        11,PRTSAV11
         BR       11
PRTSAV11 DS       F
*
*   MODULE 340:    PRINT HEADING LINES
*
REORD340 ST       11,HDSAV11
         MVC      PRTAREA,HDGLINE1
         BAL      11,REORD350
         MVC      PRTAREA,HDGLINE2
         BAL      11,REORD350
         MVC      PRTAREA,HDGLINE3
         BAL      11,REORD350
         ZAP      LINECNT,=P'0'
         MVI      PRTDCTL,C'0'
         L        11,HDSAV11
         BR       11
HDSAV11  DS       F
*
*   MODULE 350:    WRITE REPORT LINE
*
REORD350 PUT      PRTOUT,PRTAREA
         AP       LINECNT,=P'1'
         BR       11
*
*   MODULE 500:    PRINT COUNT LINE
*
REORD500 ST       11,CNTSAV11
         ED       CNTPATRN,COUNT
         MVC      PRTAREA,CNTLINE
         BAL      11,REORD350
         L        11,CNTSAV11
         BR       11
CNTSAV11 DS       F
```

Figure 19-4   The source listing for the structured reorder-listing program that is planned by the pseudocode in figure 19-3 (part 2 of 4)

```
❖
❖ FILE DEFINITIONS
❖
INVMAST    DTFSD BLKSIZE=500,                                              X
                 RECFORM=FIXBLK,                                          X
                 RECSIZE=50,                                              X
                 IOAREA1=INVIO1,                                          X
                 IOAREA2=INVIO2,                                          X
                 EOFADDR=INVEOF,                                          X
                 WORKA=YES
❖
PRTOUT     DTFPR DEVADDR=SYSLST,                                          X
                 IOAREA1=PRTWRKA,                                         X
                 WORKA=YES,                                               X
                 BLKSIZE=133,                                             X
                 CTLCHR=ASA
❖
❖I/O AREAS
❖
INVIO1     DS    CL500
INVIO2     DS    CL500
❖
❖ WORK AREAS
❖
INVWRKA    DS    0CL50
INVITNBR DS      CL5
INVITDES DS      CL20
         DS      CL5
INVPRICE DS      CL5
INVORDPT DS      CL5
INVONHND DS      CL5
INVONORD DS      CL5
❖
PRTWRKA    DS    CL133
❖
HDGLINE1 DS      0CL133
         DC      C'1'
         DC      C'DATE:  '
HDG1DATE DS      CL8
         DC      9C' '
         DC      C'REORDER LISTING'
         DC      12C' '
         DC      C'TIME:'
HDG1TIME DS      CL7
         DC      69C' '
❖
HDGLINE2 DS      0CL133
         DC      C'0'
         DC      C' ITEM            ITEM            UNIT              X
                   REORDER'
         DC      69C' '
❖
HDGLINE3 DS      0CL133
         DC      C' '
         DC      C' NO.       DESCRIPTION       PRICE       AVAILABLEX
                   POINT'
         DC      70C' '
```

Figure 19-4   The source listing for the structured reorder-listing program that is planned by the pseudocode in figure 19-3 (part 3 of 4)

```
*
PRTDETL   DS      OCL133
PRTDCTL   DS      CL1
PRTITNBR  DS      CL6
          DC      5C' '
PRTITDES  DS      CL20
          DC      4C' '
PRTPRICE  DS      CL7
          DC      4C' '
PRTAVAIL  DS      CL6
          DC      4C' '
PRTORDPT  DS      CL6
          DC      70C' '
*
CNTLINE   DS      OCL133
          DC      C'-'
CNTPATRN  DC      X'4020206B202020'
          DC      C' RECORDS IN THE INPUT DECK'
          DC      99C' '
*
* SWITCHES
*
EOFSWTCH  DC      X'00'
*
* WORK FIELDS
*
TIME      DS      F
WRKAVAIL  DS      PL3
WRKONORD  DS      PL3
WRKORDPT  DS      PL3
PACKAREA  DS      PL3
*
* COUNT FIELDS
*
COUNT     DC      PL3'0'
*
* PRINT FIELDS
*
PRTAREA   DS      CL133
LINECNT   DC      P'54'
*
* PATTERNS
*
PATTERN1  DC      X'402020202020'
PATTERN2  DC      X'40202021482020'
*
          END     BEGIN
```

Figure 19-4 The source listing for the structured reorder-listing program that is planned by the pseudocode in figure 19-3 (part 4 of 4)

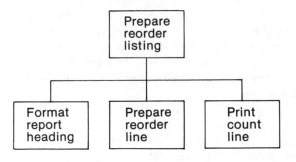

Figure 19-5   A structure chart showing the first two levels of the reorder-listing program

Step 1:   Draw the function boxes for the first two levels

To design a structure chart, you start with a top-level module that represents the entire program. Next, you decide on the one primary functional module that will be performed repeatedly during the execution of the program, and you draw this module at the second level of the chart. Next, decide whether your program requires any functional modules that need to be performed before and after this primary module. If so, you draw boxes for these functions to the left or the right of the primary module at the second level.

To illustrate, figure 19-5 represents the first two levels of the chart for the reorder-listing program. The top-level box is named "prepare reorder listing," and the primary module at the second level is named "prepare reorder line." The prepare-reorder-line module is the primary module because it will be executed repeatedly during the execution of the program. It will be executed one time for each master record until all records in the master file have been read and processed. In other words, the primary module represents the processing for one input record or one set of input records.

Because the reorder-listing program must get the date and time for the first heading line of the reorder listing, the module to the left of the prepare-reorder-line module is named "format report heading." This module will get the date and time and edit them into the appropriate fields in the first heading line. If other functions must be performed before the primary module is executed, they can also be drawn to the left of the primary module. For instance, a program that uses a table might require a module to load the table from a file into storage at the start of the program.

Because the reorder-listing program must print a count line after all reorder lines have been printed, the module to the right of the prepare-reorder-line module is named "print count line." If other functions must be performed after the function of the primary module has been completed, they can also be drawn to the right of the primary module.

As you get more experience with structured program development, you'll realize that all programs can be charted at the first two levels with a structure similar to the one in figure 19-5. Every program has one primary function, although it may not be related to a set of input records. And most programs require functions that must be performed before or after the primary function.

**Step 2:   Design the subordinate function boxes
until each module of the program can be coded in 30 lines or fewer**

Step 2 is to divide the modules at the second level into their subordinate functions and subfunctions until each module of the program can be coded in 30 lines or fewer. To illustrate, figure 19-6 shows the functions and subfunctions that I designed for the modules in figure 19-5.

To start, I asked what subordinate modules (if any) the format-report-heading module required. Since I knew a subprogram named GETIME was available for formatting the system's time, I drew the GETIME box as a subordinate function. At that point, I knew that I could code the format-report-heading line box in 30 lines or fewer so it didn't require other subordinates.

Next, I designed the subordinate functions for the prepare-reorder-line module. As you can see in figure 19-6, I designed three functions subordinate to this module in the third level of the chart. Each time the prepare-reorder-line module is executed, it must (1) read an inventory record, (2) calculate available, and (3) print a reorder line if available is less than reorder point. I then asked if any of these modules required subordinates, and I decided that only the print-reorder-line module needed one. Whenever page overflow is required, the report headings must be printed on the new page. As a result, the print-report-heading module is subordinate to the print-reorder-line module.

If the read or calculate modules required subordinates, of course, I would have drawn them at the next level of the chart. And I would have continued this process until I had designed down to the lowest level. For this simple program, though, figure 19-6 represents all the functional modules that are required by the prepare-reorder-line module.

Last, I asked whether the print-count-line module required any subordinates. I decided that it didn't. As a result, figure 19-6 represents all the functional modules required by the reorder-listing program. And I'm confident that I can code any one of them in 30 lines or fewer.

Of course, the number 30 is arbitrary. I chose it because modules of this size can be coded and tested with relative ease by the average programmer. In contrast, modules become increasingly more difficult to code as their size increases. So a 60 line module may be four times as difficult to code as a 30 line module. Nevertheless, as you get more experience with assembler language, you may want to change this arbitrary number to suit your style or your shop. From a practical point of view, though, I don't think you should use a number that is less than 20 or greater than 50.

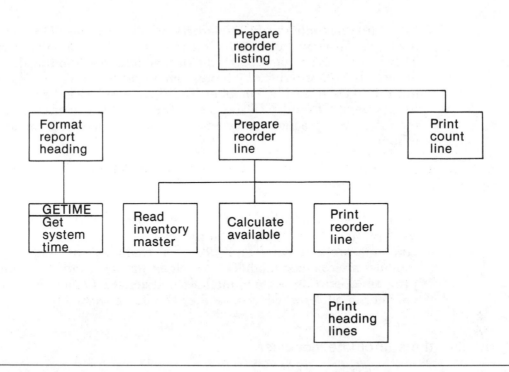

Figure 19-6   The expanded structure chart for the reorder-listing program

When you draw modules on a structure chart, keep in mind that a left-to-right sequence of execution is expected at each level of subordination. At the third level in figure 19-6, for example, you would expect the subordinates for the prepare-reorder-line module to be executed in the sequence of read, calculate, and print. However, when you actually code the program, that may not be the case. So the expected sequence can be varied as required by the program specifications. In other words, you can't always tell what the sequence will be at the time that you design a program's modules.

Step 3:   Add one function box for each I/O operation

In step 3, you add one function box for each I/O operation required by a program. This makes it possible to code a program with only one GET or PUT instruction for each I/O operation. If you look at the chart in figure 19-2, for example, you can see that I added three write modules for the printer file in step 3 of the design procedure. I didn't add a read module for the inventory master file, because the chart already had one.

When you isolate the I/O instructions in their own modules like this, you end up with a more efficient program. For instance, the program in figure 19-4 has only one PUT instruction for the printer file in contrast to the five PUT instructions used in the reorder-listing program in chapter 5. This also makes it easier to provide for functions like counting the number of records read or written by a program, because you can code functions like this in the related I/O module. The alternative in a large program is to have several GET or PUT statements for each file dispersed throughout the program, a practice that can make the logic of the program difficult to follow.

Step 4:   Shade the common modules

In step 4, you shade the upper righthand corners of the modules that are used in more than once place in the program. These modules are called *common modules*. In figure 19-2, for example, the write-report-line modules are common modules, so their corners are shaded. Although this program doesn't illustrate it, modules that aren't I/O modules can also be common modules in which case they should be shaded too.

Step 5:   Number the subroutine modules

In step 5, you number all of the modules that represent subroutines. That includes all of the modules except the subprogram modules. For most programs, a simple numbering system like the one used in figure 19-2 is adequate. That means you give the top-level module number 000. Next, you number the modules in the second level by 100s, but you leave enough space between the hundreds so it will provide for the modules at the lower levels of the chart. Finally, you number the modules at the next levels by 10s.

Note that the numbers do *not* indicate at what level a module can be found. This means that you can add modules to the chart at any level without changing the numbers of any of the other modules. For instance, you could add a module 150 as a subordinate to module 000. You could add a module 325 as a subordinate to module 300. Or, you could add a module 335 as a subordinate to module 330. As a result, a structure chart like this is easy to enhance or modify.

HOW TO PLAN THE MODULES OF A PROGRAM USING PSEUDOCODE

Once you have completed the structure chart for a program, you can use pseudocode to plan the code for the modules of the program before you actually code them. For instance, figure 19-3 gives the pseudocode for all of the modules charted in figure 19-2. Pseudocode is a language that you can use as a replacement for flowcharting. It lets you plan the operations and logic of a module using only the legal structures of structured programming. And it lets you plan the modules quickly and easily.

When you use pseudocode, you should remember that it is a personal language. As a result, you don't have to follow rigid coding rules. In general, you should capitalize all of the structure words like DO, UNTIL, IF, and ELSE. And you probably should capitalize assembler language names like REORD000 and EOFSWTCH. Beyond this, you simply try to state what each module must do in a style that you feel comfortable with.

When you use pseudocode, you should use indentation to make the code as readable as possible. This is illustrated by the code in figure 19-3. In the DO-UNTIL statement in module 300, for example, the UNTIL portion is indented four spaces. Similarly, in the IF statement in module 310, the IF and ELSE portions are indented to show their relationships.

In module 300, you can see *nested IF statements*. This refers to the fact that one IF statement is coded within another one. In this case, I used indentation to show the nesting of the statements. If these statements had ELSE portions, I would have used indentation to highlight the IF and ELSE portions of each statement as well as the nesting.

When you use pseudocode, you should realize that you don't have to plan every aspect of a module. You'll note in figure 19-3, for example, that none of the modules show the code that is required for subroutine linkage. I didn't show this code because it obviously is required and because the linkage is going to be coded in a standard way. Similarly, you may decide that the "format" statements in modules 330 and 500 are obvious so you don't have to show them in your pseudocode.

If you look closely at the pseudocode in figure 19-3, you can see that I/O modules can be used for more than just the I/O function. For instance, the read module is used to count the number of records read by the program and the write module is used to count the number of lines printed on a page. Since the write module counts both heading and detail lines, the IF statement in module 330 compares the line count with 54 rather than with 50 as used in the earlier versions of the reorder-listing program. When there is a separate I/O module for each I/O operation, it is easy to place the code for counting occurrences that are related to I/O operations.

When you use pseudocode for module planning, you don't necessarily have to plan every module in a program. For instance, modules 100, 320, 330, 340, 350, and 500 in figure 19-3 are relatively trivial. As a result, you may only want to plan modules 000, 300, and 310 for this program. When you design a structured program, you'll usually find that just a few modules are complicated enough to require planning, because all of the modules will be relatively short. On the other hand, if you're not sure how a module should be coded, it's worth taking the time to plan it with pseudocode.

HOW TO CODE A STRUCTURED PROGRAM IN ASSEMBLER LANGUAGE

When it comes to coding, structured programming implies three things. First, it implies that you have a structured design for the program. Second, it implies that the program will be coded using only the accepted structures of structured programming. And third, it implies a style of coding that is designed to increase the readability of a program.

Since you should already have some idea of how to design a structured program and how to plan the modules using only the valid structures, I will now show you how to code a structured program in assembler language. First, I will show you how to code the basic structures in assembler language. Then, I will give you some guidelines for using assembler language in a readable manner.

The basic structures in assembler language

To review, the basic structures of structured programming are the sequence, iteration, and selection structures. In addition, structured programming requires a facility for calling subordinate modules; this can be referred to as a *DO structure*. As you will see, the sequence structure presents no special problems in assembler language, but the best you can do with the other structures is to simulate them.

Figure 19-7 shows you how to code each of the basic structures in assembler language. Of course, you can code these structures in other ways. But the coding in figure 19-7 is relatively easy to use and understand, and it will get you started writing structured assembler language. Once you get used to this coding, you can modify it to suit your style. Later on, if you want to work at a more sophisticated level, you can write macro definitions for the iteration and selection structures using the techniques presented in chapter 11.

The sequence structure   In assembler language, any non-conditional, non-branching statement is a sequence structure. Similarly, a succession of two or more of these statements is a sequence structure. Thus, a series of move instructions is a sequence structure, and a series of arithmetic statements is a sequence structure. As a result, coding a sequence structure in assembler language doesn't require any special effort.

The DO structure   A DO structure in assembler language is a call to a subroutine and a return from the subroutine to the next instruction in the calling module. In chapter 8, you learned how to provide this linkage with a branch-and-link instruction like this:

```
BAL    11,REORD100
```

Before the branch takes place, the address of the next instruction to be executed is saved in the specified register (in this case, register 11). Then, when the subroutine completes its processing, it branches back to the saved address using a branch instruction like this:

```
BR    11
```

The sequence structure

```
PACK   WRKAVAIL,INVONORD
PACK   WRKONORD,INVONORD
AP     WRKAVAIL,WRKONORD
```

The DO structure

```
         BAL   11,REORD100           DO REORD100
         .
         .
REORD100 .
         .
         BR    11                    RETURN TO CALLING MODULE
```

The DO UNTIL structure

```
DU000N1  BAL   11,REORD300           DO REORD300
         CLI   EOFSWTCH,X'FF'           UNTIL EOFSWTCH=X'FF'
         BNE   DU000N1
         .
         .
REORD300 .
         .
         BR    11                    RETURN TO CALLING MODULE
```

The IF structure

```
IF300N1  CLC   FIELDA,FIELDB         IF FIELDA NOT = FIELDB
         BE    IF300N1B
IF300N1A .                              THEN DO STATEMENT GROUP A
         .
         B     IF300N1E
IF300N1B .                              ELSE DO STATEMENT GROUP B
         .
IF300N1E .                           END IF
         .
         .
         .
```

Figure 19-7　　One way to code the basic structures in assembler language

When you use a DO structure, there are a couple things to keep in mind. First, to comply with the principles of structured programming, each module (subroutine) can only have one entry and one exit point. Second, the last instruction of a subroutine *must* be an unconditional branch instruction. Although the theory of structured programming prohibits branching like this, you have no other choice in assembler language. Just be sure that the final branch instruction in the subroutine returns control to the instruction after the calling instruction.

The iteration structure　　When you use the iteration structure in assembler language, you can use any one of the three variations in figure

19-1. One of these variations, the DO UNTIL, is shown in figure 19-7. When you use it, a module is performed *until* a condition is satisfied.

Since there's no statement like the DO UNTIL in assembler language, you have to simulate it using code like the code shown in figure 19-7. Here, the branch-and-link instruction is used to branch to the module that is to be executed until the condition is met. Then, when the called module branches back to the calling routine, the calling routine tests to see if the condition has been met. If it has, processing continues with the next instruction in sequence. If it hasn't, the calling routine branches back to the start of the DO-UNTIL structure so the called module can be called again.

In figure 19-7, you can see that I used the name DU000N1 as the label for the start of the DO-UNTIL structure. This is DU (for DO UNTIL) followed by the number of the module that contains the structure (000) followed by the number of the DO-UNTIL structure in that module (N1 for number 1). If the module required a second DO-UNTIL structure, I would have named it DU000N2. And so on. Although you can modify this naming convention to suit your style, it is a simple one that easily identifies the DO-UNTIL structures that you use.

The selection structure   Since there's no statement like the IF statement in assembler language, you have to simulate it using code like the code shown in figure 19-7. Here, the structure starts with a comparison of two fields. Then, based on this comparison, the program either branches to a group of instructions that starts with the label IF300N1B or it falls through to a group of instructions that starts with the label IF300N1A. To make sure the structure has only one entry and one exit point, a branch instruction at the end of statement group A branches to the end of the selection structure, which is named IF300N1E.

I hope that the naming conventions used in this IF structure are obvious. Each IF structure starts with a label like IF300N1; that is, IF followed by the module number that contains the structure followed by the number of the IF statement in that module. Then, the label at the start of statement group A is the same label followed by the letter A; the label at the start of statement group B is the same label followed by the letter B; and the label of the exit point (or the label of the first instruction following the IF structure) is the same label followed by the letter E.

You can see how this labelling convention works in module 300 of the reorder-listing program in figure 19-4. Here, two IF structures are coded in the same module. However, neither IF statement has an ELSE portion (both are null) so there is no statement group B for either structure. In addition, the exit points for both IF statements are the same because the IF statements are nested. Finally, since the exit points of the IF statements are the same as the exit point for the entire module, I used the name of the subroutine exit (R300EXIT) as the label for the exit points of the IF statements.

When selection structures are nested, you code one selection structure within either statement group A or B of another selection structure.

Although this can become quite complicated, you can keep it manageable if you use strict naming conventions. If your selection structures are nested several levels deep, however, the coding can get out of control. In this case, you can often cut down the number of levels of nesting by modifying the structure chart.

Guidelines for readability

A primary goal of structured programming is to create code that is easy to read because a program that is readable is easier to develop, test, debug, and maintain than one that isn't. Here, then, are some guidelines that will help you create more readable code.

Use module names that refer back to the structure chart   When you code a module, the name you give it should relate it to a box on your structure chart. In the reorder-listing program in figure 19-4, you can see that all of the modules consist of the prefix REORD followed by the module number taken from the structure chart in figure 19-2. That way the structure chart becomes a directory to the modules that are coded in the assembly listing. Then, if you have to maintain a program, the structure chart will point you to the code that needs to be modified.

Put the source code modules in sequence by module number   Theoretically, it doesn't matter in what sequence the subroutines of a program are placed in the source code as long as the system starts executing the first instruction of the top-level module. If the sequence is arbitrary, though, both the original programmer and subsequent maintenance programmers will have a difficult time locating modules in the assembly listing. That's why we recommend that the modules be in sequence by module number as shown in the program in figure 19-4.

Group related data items   If you group data items by type, the data portion of your program will have a structure of its own. That way, it will be easier for you to locate data items in the program when you need to do so. Data items that you can group include switches, save areas, print control fields, editing patterns, and so on. In figure 19-4, you can see how I grouped these items in the reorder-listing program.

If you do a lot of assembler language programming, you may also want to adopt a standard sequence for data groups in your programs. For example, you may want to code your data groups in this sequence: save areas, input areas, output areas, input work areas, output work areas, printer work areas, switches, edit patterns, and other work areas. That way it will be easier for you to find a group of data items as you move from one program to the next.

Code local data names in the modules that use them   If a data name is only used in one module, you can call it a *local data name* (or a *local variable*). Then, if you code local data names in the modules that use them, you simplify the data descriptions that apply to more than one module. In the program in figure 19-4, for example, the one word save areas used by modules 300, 330, 340, and 500 are all described in these modules. Otherwise, they would be described along with all the other data names at the end of the program.

Although the reorder-listing program only uses save areas as local data names, some programs will use other types of fields and areas as local data names. Then, there is more benefit to describing these names within the modules that use them.

Use meaningful data names   When you create data names, you should make them as descriptive as you can. Of course, that isn't always easy in assembler language because of its restrictions. Nevertheless, the clearer you make your data names, the more readable your programs will be.

At the least, when data items are part of the same group or structure, you should add a prefix or a suffix to each name to identify the item as part of the group. For example, each data name in the description for the inventory master record in figure 19-4 starts with the letters INV. Using prefixes and suffixes for related fields helps you cut down on coding errors.

Use comment lines to highlight modules and data groups   If you look at the reorder-listing program in figure 19-4, you can see that three comment lines have been used before each module of the program and before each data group. In each case, the first and third comment lines are blank, while the second comment line identifies the module or data group. This makes these blocks of code easy to find.

Don't use comments unless they are necessary   Comments are the notes you can put in assembler language instructions to the right of the operands. Because unstructured assembler language can be extremely difficult to follow, comments have traditionally been used to clarify code. However, it takes time to put them into a program, and, if they are coded incorrectly, they can make a program even more difficult to follow. To illustrate, imagine a comment that says BRANCH WHEN EQUAL in an instruction with an operation code of BNE. This type of contradiction can originate during debugging when you change an operation code, but not the related comment.

In contrast to traditional practices, then, we recommend that you avoid using comments unless they are necessary. In fact, we don't even recommend comments like those in figure 19-7. If you use structured design, your modules should consist of 30 lines or fewer so they should be relatively easy to read in the first place. Then, if you code your basic structures using a style like that shown in figure 19-7, your code should be largely self-documenting.

HOW TO TEST A PROGRAM USING TOP-DOWN TESTING

When you design a program on a top-down basis using structured design, you can develop it using *top-down coding and testing*. In fact, we recommend that you use top-down coding and testing on any program that takes more than a day to develop.

When you use top-down coding and testing, you don't code the entire program and then test it. Instead, you code and test in phases. You normally start by coding the top-level module and one or more of the modules in the second level. Then, after correcting any bugs, you add one or more modules to this coding and test again. When this much of the program runs correctly, you code a few more modules, add them to what you have, and test again. You continue in this way until all the modules have been coded and you are testing the entire program. Because top-down coding and testing always go together, the phrase *top-down testing* implies top-down coding.

The primary benefit of top-down testing is improved testing efficiency (or improved productivity). To illustrate, imagine an assembler language program of 1000 lines or more. If you test the entire program at once with all of its bugs, it's likely that your testing will proceed very inefficiently. For example, it may take several days of testing just to debug a couple of minor clerical errors. But if you test on a top-down basis, testing proceeds in increments of a few modules, perhaps 50 instructions or fewer at a time. Then, it is relatively easy to find any bugs that are discovered during a test phase because they almost have to be in the modules just added or in the interfaces between the old modules and the new.

How to create a top-down test plan

When you use top-down testing, you start by developing a top-down test plan like the one in figure 19-8. In this plan for the reorder-listing program that is charted in figure 19-2, five modules are tested in phase 1, two more are added in phase 2, the last two are added in phase 3, and phase 4 is a volume test. Since the read module isn't tested until phase 3, no test data is needed for the first two phases.

When you create a test plan, you have considerable choice as to what modules you test in each phase. As long as you proceed from the top down and add one or more modules in each phase, you are adhering to the principles of top-down testing. Whether you add one, two, or more modules at a time depends on your experience and on the length and complexity of the modules. In a short program like the reorder-listing program, it doesn't matter too much what sequence you use, but in a larger, more realistic program you must carefully plan the development sequence.

In general, your goal should be to use the sequence of testing that will be most efficient in terms of coding and testing. When you develop your test plan, then, you should ask questions like: Where are the major module interfaces in the program? Where, if anywhere, in the structure chart do I have doubts about the design? In what modules do I have doubts about how the coding should be done? In most cases, you should try to code and resolve the major problems first.

After you test the first two or three levels of a program, it often becomes a case of mop up. Eventually, you have to code and test all of the modules, so you may as well take them one group at a time, introducing data that applies to each group as you go along.

Incidentally, you don't have to code the file or data definitions required by a module until you add the module to the program. For instance, since the read module in figure 19-8 isn't added to the program until phase 3, you don't have to code the DTF for the inventory master file until phase 3. On the other hand, since module 330 requires the data in the work area for the inventory master file, you have to code the data definitions for this area as part of your coding for phase 2.

How to code program stubs

To use top-down testing, you must code *program stubs*, or *dummy modules*, for the modules in a phase that are called, but not tested. Using the test plan in figure 19-8, for example, modules 310, 320, and 330 are dummy modules in phase 1 so you must code program stubs for them. Similarly, modules 310 and 320 are dummy modules in phase 2.

In phase 1 of figure 19-8, the program stubs for modules 310, 320, and 330 don't have to do anything other than provide the subroutine linkage because the modules that are being tested don't require any data that is developed by them. As a result, you can code the program stub for module 310 like this:

```
REORD310 BR      11
```

Similarly, you can code the stubs for modules 320 and 330 in the same way. This code simply passes control back to the calling module.

If you want to make sure that the linkage works correctly during your test run, you can code program stubs that print messages showing that the subroutines were called properly. For instance, you can code this stub for module 310:

```
REORD310 PUT     PRTOUT,R310MSG
         BR      11
R310MSG  DC      CL133' 310   READ INVENTORY RECORD'
```

When executed, this stub will print the number and name of the module to show that it has been executed. Then, if you code modules 320 and 330 in the same way, the printed output will indicate whether the dummy modules have been called properly.

In phase 2 of figure 19-8, the program stubs should develop some data in order to test module 330. To do this, the program stubs can be coded as in figure 19-9. Here, module 310 simulates the reading of one input record the first time it is executed. The second time it is executed, it moves hex FF to EOFSWTCH indicating that all records in the file have been read. Similarly, module 320 simulates the calculation of available by moving a value into WRKAVAIL. If the stubs are coded like this, module 330 can print the data for one reorder line so all of the modules except the stubs will get tested.

Program: REORDLST	Prepare Reorder Listing	Page: 1
Designer: Anne Prince		Date: 10-31-85

Test phase	Data	Data source
1. Modules 000, 100, 300, 500 and 350	None	Not applicable
2. Add modules 330 and 340	None	Not applicable
3. Add modules 310 and 320	Three inventory master records; one with available = reorder point, one with available > reorder point, and one with available < reorder point	Self
4. Volume test	Enough inventory master records to cause page overflow	Test data generator

Figure 19-8   A top-down test plan for the program that is charted in figure 19-2

When you code program stubs, you must try to be practical. At some point, it becomes more practical to code the actual module than it is to simulate the function of the module. If, for example, you look at the stub for the read module in figure 19-9, you can see that the code for the stub is longer than the code for the actual module will be. So is it worth coding this stub? Similarly, the actual code for the calculate module is only four lines while the stub is two lines, so is it worth coding the stub? That, of course, depends on the program, the module, and your experience. In the case of the stubs in figure 19-9, I think it's worth coding the read stub that way, because you simulate a one record file before you even have to create a test file. On the other hand, I don't think it's worth coding the calculate stub that way because the coding for the actual module will work just as well.

DISCUSSION   Although this chapter is just an introduction to the techniques of structured programming, I hope you can see how they can help you improve your productivity as well as the quality of your programs. You should realize, though, that this chapter has presented but one set of techniques for structured program development. If you read the literature on structured programming, you will learn that there are several different approaches to structured programming in assembler language. In these development systems, several different types of charts are used for structured design. The numbering and naming conventions used for the modules of a program vary. And even the approaches to determining the modules of a program vary. Similarly, there are other ways to go about structured module planning, structured coding, and top-down testing.

Nevertheless, we believe that the methods presented in this chapter are at least as good as any of the other methods. We believe that the methods presented in this chapter will help you reach a professional level of productivity. And, we believe that these methods will help you write programs that meet professional standards for reliability and maintainability.

Terminology

structured programming	nested IF statements
sequence structure	DO structure
selection structure	local data name
iteration structure	local variable
proper program	top-down coding and testing
structure chart	top-down testing
pseudocode	program stub
common module	dummy module

Objectives

1. Explain the theory of structured programming.

2. Given program specifications, use structured development techniques to design the program, plan the coding of its modules, code it in structured style, and test it using top-down testing.

Module 310: Read inventory master

```
REORD310 CP     COUNT,=P'1'                          STUB
         BE     INVEOF                               STUB
         MVC    INVITNBR,=C'00123'                   STUB
         MVC    INVITDES,=C'DUMMY RECORD 1'          STUB
         MVC    INVPRICE,=C'00005'                   STUB
         MVC    INVORDPT,=C'01000'                   STUB
         MVC    INVONHND,=C'00500'                   STUB
         MVC    INVONORD,=C'00250'                   STUB
         AP     COUNT,=P'1'
         B      R310EXIT
INVEOF   MVI    EOFSWTCH,X'FF'
R310EXIT BR     11
```

Module 320: Calculate available

```
REORD320 MVC    WRKAVAIL,=P'00750'                   STUB
         BR     11
```

Figure 19-9   Program stubs for phase 2 of the test plan in figure 19-8

Appendix A

Assembler language reference summary

This appendix presents a summary of the instructions and commands presented in this text. In sequence, you will find the following:

DTFSD operand summary
DTFPR operand summary
Common EBCDIC codes in binary and hexadecimal
DS and DC type codes
Common editing characters
ASA printer control characters
Instruction formats for a general subset
Instruction formats for decimal arithmetic
Instruction formats for bit manipulation and
    translation
Instruction formats for register operations and
    fixed-point arithmetic
Instruction formats for floating-point arithmetic
Mnemonic operation codes for branching
Standard macros
Assembler commands for controlling an assembly listing
Assembler commands for controlling an assembly
Assembler commands for macro definition and
    conditional assembly

Of course, assembler language consists of many more instructions, macros, and commands than those presented in this book.

Although this appendix presents operand summaries for the DTFSD and DTFPR macros, it does not present any reference materials for the ISAM, DAM, or VSAM access methods. Instead, we recommend that you use the figures in chapters 14 through 16 as reference materials for these access methods.

Priority	Keyword	Programmer code	Remarks
Required	BLKSIZE	Length of I/O area	Block length; for output files, it must include 8 bytes for the count area.
Optional	RECFORM	FIXUNB FIXBLK VARUNB VARBLK	FIXBLK for fixed-length blocked records; VARBLK for variable-length blocked records; FIXUNB is the default.
Optional	RECSIZE	Record length	Use only if RECFORM is FIXBLK.
Optional	TYPEFLE	INPUT OUTPUT	INPUT is the default so this operand is usually omitted for input files.
Optional	UPDATE	YES	Used only when records are to be updated in place; TYPEFLE must be INPUT.
Required	IOAREA1	Name of first I/O area	Length must equal block length.
Optional	IOAREA2	Name of second I/O area	Must be same length as first I/O area.
Optional	WORKA	YES	When used, records will be read into or written from the area named in the related GET or PUT statement. Don't use if IOREG is specified.
Optional	IOREG	Register number (nn)	When used, the register will give the address of the next record to be processed. Don't use if WORKA = YES is specified.
Required for input files	EOFADDR	Label of first instruction of EOF routine	Required for input files.
Optional	DEVADDR	Logical unit name in form SYSxxx	Programmer logical units are commonly used; only required when no EXTENT statement is used in the JCL for the file.

DTFSD operand summary

Priority	Keyword	Programmer code	Remarks
Optional	BLKSIZE	Length of I/O area	Usually, 133 when ASA control characters are used. The default is 121.
Required	IOAREA1	Name of first I/O area	Length must equal block length.
Optional	IOAREA2	Name of second I/O area	Must be same length as first I/O area.
Optional	WORKA	Yes	When used, records will be written from the work area named in the related PUT statement.
Required	DEVADDR	Logical unit name in form SYSxxx	SYSLST is commonly used.
Optional	CTLCHR	ASA or YES	ASA characters are commonly used. YES means System/370 characters are used.
Optional	DEVICE	Device number or PRT1	Code PRT1 for 3202-4, 3203-5, 3211, 3262, and 3289-4 printers. For other printers, code the device number. The default value is 1403.

DTFPR operand summary

Character	Zone bits	Digit bits	Hexadecimal code
blank	0100	0000	40
.	0100	1011	4B
(	0100	1101	4D
+	0100	1110	4E
&	0101	0000	50
$	0101	1011	5B
*	0101	1100	5C
)	0101	1101	5D
;	0101	1110	5E
-	0110	0000	60
/	0110	0001	61
,	0110	1011	6B
%	0110	1100	6C
?	0110	1111	6F
:	0111	1010	7A
#	0111	1011	7B
'	0111	1101	7D
=	0111	1110	7E
"	0111	1111	7F
A	1100	0001	C1
B	1100	0010	C2
C	1100	0011	C3
D	1100	0100	C4
E	1100	0101	C5
F	1100	0110	C6
G	1100	0111	C7
H	1100	1000	C8
I	1100	1001	C9
J	1101	0001	D1
K	1101	0010	D2
L	1101	0011	D3
M	1101	0100	D4
N	1101	0101	D5
O	1101	0110	D6
P	1101	0111	D7
Q	1101	1000	D8
R	1101	1001	D9

Common EBCDIC codes in binary and hexadecimal (part 1 of 2)

Character	Zone bits	Digit bits	Hexadecimal code
S	1110	0010	E2
T	1110	0011	E3
U	1110	0100	E4
V	1110	0101	E5
W	1110	0110	E6
X	1110	0111	E7
Y	1110	1000	E8
Z	1110	1001	E9
0	1111	0000	F0
1	1111	0001	F1
2	1111	0010	F2
3	1111	0011	F3
4	1111	0100	F4
5	1111	0101	F5
6	1111	0110	F6
7	1111	0111	F7
8	1111	1000	F8
9	1111	1001	F9

Common EBCDIC codes in binary and hexadecimal (part 2 of 2)

Code	Type	Implied length	Truncation/ padding	Alignment if ALIGN is on
C	Characters	None	Right	None
X	Hexadecimal	None	Left	None
B	Binary	None	Left	None
F	Fullword (fixed-point)	4 bytes	Left	Fullword
H	Halfword (fixed-point)	2 bytes	Left	Halfword
E	Short floating-point	4 bytes	Right	Fullword
D	Long floating-point	8 bytes	Right	Doubleword
P	Packed decimal	None	Left	None
Z	Zoned decimal	None	Left	None
A	Address constant (adcon)	4 bytes	Left	Fullword
V	Externally defined adcon	4 bytes	Left	Fullword

DS and DC type codes

Hex code	Meaning
20	Digit selector
21	Significance starter
22	Field separator
40	Blank
4B	Period
5B	Dollar sign
5C	Asterisk
6B	Comma
60	–
C3D9	CR
C4C2	DB

Common editing characters

Code	Action before printing
blank	Space 1 line
0	Space 2 lines
–	Space 3 lines
+	Suppress spacing
1	Skip to first line on new page

ASA printer control characters

Instruction	Mnemonic operation	Type	Explicit operand format
Branch and link	BAL	RX	R1,D2(X2,B2)
Branch and link register	BALR	RR	R1,R2
Branch on condition	BC	RX	M1,D2(X2,B2)
Compare logical characters	CLC	SS	D1(L,B1),D2(B2)
Compare logical immediate	CLI	SI	D1(B1),I2
Edit	ED	SS	D1(L,B1),D2(B2)
Edit and mark	EDMK	SS	D1(L,B1),D2(B2)
Move characters	MVC	SS	D1(L,B1),D2(B2)
Move immediate	MVI	SI	D1(B1),I2
Move numerics	MVN	SS	D1(L,B1),D2(B2)
Move with offset	MVO	SS	D1(L1,B1),D2(L2,B2)
Move zones	MVZ	SS	D1(L,B1),D2(B2)

Instruction formats for a general subset

Instruction	Mnemonic operation	Type	Explicit operand format
Add decimal	AP	SS	D1(L1,B1),D2(L2,B2)
Compare decimal	CP	SS	D1(L1,B1),D2(L2,B2)
Divide decimal	DP	SS	D1(L1,B1),D2(L2,B2)
Multiply decimal	MP	SS	D1(L1,B1),D2(L2,B2)
Subtract decimal	SP	SS	D1(L1,B1),D2(L2,B2)
Zero and add decimal	ZAP	SS	D1(L1,B1),D2(L2,B2)
Pack	PACK	SS	D1(L1,B1),D2(L2,B2)
Unpack	UNPK	SS	D1(L1,B1),D2(L2,B2)
Shift and round decimal	SRP	SS	D1(L1,B1),D2(B2),I3

Instruction formats for decimal arithmetic

Instruction	Mnemonic operation	Type	Explicit operand format
AND logical	N	RX	R1,D2(X2,B2)
AND logical	NC	SS	D1(L,B1),D2(B2)
AND logical immediate	NI	SI	D1(B1),I2
AND logical	NR	RR	R1,R2
Execute	EX	RX	R1,D2(X2,B2)
OR logical	O	RX	R1,D2(X2,B2)
OR logical	OC	SS	D1(L,B1),D2(B2)
OR logical immediate	OI	SI	D1(B1),I2
OR logical	OR	RR	R1,R2
Test under mask	TM	SI	D1(B1),I2
Translate	TR	SS	D1(L,B1),D2(B2)
Translate and test	TRT	SS	D1(L,B1),D2(B2)

Instruction formats for bit manipulation and translation

Instruction	Mnemonic operation	Type	Explicit operand format
Add	A	RX	R1,D2(X2,B2)
Add halfword	AH	RX	R1,D2(X2,B2)
Add register	AR	RR	R1,R2
Branch on count	BCT	RX	R1,D2(X2,B2)
Branch on count register	BCTR	RR	R1,R2
Compare	C	RX	R1,D2(X2,B2)
Compare halfword	CH	RX	R1,D2(X2,B2)
Compare logical long	CLCL	RR	R1,R2
Compare register	CR	RR	R1,R2
Convert to binary	CVB	RX	R1,D2(X2,B2)
Convert to decimal	CVD	RX	R1,D2(X2,B2)
Divide	D	RX	R1,D2(X2,B2)
Divide register	DR	RR	R1,R2
Insert characters under mask	ICM	RS	R1,M3,D2(B2)
Load	L	RX	R1,D2(X2,B2)
Load address	LA	RX	R1,D2(X2,B2)
Load halfword	LH	RX	R1,D2(X2,B2)
Load multiple	LM	RS	R1,R3,D2(B2)
Load register	LR	RR	R1,R2
Load and test register	LTR	RR	R1,R2
Move characters long	MVCL	RR	R1,R2
Multiply	M	RX	R1,D2(X2,B2)
Multiply halfword	MH	RX	R1,D2(X2,B2)
Multiply register	MR	RR	R1,R2
Store	ST	RX	R1,D2(X2,B2)
Store characters under mask	STCM	RS	R1,M3,D2(B2)
Store halfword	STH	RX	R1,D2(X2,B2)
Store multiple	STM	RS	R1,R3,D2(B2)
Subtract	S	RX	R1,D2(X2,B2)
Subtract halfword	SH	RX	R1,D2(X2,B2)
Subtract register	SR	RR	R1,R2

Instruction formats for register operations and fixed-point arithmetic

Instruction	Mnemonic operation	Type	Explicit operand format
Add normalized short	AE	RX	R1,D2(X2,B2)
Add normalized long	AD	RX	R1,D2(X2,B2)
Add normalized short	AER	RR	R1,R2
Add normalized long	ADR	RR	R1,R2
Compare short	CE	RX	R1,D2(X2,B2)
Compare long	CD	RX	R1,D2(X2,B2)
Compare short	CER	RR	R1,R2
Compare long	CDR	RR	R1,R2
Divide short	DE	RX	R1,D2(X2,B2)
Divide long	DD	RX	R1,D2(X2,B2)
Divide short	DER	RR	R1,R2
Divide long	DDR	RR	R1,R2
Load short	LE	RX	R1,D2(X2,B2)
Load long	LD	RX	R1,D2(X2,B2)
Load short	LER	RR	R1,R2
Load long	LDR	RR	R1,R2
Load positive short	LPER	RR	R1,R2
Load positive long	LPDR	RR	R1,R2
Load negative short	LNER	RR	R1,R2
Load negative long	LNDR	RR	R1,R2
Load complement short	LCER	RR	R1,R2
Load complement long	LCDR	RR	R1,R2
Multiply short	ME	RX	R1,D2(X2,B2)
Multiply long	MD	RX	R1,D2(X2,B2)
Multiply short	MER	RR	R1,R2
Multiply long	MDR	RR	R1,R2
Store short	STE	RX	R1,D2(X2,B2)
Store long	STD	RX	R1,D2(X2,B2)
Subtract normalized short	SE	RX	R1,D2(X2,B2)
Subtract normalized long	SD	RX	R1,D2(X2,B2)
Subtract normalized short	SER	RR	R1,R2
Subtract normalized long	SDR	RR	R1,R2

Instruction formats for floating-point arithmetic

Use	Code	Meaning
General	B or BR	Unconditional branch
After	BH or BHR	Branch on A high
Compare	BL or BLR	Branch on A low
Instructions	BE or BER	Branch on A equal B
(A:B)	BNH or BNHR	Branch on A not high
	BNL or BNLR	Branch on A not low
	BNE or BNER	Branch on A not equal B
After	BO or BOR	Branch on overflow
Arithmetic	BP or BPR	Branch on plus
Instructions	BM or BMR	Branch on minus
	BZ or BZR	Branch on zero
	BNP or BNPR	Branch on not plus
	BNM or BNMR	Branch on not minus
	BNZ or BNZR	Branch on not zero
After the	BO or BOR	Branch if ones
Test under	BM or BMR	Branch if mixed
Mask	BZ or BZR	Branch if zeros
Instruction	BNO or BNOR	Branch if not ones

Mnemonic operation codes for branching

Code	Operands	Meaning
EOJ	none	End the program and pass control to the supervisor.
COMRG	none	Store the address of the communication region in register 1.
GETIME	STANDARD BINARY TU	Store the time in register 1 in one of three formats. The default is STANDARD. STANDARD format is HHMMSS in packed decimal; BINARY is number of seconds since midnight in binary; and TU is number of 1/300ths of a second since midnight in binary.
CANCEL	none	Cancel the program and print a dump of the registers and all storage.
DUMP	none	Cancel the program and print a dump of the registers and the user's partition only.
PDUMP	address-1,address-2	Print a dump of the registers and the storage area between the two addresses given in the macro. The addresses can be coded as labels.
SAVE	(register-1,register-2)	Store the contents of the registers from register-1 through register-2 in an 18-word standard save area. The address of the save area must be in register 13. The wrap-around concept applies.
CALL	subprogram,(label-1,...)	Construct an address list for the labels given in the second operand. Store the address of this list in register 1. Store the address of the subprogram in register 15. Store the return address in register 14. Branch to the address in register 15.
RETURN	(register-1,register-2)	Load the contents of the registers from register-1 through register-2 from an 18-word standard save area. The address of the save area must be in register 13. The wrap-around concept applies. Then, branch to the address in register 14.

Standard macros

Code	Operands	Meaning
EJECT	none	Skip to the first line of a new page of the assembly listing.
PRINT	ON	Print the assembly listing.
	OFF	Don't print the assembly listing.
	GEN	Print the instructions generated by macros.
	NOGEN	Don't print the instructions generated by macros.
	DATA	Print all DC and literal data.
	NODATA	Print only the first eight bytes of the data defined by each DC or literal.
SPACE	number	Space the assembly listing the specified number of lines. If the number is more than the number of lines remaining on the page, skip to the first line of a new page.
TITLE	'title'	Print the specified title on each page of the assembly listing.

Assembler commands for controlling an assembly listing

Code	Operands	Meaning
COPY	bookname	Insert the code from the specified book in the source statement library into the source program.
CSECT	none	Restore the location counter after a DSECT. The label should be the same as the program name given in the label of the START instruction.
DSECT	none	Signal the start of a dummy section. The label must be assigned to a base register by a USING command.
END	entry-point	Signal the end of a source program. The operand names the entry point of the program.
ENTRY	entry-point	Identify the entry point of a subprogram.
EQU	label or expression	Assign the address and length of the operand to the label of the macro.
EXTRN	external-name	The specified name is defined outside the program so it should be resolved by the linkage editor.
LTORG	none	Define all literals used to this point in the program at this point in the program.
ORG	label or expression	Change the location counter value to the address of the label or to the value of the expression given as the operand.
START	self-defining term	Start the assembly of the program using the value of the operand as the starting location counter value.
USING	*,register-1,register-2	Use the registers from register-1 through register-2 as the base registers for this program.
USING	dsect-name,register	Use the register number given in the second operand as the base register for the DSECT named.

Assembler commands for controlling an assembly

Code	Operands	Meaning
AGO	sequence symbol	Branch to the specified sequence symbol.
AIF	(logical expression) sequence symbol	Branch to the specified sequence symbol if the logical expression is true.
GBLA	symbol-1,...	Declare arithmetic global SET symbols.
GBLB	symbol-1,...	Declare binary global SET symbols.
GBLC	symbol-1,...	Declare character global SET symbols.
LCLA	symbol-1,...	Declare arithmetic local SET symbols.
LCLB	symbol-1,...	Declare binary local SET symbols.
LCLC	symbol-1,...	Declare character local SET symbols.
MACRO	none	Start a macro definition.
MEND	none	End a macro definition.
MEXIT	none	Terminate macro expansion.
MNOTE	severity-code,'message'	Print a message during macro expansion. If a severity code is present, print the message in the diagnostic listing too.
SETA	arithmetic expression	Assign the operand value to the arithmetic SET symbol coded as the label of the command.
SETB	0 or 1	Assign the value of 0 or 1 to the binary SET symbol coded as the label of the command.
	logical expression	If the expression is true, assign a value of 1 to the binary SET symbol coded as the label of the command. If the expression is false, assign a value of 0 to the symbol.
SETC	'character expression'	Assign the operand value to the character SET symbol coded as the label of the command.

Assembler commands for macro definition and conditional assembly

Appendix B

A comprehensive case study

The case study that follows asks you to develop one program after you finish chapter 5 in the text. Then, for chapters 6 through 16, you will be asked to enhance this program in many different ways. By the time you code and test all the enhancements, you will have coded over 600 lines of code. And you will have used most of the functions provided for by assembler language.

If you don't have time to complete all of the tasks in the case study, you should at least do the tasks for chapters 5 through 8. Since these chapters present a professional subset of assembler language, you will have a useful background in assembler language once you complete the tasks for these chapters.

Instead of doing one program enhancement at a time, you may prefer to do the tasks for several chapters as a single work unit. This should reduce the number of assemblies and test runs you will have to make for the case study. But whether or not you combine tasks will depend on your working style, how much access you have to a computer terminal, and the instructions given you by your instructor.

Even if you don't have access to a DOS/VSE computer system, we still recommend that you code the phases of this case study because that's a critical test of your learning progress. If you can code all phases of this case study with confidence that your coding will work correctly, we're confident that you will have met the objectives of this book.

Input/output specifications

File	Description	Use
CUSTMST	Customer master file	Input
SLSRPT	Print file: Sales report	Output
CUSTEXT	Customer extension file (used only for the tasks in section 4)	Input

Process specifications

This program prepares a year-to-date (YTD) sales report from a file of customer records. The records are in sequence by customer key and the report should be printed in the same sequence. The program should print headings at the top of each page of the report and skip to a new page after 50 detail lines have been printed on a page.

The customer key is not a numeric field, so a key like NOR101 is valid. Since net sales = gross sales − returns, any of the net sales fields can be negative. As a result, a minus sign should be printed after a number to show that it is negative, as indicated by the minus signs on the print chart in positions 77, 92, and 109. If a number is positive, nothing should be printed in these positions.

This program is designed so you can add code to it as you proceed through the book. When you complete chapter 5, for example, you aren't expected to be able to write a program that produces the shaded portions of the print chart. As a result, your program should only produce the unshaded data. Then, when you complete chapter 6, you'll be able to enhance your program so it produces the shaded data in the first two heading lines and all of total line 2. When you complete chapter 7, you'll be able to enhance your program so it produces the shaded data in print positions 79-92. And so on.

Disk file specifications

You will need to get the following specifications from your instructor related to the disk file you'll be using for this program:

Block size:
Device:
Logical unit name:
Device address:
File-id:

Otherwise, assume that the block size is 800 (record size is 400), the device is the 2311, and the logical unit name is SYS008.

Record Layout for the Customer Master Record (CUSTMST)

Field name	Field description	Characteristics
CMKEY	Customer key	CL6
CMNAME	Customer name	CL31
CMADDR	Customer address	CL31
CMCITY	Customer city	CL18
CMSTATE	State code	CL2
CMZIP5	Zip code (5 digits)	CL5
CMZIPX	Zip code extension (4 digits)	CL4
CMYSLSD	YTD $ gross sales	CL8 (two decimal positions)
CMYSLSQ	YTD quantity gross sales	CL5
CMYRTNSD	YTD $ returns	CL7 (two decimal positions)
CMYRTNSQ	YTD quantity returns	CL4
CMMONSLS	12 monthly sales segments	CL252
	Monthly $ gross sales	ZL7 (two decimal positions)
	Monthly $ returns	ZL7 (two decimal positions)
	Monthly $ net sales	ZL7 (two decimal positions)
	Unused	CL27

Record Layout for the Customer Extension Record (CUSTEXT)

Field name	Field description	Characteristics
CESTATUS	Record status	CL1
CEKEY	Customer key	CL6
CELYSLS	12 monthly YTD sales segments	OL100
	Last YTD $ gross sales	PL5 (two decimal positions)
	Last YTD $ returns	PL4 (two decimal positions)
	Last YTD $ net sales	PL5 (two decimal positions)
	Unused	CL25

Document name Sales by customer   Date 11-13-85

Program name CUST5230   Designer AMP

Record Name

Record Name		
Heading line 1 (CC)	1	DATE: MM/DD/YY YTD SALES BY CUSTOMER IN DOLLARS (C$ XX,000 OR MORE) PAGE: XXX
Heading line 2 (CC)	2	TIME: HH:MM CUST5230
Heading line 3	3	
	4	KEY CUSTOMER NAME YTD SALES YTD RETURNS YTD NET SLS NET SLS 3 POS NET LAST YTD FILE MAINTENANCE
	5	
Detail lines	6	XXXXXX XXXXXXXXXXXXXXXXXXXXX XXX,XXX.XX XX,XXX.XX XXX,XXX.XX XXX,XXX.XX- X,XXX,XXX.XXX INVALID STATE CODE
	7	XXXXXX XXXXXXXXXXXXXXXXXXXXX XXX,XXX.XX XX,XXX.XX XXX,XXX.XX XXX,XXX.XX- X,XXX,XXX.XX INVALID ZIP CODE
	8	XXXXXX XXXXXXXXXXXXXXXXXXXXX XXX,XXX.XX XX,XXX.XX XXX,XXX.XX XXX,XXX.XX- X,XXX,XXX.XX ZIP CODE NOT NUMERIC
	9	XXXXXX XXXXXXXXXXXXXXXXXXXXX XXX,XXX.XX XX,XXX.XX XXX,XXX.XX XXX,XXX.XX- X,XXX,XXX.XX NO EXTENSION RECORD
	10	
Total line 1	11	RECORDS IN CUSTOMER FILE = XX,XXX
Total line 2 (CC)	12	AVG. NET SALES/CUSTOMER = XXX,XXX.XX
	13	

(C7)   (Section #)   (C11 and Section #)

Development tasks by chapter

Section 2   A professional subset of assembler language

Chapter 5   An introductory subset of assembler language

When you finish chapter 5 in the text, develop a program that produces the report represented by the unshaded portion of the print chart. When you get your first assembly listing, you will want to read chapter 17 to learn how to read the output and correct the diagnostics. When you test your program, you will want to read chapter 18 to learn how to solve your debugging problems.

If you want to start this case study before you finish chapter 5, you can write a program to produce just the detail lines of the report after you finish topic 1 of chapter 5. If the input file you'll be using is blocked, you'll have to look ahead to topic 2 to see how the DTF and I/O areas are coded for blocked records.

Chapter 6   Completing a basic subset of assembler language

Topic 1   Enhance your program to produce total line 2. Average net sales is YTD net sales divided by the number of records in the customer file. But note that average sales is rounded to the nearest whole dollar.

Also, use relative addressing and explicit lengths to set the detail line to blanks. Modify the detail line definition appropriately.

Topic 2   Enhance your program to produce the date and time data in the first two heading lines of the report. Then, use the appropriate macro to print a snapshot dump of your data definitions (not including the I/O areas) after all records have been processed but before your program ends. After you've produced this dump output once, remove the dump macro from your program so you won't produce this unnecessary output when you test subsequent enhancements of your program.

Topic 3   Replace your data definitions for the customer master record's work area with a COPY instruction. This instruction should insert the copy book named CUSTMST into your program. Find out what library this book is going to be in and use the LIBDEF statement in your JCL if it is necessary.

Also, use the assembler commands (1) to skip to the top of a new page in the assembly listing between the instructions of the program and the DTFs and data definitions, and (2) to suppress the printing of instructions generated by macros. If your program requires more than one base register, code the USING command and adcons to provide for the additional registers.

Chapter 7   Register operations, binary arithmetic, and storage definition techniques

Enhance your program to produce the data in print positions 79-92 on the print chart. This column of data is the sales total for the last 3-month period. To derive this total, you use the net sales fields in the monthly sales segments in the master records. There are 12 of these segments, one for each of the last 12 months. In your program, then, you want to accumulate the data for the last three segments, segments 10, 11, and 12.

Use a DSECT to provide for the processing of the fields in the segments. Also, use binary arithmetic to accumulate the 3-month total for each customer. This will give you experience with the conversion requirements for binary arithmetic.

Chapter 8   Using subroutines and subprograms

Topic 1   At this point, redesign your program using modular program design. Then, modify the code so the program uses one subroutine for each of the modules of the program. Your program should consist of a mainline module and at least these three other modules: a read module, a process module, and a print module. The more thoughtful your design is, the easier it will be to make the program enhancements required for the remaining chapters of the book.

Alternative for topic 1   Instead of redesigning your program using modular program design, redesign it using structured design as described in chapter 19. This will make it easier for you to modify your program and to add modules to it as you do the tasks for chapters 9 through 16. If you choose this option or your instructor requires it, skip to the task for chapter 19 at this time.

Topic 2   Modify your program so it calls a subprogram called GETIME to put the time in the form of HH:MM into a field described as CL5. In other words, your program passes a five-character field to the subprogram and the subprogram puts the time into this field. After you modify your program, write the subprogram to perform this function. You can test your subprogram and your linkage by assembling both calling program and subprogram in a single job as described in the text.

After you test your subprogram, you can use the subprogram called GETIME that's already available in one of the relocatable libraries. Then, you can remove your own subprogram from the assemble-and-test job as you proceed with the development tasks that follow. To use the system's GETIME subprogram, be sure you have identified the correct relocatable library in your search chain. So find out what the name of this library is.

Section 3 Assembler language capabilities by function

Chapter 9 Table handling

A copy book named STATABLE is available in one of the source statement libraries. It contains 51 DCs, one for each of the 50 states and one containing hex Fs to indicate the last entry. For instance, the first three DCs are these:

```
DC      CL12'AL3500036999'
DC      CL12'AK9950099999'
DC      CL12'AZ8500086599'
```

This table can be used to check the validity of the state codes and the five-digit zip codes used in an address. For a state code to be valid, it must match one of the 50 state code entries (bytes 1-2 in each DC). For a zip code to be valid, it must be equal to or greater than the first zip code value given for a state (bytes 3-7 in each DC) and it must be equal to or less than the second zip code (bytes 8-12).

Using this table, enhance your program to produce the shaded data in print positions 112-129 of the print chart. To produce this data, the program first checks each record's state code for validity. If it is invalid, the program prints INVALID STATE CODE in the FILE MAINTENANCE area; in this case, the program doesn't do the validity checking for the zip code. But if the state code is valid, the program checks the zip code. If it is invalid, it prints INVALID ZIP CODE in the FILE MAINTENANCE area of the report; if it isn't, the program prints nothing in this area.

Chapter 10 Editing, bit manipulation, and translation

Editing   Modify your program so the net sales per customer amount in total line 2 is printed with a floating dollar sign to its left. Also, change the edit patterns used for the net sales fields so a negative amount is indicated by CR instead of a minus sign.

Bit manipulation   If you refer to figure 6-7 in the text, you can see that byte 23 of the communication region contains program switches, or UPSI switches. This byte consists of eight one-bit switches that can be turned on and off by an UPSI statement in your JCL. For instance, this UPSI statement turns on the first bit in byte 23 of the communication region:

```
// UPSI 10000000
```

It also turns off bits 2-8. Similarly, this statement turns bit 1 off and leaves the other seven bits unchanged:

```
// UPSI 0XXXXXXX
```

The UPSI switches have traditionally been used to direct the processing done by a program. For instance, a program can be coded so it performs a function one way if UPSI switch 1 is on, another way if it is off.

With this as background, modify your program based on the setting of UPSI switch 1. If it is off, print the report as usual with one detail line per customer. But if it is on, your program should only list the customers that have a net YTD sales of $2000 or more per month. To calculate the amount that the customers' net sales should equal or exceed, multiply the current month by $2000. Thus, the base value for a report that is printed in month 9 should be $18,000. To identify this form of the report, print positions 77-94 of heading line 2 should show

```
($ XX,000 OR MORE)
```

where XX is the number of thousands used as the base value for the selection.

Translation   To give you some practice with character manipulation, modify your program so it prints the words in a customer's name with one word per line after the YTD sales line as in this example:

```
KEY        CUSTOMER NAME                        YTD SALES

MMAINC     MIKE MURACH & ASSOCIATES, INC.       12,345.67
           MIKE
           MURACH
           &
           ASSOCIATES
           INC
```

To identify words, your program must search for blanks within the name field. For this to work properly, it must determine the actual length of each name before it performs the translation so that trailing blanks aren't processed. Your program should also ignore commas and periods as in the above example. So the listing will be easy to read, your program should double space after the last word in a name.

Chapter 11   Writing macro definitions

A GETIME macro   Write a macro definition that will generate instructions to get the time and store it in a five-byte field in the form HH:MM. The macro code should be GETIME and its operand should be the name of the five-byte field as in this macro instruction:

```
GETIME HTIME
```

After you've written this macro, modify your program so it gets the time with the GETIME macro rather than with the GETIME subprogram.

An EDIT macro   Write a macro definition that will generate instructions to check a field to make sure that it contains valid zoned decimal data. Specifically, the macro should check to make sure that each byte has hex F in its zone portion and a hex digit from 0 through 9 in its digit portion. If the field is valid, the macro should move hex 40 into a switch field specified in the macro instruction. If the field is invalid, the macro should move hex FF into the switch field.

In the first version of this macro, assume that the field to be edited is five-bytes long. Then, the macro will have two operands as in this example:

```
ZDTEST FIELDA,SWITCHA
```

After you write this macro definition, modify your program so it uses this macro to test the zip code field before the zip code is tested by using the zip code table described in the task for chapter 9. If the macro finds the zip code to be valid, continue with the table lookup. Otherwise, this message should be printed in the FILE MAINTENANCE area:

```
ZIP CODE NOT NUMERIC
```

After you get this first version of the macro working, modify the macro so it will test a field of any length. In this case, the macro instruction has three operands as in this example:

```
ZDTEST FIELDA,SWITCHA,7
```

In this case, the third operand is a number that gives the length of the field to be tested. Assume that the maximum field length is 16.

Once you have this version of the macro working, enhance your macro definition so it checks to make sure the operands are valid. Specifically, the first two operands should be labels and the third one should be a number between 1 and 16 that is equal to the length of the first operand. If the operands aren't valid, generate appropriate error messages.

Section 4   Assembler language for the DASD access methods

For all of the tasks required in this section, assume that a customer extension file (CUSTEXT) is available. This file is defined on the record layout page in the program specifications. For each record in the master file, there should be a record with matching key in the extension file.

If you review its record layout, you can see that the customer extension file contains the year-to-date data from the previous year. The first year-to-date segment contains the YTD data through January of the previous year; the second segment contains the data through February; and so on. This data is in a separate file because it is only needed for occasional reports.

The extension file is used to produce the data in print positions 97-109 of the print chart. To produce this data, your program must read the extension record that matches a customer master record. Then, your program should get the net YTD data from the appropriate segment of the extension record and print it in the NET LAST YTD column of the report. The appropriate segment is the segment that is equal to the current month.

All of the program enhancements that follow use the extension file. However, each one uses a different VSE access method to get the file. In other words, the extension file is available in four different forms: as a sequential file, as an ISAM file, as a DAM file, and as a key-sequenced VSAM file.

No matter what access method your program is using, if it can't find a matching extension record for a customer master record, it should print this message in positions 112-130 of the report:

    NO EXTENSION RECORD

In this case, print positions 97-109 in the detail line should be blank.

Chapter 13   The Sequential Access Method (SAM)

Modify your program so it reads one extension record for each master record and prints the last YTD data in print positions 97-109 of the report. For this task, the extension file is a sequential file, so you must get the following specifications for it:

    Block size:
    Device:
    Logical unit name:
    Device address:
    File-id:

Chapter 14   The Indexed Sequential Access Method (ISAM)

Modify your program so it reads one extension record for each master record and prints the last YTD data in print positions 97-109 of the report. For this problem, the extension file is an indexed sequential file. The keys are embedded in the record as shown in the record layout in the program specifications. When applicable, the keys are also in the key areas.

You should do this problem in two parts: one using sequential access, the other using random access. Before you can code and test the program modifications either way, though, you must get the following specifications for the extension file:

Block size:
Device:
Logical unit name:
Device address:
Number of tracks used for cylinder overflow:
Location of master index area (if any):
Location of cylinder index area:
Location of prime data area:
Location of independent overflow area (if any):
File-id:

Sequential access   Code the program so the ISAM extension file is accessed on a sequential basis. In other words, your program logic will be the same as it was in the program enhancement for chapter 13.

Random access   Code the program so the ISAM extension file is accessed on a random basis. The program logic for random access should be quite a bit different than that used for sequential access. In fact, it should be quite a bit simpler.

Chapter 15   The Direct Access Method (DAM)

Modify your program so it reads one extension record for each master record and prints the last YTD data in print positions 97-109 of the report. For this problem, the extension file is a direct file with unblocked records.

The steps used in the randomizing algorithm for this file follow:

1.   Convert the zone halfs of the bytes in the customer key in the customer master record to hex Fs. This converts the alphanumeric field to a zoned decimal field.

2. Divide the zoned-decimal key field by 19 and save the remainder. This remainder identifies the relative track for the matching extension record.

3. Search the relative track for a record with a key that matches the original key in the customer master record. If your program doesn't find the matching record on this track and the track is full, add 1 to the relative track number and search the next track. If your program still can't find the matching record, assume that there is no matching extension record.

Before you can code and test the program modifications for this task, you must get the following specifications for the extension file:

Device:
Logical unit name:
Device address:
Location of file:
File-id:

Chapter 16   The Virtual Storage Access Method (VSAM)

Modify your program so it reads one extension record for each master record and prints the last YTD data in print positions 97-109 of the report. For this problem, the extension file is a key-sequenced VSAM file (a KSDS).

You should do this problem in two parts: one using sequential access, the other using random access. Before you can code and test the program modifications either way, though, you must get the following specifications for the extension file:

File-id:
User catalog:

Sequential access   Code the program so the KSDS extension file is accessed on a sequential basis. In other words, your program logic will be the same as it was for the program enhancement for chapter 13.

Random access   Code the program so the KSDS extension file is accessed on a random basis. The program logic for random access should be quite a bit different than that used for sequential access. In fact, it should be quite a bit simpler.

Section 5   Program development techniques

Chapter 19   An introduction to structured program development

You can do the task for this chapter any time after you read chapter 8 in the text. No matter what stage your program is at, though, the task is to redesign the program using structured design. The result should be a structure chart that consists of at least three levels and at least seven modules. If you design your program in this way before you do the tasks for chapters 8 through 16, it should be easier for you to make the required program enhancements.

After you've redesigned your program using structured design, you should code it so the program uses one subroutine for each of the modules of the structure chart. Be sure to code each subroutine module so it has only one entry and one exit point. As you reorganize your code into modules, you should also modify it so it becomes more readable.

Index

Comment Form

Your opinions count

Your opinions today will affect our future products and policies. So if you have questions, criticisms, or suggestions, I'm eager to get them. You can expect a response within a week of the time we receive your comments.

Also, if you discover any errors in this book, typographical or otherwise, please point them out. We'll correct them when the book is reprinted.

Thanks for your help!

Mike Murach, President
Mike Murach and Associates, Inc.

Book title: DOS/VSE Assembler Language

Dear Mike: _____

_____

_____

_____

_____

_____

_____

_____

_____

_____

_____

_____

_____

_____

Name and Title _____

Company (if any) _____

Address _____

City, State, Zip _____

Fold where indicated and staple.
No postage necessary if mailed in the U.S.

fold

fold

BUSINESS REPLY MAIL

FIRST-CLASS MAIL   PERMIT NO. 3063   FRESNO, CA

POSTAGE WILL BE PAID BY ADDRESSEE

Mike Murach & Associates, Inc.

4697 West Jacquelyn Avenue
Fresno, CA 93722-9986

Order Form

Our Unlimited Guarantee

To our customers who order directly from us: You must be satisfied. Our books must work for you, or you can send them back for a full refund . . . no matter how many you buy, no matter how long you've had them.

Name & Title _____

Company (if company address) _____

Address_____

City, State, Zip _____

Phone number (including area code) _____

Qty	Product code and title	Price
Assembler Language		
_____ VBAL	DOS/VSE Assembler Language	$30.00
_____ VBIG	DOS/VSE Assembler Instructor's Guide	75.00
_____ MBAL	MVS Assembler Language	30.00
_____ MBIG	MVS Assembler Instructor's Guide	75.00
DOS/VSE Subjects		
_____ VJCL	DOS/VSE JCL	$30.00
_____ ICCF	DOS/VSE ICCF	25.00
COBOL Language Elements		
_____ SC1R	Structured ANS COBOL: Part 1	$25.00
_____ SC2R	Structured ANS COBOL: Part 2	25.00
_____ RW	Report Writer	13.50
COBOL Program Development		
_____ DDCP	How to Design and Develop COBOL Programs	$30.00
_____ CPHB	The COBOL Programmer's Handbook	20.00

Qty	Product code and title	Price
VSAM		
_____ VSMX	VSAM: Access Method Services and Application Programming	$25.00
_____ VSAM	VSAM for the COBOL Programmer	15.00
CICS		
_____ CIC1	CICS for the COBOL Programmer: Part 1	$25.00
_____ CIC2	CICS for the COBOL Programmer: Part 2	25.00
_____ CREF	The CICS Programmer's Desk Reference	32.50
Data Base Processing		
_____ IMS1	IMS for the COBOL Programmer Part 1: DL/I Data Base Processing	$30.00
_____ IMS2	IMS for the COBOL Programmer Part 2: Data Communications and MFS	30.00
OS Subjects		
_____ MJCL	MVS JCL	$32.50
_____ TSO	MVS TSO	25.00
_____ OSUT	OS Utilities	15.00
_____ OSDB	OS Debugging for the COBOL Programmer	20.00

☐ Bill me the appropriate price plus UPS shipping and handling (and sales tax in California) for each book ordered.

☐ Bill the appropriate book prices plus UPS shipping and handling (and sales tax in California) to my
_____VISA _____MasterCard:

Card number_____

Valid thru (month/year) _____

Cardowner's signature_____
                              (not valid without signature)

☐ I want to **save** UPS shipping and handling charges. Here's my check or money order for $_____. California residents, please add 6% sales tax to your total. (Offer valid in the U.S. only.)

To order more quickly,

Call **toll-free** 1-800-221-5528

(Weekdays, 9 to 4 Pacific Std. Time)

In California, call 1-800-221-5527

Mike Murach & Associates, Inc.
4697 West Jacquelyn Avenue
Fresno, California 93722
(209) 275-3335